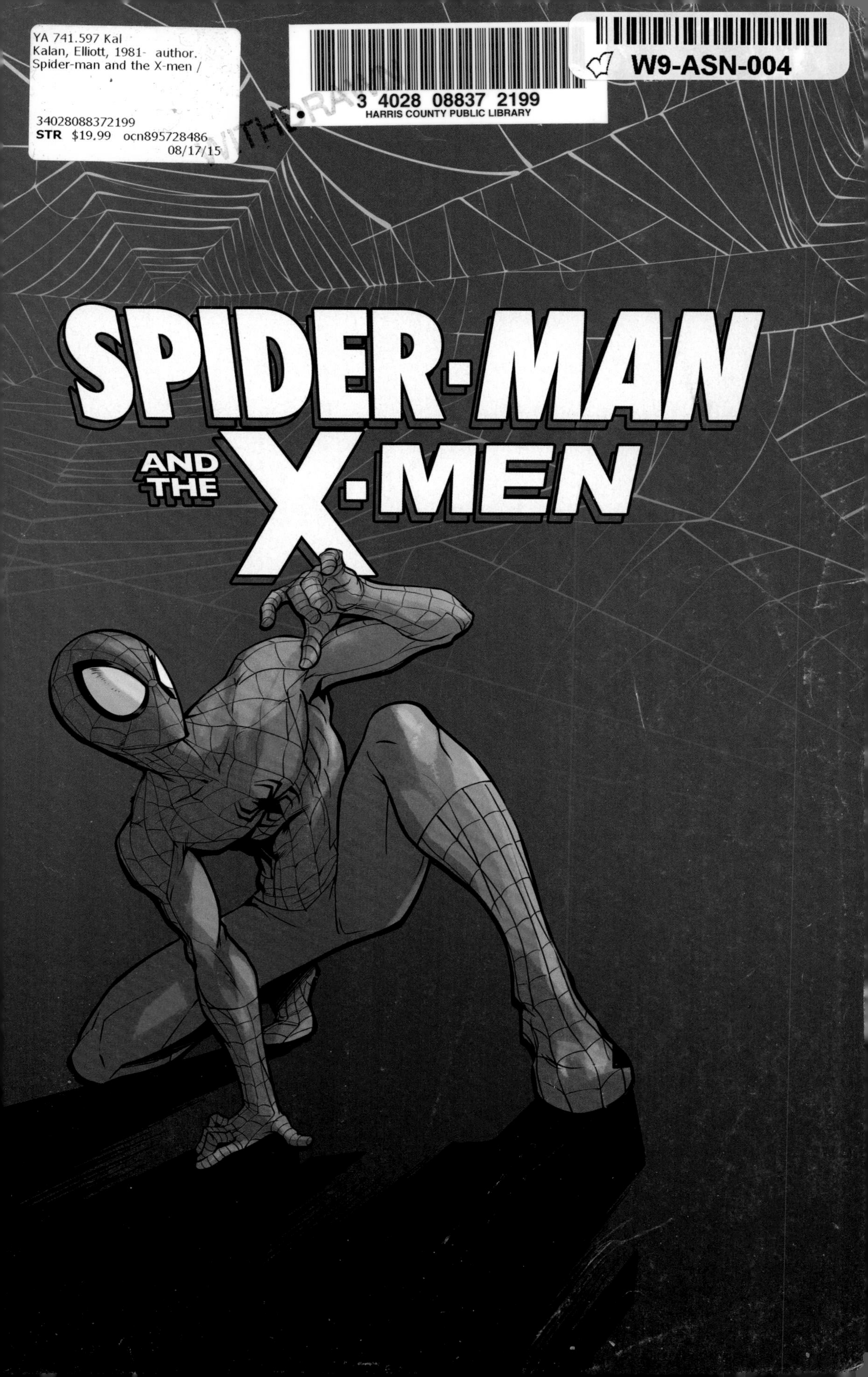
SPIDER-MAN
AND THE
X-MEN

SANTO VACCARRO
ROCKSLIDE

MARTHA JOHANSSON
NO-GIRL

JULIAN KELLER
HELLION

ROBERT HERMAN
GLOB HERMAN

LARA DOS SANTOS
SHARK-GIRL

ERNST
ERNST

TREVOR HAWKIN
EYE BOY

SPIDER-MAN & THE X-MEN. Contains material originally published in magazine form as SPIDER-MAN & THE X-MEN #1-6. First printing 2015. ISBN# 978-0-7851-9700-3. Published by MARVEL WORLDWIDE, INC., a subsidiary of MARVEL ENTERTAINMENT, LLC. OFFICE OF PUBLICATION: 135 West 50th Street, New York, NY 10020. Copyright © 2015 MARVEL No similarity between any of the names, characters, persons, and/or institutions in this magazine with those of any living or dead person or institution is intended, and any such similarity which may exist is purely coincidental. **Printed in the U.S.A.** ALAN FINE, President, Marvel Entertainment; DAN BUCKLEY, President, TV, Publishing and Brand Management; JOE QUESADA, Chief Creative Officer; TOM BREVOORT, SVP of Publishing; DAVID BOGART, SVP of Operations & Procurement, Publishing; C.B. CEBULSKI, VP of International Development & Brand Management; DAVID GABRIEL, SVP Print, Sales & Marketing; JIM O'KEEFE, VP of Operations & Logistics; DAN CARR, Executive Director of Publishing Technology; SUSAN CRESPI, Editorial Operations Manager; ALEX MORALES, Publishing Operations Manager; STAN LEE, Chairman Emeritus. For information regarding advertising in Marvel Comics or on Marvel.com, please contact Jonathan Rheingold, VP of Custom Solutions & Ad Sales, at jrheingold@marvel.com. For Marvel subscription inquiries, please call 800-217-9158. **Manufactured between 5/1/2015 and 6/8/2015 by SOLISCO PRINTERS, SCOTT, QC, CANADA.**

10 9 8 7 6 5 4 3 2 1

SPIDER-MAN AND THE X-MEN

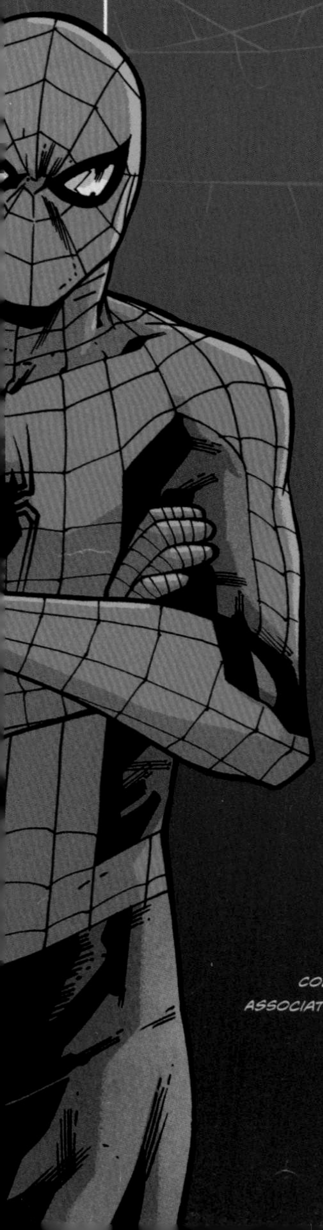

WRITER
ELLIOTT KALAN

ARTIST
ISSUES #1-3 & 5-6
MARCO FAILLA
WITH DIOGO SAITO (#6)

ISSUE #4
PENCILER RB SILVA
INKER ROB LEAN

COLORIST IAN HERRING
LETTERERS VC'S CLAYTON COWLES

COVER ART
NICK BRADSHAW & IAN HERRING (#1-3)
AND STACEY LEE (#4-6)

ASSISTANT EDITOR
CHRISTINA HARRINGTON
EDITOR KATIE KUBERT
X-MEN GROUP EDITOR MIKE MARTS

SPECIAL THANKS TO IRMA KNIIVILA
SPIDER-MAN CREATED BY STAN LEE & STEVE DITKO
X-MEN CREATED BY STAN LEE & JACK KIRBY

COLLECTION EDITOR JENNIFER GRÜNWALD ASSISTANT EDITOR SARAH BRUNSTAD
ASSOCIATE MANAGING EDITOR ALEX STARBUCK EDITOR, SPECIAL PROJECTS MARK D. BEAZLEY
SENIOR EDITOR, SPECIAL PROJECTS JEFF YOUNGQUIST
SVP PRINT, SALES & MARKETING DAVID GABRIEL BOOK DESIGNER JAY BOWEN

EDITOR IN CHIEF AXEL ALONSO CHIEF CREATIVE OFFICER JOE QUESADA
PUBLISHER DAN BUCKLEY EXECUTIVE PRODUCER ALAN FINE

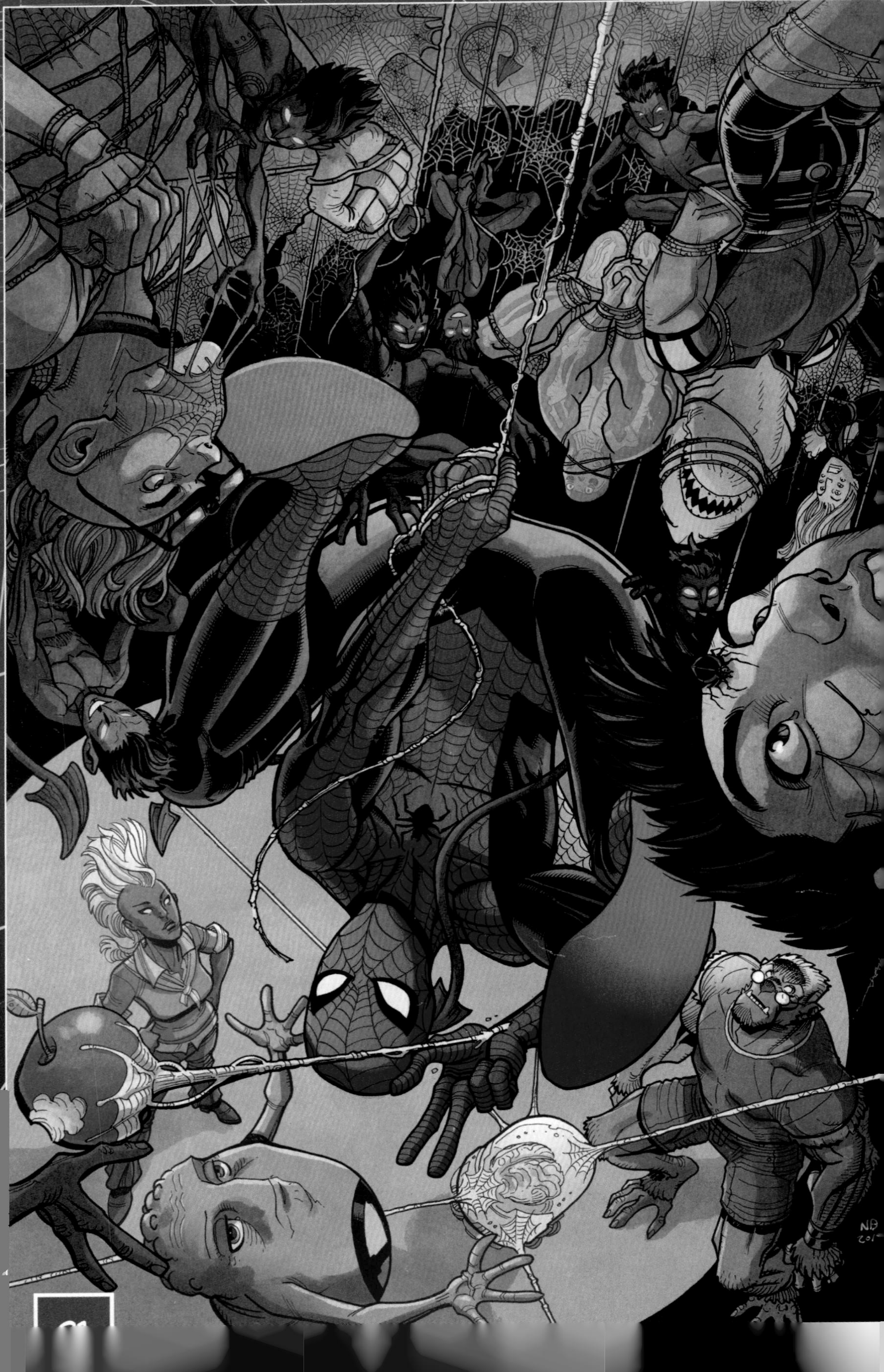

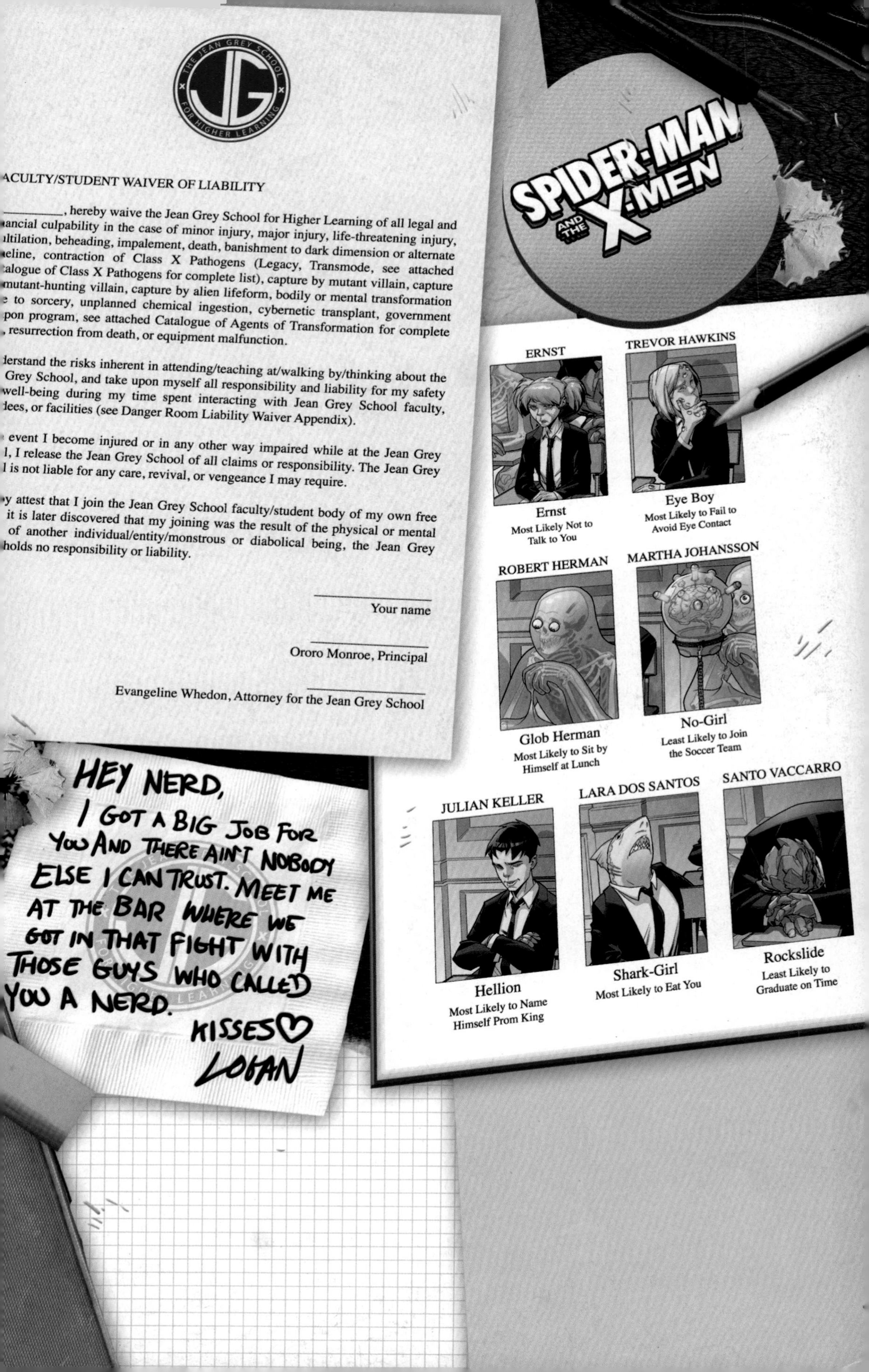

ACULTY/STUDENT WAIVER OF LIABILITY

__________, hereby waive the Jean Grey School for Higher Learning of all legal and ancial culpability in the case of minor injury, major injury, life-threatening injury, ıtilation, beheading, impalement, death, banishment to dark dimension or alternate eline, contraction of Class X Pathogens (Legacy, Transmode, see attached talogue of Class X Pathogens for complete list), capture by mutant villain, capture mutant-hunting villain, capture by alien lifeform, bodily or mental transformation e to sorcery, unplanned chemical ingestion, cybernetic transplant, government pon program, see attached Catalogue of Agents of Transformation for complete , resurrection from death, or equipment malfunction.

lerstand the risks inherent in attending/teaching at/walking by/thinking about the Grey School, and take upon myself all responsibility and liability for my safety well-being during my time spent interacting with Jean Grey School faculty, dees, or facilities (see Danger Room Liability Waiver Appendix).

event I become injured or in any other way impaired while at the Jean Grey l, I release the Jean Grey School of all claims or responsibility. The Jean Grey l is not liable for any care, revival, or vengeance I may require.

y attest that I join the Jean Grey School faculty/student body of my own free it is later discovered that my joining was the result of the physical or mental of another individual/entity/monstrous or diabolical being, the Jean Grey holds no responsibility or liability.

Your name

Ororo Monroe, Principal

Evangeline Whedon, Attorney for the Jean Grey School

THE JEAN GREY SCHOOL FOR HIGHER LEARNING
JG
SPIDER-MAN AND THE X-MEN
ERNST
Ernst
Most Likely Not to Talk to You
TREVOR HAWKINS
Eye Boy
Most Likely to Fail to Avoid Eye Contact
ROBERT HERMAN
Glob Herman
Most Likely to Sit by Himself at Lunch
MARTHA JOHANSSON
No-Girl
Least Likely to Join the Soccer Team
JULIAN KELLER
Hellion
Most Likely to Name Himself Prom King
LARA DOS SANTOS
Shark-Girl
Most Likely to Eat You
SANTO VACCARRO
Rockslide
Least Likely to Graduate on Time
HEY NERD,
I GOT A BIG JOB FOR YOU AND THERE AIN'T NOBODY ELSE I CAN TRUST. MEET ME AT THE BAR WHERE WE GOT IN THAT FIGHT WITH THOSE GUYS WHO CALLED YOU A NERD.
KISSES♡
LOGAN

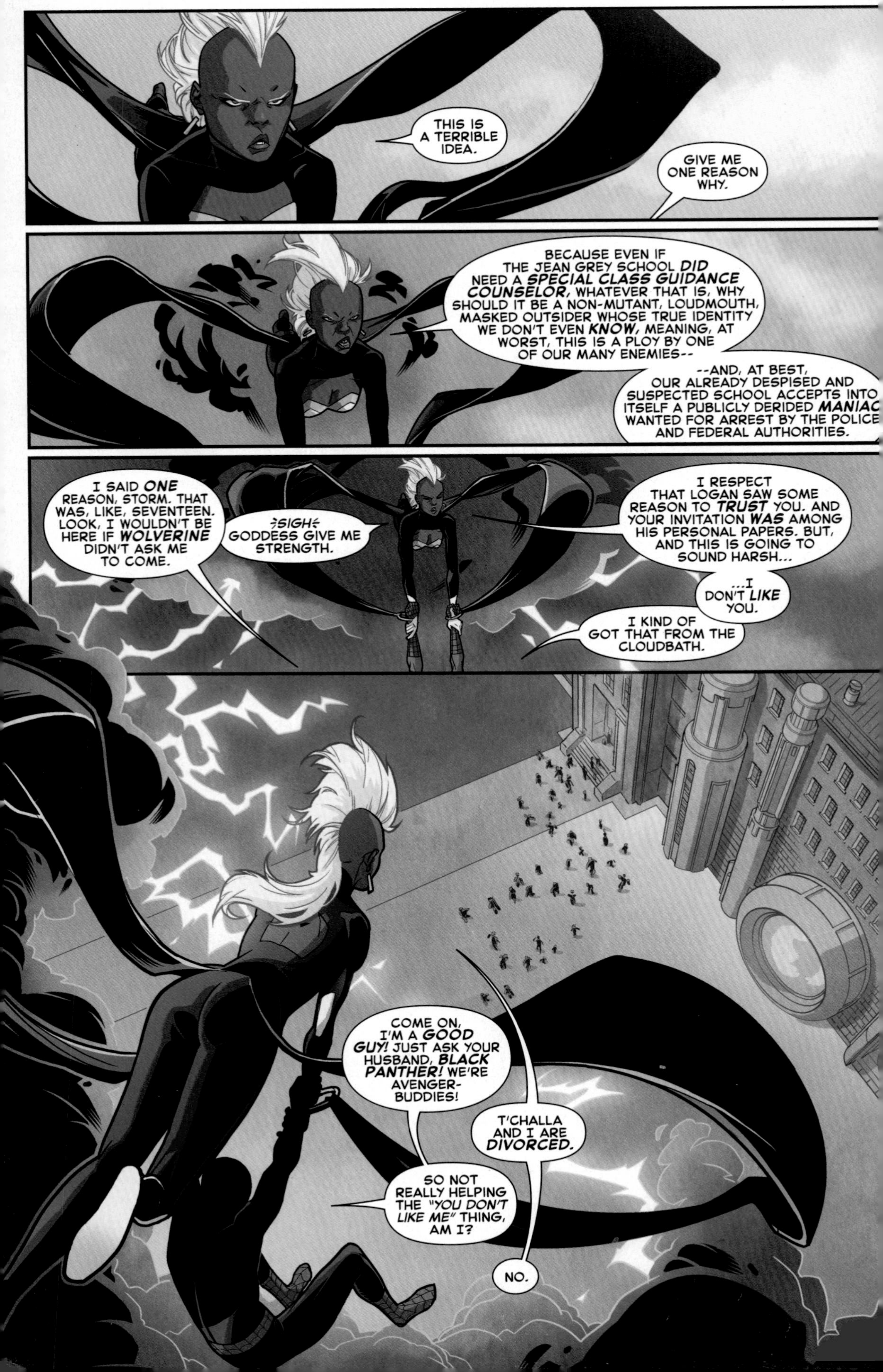
THIS IS A TERRIBLE IDEA.
GIVE ME ONE REASON WHY.
BECAUSE EVEN IF THE JEAN GREY SCHOOL DID NEED A SPECIAL CLASS GUIDANCE COUNSELOR, WHATEVER THAT IS, WHY SHOULD IT BE A NON-MUTANT, LOUDMOUTH, MASKED OUTSIDER WHOSE TRUE IDENTITY WE DON'T EVEN KNOW, MEANING, AT WORST, THIS IS A PLOY BY ONE OF OUR MANY ENEMIES--
--AND, AT BEST, OUR ALREADY DESPISED AND SUSPECTED SCHOOL ACCEPTS INTO ITSELF A PUBLICLY DERIDED MANIAC WANTED FOR ARREST BY THE POLICE AND FEDERAL AUTHORITIES.
I SAID ONE REASON, STORM. THAT WAS, LIKE, SEVENTEEN. LOOK, I WOULDN'T BE HERE IF WOLVERINE DIDN'T ASK ME TO COME.
SIGH GODDESS GIVE ME STRENGTH.
I RESPECT THAT LOGAN SAW SOME REASON TO TRUST YOU. AND YOUR INVITATION WAS AMONG HIS PERSONAL PAPERS. BUT, AND THIS IS GOING TO SOUND HARSH...
...I DON'T LIKE YOU.
I KIND OF GOT THAT FROM THE CLOUDBATH.
COME ON, I'M A GOOD GUY! JUST ASK YOUR HUSBAND, BLACK PANTHER! WE'RE AVENGER-BUDDIES!
T'CHALLA AND I ARE DIVORCED.
SO NOT REALLY HELPING THE "YOU DON'T LIKE ME" THING, AM I?
NO.

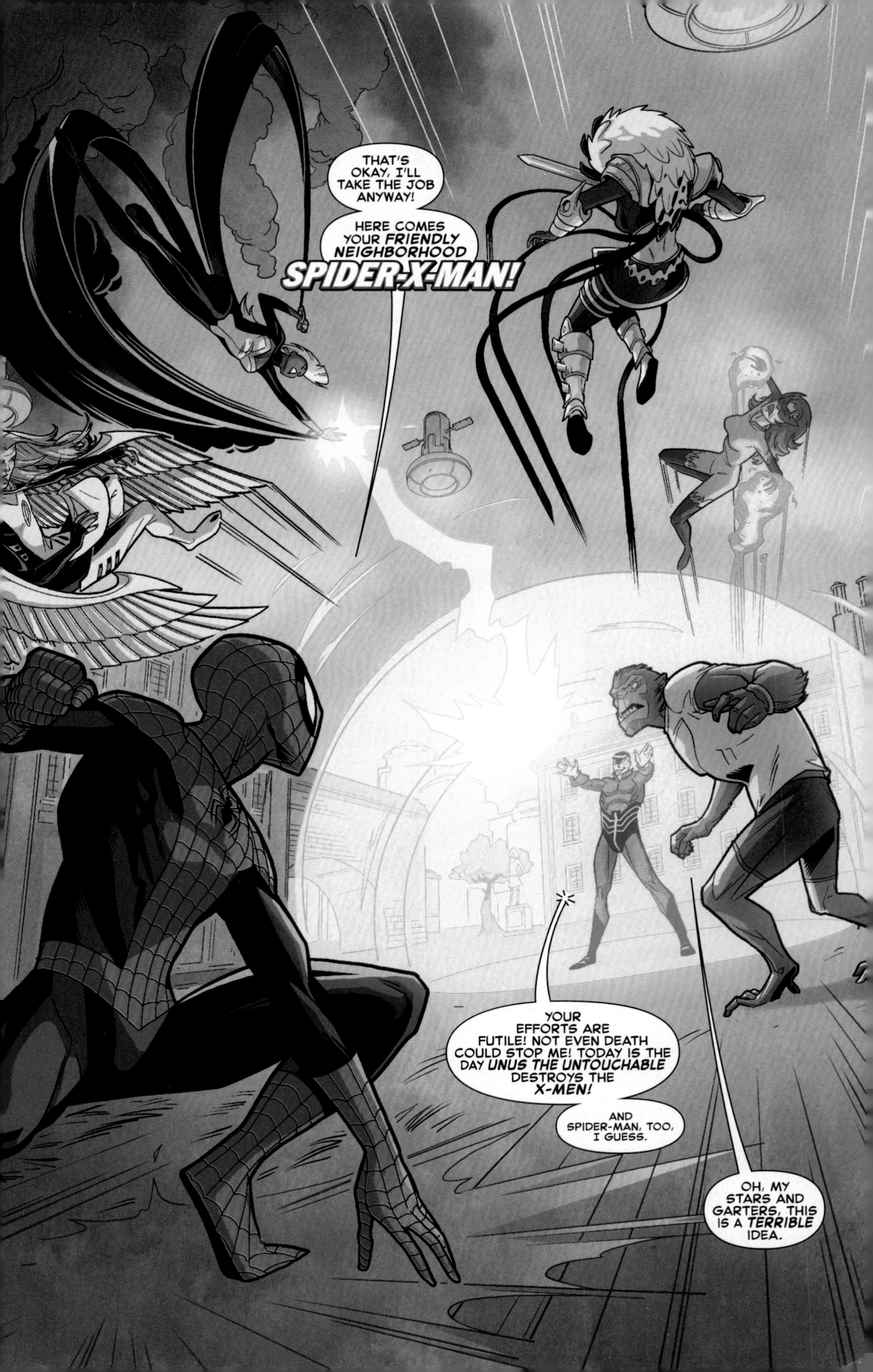
THAT'S OKAY, I'LL TAKE THE JOB ANYWAY!
HERE COMES YOUR FRIENDLY NEIGHBORHOOD
SPIDER-X-MAN!
YOUR EFFORTS ARE FUTILE! NOT EVEN DEATH COULD STOP ME! TODAY IS THE DAY UNUS THE UNTOUCHABLE DESTROYS THE X-MEN!
AND SPIDER-MAN, TOO, I GUESS.
OH, MY STARS AND GARTERS, THIS IS A TERRIBLE IDEA.

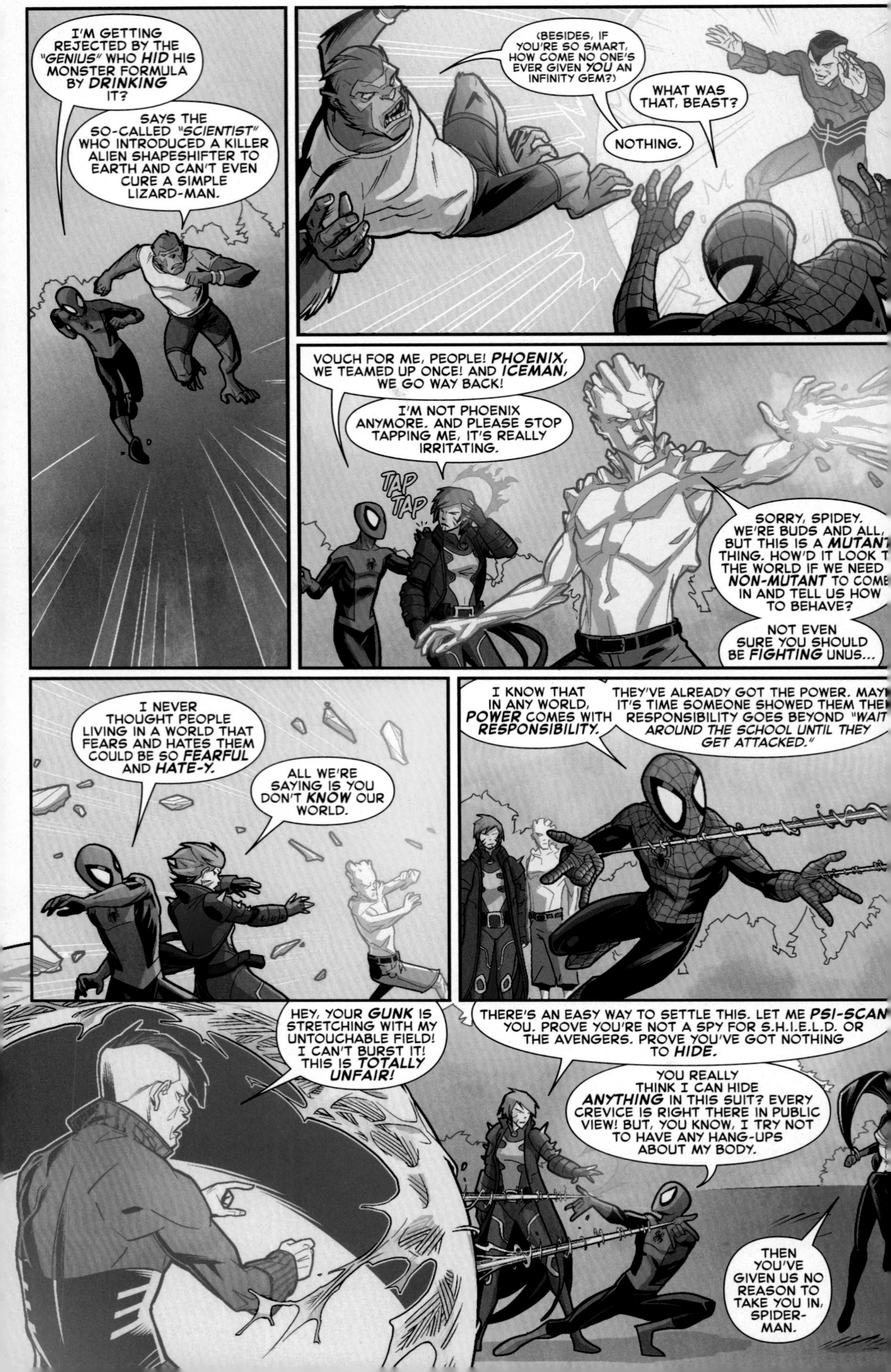

I'M GETTING REJECTED BY THE "GENIUS" WHO HID HIS MONSTER FORMULA BY DRINKING IT?
SAYS THE SO-CALLED "SCIENTIST" WHO INTRODUCED A KILLER ALIEN SHAPESHIFTER TO EARTH AND CAN'T EVEN CURE A SIMPLE LIZARD-MAN.
(BESIDES, IF YOU'RE SO SMART, HOW COME NO ONE'S EVER GIVEN YOU AN INFINITY GEM?)
WHAT WAS THAT, BEAST?
NOTHING.
VOUCH FOR ME, PEOPLE! PHOENIX, WE TEAMED UP ONCE! AND ICEMAN, WE GO WAY BACK!
I'M NOT PHOENIX ANYMORE. AND PLEASE STOP TAPPING ME, IT'S REALLY IRRITATING.
TAP TAP
SORRY, SPIDEY. WE'RE BUDS AND ALL, BUT THIS IS A MUTANT THING. HOW'D IT LOOK T THE WORLD IF WE NEED NON-MUTANT TO COME IN AND TELL US HOW TO BEHAVE?
NOT EVEN SURE YOU SHOULD BE FIGHTING UNUS...
I NEVER THOUGHT PEOPLE LIVING IN A WORLD THAT FEARS AND HATES THEM COULD BE SO FEARFUL AND HATE-Y.
ALL WE'RE SAYING IS YOU DON'T KNOW OUR WORLD.
I KNOW THAT IN ANY WORLD, POWER COMES WITH RESPONSIBILITY.
THEY'VE ALREADY GOT THE POWER. MAY IT'S TIME SOMEONE SHOWED THEM THE RESPONSIBILITY GOES BEYOND "WAIT AROUND THE SCHOOL UNTIL THEY GET ATTACKED."
HEY, YOUR GUNK IS STRETCHING WITH MY UNTOUCHABLE FIELD! I CAN'T BURST IT! THIS IS TOTALLY UNFAIR!
THERE'S AN EASY WAY TO SETTLE THIS. LET ME PSI-SCAN YOU. PROVE YOU'RE NOT A SPY FOR S.H.I.E.L.D. OR THE AVENGERS. PROVE YOU'VE GOT NOTHING TO HIDE.
YOU REALLY THINK I CAN HIDE ANYTHING IN THIS SUIT? EVERY CREVICE IS RIGHT THERE IN PUBLIC VIEW! BUT, YOU KNOW, I TRY NOT TO HAVE ANY HANG-UPS ABOUT MY BODY.
THEN YOU'VE GIVEN US NO REASON TO TAKE YOU IN, SPIDER-MAN.

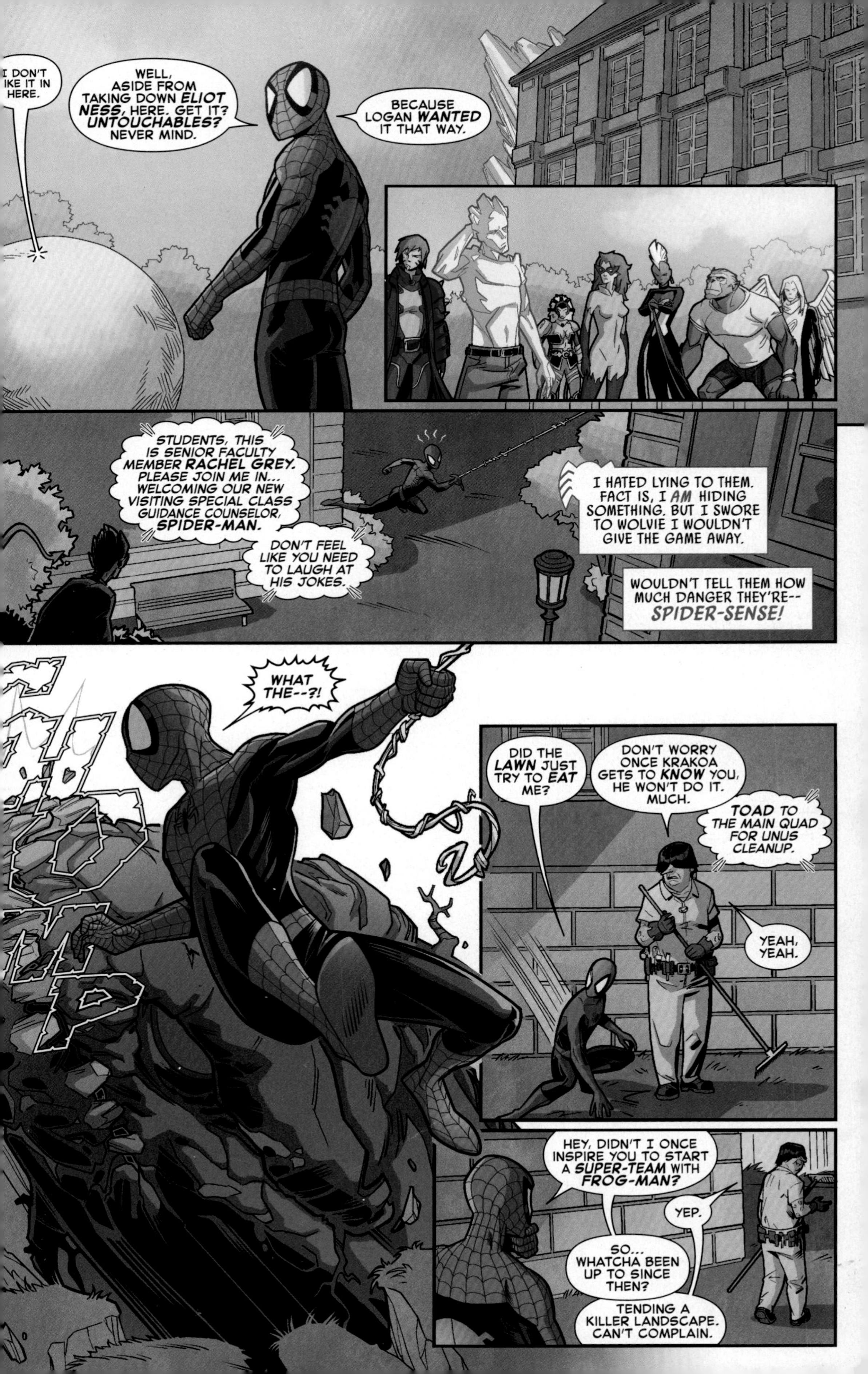
I DON'T LIKE IT IN HERE.
WELL, ASIDE FROM TAKING DOWN ELIOT NESS, HERE. GET IT? UNTOUCHABLES? NEVER MIND.
BECAUSE LOGAN WANTED IT THAT WAY.
STUDENTS, THIS IS SENIOR FACULTY MEMBER RACHEL GREY. PLEASE JOIN ME IN... WELCOMING OUR NEW VISITING SPECIAL CLASS GUIDANCE COUNSELOR, SPIDER-MAN.
DON'T FEEL LIKE YOU NEED TO LAUGH AT HIS JOKES.
I HATED LYING TO THEM. FACT IS, I AM HIDING SOMETHING. BUT I SWORE TO WOLVIE I WOULDN'T GIVE THE GAME AWAY.
WOULDN'T TELL THEM HOW MUCH DANGER THEY'RE-- SPIDER-SENSE!
WHAT THE--?!
DID THE LAWN JUST TRY TO EAT ME?
DON'T WORRY ONCE KRAKOA GETS TO KNOW YOU, HE WON'T DO IT. MUCH.
TOAD TO THE MAIN QUAD FOR UNUS CLEANUP.
YEAH, YEAH.
HEY, DIDN'T I ONCE INSPIRE YOU TO START A SUPER-TEAM WITH FROG-MAN?
YEP.
SO... WHATCHA BEEN UP TO SINCE THEN?
TENDING A KILLER LANDSCAPE. CAN'T COMPLAIN.

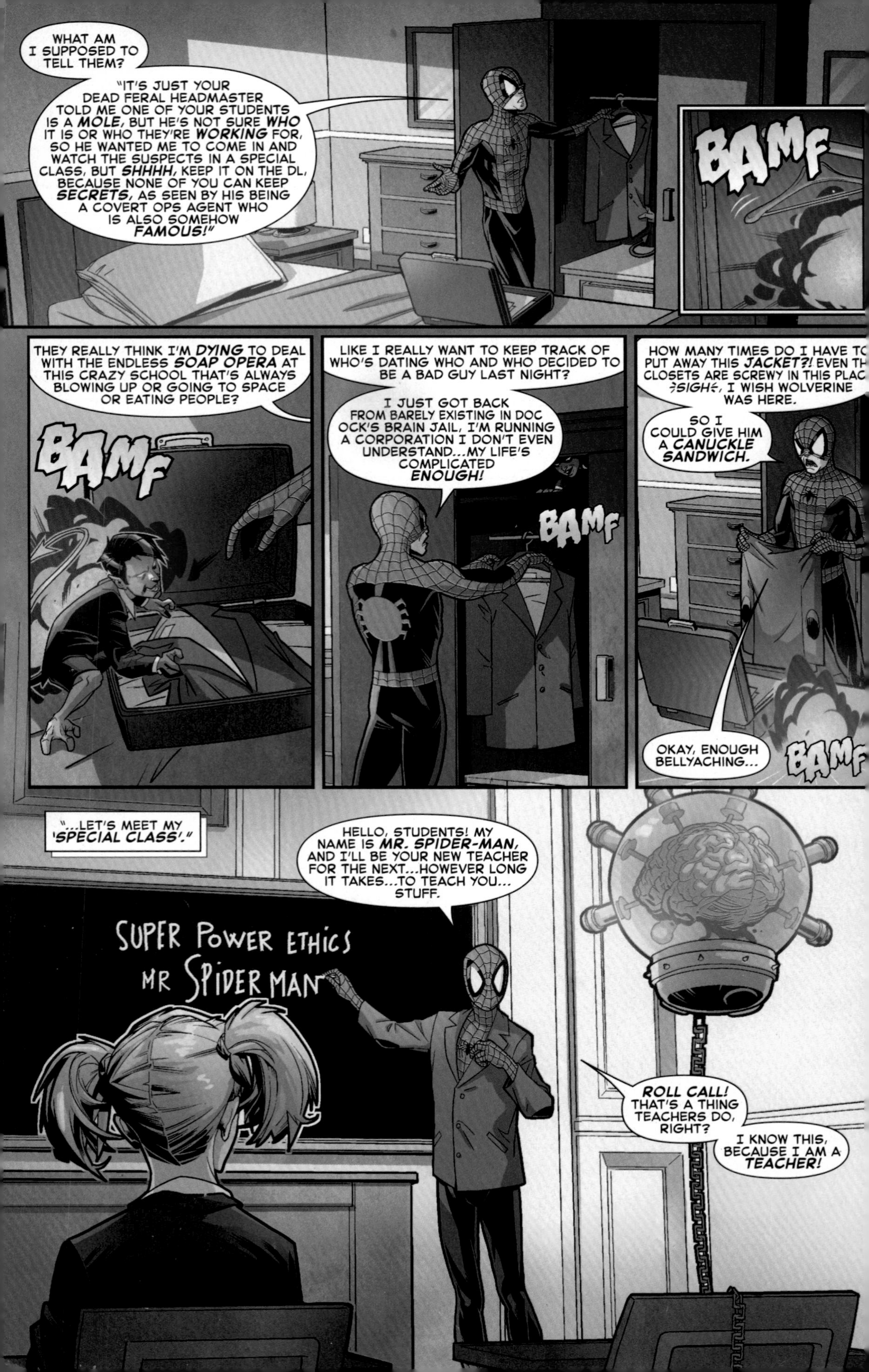
WHAT AM I SUPPOSED TO TELL THEM?
"IT'S JUST YOUR DEAD FERAL HEADMASTER TOLD ME ONE OF YOUR STUDENTS IS A MOLE, BUT HE'S NOT SURE WHO IT IS OR WHO THEY'RE WORKING FOR, SO HE WANTED ME TO COME IN AND WATCH THE SUSPECTS IN A SPECIAL CLASS, BUT SHHHH, KEEP IT ON THE DL, BECAUSE NONE OF YOU CAN KEEP SECRETS, AS SEEN BY HIS BEING A COVERT OPS AGENT WHO IS ALSO SOMEHOW FAMOUS!"
BAMF
THEY REALLY THINK I'M DYING TO DEAL WITH THE ENDLESS SOAP OPERA AT THIS CRAZY SCHOOL THAT'S ALWAYS BLOWING UP OR GOING TO SPACE OR EATING PEOPLE?
BAMF
LIKE I REALLY WANT TO KEEP TRACK OF WHO'S DATING WHO AND WHO DECIDED TO BE A BAD GUY LAST NIGHT?
I JUST GOT BACK FROM BARELY EXISTING IN DOC OCK'S BRAIN JAIL, I'M RUNNING A CORPORATION I DON'T EVEN UNDERSTAND...MY LIFE'S COMPLICATED ENOUGH!
BAMF
HOW MANY TIMES DO I HAVE TO PUT AWAY THIS JACKET?! EVEN TH CLOSETS ARE SCREWY IN THIS PLAC *SIGH*, I WISH WOLVERINE WAS HERE.
SO I COULD GIVE HIM A CANUCKLE SANDWICH.
OKAY, ENOUGH BELLYACHING...
BAMF
"...LET'S MEET MY 'SPECIAL CLASS'."
HELLO, STUDENTS! MY NAME IS MR. SPIDER-MAN, AND I'LL BE YOUR NEW TEACHER FOR THE NEXT...HOWEVER LONG IT TAKES...TO TEACH YOU... STUFF.
SUPER POWER ETHICS
MR SPIDER MAN
ROLL CALL! THAT'S A THING TEACHERS DO, RIGHT?
I KNOW THIS, BECAUSE I AM A TEACHER!

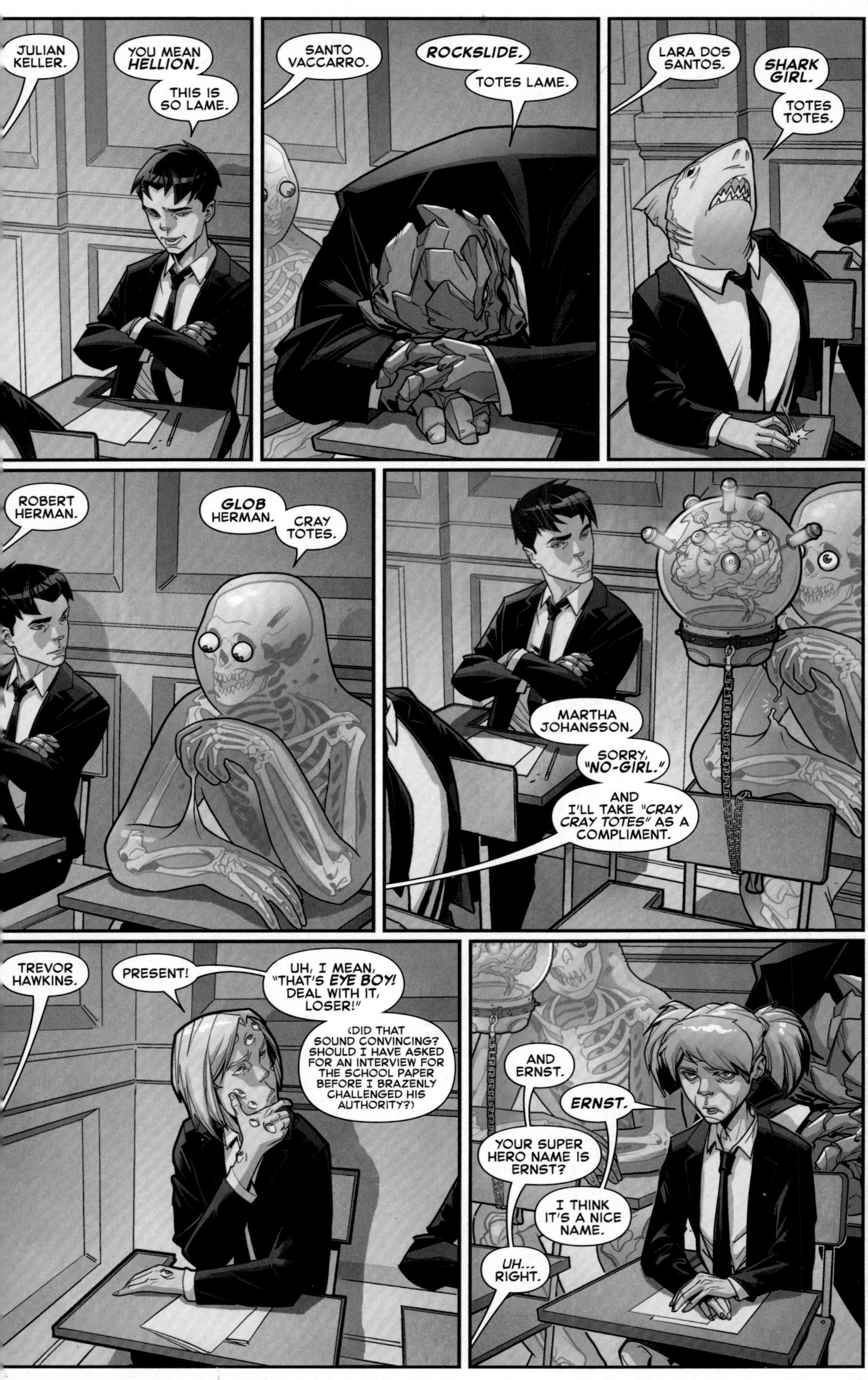

JULIAN KELLER.
YOU MEAN HELLION.
THIS IS SO LAME.
SANTO VACCARRO.
ROCKSLIDE.
TOTES LAME.
LARA DOS SANTOS.
SHARK GIRL.
TOTES TOTES.
ROBERT HERMAN.
GLOB HERMAN.
CRAY TOTES.
MARTHA JOHANSSON.
SORRY, "NO-GIRL."
AND I'LL TAKE "CRAY CRAY TOTES" AS A COMPLIMENT.
TREVOR HAWKINS.
PRESENT!
UH, I MEAN, "THAT'S EYE BOY! DEAL WITH IT, LOSER!"
(DID THAT SOUND CONVINCING? SHOULD I HAVE ASKED FOR AN INTERVIEW FOR THE SCHOOL PAPER BEFORE I BRAZENLY CHALLENGED HIS AUTHORITY?)
AND ERNST.
ERNST.
YOUR SUPER HERO NAME IS ERNST?
I THINK IT'S A NICE NAME.
UH... RIGHT.

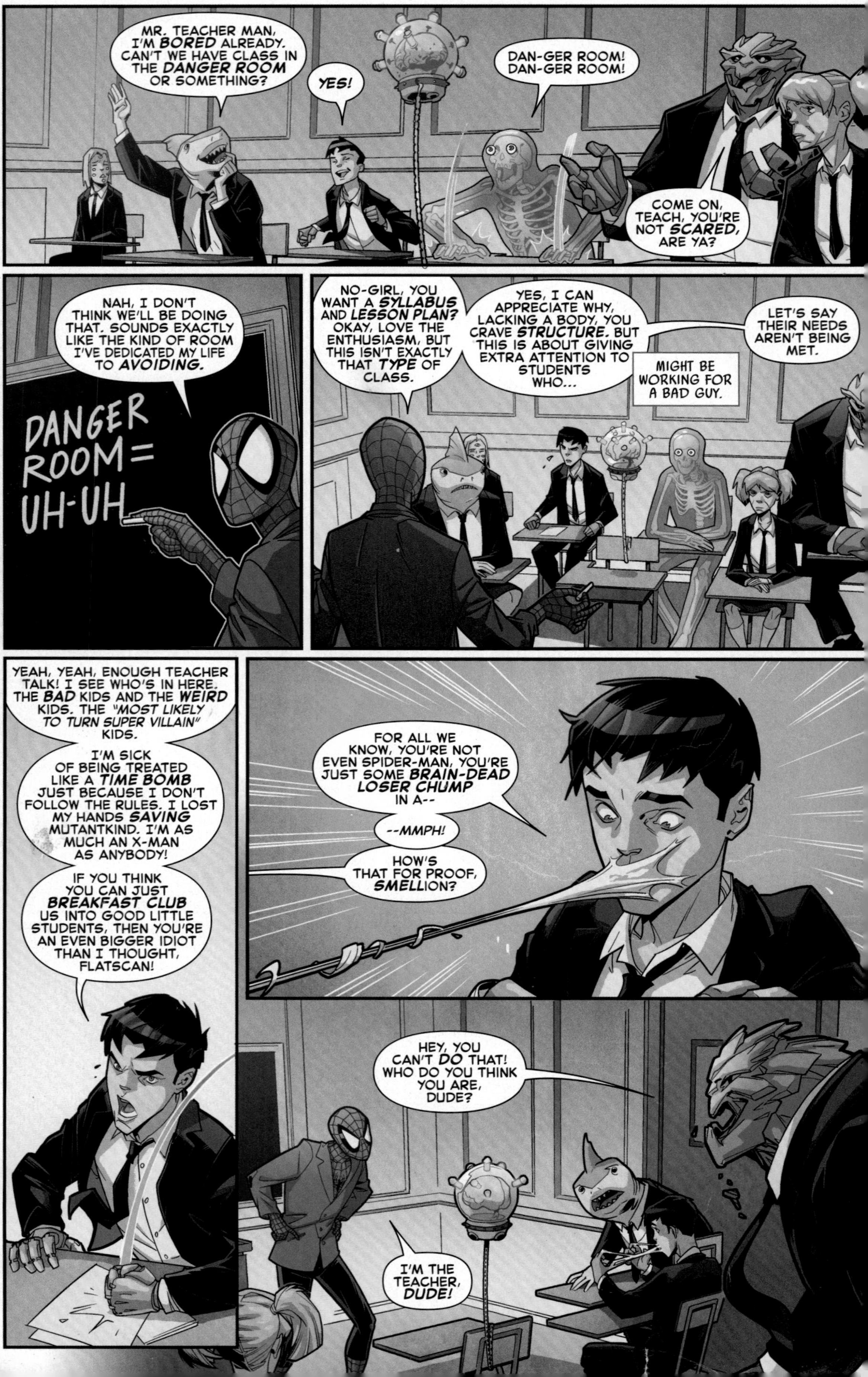
MR. TEACHER MAN, I'M BORED ALREADY. CAN'T WE HAVE CLASS IN THE DANGER ROOM OR SOMETHING?
YES!
DAN-GER ROOM! DAN-GER ROOM!
COME ON, TEACH, YOU'RE NOT SCARED, ARE YA?
NAH, I DON'T THINK WE'LL BE DOING THAT. SOUNDS EXACTLY LIKE THE KIND OF ROOM I'VE DEDICATED MY LIFE TO AVOIDING.
DANGER ROOM= UH-UH
NO-GIRL, YOU WANT A SYLLABUS AND LESSON PLAN? OKAY, LOVE THE ENTHUSIASM, BUT THIS ISN'T EXACTLY THAT TYPE OF CLASS.
YES, I CAN APPRECIATE WHY, LACKING A BODY, YOU CRAVE STRUCTURE. BUT THIS IS ABOUT GIVING EXTRA ATTENTION TO STUDENTS WHO...
LET'S SAY THEIR NEEDS AREN'T BEING MET.
MIGHT BE WORKING FOR A BAD GUY.
YEAH, YEAH, ENOUGH TEACHER TALK! I SEE WHO'S IN HERE. THE BAD KIDS AND THE WEIRD KIDS. THE "MOST LIKELY TO TURN SUPER VILLAIN" KIDS.
I'M SICK OF BEING TREATED LIKE A TIME BOMB JUST BECAUSE I DON'T FOLLOW THE RULES. I LOST MY HANDS SAVING MUTANTKIND. I'M AS MUCH AN X-MAN AS ANYBODY!
IF YOU THINK YOU CAN JUST BREAKFAST CLUB US INTO GOOD LITTLE STUDENTS, THEN YOU'RE AN EVEN BIGGER IDIOT THAN I THOUGHT, FLATSCAN!
FOR ALL WE KNOW, YOU'RE NOT EVEN SPIDER-MAN, YOU'RE JUST SOME BRAIN-DEAD LOSER CHUMP IN A--
--MMPH!
HOW'S THAT FOR PROOF, SMELLION?
HEY, YOU CAN'T DO THAT! WHO DO YOU THINK YOU ARE, DUDE?
I'M THE TEACHER, DUDE!

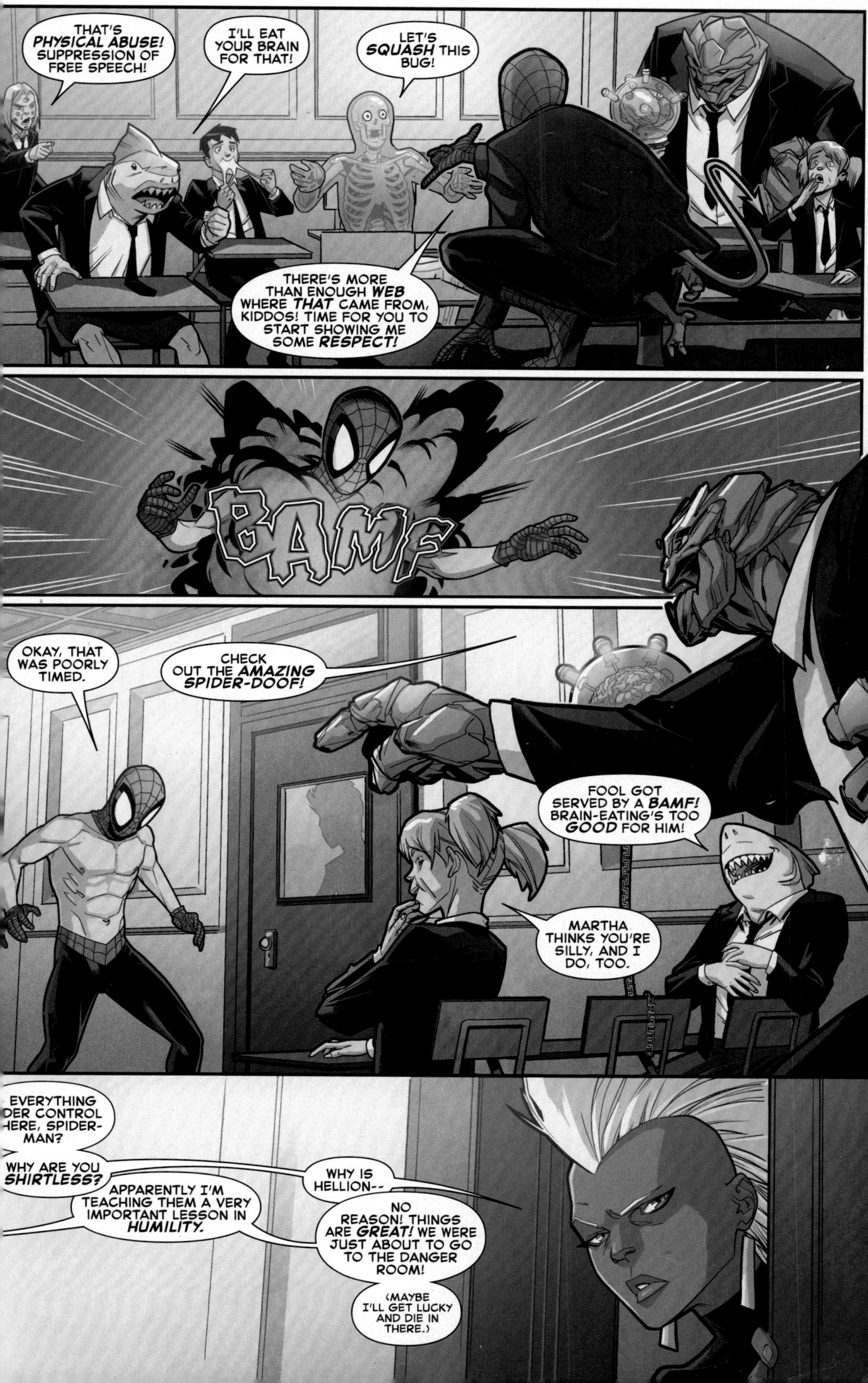
THAT'S PHYSICAL ABUSE! SUPPRESSION OF FREE SPEECH!
I'LL EAT YOUR BRAIN FOR THAT!
LET'S SQUASH THIS BUG!
THERE'S MORE THAN ENOUGH WEB WHERE THAT CAME FROM, KIDDOS! TIME FOR YOU TO START SHOWING ME SOME RESPECT!
BAMF
OKAY, THAT WAS POORLY TIMED.
CHECK OUT THE AMAZING SPIDER-DOOF!
FOOL GOT SERVED BY A BAMF! BRAIN-EATING'S TOO GOOD FOR HIM!
MARTHA THINKS YOU'RE SILLY, AND I DO, TOO.
EVERYTHING DER CONTROL HERE, SPIDER-MAN?
WHY ARE YOU SHIRTLESS?
WHY IS HELLION--
APPARENTLY I'M TEACHING THEM A VERY IMPORTANT LESSON IN HUMILITY.
NO REASON! THINGS ARE GREAT! WE WERE JUST ABOUT TO GO TO THE DANGER ROOM!
(MAYBE I'LL GET LUCKY AND DIE IN THERE.)

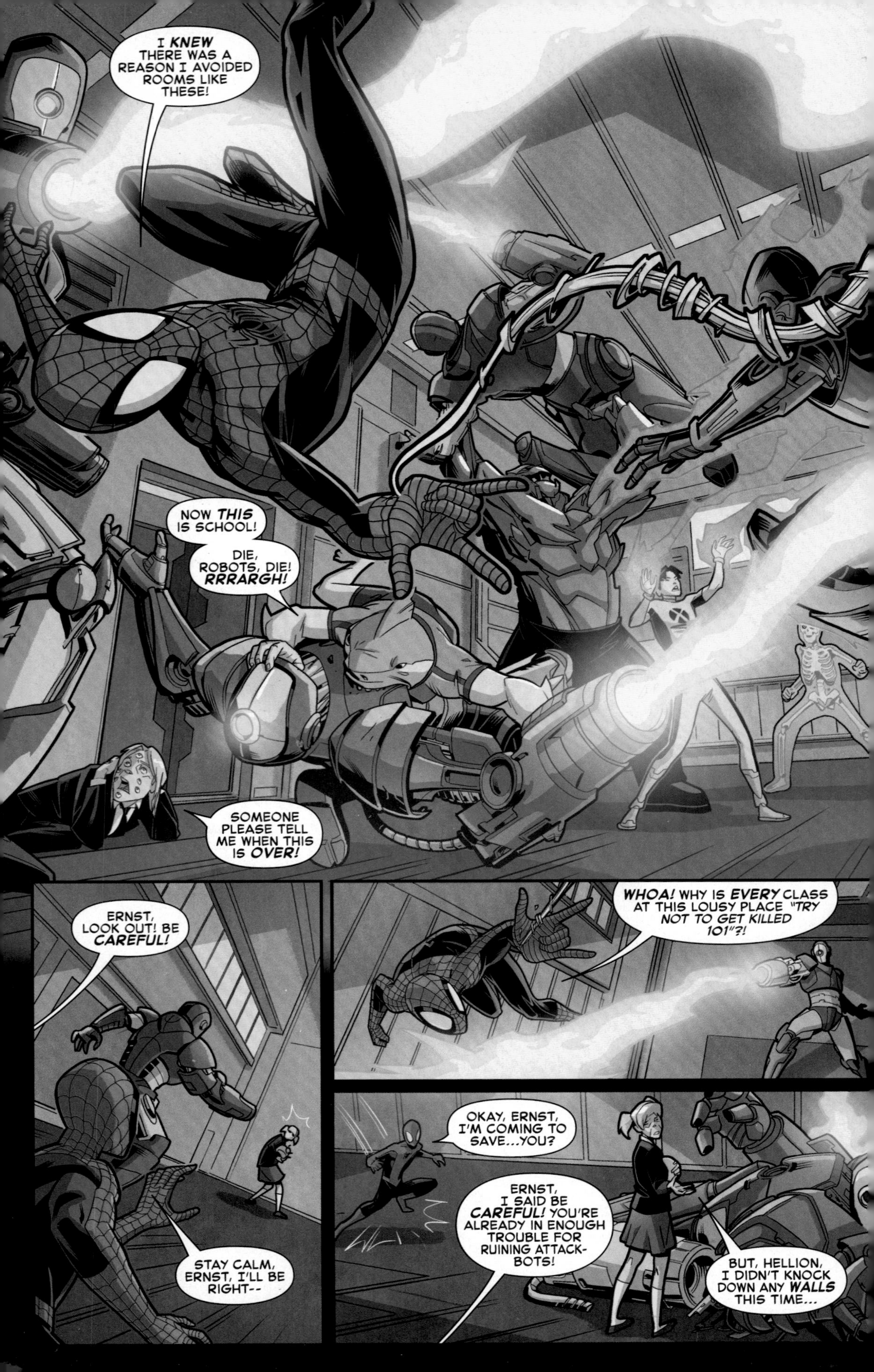
I KNEW THERE WAS A REASON I AVOIDED ROOMS LIKE THESE!
NOW THIS IS SCHOOL!
DIE, ROBOTS, DIE! RRRARGH!
SOMEONE PLEASE TELL ME WHEN THIS IS OVER!
ERNST, LOOK OUT! BE CAREFUL!
STAY CALM, ERNST, I'LL BE RIGHT--
WHOA! WHY IS EVERY CLASS AT THIS LOUSY PLACE "TRY NOT TO GET KILLED 101"?!
OKAY, ERNST, I'M COMING TO SAVE...YOU?
ERNST, I SAID BE CAREFUL! YOU'RE ALREADY IN ENOUGH TROUBLE FOR RUINING ATTACK-BOTS!
BUT, HELLION, I DIDN'T KNOCK DOWN ANY WALLS THIS TIME...

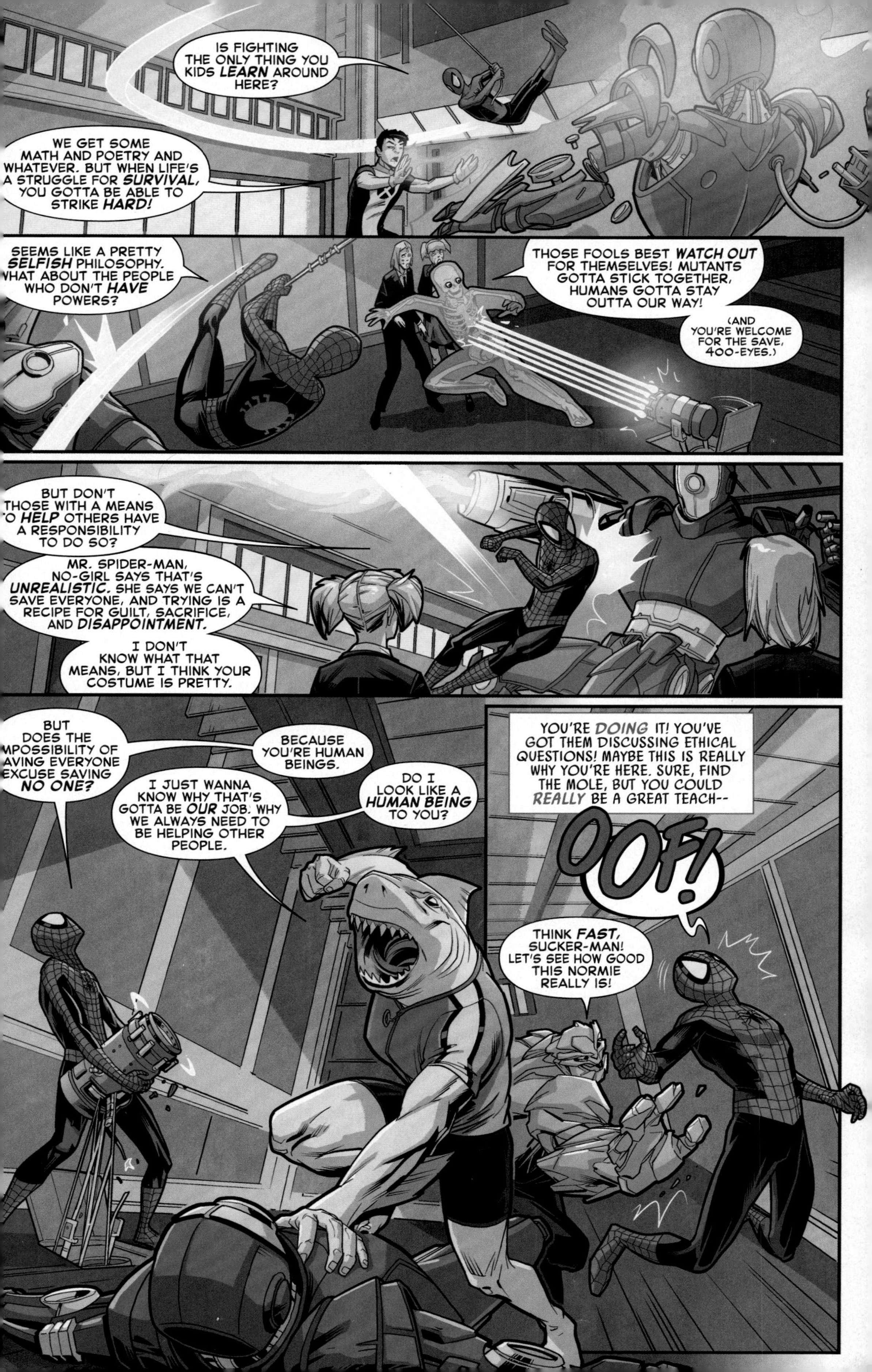

IS FIGHTING THE ONLY THING YOU KIDS LEARN AROUND HERE?
WE GET SOME MATH AND POETRY AND WHATEVER. BUT WHEN LIFE'S A STRUGGLE FOR SURVIVAL, YOU GOTTA BE ABLE TO STRIKE HARD!
SEEMS LIKE A PRETTY SELFISH PHILOSOPHY. WHAT ABOUT THE PEOPLE WHO DON'T HAVE POWERS?
THOSE FOOLS BEST WATCH OUT FOR THEMSELVES! MUTANTS GOTTA STICK TOGETHER, HUMANS GOTTA STAY OUTTA OUR WAY!
(AND YOU'RE WELCOME FOR THE SAVE, 400-EYES.)
BUT DON'T THOSE WITH A MEANS TO HELP OTHERS HAVE A RESPONSIBILITY TO DO SO?
MR. SPIDER-MAN, NO-GIRL SAYS THAT'S UNREALISTIC. SHE SAYS WE CAN'T SAVE EVERYONE, AND TRYING IS A RECIPE FOR GUILT, SACRIFICE, AND DISAPPOINTMENT.
I DON'T KNOW WHAT THAT MEANS, BUT I THINK YOUR COSTUME IS PRETTY.
BUT DOES THE IMPOSSIBILITY OF SAVING EVERYONE EXCUSE SAVING NO ONE?
BECAUSE YOU'RE HUMAN BEINGS.
I JUST WANNA KNOW WHY THAT'S GOTTA BE OUR JOB. WHY WE ALWAYS NEED TO BE HELPING OTHER PEOPLE.
DO I LOOK LIKE A HUMAN BEING TO YOU?
YOU'RE DOING IT! YOU'VE GOT THEM DISCUSSING ETHICAL QUESTIONS! MAYBE THIS IS REALLY WHY YOU'RE HERE. SURE, FIND THE MOLE, BUT YOU COULD REALLY BE A GREAT TEACH--
OOF!
THINK FAST, SUCKER-MAN! LET'S SEE HOW GOOD THIS NORMIE REALLY IS!

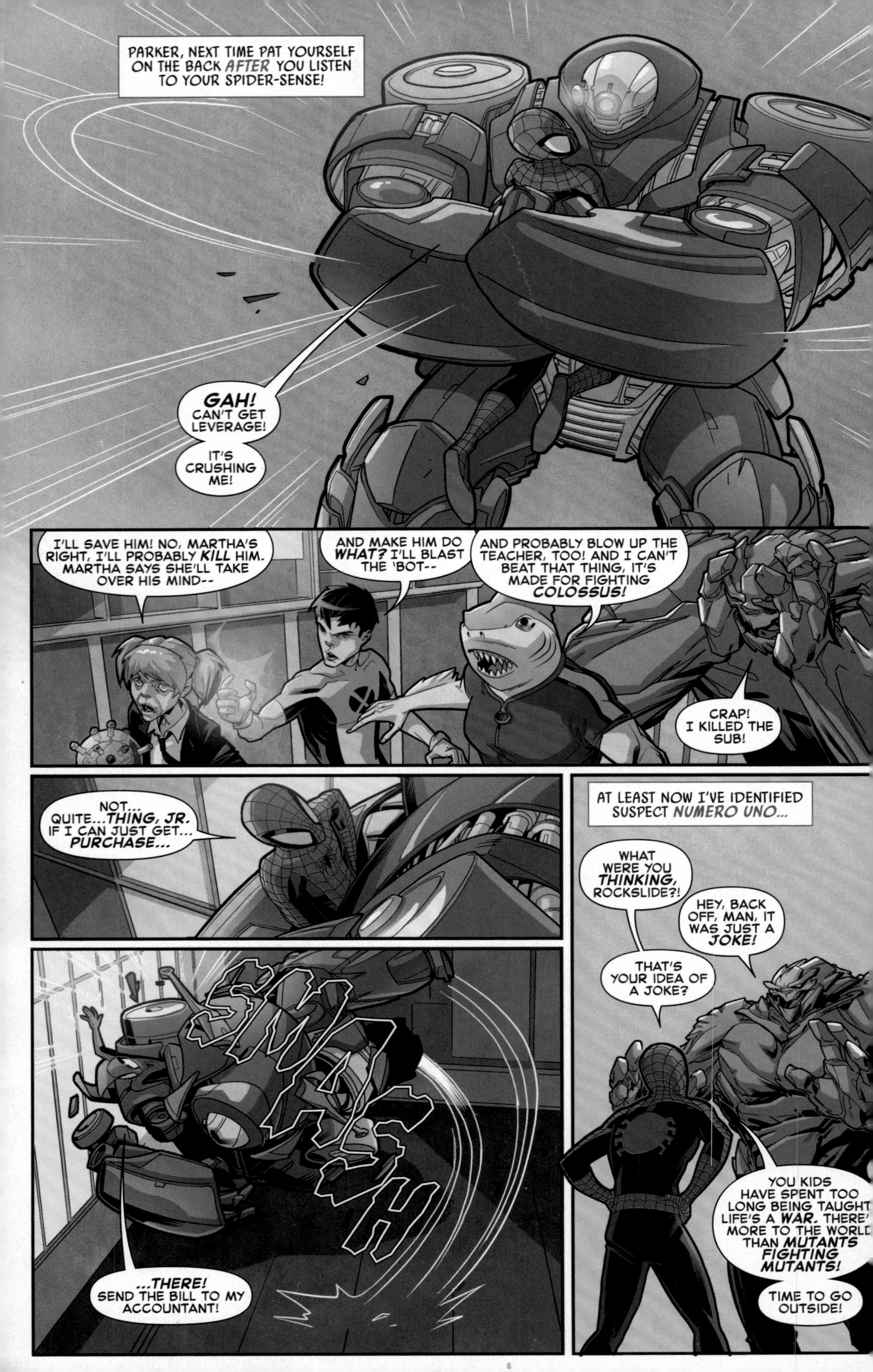

PARKER, NEXT TIME PAT YOURSELF ON THE BACK AFTER YOU LISTEN TO YOUR SPIDER-SENSE!
GAH! CAN'T GET LEVERAGE!
IT'S CRUSHING ME!
I'LL SAVE HIM! NO, MARTHA'S RIGHT, I'LL PROBABLY KILL HIM. MARTHA SAYS SHE'LL TAKE OVER HIS MIND--
AND MAKE HIM DO WHAT? I'LL BLAST THE 'BOT--
AND PROBABLY BLOW UP THE TEACHER, TOO! AND I CAN'T BEAT THAT THING, IT'S MADE FOR FIGHTING COLOSSUS!
CRAP! I KILLED THE SUB!
NOT... QUITE...THING, JR. IF I CAN JUST GET... PURCHASE...
SMASH
...THERE! SEND THE BILL TO MY ACCOUNTANT!
AT LEAST NOW I'VE IDENTIFIED SUSPECT NUMERO UNO...
WHAT WERE YOU THINKING, ROCKSLIDE?!
HEY, BACK OFF, MAN, IT WAS JUST A JOKE!
THAT'S YOUR IDEA OF A JOKE?
YOU KIDS HAVE SPENT TOO LONG BEING TAUGHT LIFE'S A WAR. THERE' MORE TO THE WORLD THAN MUTANTS FIGHTING MUTANTS!
TIME TO GO OUTSIDE!

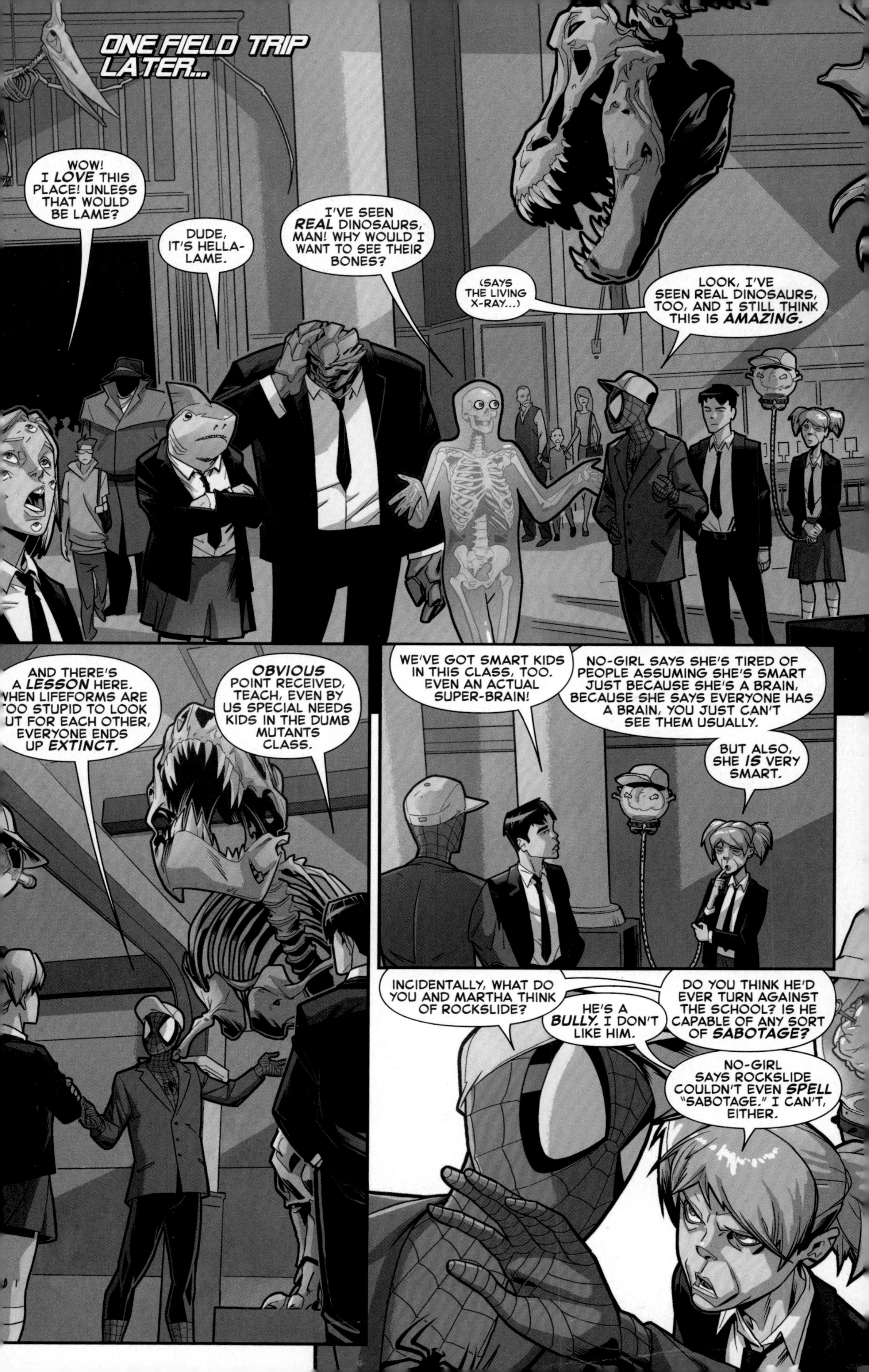
ONE FIELD TRIP LATER...
WOW! I LOVE THIS PLACE! UNLESS THAT WOULD BE LAME?
DUDE, IT'S HELLA-LAME.
I'VE SEEN REAL DINOSAURS, MAN! WHY WOULD I WANT TO SEE THEIR BONES?
(SAYS THE LIVING X-RAY...)
LOOK, I'VE SEEN REAL DINOSAURS, TOO, AND I STILL THINK THIS IS AMAZING.
AND THERE'S A LESSON HERE. WHEN LIFEFORMS ARE TOO STUPID TO LOOK OUT FOR EACH OTHER, EVERYONE ENDS UP EXTINCT.
OBVIOUS POINT RECEIVED, TEACH, EVEN BY US SPECIAL NEEDS KIDS IN THE DUMB MUTANTS CLASS.
WE'VE GOT SMART KIDS IN THIS CLASS, TOO. EVEN AN ACTUAL SUPER-BRAIN!
NO-GIRL SAYS SHE'S TIRED OF PEOPLE ASSUMING SHE'S SMART JUST BECAUSE SHE'S A BRAIN, BECAUSE SHE SAYS EVERYONE HAS A BRAIN, YOU JUST CAN'T SEE THEM USUALLY.
BUT ALSO, SHE IS VERY SMART.
INCIDENTALLY, WHAT DO YOU AND MARTHA THINK OF ROCKSLIDE?
HE'S A BULLY. I DON'T LIKE HIM.
DO YOU THINK HE'D EVER TURN AGAINST THE SCHOOL? IS HE CAPABLE OF ANY SORT OF SABOTAGE?
NO-GIRL SAYS ROCKSLIDE COULDN'T EVEN SPELL "SABOTAGE." I CAN'T, EITHER.

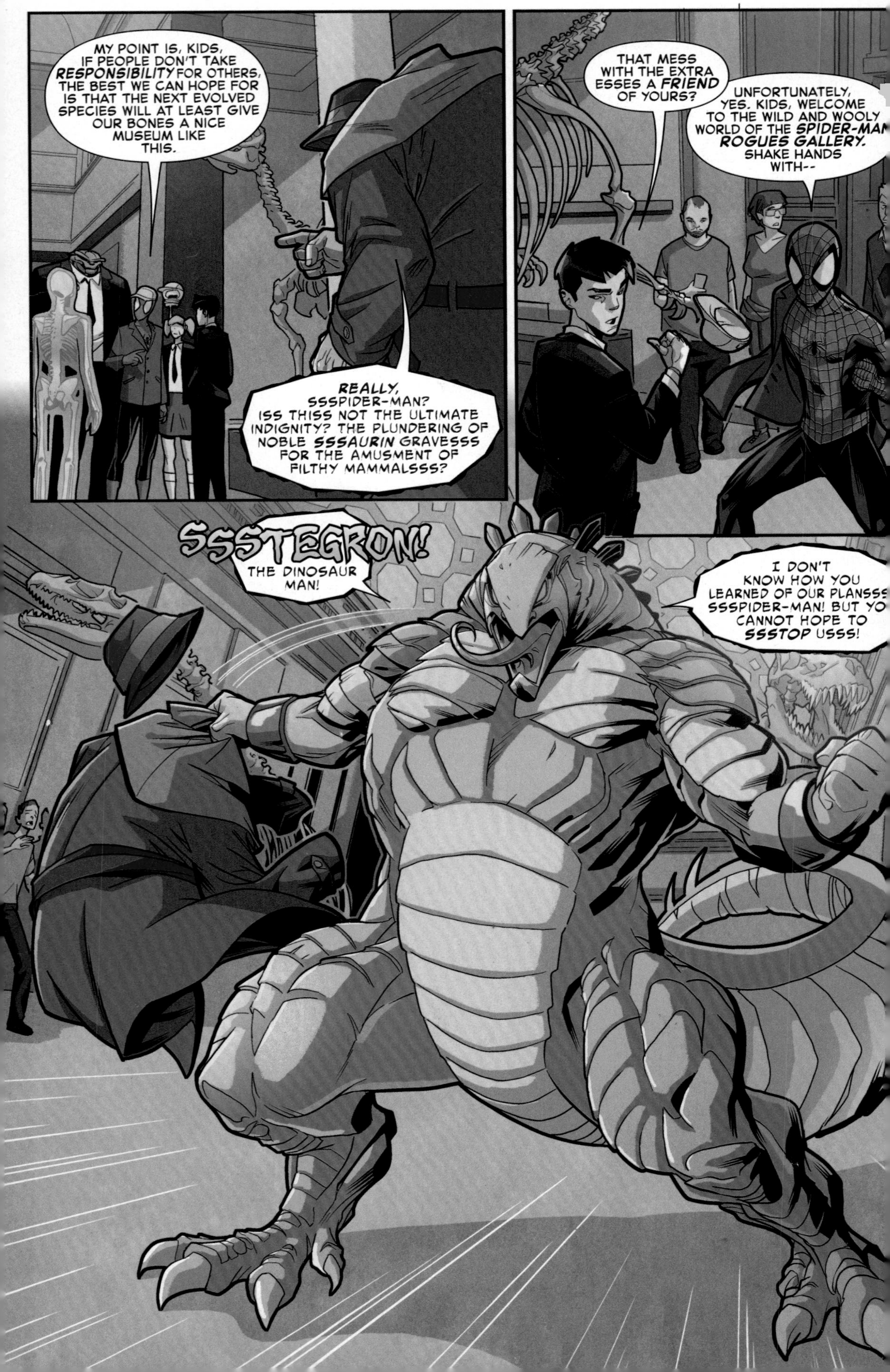
MY POINT IS, KIDS, IF PEOPLE DON'T TAKE RESPONSIBILITY FOR OTHERS, THE BEST WE CAN HOPE FOR IS THAT THE NEXT EVOLVED SPECIES WILL AT LEAST GIVE OUR BONES A NICE MUSEUM LIKE THIS.
REALLY, SSSPIDER-MAN? ISS THISS NOT THE ULTIMATE INDIGNITY? THE PLUNDERING OF NOBLE SSSAURIN GRAVESSS FOR THE AMUSMENT OF FILTHY MAMMALSSS?
THAT MESS WITH THE EXTRA ESSES A FRIEND OF YOURS?
UNFORTUNATELY, YES. KIDS, WELCOME TO THE WILD AND WOOLY WORLD OF THE SPIDER-MAN ROGUES GALLERY. SHAKE HANDS WITH--
SSSTEGRON!
THE DINOSAUR MAN!
I DON'T KNOW HOW YOU LEARNED OF OUR PLANSSS SSSPIDER-MAN! BUT YOU CANNOT HOPE TO SSSTOP USSS!

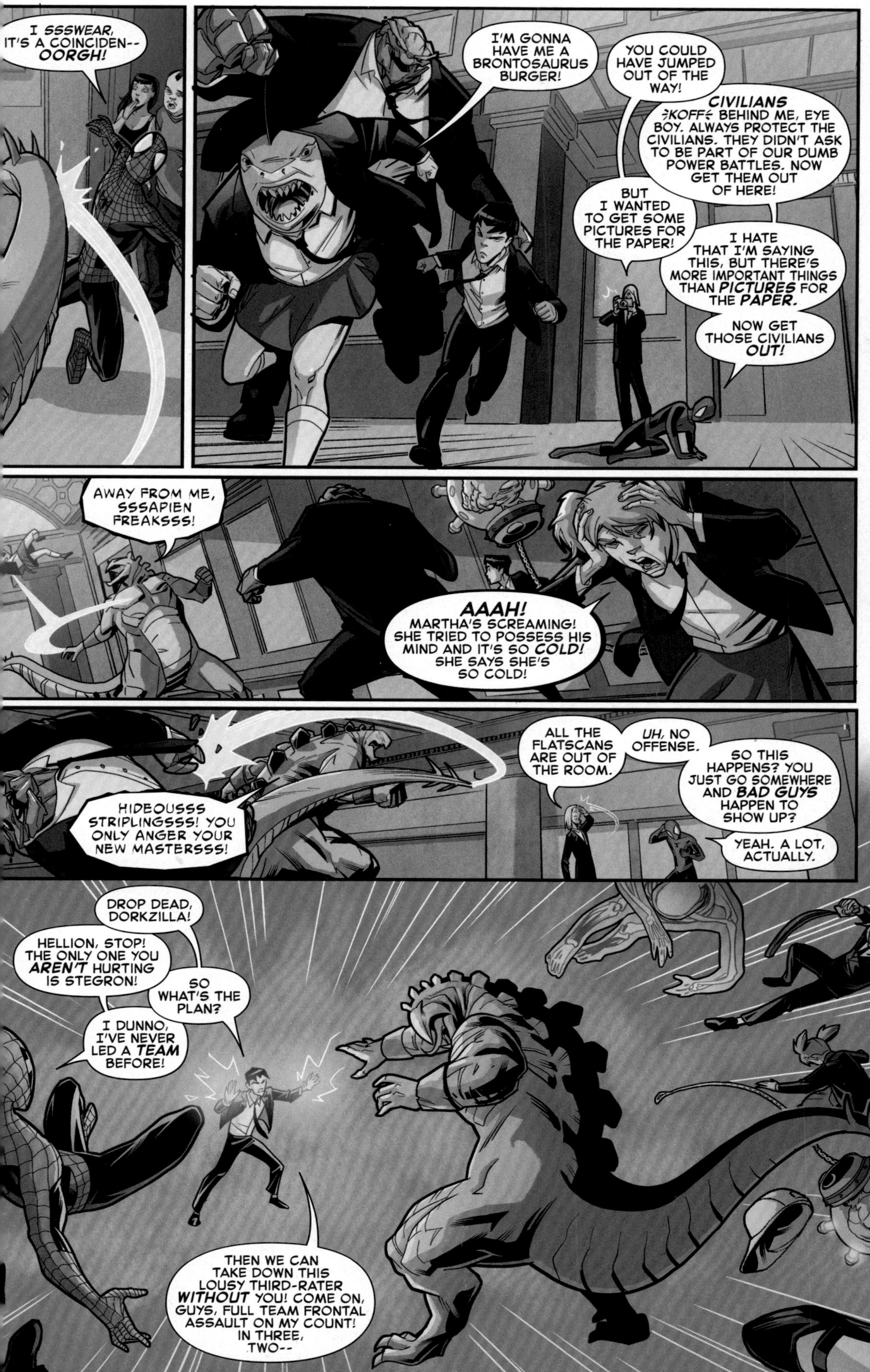
I SSSWEAR, IT'S A COINCIDEN-- OORGH!
I'M GONNA HAVE ME A BRONTOSAURUS BURGER!
YOU COULD HAVE JUMPED OUT OF THE WAY!
CIVILIANS *KOFF* BEHIND ME, EYE BOY. ALWAYS PROTECT THE CIVILIANS. THEY DIDN'T ASK TO BE PART OF OUR DUMB POWER BATTLES. NOW GET THEM OUT OF HERE!
BUT I WANTED TO GET SOME PICTURES FOR THE PAPER!
I HATE THAT I'M SAYING THIS, BUT THERE'S MORE IMPORTANT THINGS THAN PICTURES FOR THE PAPER.
NOW GET THOSE CIVILIANS OUT!
AWAY FROM ME, SSSAPIEN FREAKSSS!
AAAH! MARTHA'S SCREAMING! SHE TRIED TO POSSESS HIS MIND AND IT'S SO COLD! SHE SAYS SHE'S SO COLD!
HIDEOUSSS STRIPLINGSSS! YOU ONLY ANGER YOUR NEW MASTERSSS!
ALL THE FLATSCANS ARE OUT OF THE ROOM.
UH, NO OFFENSE.
SO THIS HAPPENS? YOU JUST GO SOMEWHERE AND BAD GUYS HAPPEN TO SHOW UP?
YEAH. A LOT, ACTUALLY.
DROP DEAD, DORKZILLA!
HELLION, STOP! THE ONLY ONE YOU AREN'T HURTING IS STEGRON!
SO WHAT'S THE PLAN?
I DUNNO, I'VE NEVER LED A TEAM BEFORE!
THEN WE CAN TAKE DOWN THIS LOUSY THIRD-RATER WITHOUT YOU! COME ON, GUYS, FULL TEAM FRONTAL ASSAULT ON MY COUNT! IN THREE, TWO--

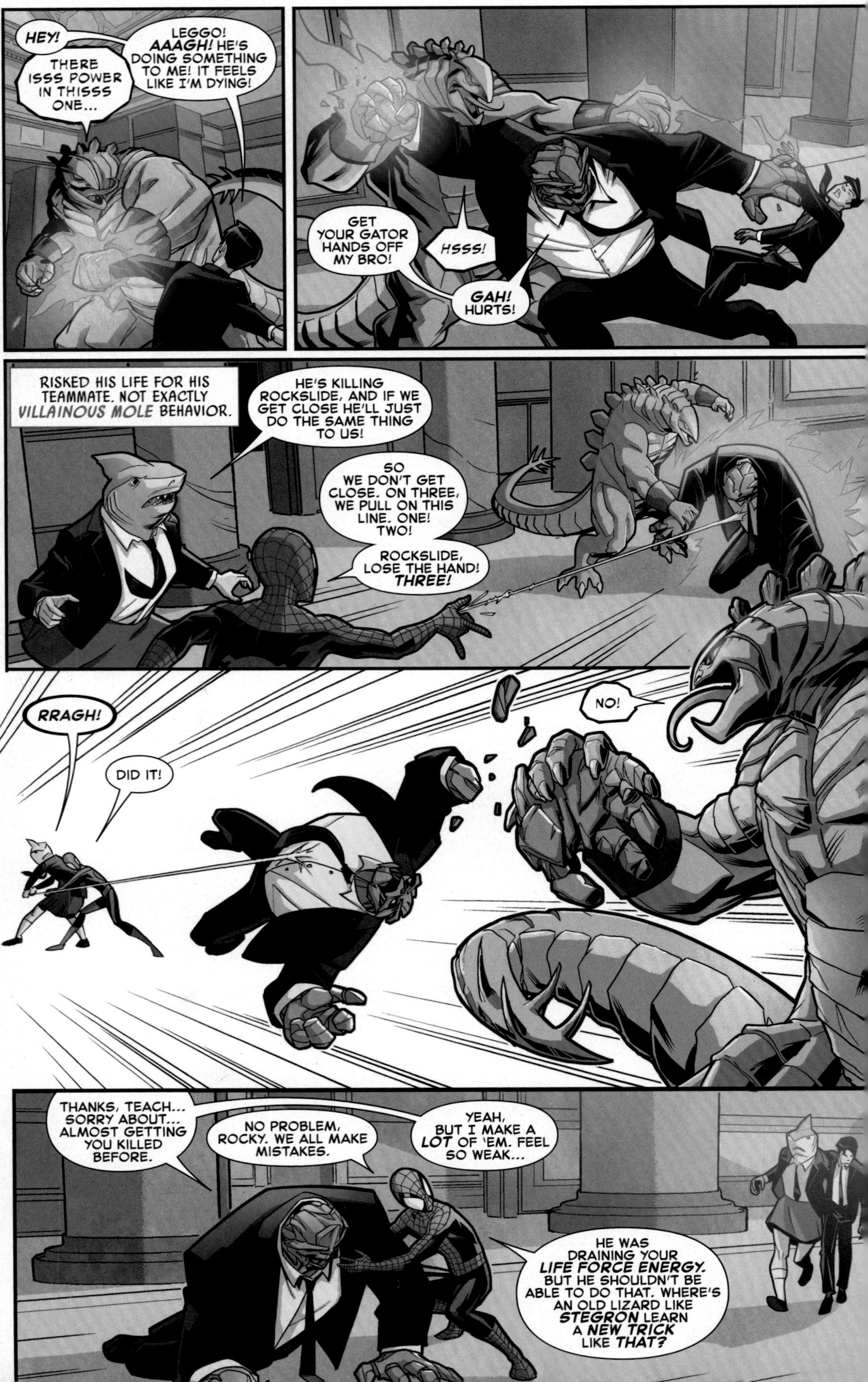
HEY!
LEGGO! AAAGH! HE'S DOING SOMETHING TO ME! IT FEELS LIKE I'M DYING!
THERE ISSS POWER IN THISSS ONE...
GET YOUR GATOR HANDS OFF MY BRO!
HSSS!
GAH! HURTS!
RISKED HIS LIFE FOR HIS TEAMMATE. NOT EXACTLY VILLAINOUS MOLE BEHAVIOR.
HE'S KILLING ROCKSLIDE, AND IF WE GET CLOSE HE'LL JUST DO THE SAME THING TO US!
SO WE DON'T GET CLOSE. ON THREE, WE PULL ON THIS LINE. ONE! TWO!
ROCKSLIDE, LOSE THE HAND! THREE!
RRAGH!
DID IT!
NO!
THANKS, TEACH... SORRY ABOUT... ALMOST GETTING YOU KILLED BEFORE.
NO PROBLEM, ROCKY. WE ALL MAKE MISTAKES.
YEAH, BUT I MAKE A LOT OF 'EM. FEEL SO WEAK...
HE WAS DRAINING YOUR LIFE FORCE ENERGY. BUT HE SHOULDN'T BE ABLE TO DO THAT. WHERE'S AN OLD LIZARD LIKE STEGRON LEARN A NEW TRICK LIKE THAT?

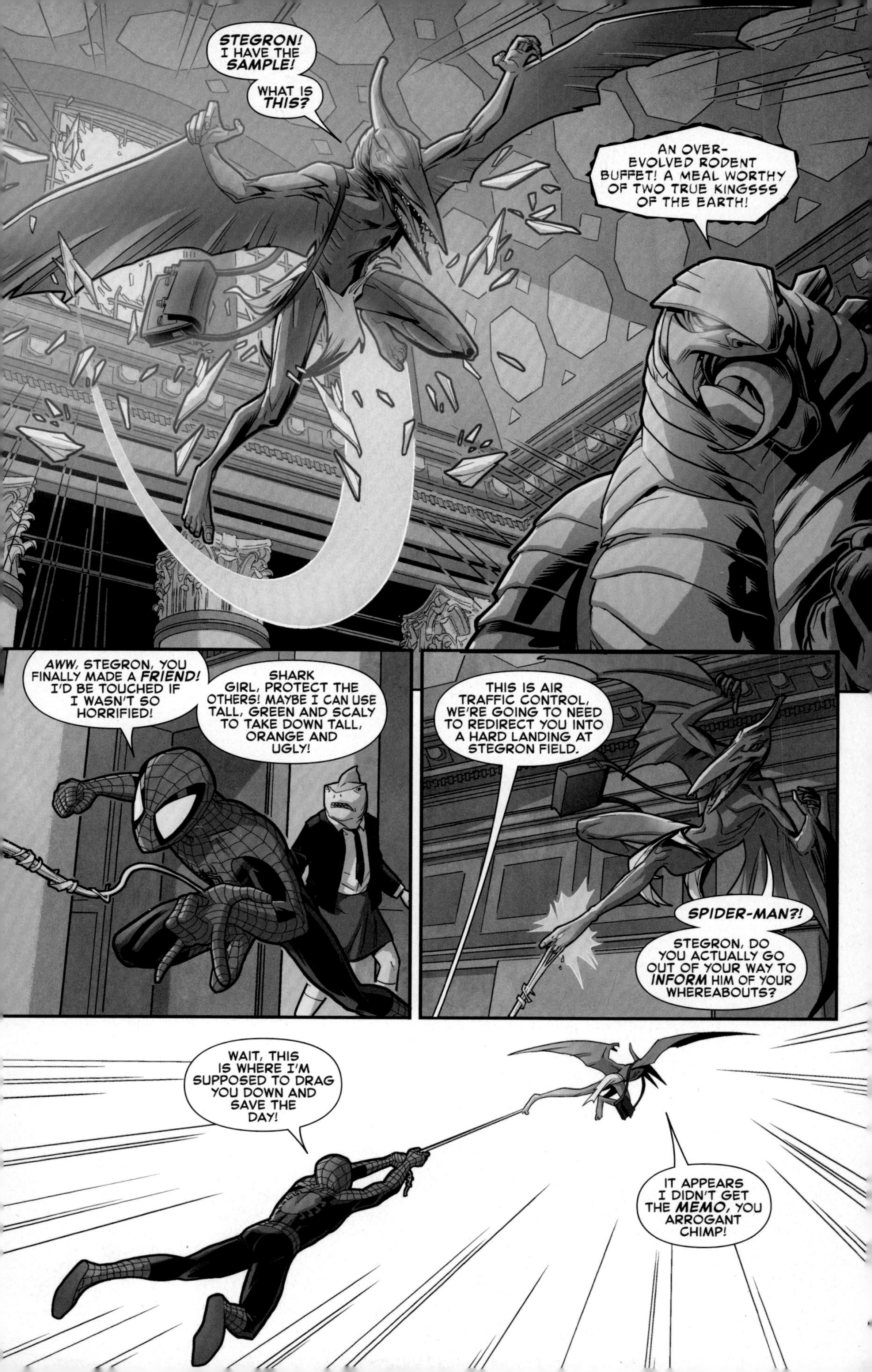
STEGRON! I HAVE THE SAMPLE!
WHAT IS THIS?
AN OVER-EVOLVED RODENT BUFFET! A MEAL WORTHY OF TWO TRUE KINGSSS OF THE EARTH!
AWW, STEGRON, YOU FINALLY MADE A FRIEND! I'D BE TOUCHED IF I WASN'T SO HORRIFIED!
SHARK GIRL, PROTECT THE OTHERS! MAYBE I CAN USE TALL, GREEN AND SCALY TO TAKE DOWN TALL, ORANGE AND UGLY!
THIS IS AIR TRAFFIC CONTROL, WE'RE GOING TO NEED TO REDIRECT YOU INTO A HARD LANDING AT STEGRON FIELD.
SPIDER-MAN?!
STEGRON, DO YOU ACTUALLY GO OUT OF YOUR WAY TO INFORM HIM OF YOUR WHEREABOUTS?
WAIT, THIS IS WHERE I'M SUPPOSED TO DRAG YOU DOWN AND SAVE THE DAY!
IT APPEARS I DIDN'T GET THE MEMO, YOU ARROGANT CHIMP!

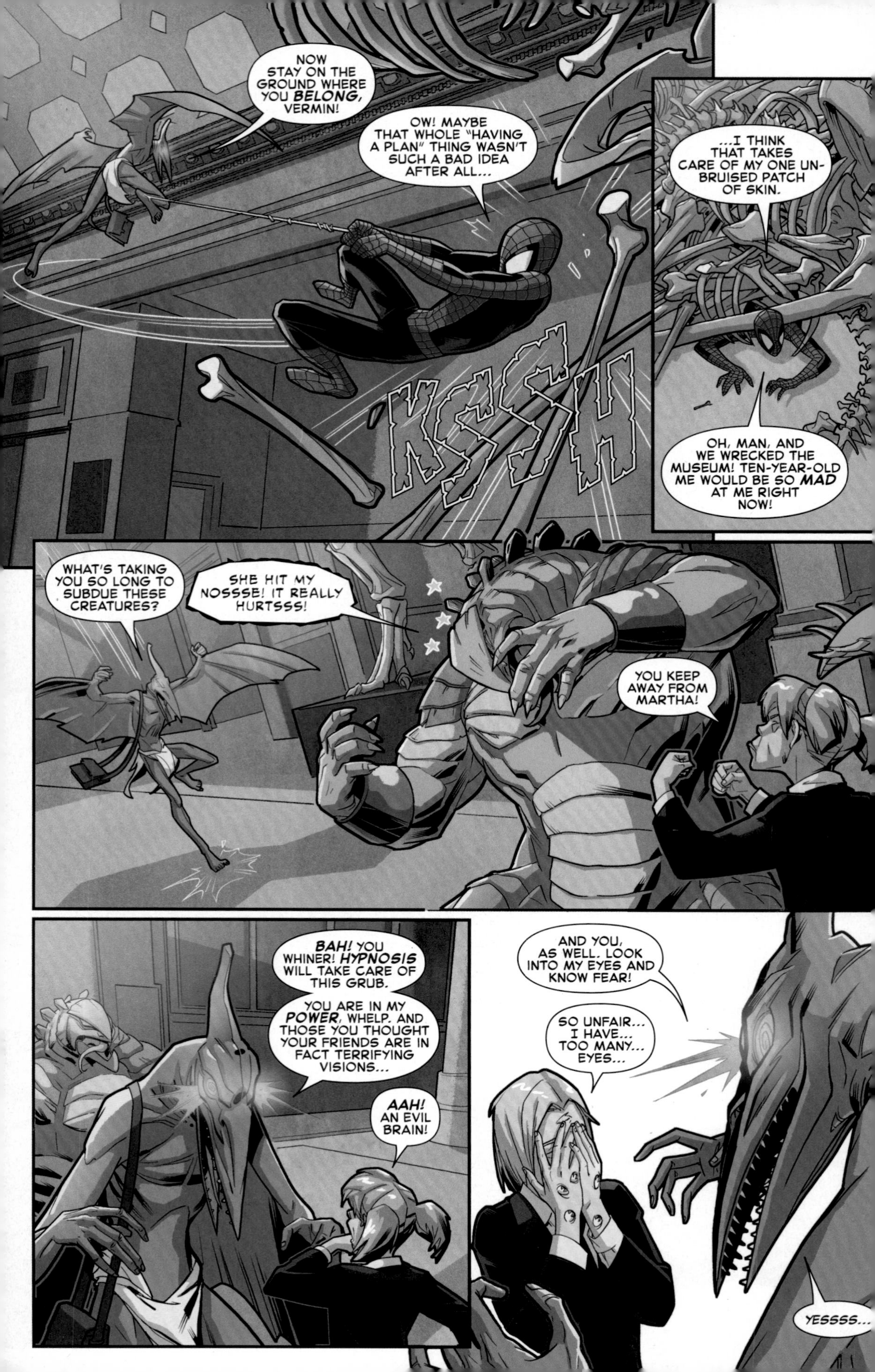

NOW STAY ON THE GROUND WHERE YOU *BELONG*, VERMIN!
OW! MAYBE THAT WHOLE "HAVING A PLAN" THING WASN'T SUCH A BAD IDEA AFTER ALL...
KSSH
...I THINK THAT TAKES CARE OF MY ONE UN-BRUISED PATCH OF SKIN.
OH, MAN, AND WE WRECKED THE MUSEUM! TEN-YEAR-OLD ME WOULD BE SO *MAD* AT ME RIGHT NOW!
WHAT'S TAKING YOU SO LONG TO SUBDUE THESE CREATURES?
SHE HIT MY NOSSSE! IT REALLY HURTSSS!
YOU KEEP AWAY FROM MARTHA!
BAH! YOU WHINER! *HYPNOSIS* WILL TAKE CARE OF THIS GRUB.
YOU ARE IN MY *POWER*, WHELP. AND THOSE YOU THOUGHT YOUR FRIENDS ARE IN FACT TERRIFYING VISIONS...
AAH! AN EVIL BRAIN!
AND YOU, AS WELL. LOOK INTO MY EYES AND KNOW FEAR!
SO UNFAIR... I HAVE... TOO MANY... EYES...
YESSSS...

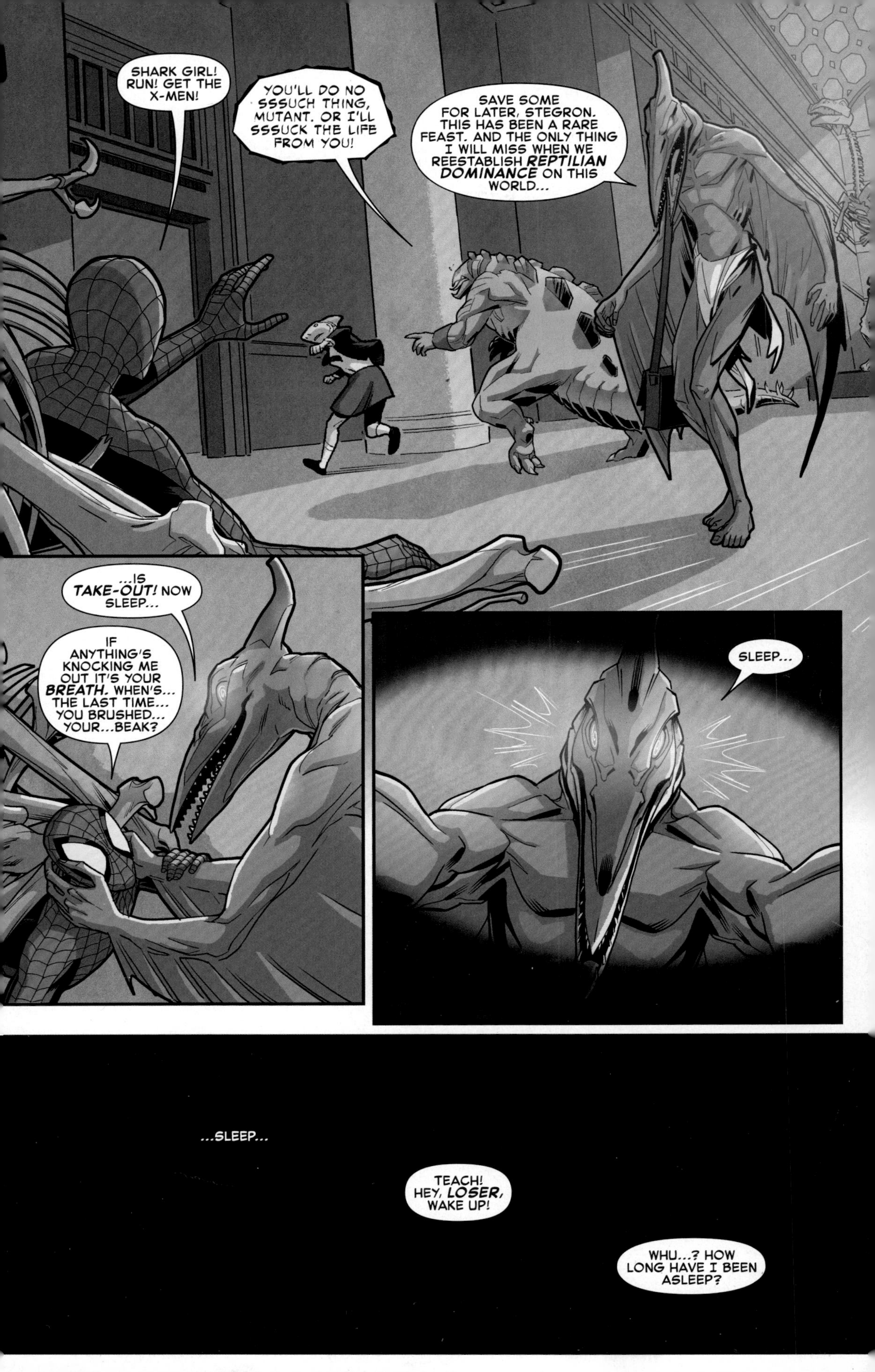
SHARK GIRL! RUN! GET THE X-MEN!
YOU'LL DO NO SSSUCH THING, MUTANT. OR I'LL SSSUCK THE LIFE FROM YOU!
SAVE SOME FOR LATER, STEGRON. THIS HAS BEEN A RARE FEAST. AND THE ONLY THING I WILL MISS WHEN WE REESTABLISH REPTILIAN DOMINANCE ON THIS WORLD...
...IS TAKE-OUT! NOW SLEEP...
IF ANYTHING'S KNOCKING ME OUT IT'S YOUR BREATH. WHEN'S... THE LAST TIME... YOU BRUSHED... YOUR...BEAK?
SLEEP...
...SLEEP...
TEACH! HEY, LOSER, WAKE UP!
WHU...? HOW LONG HAVE I BEEN ASLEEP?

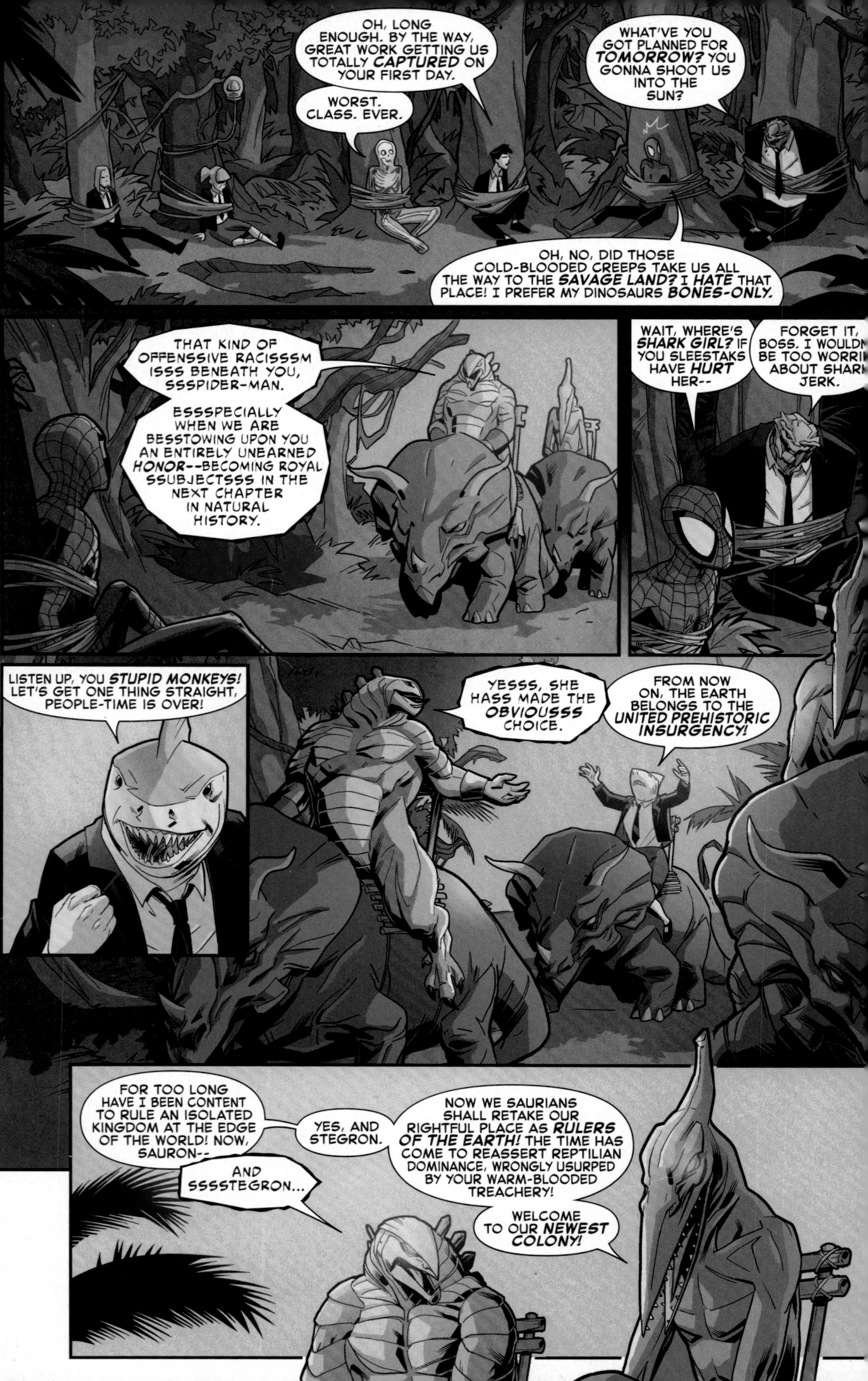
OH, LONG ENOUGH. BY THE WAY, GREAT WORK GETTING US TOTALLY CAPTURED ON YOUR FIRST DAY.
WORST. CLASS. EVER.
WHAT'VE YOU GOT PLANNED FOR TOMORROW? YOU GONNA SHOOT US INTO THE SUN?
OH, NO, DID THOSE COLD-BLOODED CREEPS TAKE US ALL THE WAY TO THE SAVAGE LAND? I HATE THAT PLACE! I PREFER MY DINOSAURS BONES-ONLY.
THAT KIND OF OFFENSSIVE RACISSSM ISSS BENEATH YOU, SSSPIDER-MAN.
ESSSPECIALLY WHEN WE ARE BESSTOWING UPON YOU AN ENTIRELY UNEARNED HONOR--BECOMING ROYAL SSUBJECTSSS IN THE NEXT CHAPTER IN NATURAL HISTORY.
WAIT, WHERE'S SHARK GIRL? IF YOU SLEESTAKS HAVE HURT HER--
FORGET IT, BOSS. I WOULDN BE TOO WORRI ABOUT SHARK JERK.
LISTEN UP, YOU STUPID MONKEYS! LET'S GET ONE THING STRAIGHT, PEOPLE-TIME IS OVER!
YESSS, SHE HASS MADE THE OBVIOUSSS CHOICE.
FROM NOW ON, THE EARTH BELONGS TO THE UNITED PREHISTORIC INSURGENCY!
FOR TOO LONG HAVE I BEEN CONTENT TO RULE AN ISOLATED KINGDOM AT THE EDGE OF THE WORLD! NOW, SAURON--
AND SSSSTEGRON...
YES, AND STEGRON.
NOW WE SAURIANS SHALL RETAKE OUR RIGHTFUL PLACE AS RULERS OF THE EARTH! THE TIME HAS COME TO REASSERT REPTILIAN DOMINANCE, WRONGLY USURPED BY YOUR WARM-BLOODED TREACHERY!
WELCOME TO OUR NEWEST COLONY!

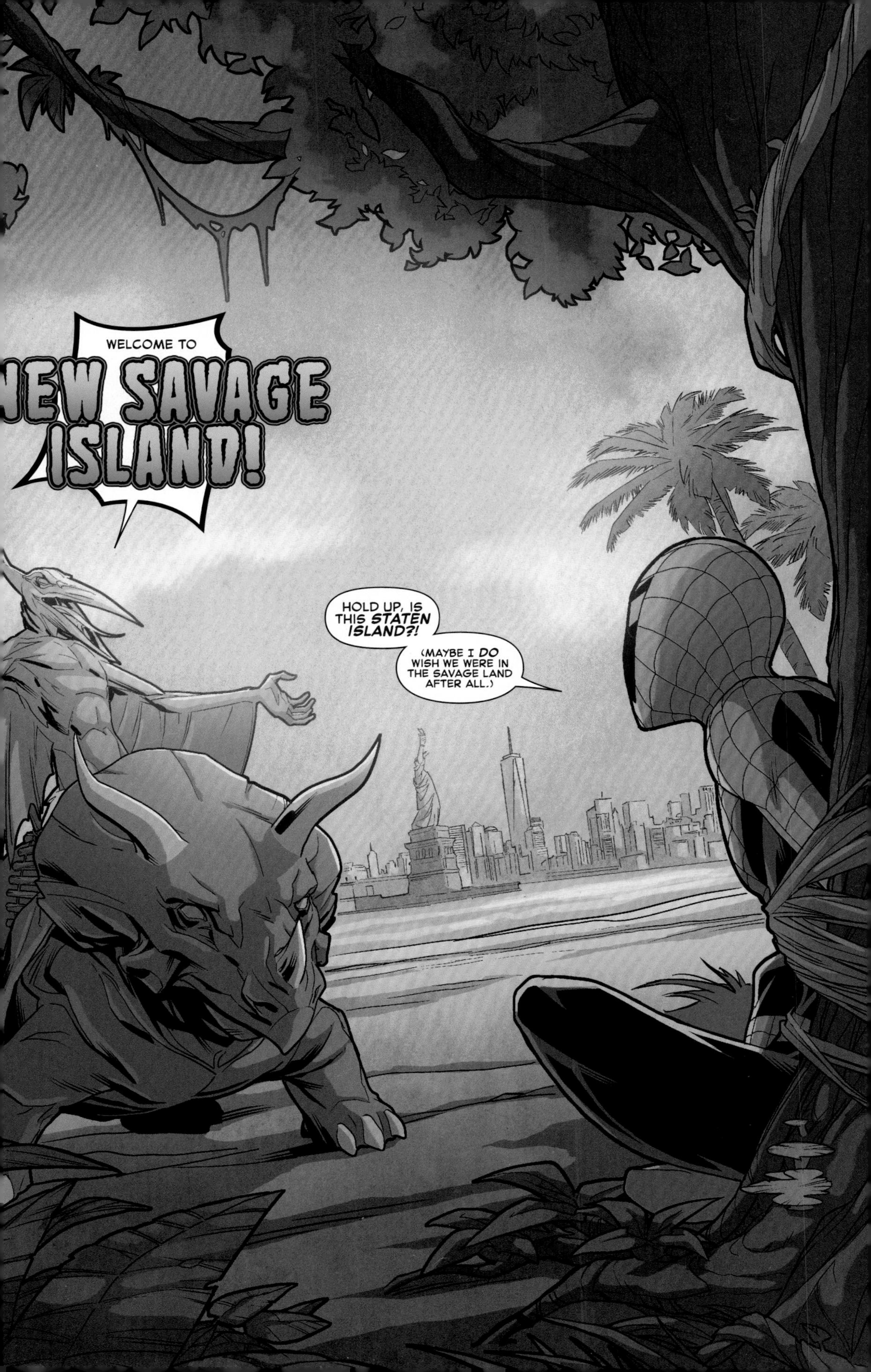
WELCOME TO
NEW SAVAGE ISLAND!
HOLD UP, IS THIS STATEN ISLAND?!
(MAYBE I DO WISH WE WERE IN THE SAVAGE LAND AFTER ALL.)

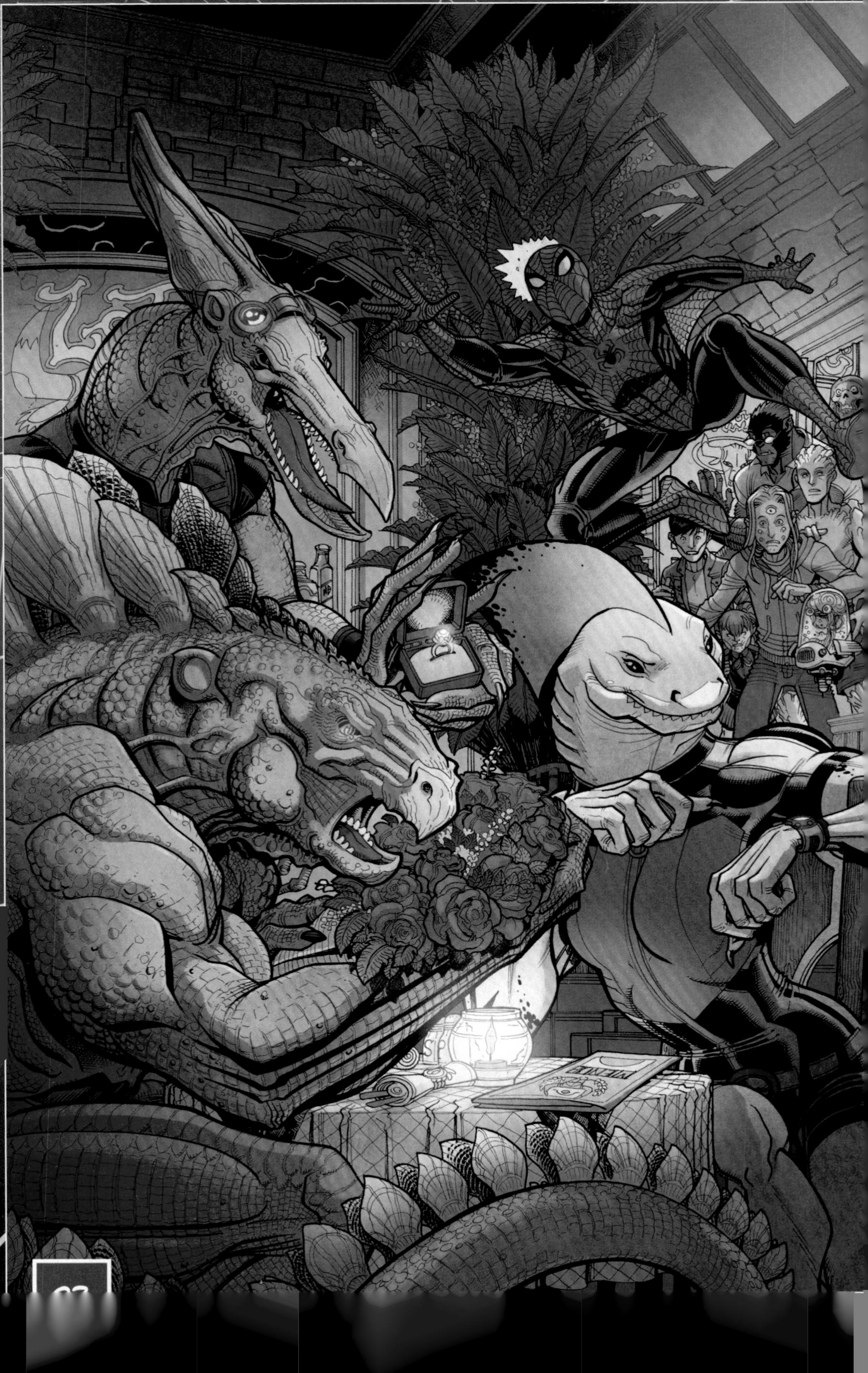
MENU

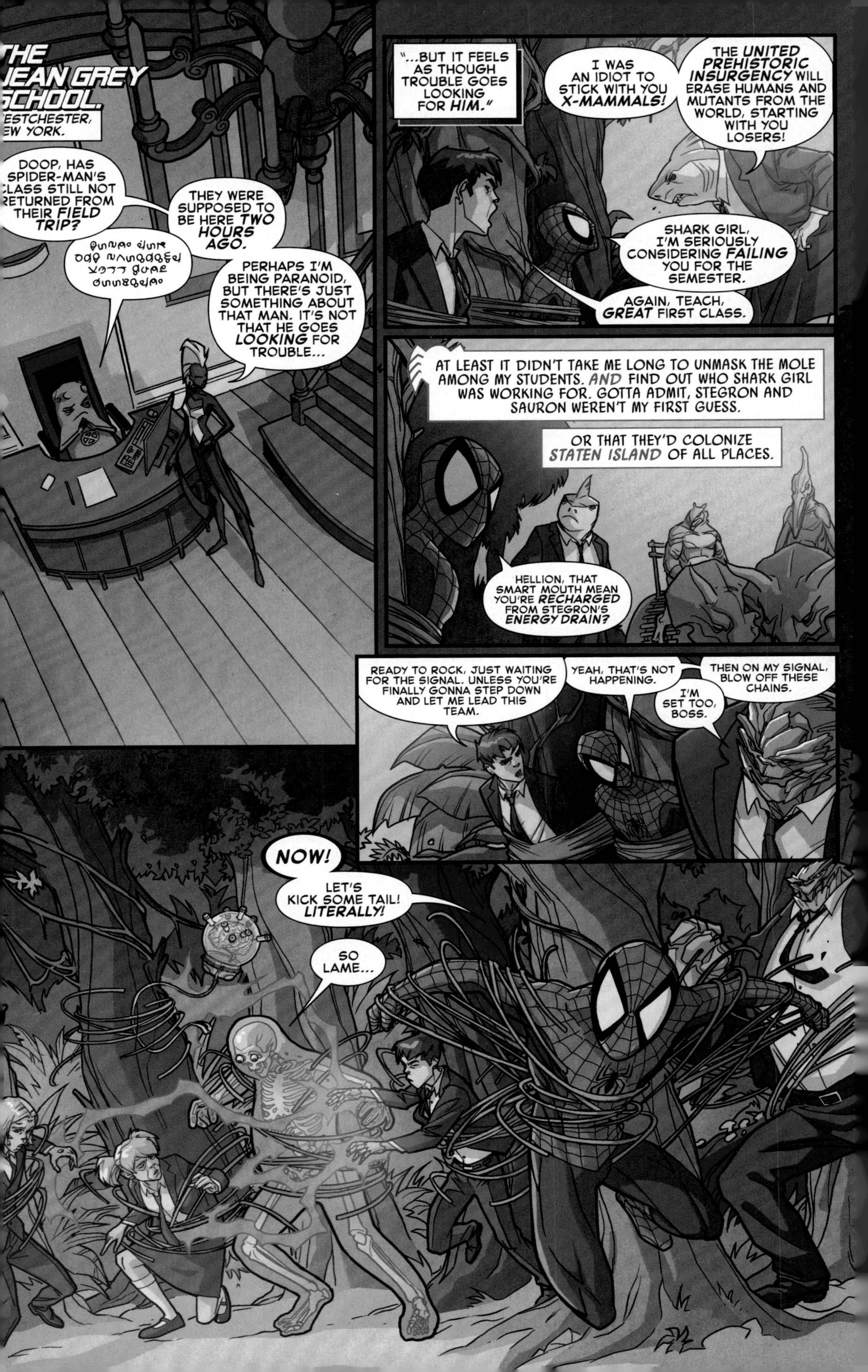

THE JEAN GREY SCHOOL. ESTCHESTER, EW YORK.
DOOP, HAS SPIDER-MAN'S CLASS STILL NOT RETURNED FROM THEIR FIELD TRIP?
THEY WERE SUPPOSED TO BE HERE TWO HOURS AGO.
PERHAPS I'M BEING PARANOID, BUT THERE'S JUST SOMETHING ABOUT THAT MAN. IT'S NOT THAT HE GOES LOOKING FOR TROUBLE...
"...BUT IT FEELS AS THOUGH TROUBLE GOES LOOKING FOR HIM."
I WAS AN IDIOT TO STICK WITH YOU X-MAMMALS!
THE UNITED PREHISTORIC INSURGENCY WILL ERASE HUMANS AND MUTANTS FROM THE WORLD, STARTING WITH YOU LOSERS!
SHARK GIRL, I'M SERIOUSLY CONSIDERING FAILING YOU FOR THE SEMESTER.
AGAIN, TEACH, GREAT FIRST CLASS.
AT LEAST IT DIDN'T TAKE ME LONG TO UNMASK THE MOLE AMONG MY STUDENTS. AND FIND OUT WHO SHARK GIRL WAS WORKING FOR. GOTTA ADMIT, STEGRON AND SAURON WEREN'T MY FIRST GUESS.
OR THAT THEY'D COLONIZE STATEN ISLAND OF ALL PLACES.
HELLION, THAT SMART MOUTH MEAN YOU'RE RECHARGED FROM STEGRON'S ENERGY DRAIN?
READY TO ROCK, JUST WAITING FOR THE SIGNAL. UNLESS YOU'RE FINALLY GONNA STEP DOWN AND LET ME LEAD THIS TEAM.
YEAH, THAT'S NOT HAPPENING.
I'M SET TOO, BOSS.
THEN ON MY SIGNAL, BLOW OFF THESE CHAINS.
NOW!
LET'S KICK SOME TAIL! LITERALLY!
SO LAME...

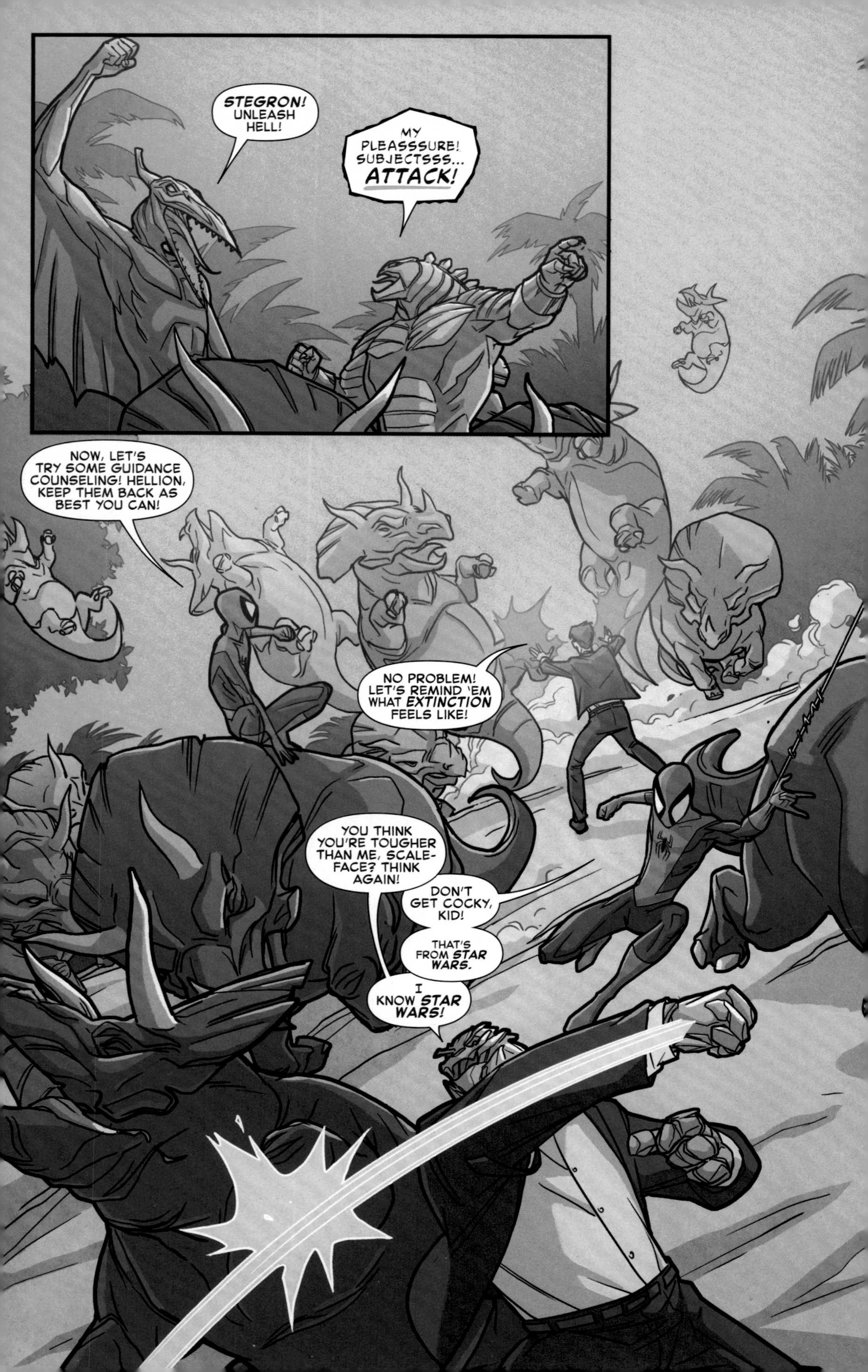

STEGRON! UNLEASH HELL!
MY PLEASSSURE! SUBJECTSSS... ATTACK!
NOW, LET'S TRY SOME GUIDANCE COUNSELING! HELLION, KEEP THEM BACK AS BEST YOU CAN!
NO PROBLEM! LET'S REMIND 'EM WHAT EXTINCTION FEELS LIKE!
YOU THINK YOU'RE TOUGHER THAN ME, SCALE-FACE? THINK AGAIN!
DON'T GET COCKY, KID!
THAT'S FROM STAR WARS.
I KNOW STAR WARS!

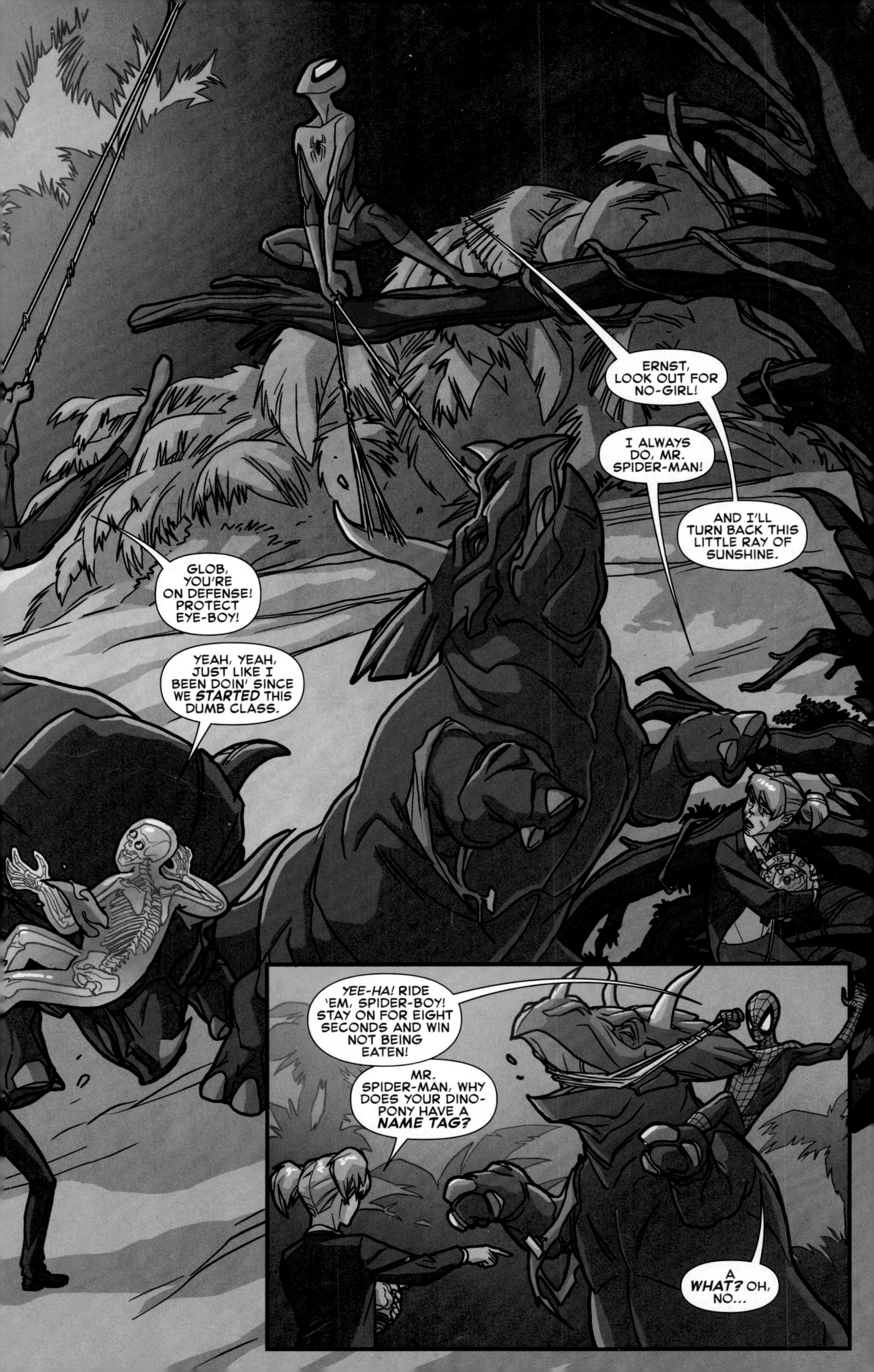
ERNST, LOOK OUT FOR NO-GIRL!
I ALWAYS DO, MR. SPIDER-MAN!
AND I'LL TURN BACK THIS LITTLE RAY OF SUNSHINE.
GLOB, YOU'RE ON DEFENSE! PROTECT EYE-BOY!
YEAH, YEAH, JUST LIKE I BEEN DOIN' SINCE WE *STARTED* THIS DUMB CLASS.
YEE-HA! RIDE 'EM, SPIDER-BOY! STAY ON FOR EIGHT SECONDS AND WIN NOT BEING EATEN!
MR. SPIDER-MAN, WHY DOES YOUR DINO-PONY HAVE A ***NAME TAG?***
A ***WHAT?*** OH, NO...

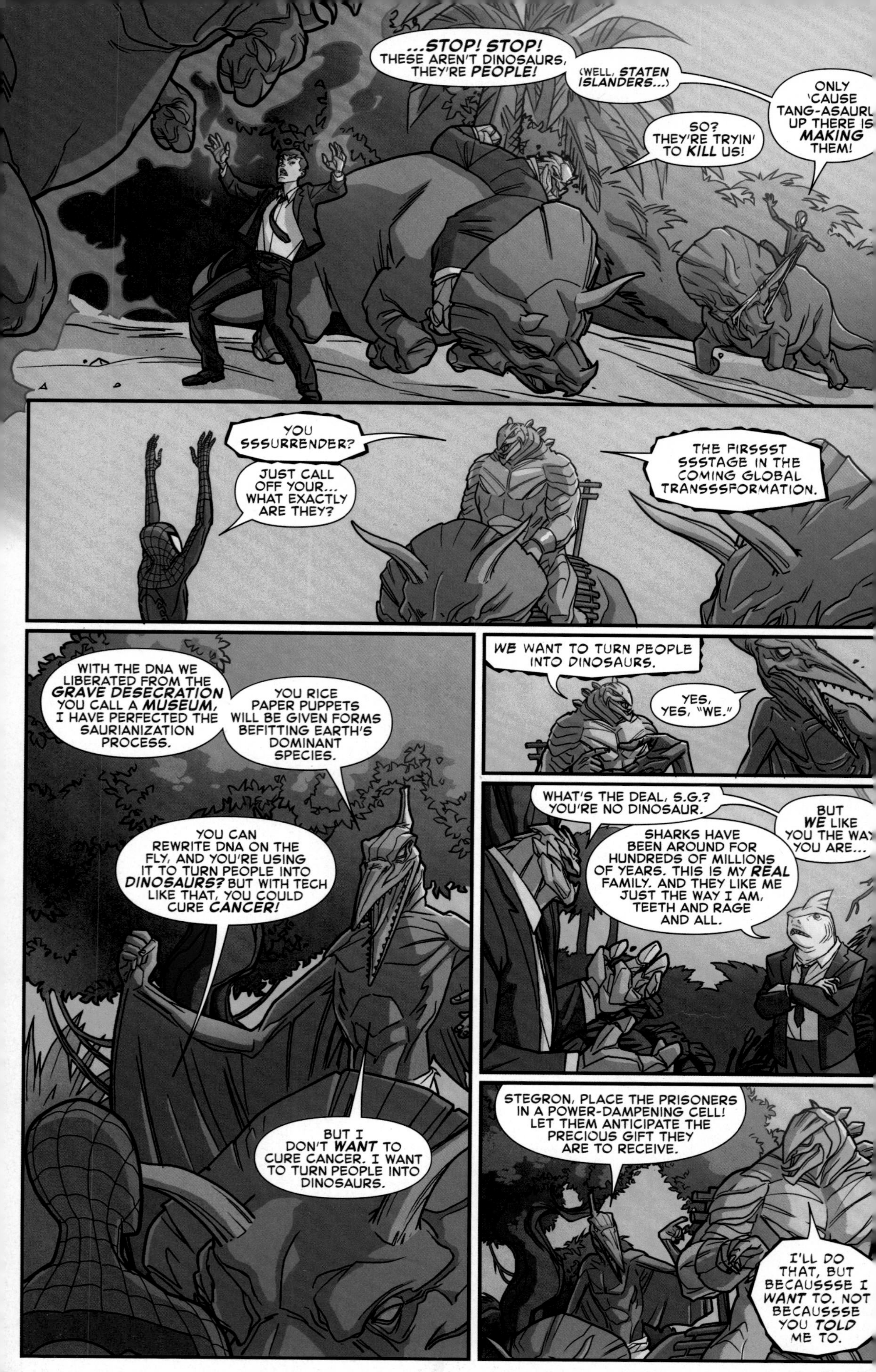
...STOP! STOP! THESE AREN'T DINOSAURS, THEY'RE PEOPLE!
(WELL, STATEN ISLANDERS...)
SO? THEY'RE TRYIN' TO KILL US!
ONLY 'CAUSE TANG-ASAURU UP THERE IS MAKING THEM!
YOU SSSURRENDER?
JUST CALL OFF YOUR... WHAT EXACTLY ARE THEY?
THE FIRSSST SSSTAGE IN THE COMING GLOBAL TRANSSSFORMATION.
WITH THE DNA WE LIBERATED FROM THE GRAVE DESECRATION YOU CALL A MUSEUM, I HAVE PERFECTED THE SAURIANIZATION PROCESS.
YOU RICE PAPER PUPPETS WILL BE GIVEN FORMS BEFITTING EARTH'S DOMINANT SPECIES.
YOU CAN REWRITE DNA ON THE FLY, AND YOU'RE USING IT TO TURN PEOPLE INTO DINOSAURS? BUT WITH TECH LIKE THAT, YOU COULD CURE CANCER!
BUT I DON'T WANT TO CURE CANCER. I WANT TO TURN PEOPLE INTO DINOSAURS.
WE WANT TO TURN PEOPLE INTO DINOSAURS.
YES, YES, "WE."
WHAT'S THE DEAL, S.G.? YOU'RE NO DINOSAUR.
SHARKS HAVE BEEN AROUND FOR HUNDREDS OF MILLIONS OF YEARS. THIS IS MY REAL FAMILY. AND THEY LIKE ME JUST THE WAY I AM, TEETH AND RAGE AND ALL.
BUT WE LIKE YOU THE WAY YOU ARE...
STEGRON, PLACE THE PRISONERS IN A POWER-DAMPENING CELL! LET THEM ANTICIPATE THE PRECIOUS GIFT THEY ARE TO RECEIVE.
I'LL DO THAT, BUT BECAUSSSE I WANT TO. NOT BECAUSSSE YOU TOLD ME TO.

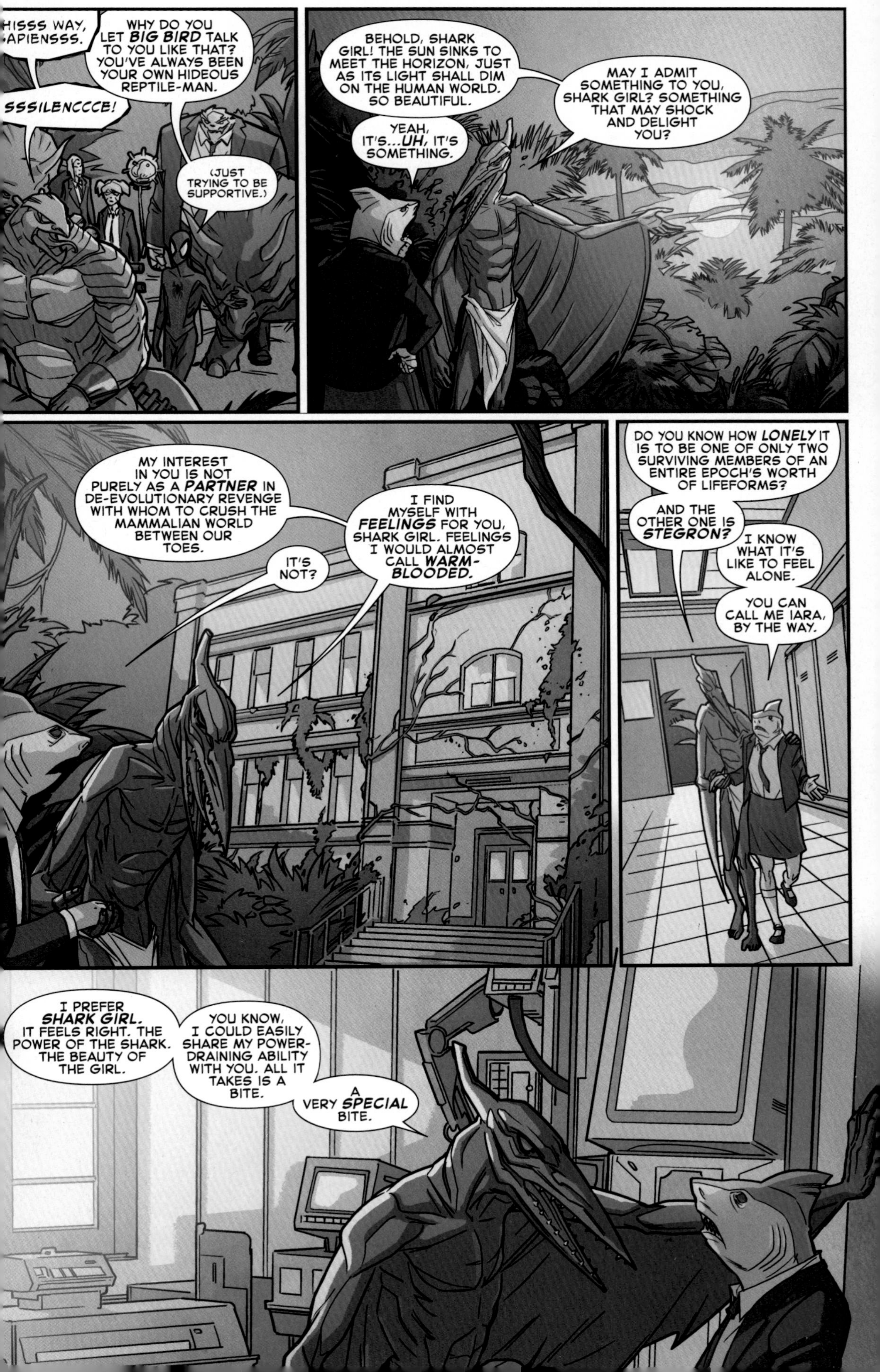
HISSS WAY, SAPIENSSS.
WHY DO YOU LET BIG BIRD TALK TO YOU LIKE THAT? YOU'VE ALWAYS BEEN YOUR OWN HIDEOUS REPTILE-MAN.
SSSILENCCCE!
(JUST TRYING TO BE SUPPORTIVE.)
BEHOLD, SHARK GIRL! THE SUN SINKS TO MEET THE HORIZON, JUST AS ITS LIGHT SHALL DIM ON THE HUMAN WORLD. SO BEAUTIFUL.
YEAH, IT'S...UH, IT'S SOMETHING.
MAY I ADMIT SOMETHING TO YOU, SHARK GIRL? SOMETHING THAT MAY SHOCK AND DELIGHT YOU?
MY INTEREST IN YOU IS NOT PURELY AS A PARTNER IN DE-EVOLUTIONARY REVENGE WITH WHOM TO CRUSH THE MAMMALIAN WORLD BETWEEN OUR TOES.
IT'S NOT?
I FIND MYSELF WITH FEELINGS FOR YOU, SHARK GIRL. FEELINGS I WOULD ALMOST CALL WARM-BLOODED.
DO YOU KNOW HOW LONELY IT IS TO BE ONE OF ONLY TWO SURVIVING MEMBERS OF AN ENTIRE EPOCH'S WORTH OF LIFEFORMS?
AND THE OTHER ONE IS STEGRON?
I KNOW WHAT IT'S LIKE TO FEEL ALONE.
YOU CAN CALL ME IARA, BY THE WAY.
I PREFER SHARK GIRL. IT FEELS RIGHT. THE POWER OF THE SHARK. THE BEAUTY OF THE GIRL.
YOU KNOW, I COULD EASILY SHARE MY POWER-DRAINING ABILITY WITH YOU. ALL IT TAKES IS A BITE.
A VERY SPECIAL BITE.

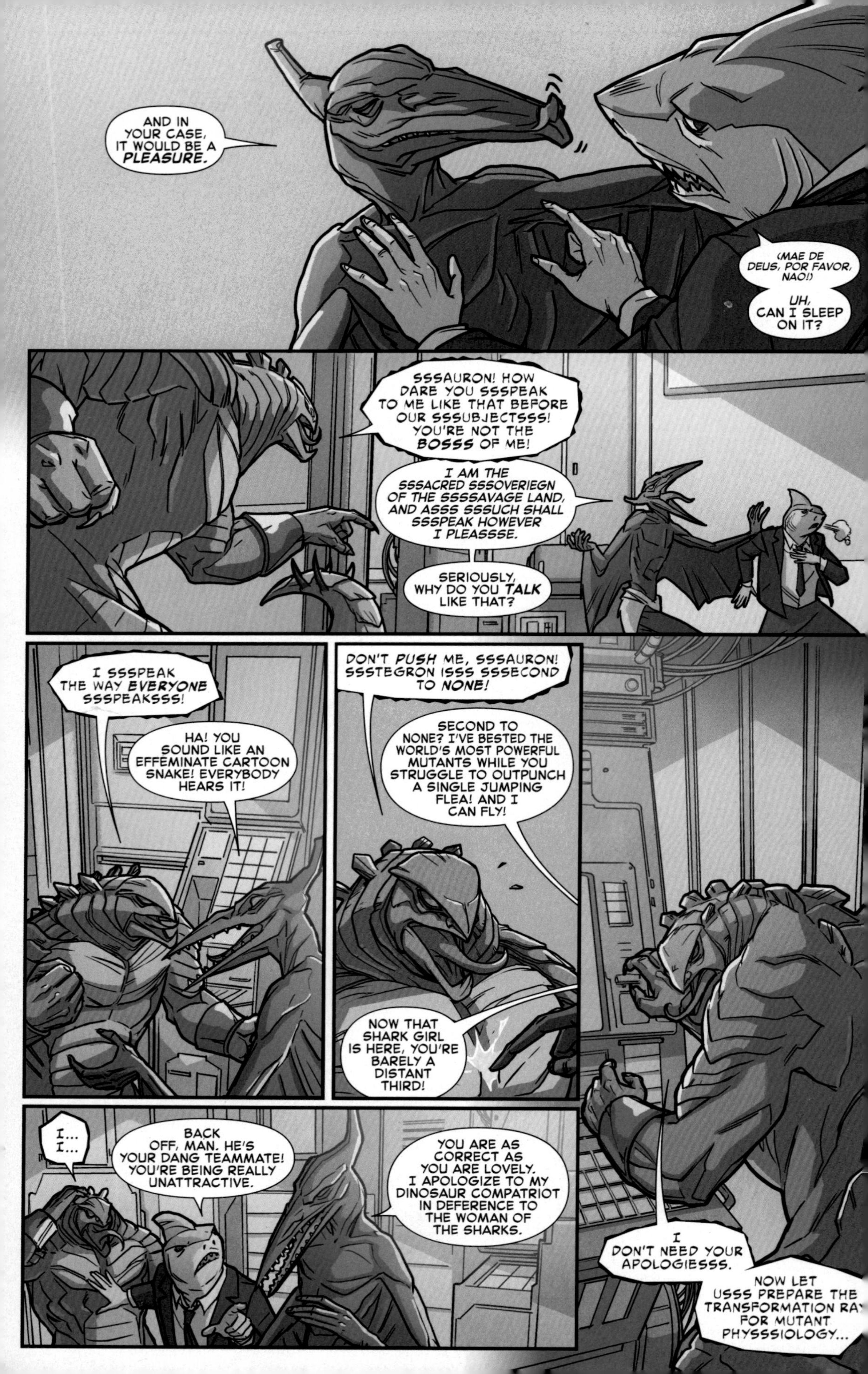

AND IN YOUR CASE, IT WOULD BE A *PLEASURE.*
(MAE DE DEUS, POR FAVOR, NAO!)
UH, CAN I SLEEP ON IT?
SSSAURON! HOW DARE YOU SSSPEAK TO ME LIKE THAT BEFORE OUR SSSUBJECTSSS! YOU'RE NOT THE *BOSSS* OF ME!
I AM THE SSSACRED SSSOVERIEGN OF THE SSSSAVAGE LAND, AND ASSS SSSUCH SHALL SSSPEAK HOWEVER I PLEASSSE.
SERIOUSLY, WHY DO YOU *TALK* LIKE THAT?
I SSSPEAK THE WAY *EVERYONE* SSSPEAKSSS!
HA! YOU SOUND LIKE AN EFFEMINATE CARTOON SNAKE! EVERYBODY HEARS IT!
DON'T *PUSH* ME, SSSAURON! SSSTEGRON ISSS SSSECOND TO *NONE!*
SECOND TO NONE? I'VE BESTED THE WORLD'S MOST POWERFUL MUTANTS WHILE YOU STRUGGLE TO OUTPUNCH A SINGLE JUMPING FLEA! AND I CAN FLY!
NOW THAT SHARK GIRL IS HERE, YOU'RE BARELY A DISTANT THIRD!
I... I...
BACK OFF, MAN. HE'S YOUR DANG TEAMMATE! YOU'RE BEING REALLY UNATTRACTIVE.
YOU ARE AS CORRECT AS YOU ARE LOVELY. I APOLOGIZE TO MY DINOSAUR COMPATRIOT IN DEFERENCE TO THE WOMAN OF THE SHARKS.
I DON'T NEED YOUR APOLOGIESSS.
NOW LET USSS PREPARE THE TRANSFORMATION RAY FOR MUTANT PHYSSSIOLOGY...

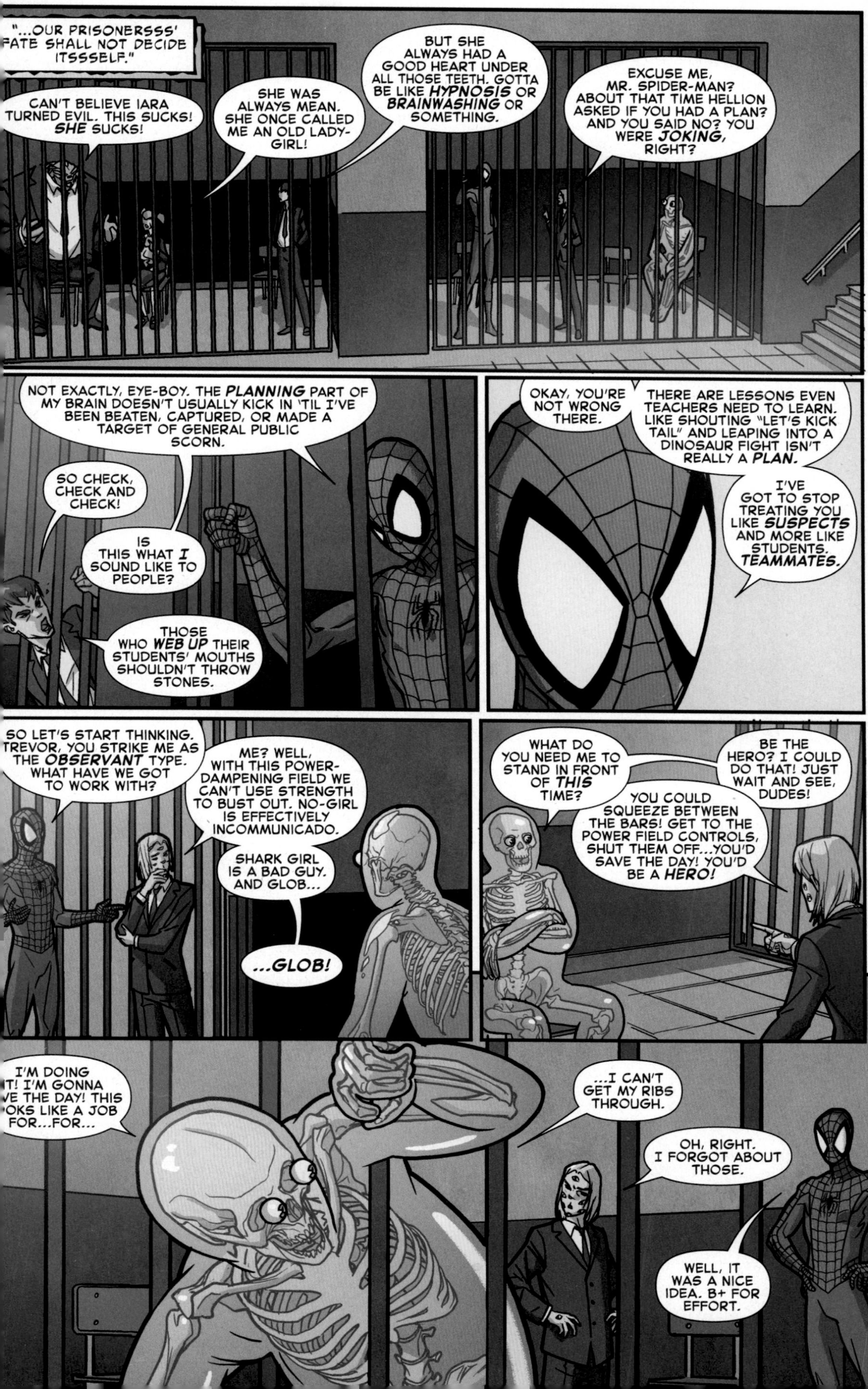
"...OUR PRISONERSSS' FATE SHALL NOT DECIDE ITSSSELF."
CAN'T BELIEVE IARA TURNED EVIL. THIS SUCKS! SHE SUCKS!
SHE WAS ALWAYS MEAN. SHE ONCE CALLED ME AN OLD LADY-GIRL!
BUT SHE ALWAYS HAD A GOOD HEART UNDER ALL THOSE TEETH. GOTTA BE LIKE HYPNOSIS OR BRAINWASHING OR SOMETHING.
EXCUSE ME, MR. SPIDER-MAN? ABOUT THAT TIME HELLION ASKED IF YOU HAD A PLAN? AND YOU SAID NO? YOU WERE JOKING, RIGHT?
NOT EXACTLY, EYE-BOY. THE PLANNING PART OF MY BRAIN DOESN'T USUALLY KICK IN 'TIL I'VE BEEN BEATEN, CAPTURED, OR MADE A TARGET OF GENERAL PUBLIC SCORN.
SO CHECK, CHECK AND CHECK!
IS THIS WHAT I SOUND LIKE TO PEOPLE?
THOSE WHO WEB UP THEIR STUDENTS' MOUTHS SHOULDN'T THROW STONES.
OKAY, YOU'RE NOT WRONG THERE.
THERE ARE LESSONS EVEN TEACHERS NEED TO LEARN. LIKE SHOUTING "LET'S KICK TAIL" AND LEAPING INTO A DINOSAUR FIGHT ISN'T REALLY A PLAN.
I'VE GOT TO STOP TREATING YOU LIKE SUSPECTS AND MORE LIKE STUDENTS. TEAMMATES.
SO LET'S START THINKING. TREVOR, YOU STRIKE ME AS THE OBSERVANT TYPE. WHAT HAVE WE GOT TO WORK WITH?
ME? WELL, WITH THIS POWER-DAMPENING FIELD WE CAN'T USE STRENGTH TO BUST OUT. NO-GIRL IS EFFECTIVELY INCOMMUNICADO.
SHARK GIRL IS A BAD GUY. AND GLOB...
...GLOB!
WHAT DO YOU NEED ME TO STAND IN FRONT OF THIS TIME?
YOU COULD SQUEEZE BETWEEN THE BARS! GET TO THE POWER FIELD CONTROLS, SHUT THEM OFF...YOU'D SAVE THE DAY! YOU'D BE A HERO!
BE THE HERO? I COULD DO THAT! JUST WAIT AND SEE, DUDES!
I'M DOING IT! I'M GONNA VE THE DAY! THIS OKS LIKE A JOB FOR...FOR...
...I CAN'T GET MY RIBS THROUGH.
OH, RIGHT. I FORGOT ABOUT THOSE.
WELL, IT WAS A NICE IDEA. B+ FOR EFFORT.

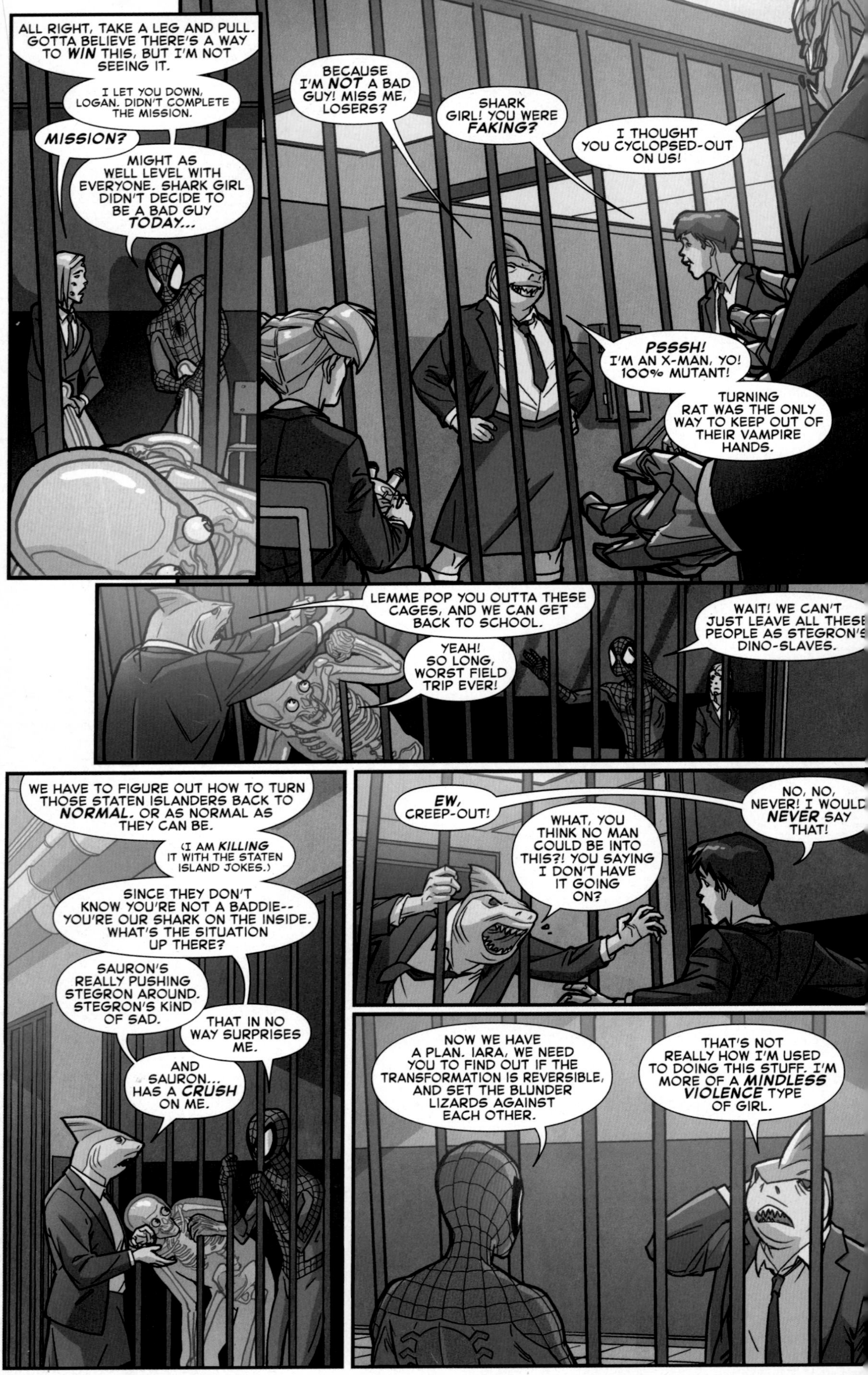
ALL RIGHT, TAKE A LEG AND PULL. GOTTA BELIEVE THERE'S A WAY TO WIN THIS, BUT I'M NOT SEEING IT.
I LET YOU DOWN, LOGAN. DIDN'T COMPLETE THE MISSION.
MISSION?
MIGHT AS WELL LEVEL WITH EVERYONE. SHARK GIRL DIDN'T DECIDE TO BE A BAD GUY TODAY...
BECAUSE I'M NOT A BAD GUY! MISS ME, LOSERS?
SHARK GIRL! YOU WERE FAKING?
I THOUGHT YOU CYCLOPSED-OUT ON US!
PSSSH! I'M AN X-MAN, YO! 100% MUTANT!
TURNING RAT WAS THE ONLY WAY TO KEEP OUT OF THEIR VAMPIRE HANDS.
LEMME POP YOU OUTTA THESE CAGES, AND WE CAN GET BACK TO SCHOOL.
YEAH! SO LONG, WORST FIELD TRIP EVER!
WAIT! WE CAN'T JUST LEAVE ALL THESE PEOPLE AS STEGRON'S DINO-SLAVES.
WE HAVE TO FIGURE OUT HOW TO TURN THOSE STATEN ISLANDERS BACK TO NORMAL. OR AS NORMAL AS THEY CAN BE.
(I AM KILLING IT WITH THE STATEN ISLAND JOKES.)
SINCE THEY DON'T KNOW YOU'RE NOT A BADDIE-- YOU'RE OUR SHARK ON THE INSIDE. WHAT'S THE SITUATION UP THERE?
SAURON'S REALLY PUSHING STEGRON AROUND. STEGRON'S KIND OF SAD.
THAT IN NO WAY SURPRISES ME.
AND SAURON... HAS A CRUSH ON ME.
EW, CREEP-OUT!
NO, NO, NEVER! I WOULD NEVER SAY THAT!
WHAT, YOU THINK NO MAN COULD BE INTO THIS?! YOU SAYING I DON'T HAVE IT GOING ON?
NOW WE HAVE A PLAN. IARA, WE NEED YOU TO FIND OUT IF THE TRANSFORMATION IS REVERSIBLE, AND SET THE BLUNDER LIZARDS AGAINST EACH OTHER.
THAT'S NOT REALLY HOW I'M USED TO DOING THIS STUFF. I'M MORE OF A MINDLESS VIOLENCE TYPE OF GIRL.

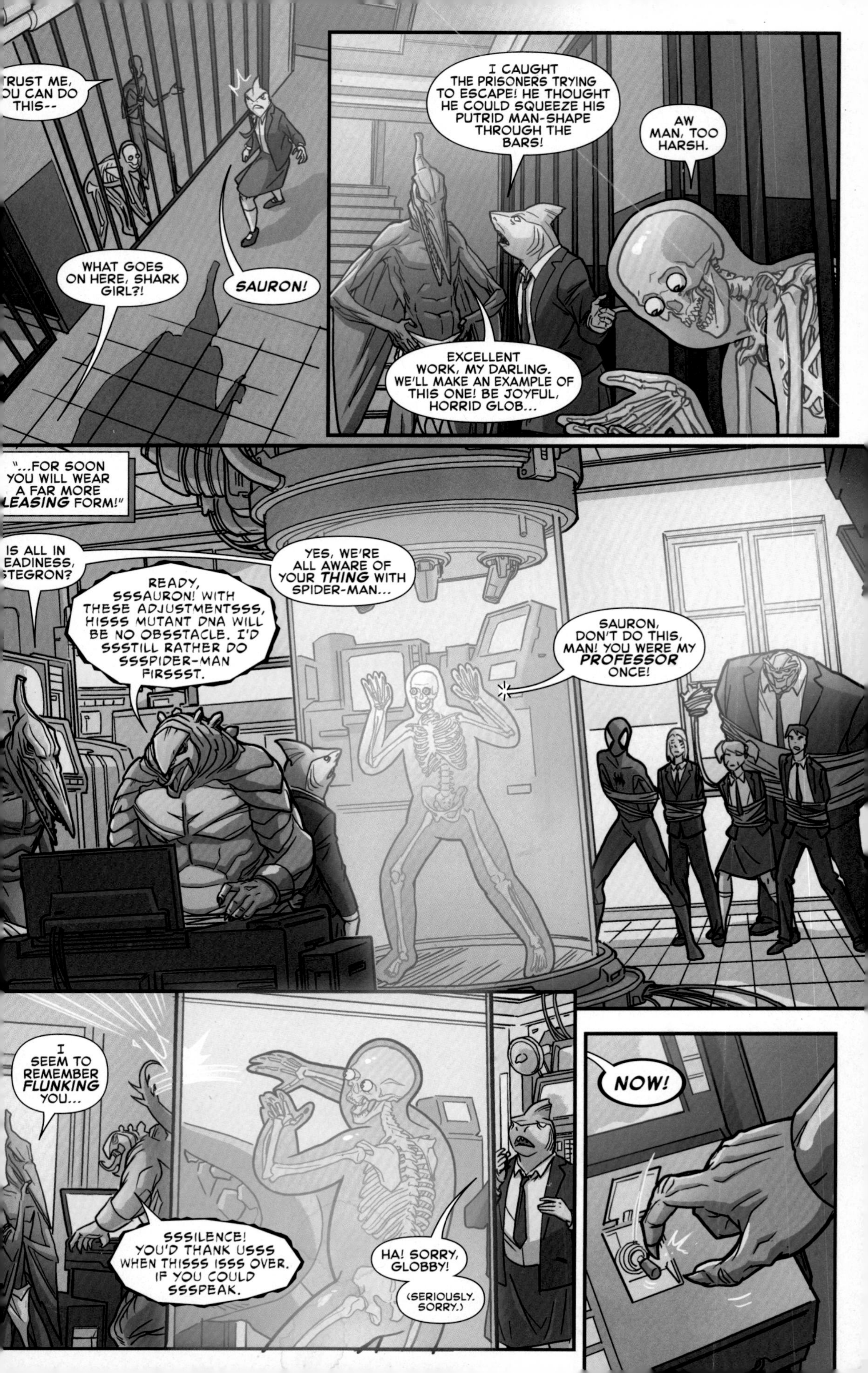
TRUST ME, YOU CAN DO THIS--
WHAT GOES ON HERE, SHARK GIRL?!
SAURON!
I CAUGHT THE PRISONERS TRYING TO ESCAPE! HE THOUGHT HE COULD SQUEEZE HIS PUTRID MAN-SHAPE THROUGH THE BARS!
AW MAN, TOO HARSH.
EXCELLENT WORK, MY DARLING. WE'LL MAKE AN EXAMPLE OF THIS ONE! BE JOYFUL, HORRID GLOB...
"...FOR SOON YOU WILL WEAR A FAR MORE PLEASING FORM!"
IS ALL IN READINESS, STEGRON?
YES, WE'RE ALL AWARE OF YOUR THING WITH SPIDER-MAN...
READY, SSSAURON! WITH THESE ADJUSTMENTSSS, HISSS MUTANT DNA WILL BE NO OBSSTACLE. I'D SSSTILL RATHER DO SSSPIDER-MAN FIRSSST.
SAURON, DON'T DO THIS, MAN! YOU WERE MY PROFESSOR ONCE!
I SEEM TO REMEMBER FLUNKING YOU...
SSSILENCE! YOU'D THANK USSS WHEN THISSS ISSS OVER. IF YOU COULD SSSPEAK.
HA! SORRY, GLOBBY!
(SERIOUSLY. SORRY.)
NOW!

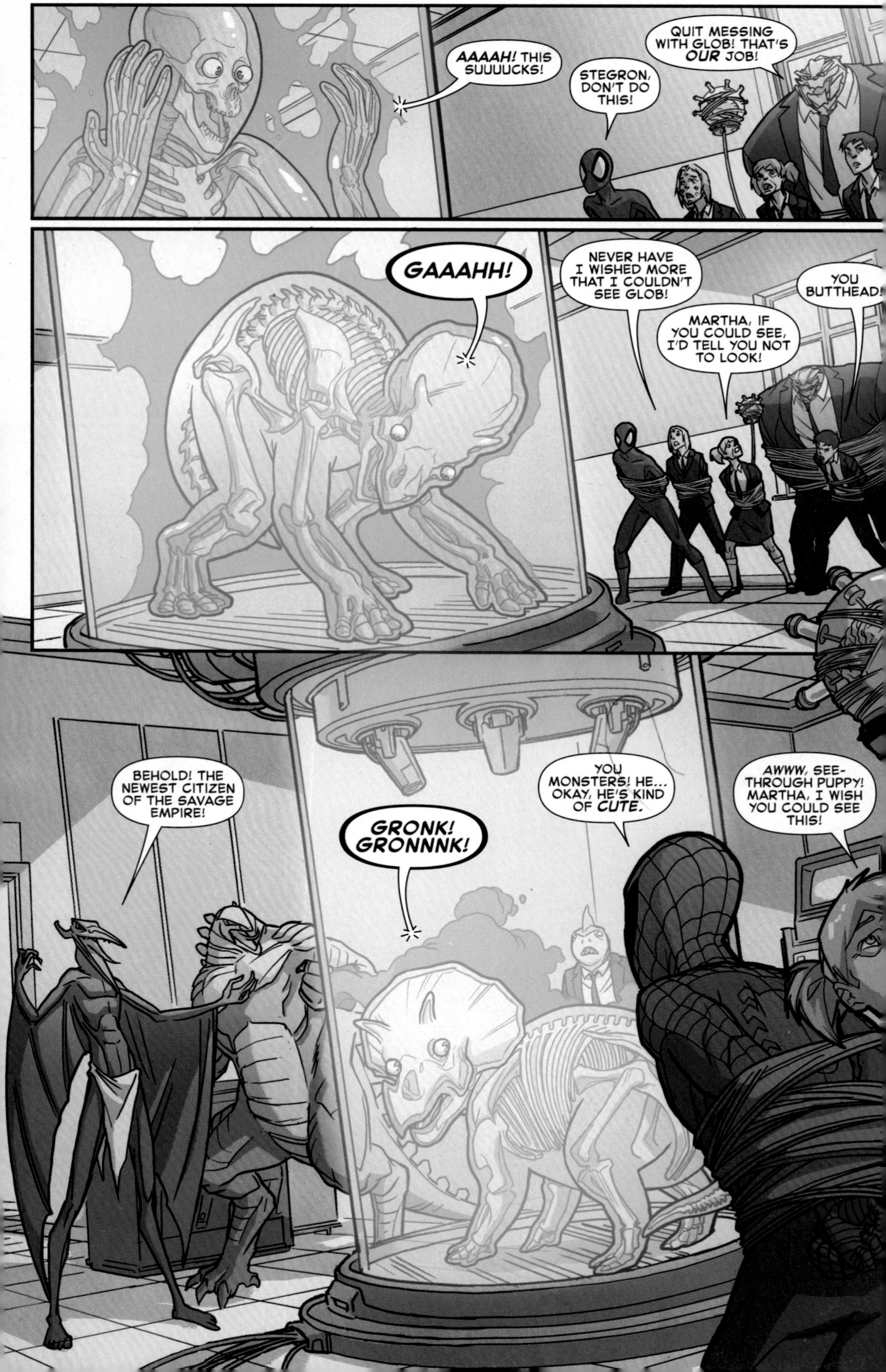
AAAAH! THIS SUUUUCKS!
STEGRON, DON'T DO THIS!
QUIT MESSING WITH GLOB! THAT'S OUR JOB!
GAAAHH!
NEVER HAVE I WISHED MORE THAT I COULDN'T SEE GLOB!
MARTHA, IF YOU COULD SEE, I'D TELL YOU NOT TO LOOK!
YOU BUTTHEAD!
BEHOLD! THE NEWEST CITIZEN OF THE SAVAGE EMPIRE!
GRONK! GRONNNK!
YOU MONSTERS! HE... OKAY, HE'S KIND OF CUTE.
AWWW, SEE-THROUGH PUPPY! MARTHA, I WISH YOU COULD SEE THIS!

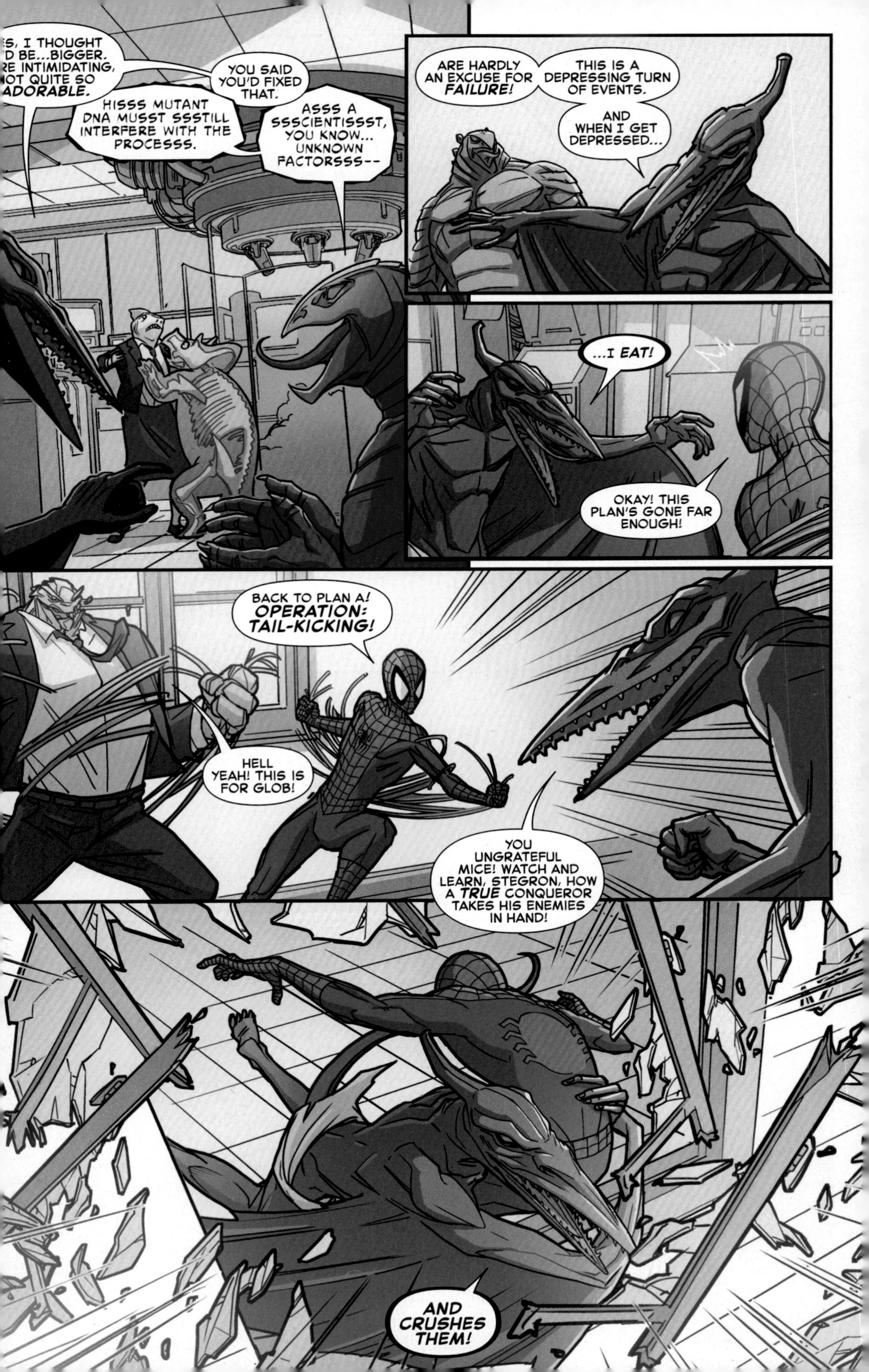

...ES, I THOUGHT ...'D BE...BIGGER. ...RE INTIMIDATING, ...NOT QUITE SO ADORABLE.
YOU SAID YOU'D FIXED THAT.
HISSS MUTANT DNA MUSST SSSTILL INTERFERE WITH THE PROCESSS.
ASSS A SSSCIENTISSST, YOU KNOW... UNKNOWN FACTORSSS--
ARE HARDLY AN EXCUSE FOR FAILURE!
THIS IS A DEPRESSING TURN OF EVENTS.
AND WHEN I GET DEPRESSED...
...I EAT!
OKAY! THIS PLAN'S GONE FAR ENOUGH!
BACK TO PLAN A! OPERATION: TAIL-KICKING!
HELL YEAH! THIS IS FOR GLOB!
YOU UNGRATEFUL MICE! WATCH AND LEARN, STEGRON, HOW A TRUE CONQUEROR TAKES HIS ENEMIES IN HAND!
AND CRUSHES THEM!

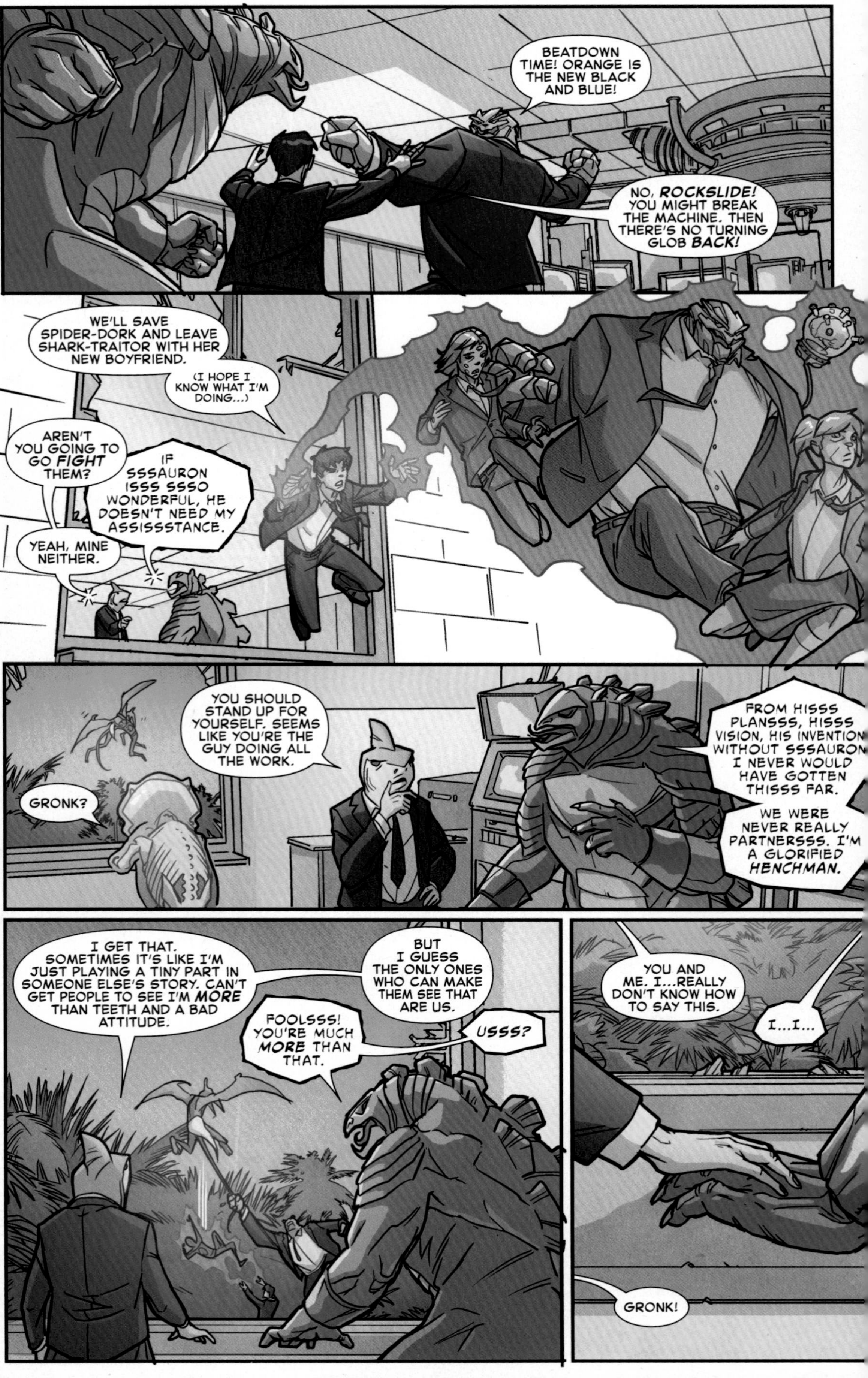
BEATDOWN TIME! ORANGE IS THE NEW BLACK AND BLUE!
NO, ROCKSLIDE! YOU MIGHT BREAK THE MACHINE. THEN THERE'S NO TURNING GLOB BACK!
WE'LL SAVE SPIDER-DORK AND LEAVE SHARK-TRAITOR WITH HER NEW BOYFRIEND.
(I HOPE I KNOW WHAT I'M DOING...)
AREN'T YOU GOING TO GO FIGHT THEM?
IF SSSAURON ISSS SSSO WONDERFUL, HE DOESN'T NEED MY ASSISSSTANCE.
YEAH, MINE NEITHER.
GRONK?
YOU SHOULD STAND UP FOR YOURSELF. SEEMS LIKE YOU'RE THE GUY DOING ALL THE WORK.
FROM HISSS PLANSSS, HISSS VISION, HIS INVENTION WITHOUT SSSAURON I NEVER WOULD HAVE GOTTEN THISSS FAR.
WE WERE NEVER REALLY PARTNERSSS. I'M A GLORIFIED HENCHMAN.
I GET THAT. SOMETIMES IT'S LIKE I'M JUST PLAYING A TINY PART IN SOMEONE ELSE'S STORY. CAN'T GET PEOPLE TO SEE I'M MORE THAN TEETH AND A BAD ATTITUDE.
BUT I GUESS THE ONLY ONES WHO CAN MAKE THEM SEE THAT ARE US.
USSS?
FOOLSSS! YOU'RE MUCH MORE THAN THAT.
YOU AND ME. I...REALLY DON'T KNOW HOW TO SAY THIS.
I...I...
GRONK!

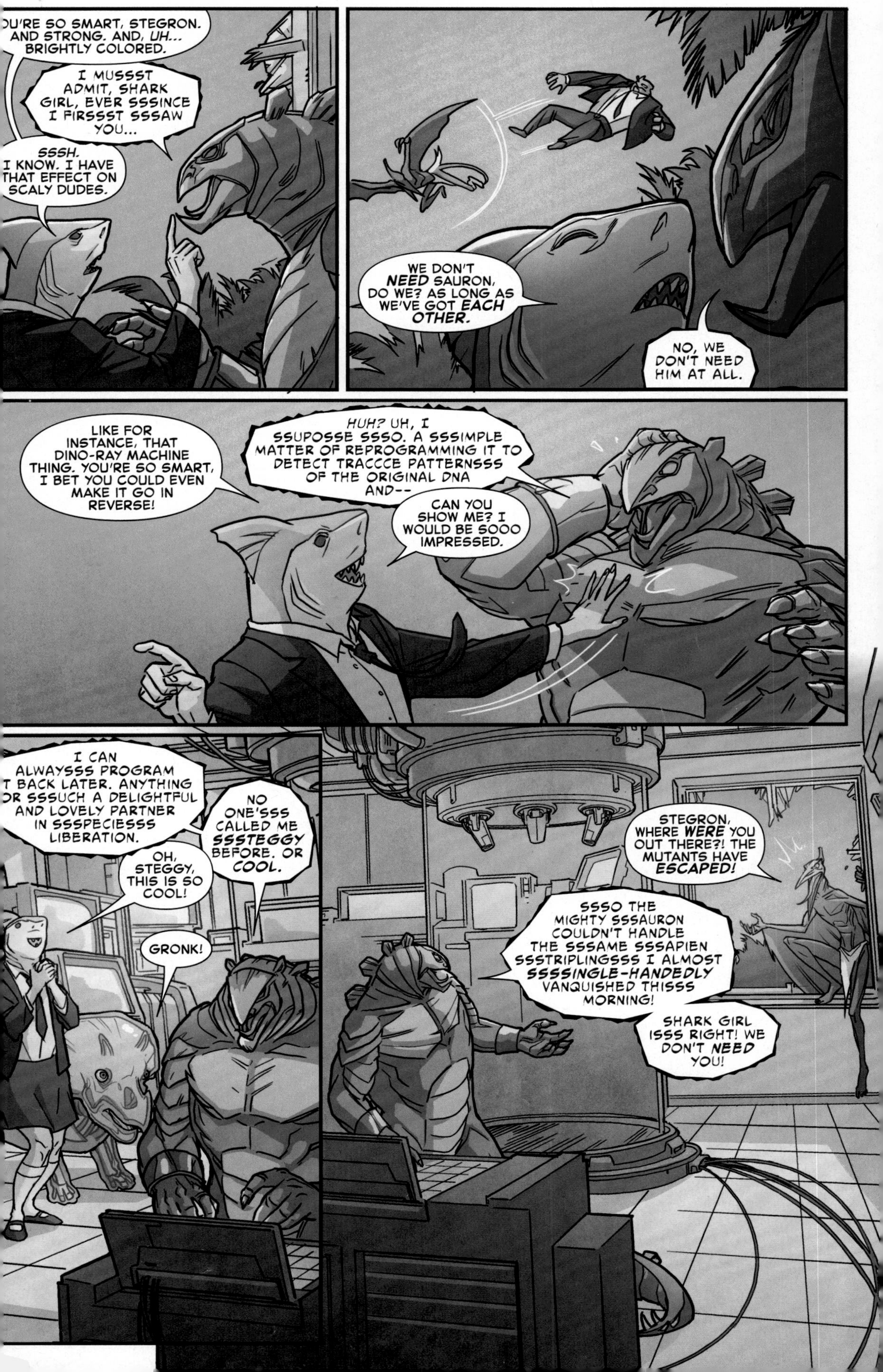

OU'RE SO SMART, STEGRON. AND STRONG. AND, UH... BRIGHTLY COLORED.
I MUSSST ADMIT, SHARK GIRL, EVER SSSINCE I FIRSSST SSSAW YOU...
SSSH. I KNOW. I HAVE THAT EFFECT ON SCALY DUDES.
WE DON'T NEED SAURON, DO WE? AS LONG AS WE'VE GOT EACH OTHER.
NO, WE DON'T NEED HIM AT ALL.
LIKE FOR INSTANCE, THAT DINO-RAY MACHINE THING. YOU'RE SO SMART, I BET YOU COULD EVEN MAKE IT GO IN REVERSE!
HUH? UH, I SSUPOSSE SSSO. A SSSIMPLE MATTER OF REPROGRAMMING IT TO DETECT TRACCCE PATTERNSSS OF THE ORIGINAL DNA AND--
CAN YOU SHOW ME? I WOULD BE SOOO IMPRESSED.
I CAN ALWAYSSS PROGRAM T BACK LATER. ANYTHING OR SSSUCH A DELIGHTFUL AND LOVELY PARTNER IN SSSPECIESSS LIBERATION.
NO ONE'SSS CALLED ME SSSTEGGY BEFORE. OR COOL.
OH, STEGGY, THIS IS SO COOL!
GRONK!
STEGRON, WHERE WERE YOU OUT THERE?! THE MUTANTS HAVE ESCAPED!
SSSO THE MIGHTY SSSAURON COULDN'T HANDLE THE SSSAME SSSAPIEN SSSTRIPLINGSSS I ALMOST SSSSINGLE-HANDEDLY VANQUISHED THISSS MORNING!
SHARK GIRL ISSS RIGHT! WE DON'T NEED YOU!

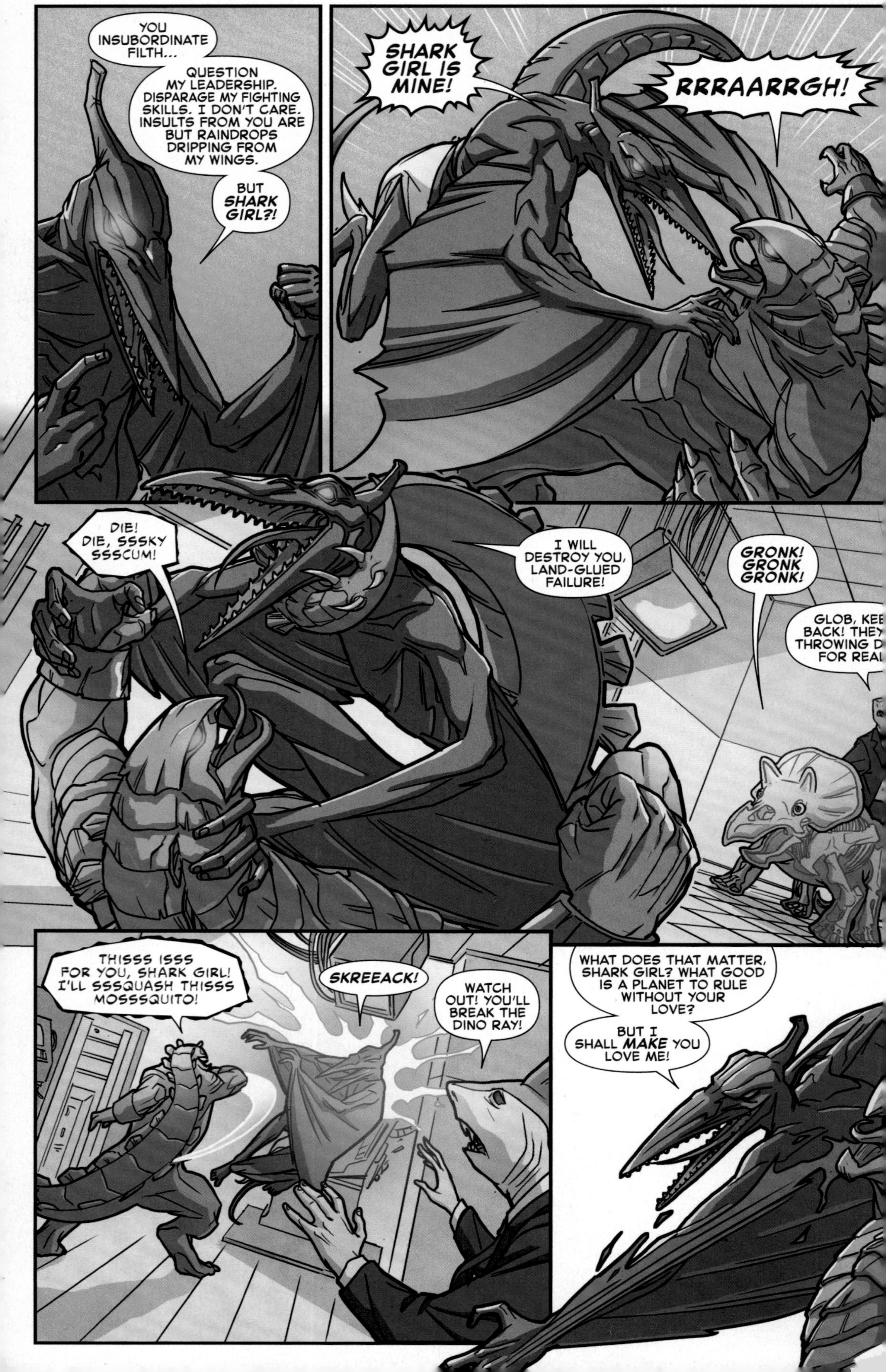

YOU INSUBORDINATE FILTH...
QUESTION MY LEADERSHIP. DISPARAGE MY FIGHTING SKILLS. I DON'T CARE. INSULTS FROM YOU ARE BUT RAINDROPS DRIPPING FROM MY WINGS.
BUT SHARK GIRL?!
SHARK GIRL IS MINE!
RRRAARRGH!
DIE! DIE, SSSKY SSSCUM!
I WILL DESTROY YOU, LAND-GLUED FAILURE!
GRONK! GRONK GRONK!
THISSS ISSS FOR YOU, SHARK GIRL! I'LL SSSQUASH THISSS MOSSSQUITO!
SKREEACK!
WATCH OUT! YOU'LL BREAK THE DINO RAY!
WHAT DOES THAT MATTER, SHARK GIRL? WHAT GOOD IS A PLANET TO RULE WITHOUT YOUR LOVE?
BUT I SHALL MAKE YOU LOVE ME!

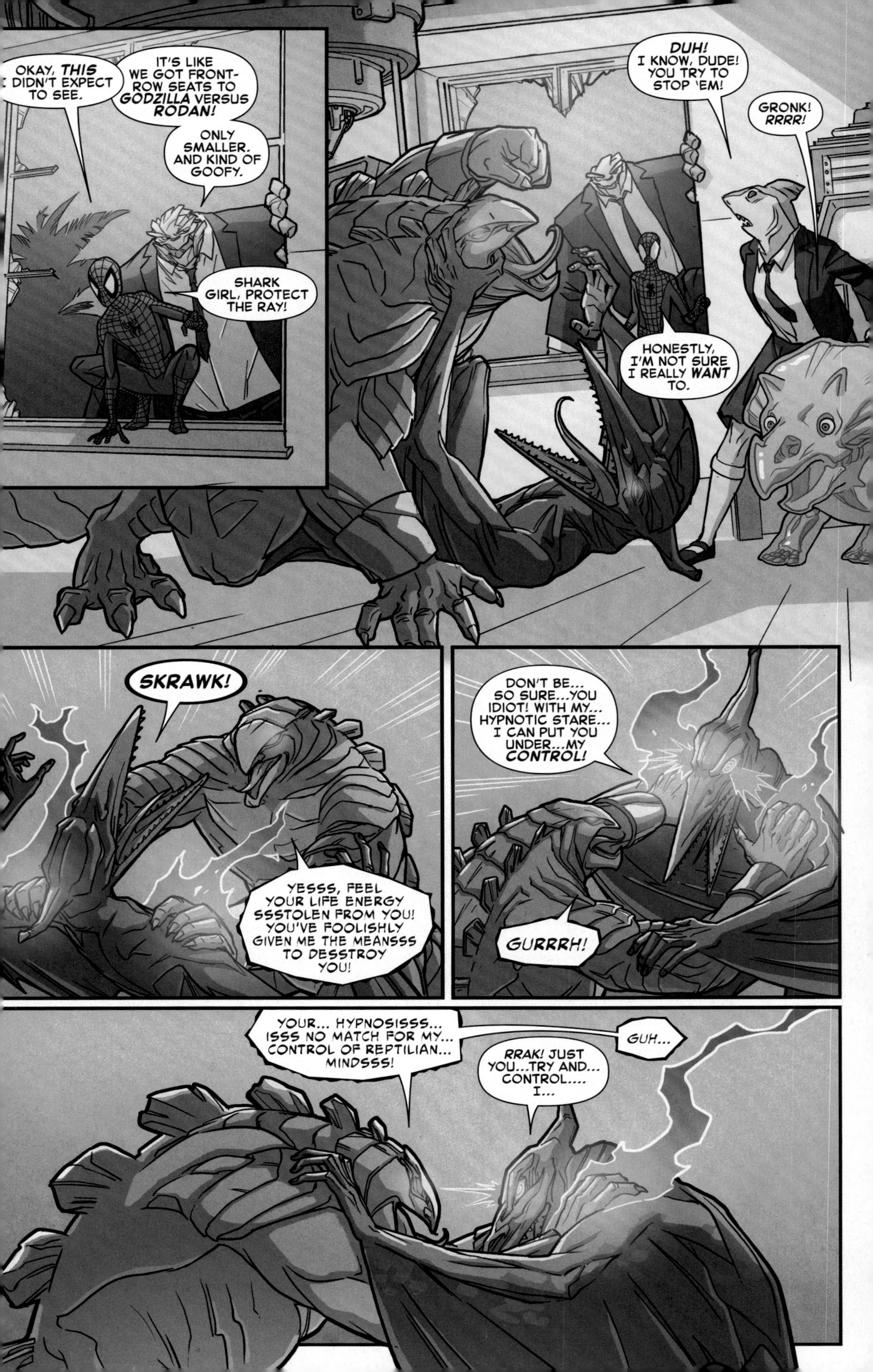

OKAY, THIS I DIDN'T EXPECT TO SEE.
IT'S LIKE WE GOT FRONT-ROW SEATS TO GODZILLA VERSUS RODAN!
ONLY SMALLER. AND KIND OF GOOFY.
SHARK GIRL, PROTECT THE RAY!
DUH! I KNOW, DUDE! YOU TRY TO STOP 'EM!
GRONK! RRRR!
HONESTLY, I'M NOT SURE I REALLY WANT TO.
SKRAWK!
YESSS, FEEL YOUR LIFE ENERGY SSSTOLEN FROM YOU! YOU'VE FOOLISHLY GIVEN ME THE MEANSSS TO DESSTROY YOU!
DON'T BE... SO SURE...YOU IDIOT! WITH MY... HYPNOTIC STARE... I CAN PUT YOU UNDER...MY CONTROL!
GURRRH!
YOUR... HYPNOSISSS... ISSS NO MATCH FOR MY... CONTROL OF REPTILIAN... MINDSSS!
GUH...
RRAK! JUST YOU...TRY AND... CONTROL.... I...

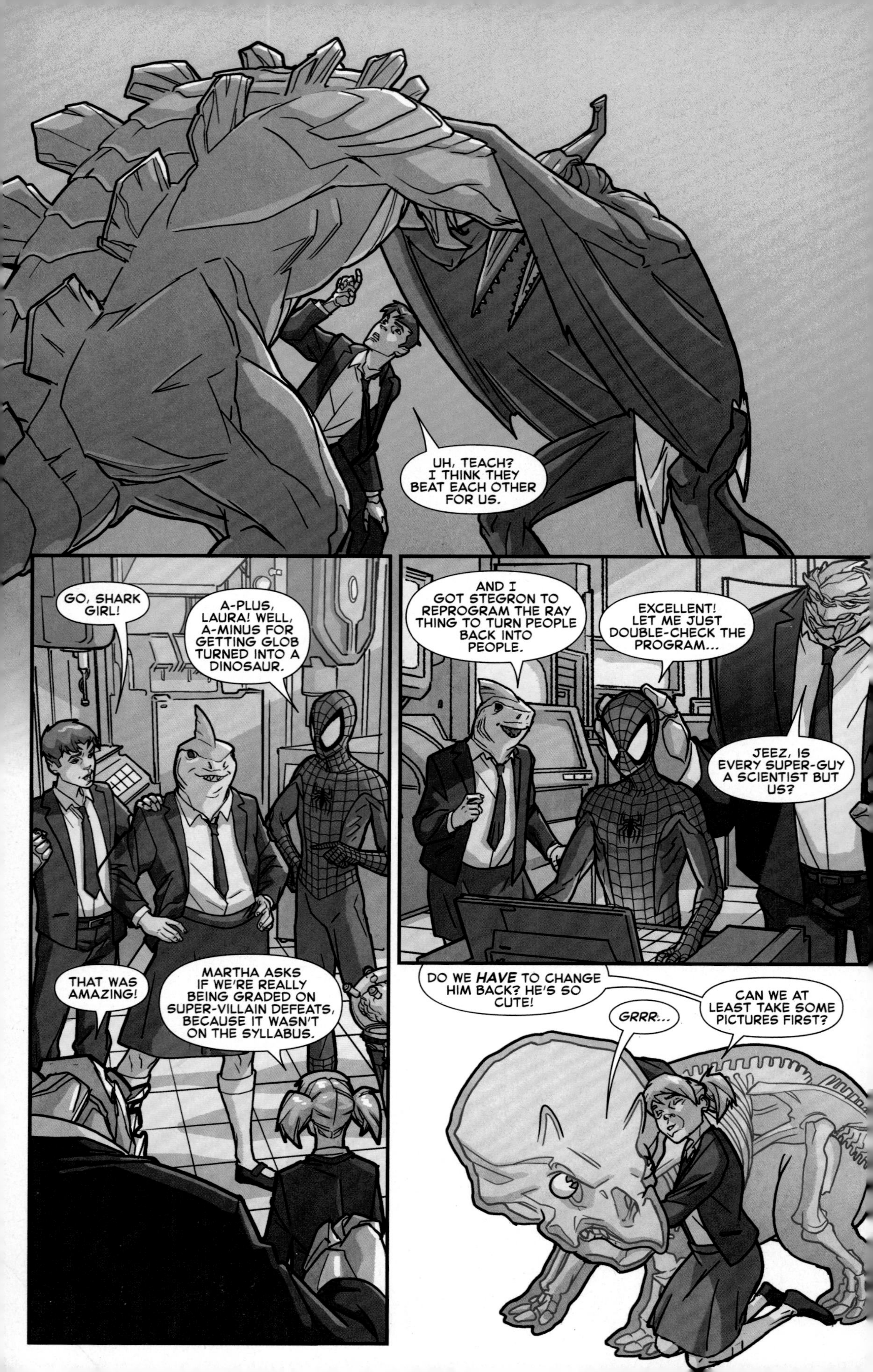
UH, TEACH? I THINK THEY BEAT EACH OTHER FOR US.
GO, SHARK GIRL!
A-PLUS, LAURA! WELL, A-MINUS FOR GETTING GLOB TURNED INTO A DINOSAUR.
AND I GOT STEGRON TO REPROGRAM THE RAY THING TO TURN PEOPLE BACK INTO PEOPLE.
EXCELLENT! LET ME JUST DOUBLE-CHECK THE PROGRAM...
JEEZ, IS EVERY SUPER-GUY A SCIENTIST BUT US?
THAT WAS AMAZING!
MARTHA ASKS IF WE'RE REALLY BEING GRADED ON SUPER-VILLAIN DEFEATS, BECAUSE IT WASN'T ON THE SYLLABUS.
DO WE *HAVE* TO CHANGE HIM BACK? HE'S SO CUTE!
GRRR...
CAN WE AT LEAST TAKE SOME PICTURES FIRST?

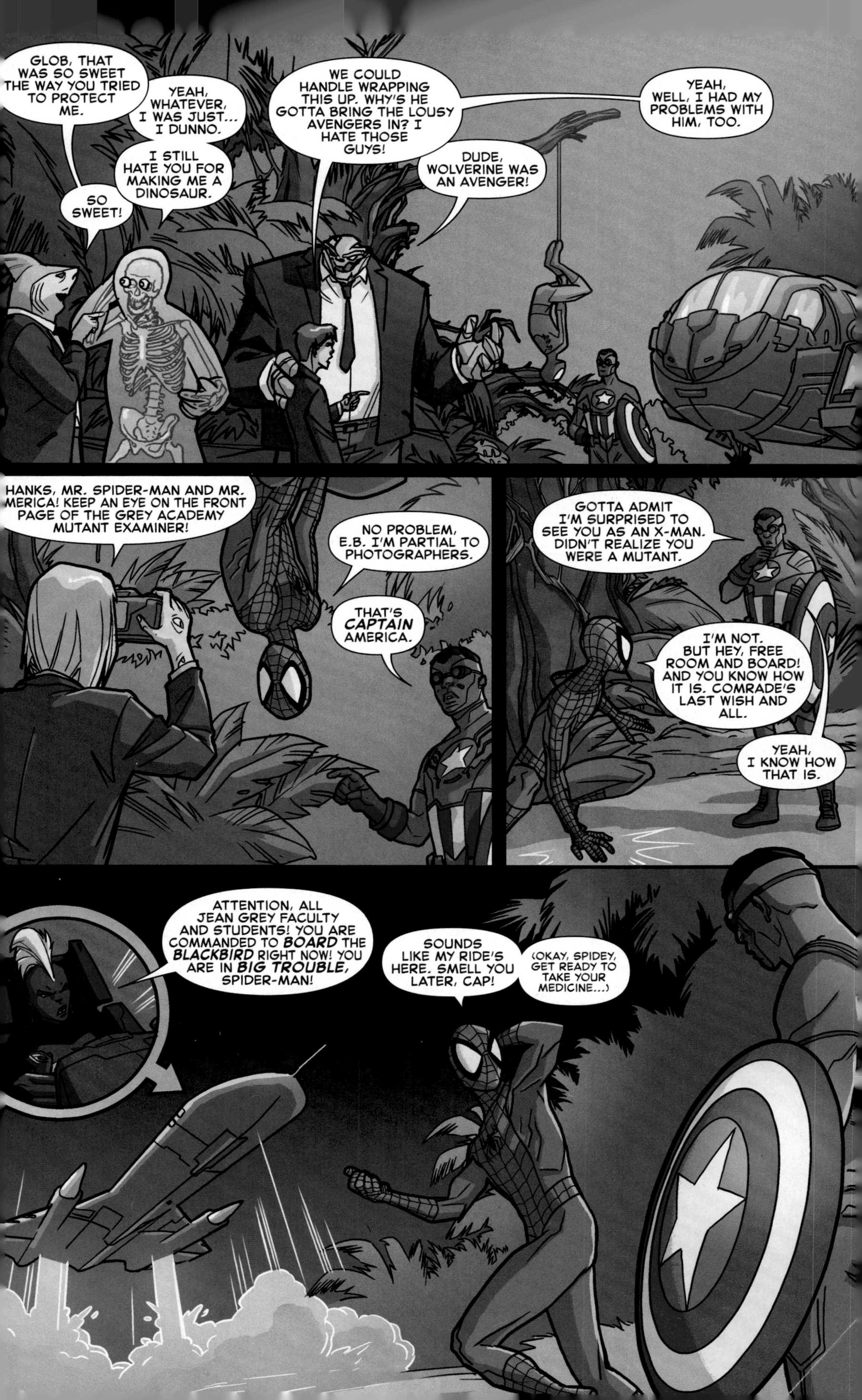
GLOB, THAT WAS SO SWEET THE WAY YOU TRIED TO PROTECT ME.
YEAH, WHATEVER, I WAS JUST... I DUNNO.
SO SWEET!
I STILL HATE YOU FOR MAKING ME A DINOSAUR.
WE COULD HANDLE WRAPPING THIS UP. WHY'S HE GOTTA BRING THE LOUSY AVENGERS IN? I HATE THOSE GUYS!
DUDE, WOLVERINE WAS AN AVENGER!
YEAH, WELL, I HAD MY PROBLEMS WITH HIM, TOO.
HANKS, MR. SPIDER-MAN AND MR. MERICA! KEEP AN EYE ON THE FRONT PAGE OF THE GREY ACADEMY MUTANT EXAMINER!
NO PROBLEM, E.B. I'M PARTIAL TO PHOTOGRAPHERS.
THAT'S CAPTAIN AMERICA.
GOTTA ADMIT I'M SURPRISED TO SEE YOU AS AN X-MAN. DIDN'T REALIZE YOU WERE A MUTANT.
I'M NOT. BUT HEY, FREE ROOM AND BOARD! AND YOU KNOW HOW IT IS. COMRADE'S LAST WISH AND ALL.
YEAH, I KNOW HOW THAT IS.
ATTENTION, ALL JEAN GREY FACULTY AND STUDENTS! YOU ARE COMMANDED TO BOARD THE BLACKBIRD RIGHT NOW! YOU ARE IN BIG TROUBLE, SPIDER-MAN!
SOUNDS LIKE MY RIDE'S HERE. SMELL YOU LATER, CAP!
(OKAY, SPIDEY, GET READY TO TAKE YOUR MEDICINE...)

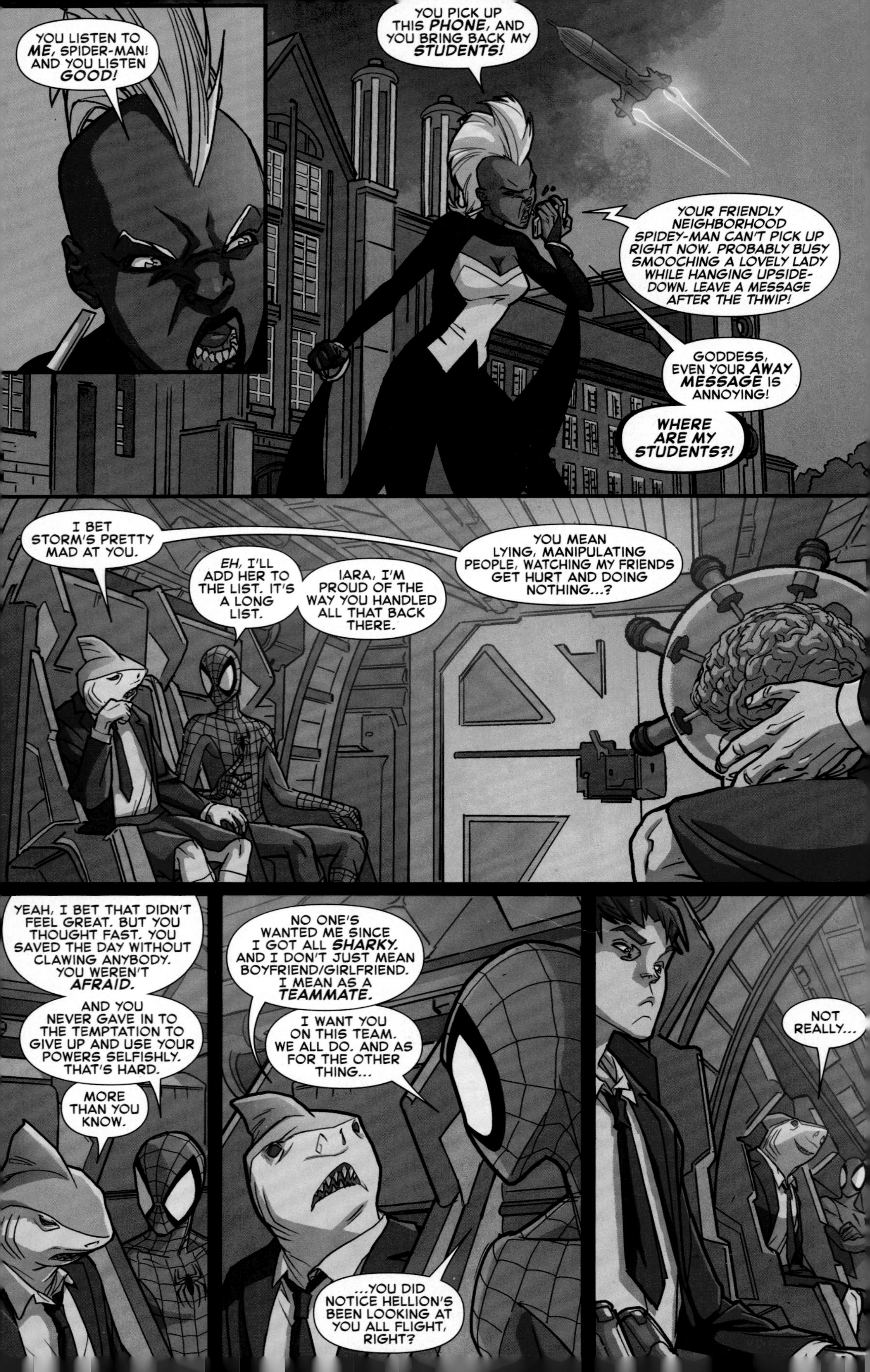
YOU LISTEN TO ME, SPIDER-MAN! AND YOU LISTEN GOOD!
YOU PICK UP THIS PHONE, AND YOU BRING BACK MY STUDENTS!
YOUR FRIENDLY NEIGHBORHOOD SPIDEY-MAN CAN'T PICK UP RIGHT NOW. PROBABLY BUSY SMOOCHING A LOVELY LADY WHILE HANGING UPSIDE-DOWN. LEAVE A MESSAGE AFTER THE THWIP!
GODDESS, EVEN YOUR AWAY MESSAGE IS ANNOYING!
WHERE ARE MY STUDENTS?!
I BET STORM'S PRETTY MAD AT YOU.
EH, I'LL ADD HER TO THE LIST. IT'S A LONG LIST.
IARA, I'M PROUD OF THE WAY YOU HANDLED ALL THAT BACK THERE.
YOU MEAN LYING, MANIPULATING PEOPLE, WATCHING MY FRIENDS GET HURT AND DOING NOTHING...?
YEAH, I BET THAT DIDN'T FEEL GREAT. BUT YOU THOUGHT FAST. YOU SAVED THE DAY WITHOUT CLAWING ANYBODY. YOU WEREN'T AFRAID.
AND YOU NEVER GAVE IN TO THE TEMPTATION TO GIVE UP AND USE YOUR POWERS SELFISHLY. THAT'S HARD.
MORE THAN YOU KNOW.
NO ONE'S WANTED ME SINCE I GOT ALL SHARKY. AND I DON'T JUST MEAN BOYFRIEND/GIRLFRIEND. I MEAN AS A TEAMMATE.
I WANT YOU ON THIS TEAM. WE ALL DO. AND AS FOR THE OTHER THING...
...YOU DID NOTICE HELLION'S BEEN LOOKING AT YOU ALL FLIGHT, RIGHT?
NOT REALLY...

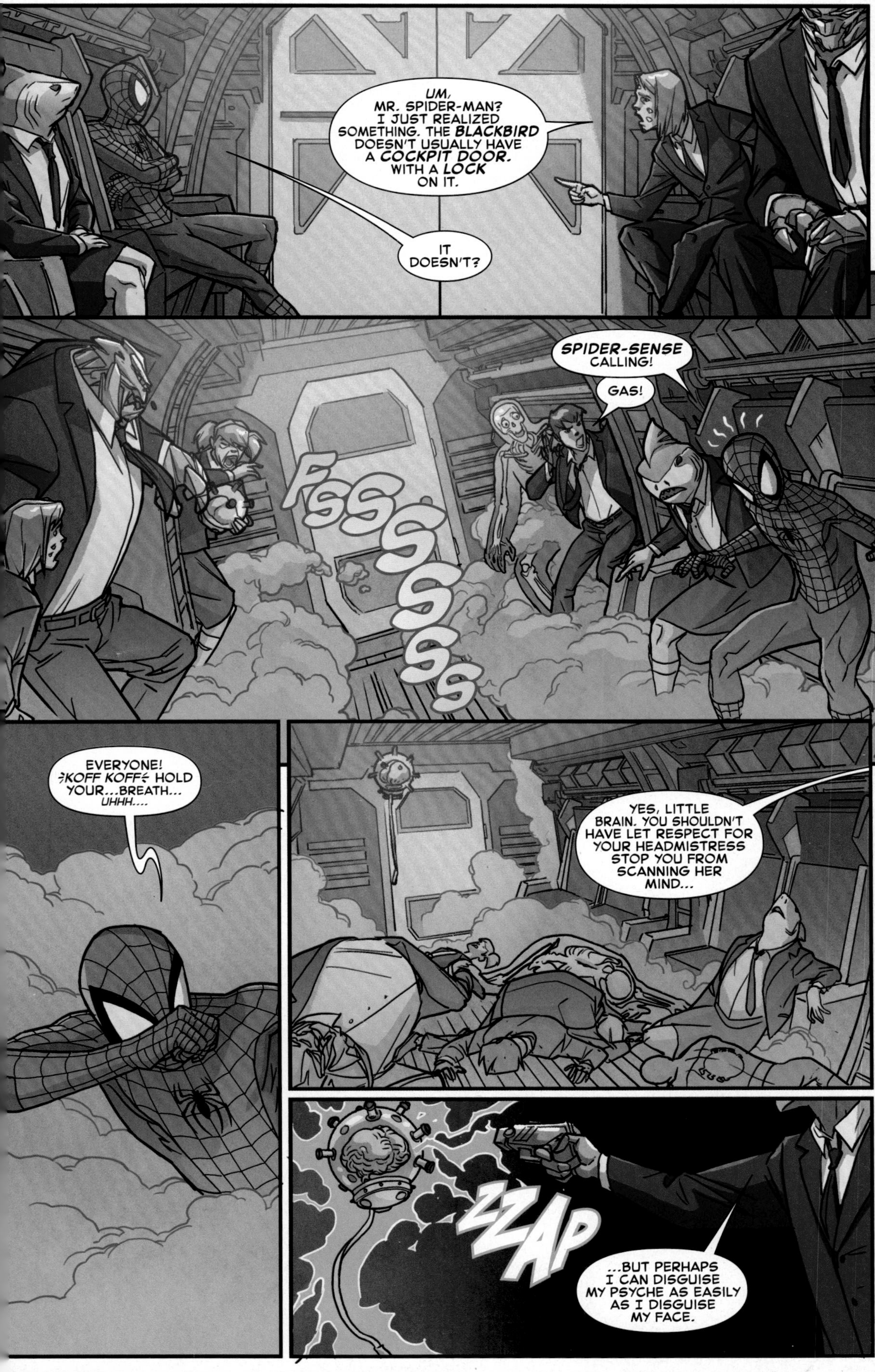
UM, MR. SPIDER-MAN? I JUST REALIZED SOMETHING. THE BLACKBIRD DOESN'T USUALLY HAVE A COCKPIT DOOR. WITH A LOCK ON IT.
IT DOESN'T?
SPIDER-SENSE CALLING!
GAS!
FSSSSSS
EVERYONE! ≠KOFF KOFF≠ HOLD YOUR...BREATH... UHHH....
YES, LITTLE BRAIN. YOU SHOULDN'T HAVE LET RESPECT FOR YOUR HEADMISTRESS STOP YOU FROM SCANNING HER MIND...
ZZAP
...BUT PERHAPS I CAN DISGUISE MY PSYCHE AS EASILY AS I DISGUISE MY FACE.

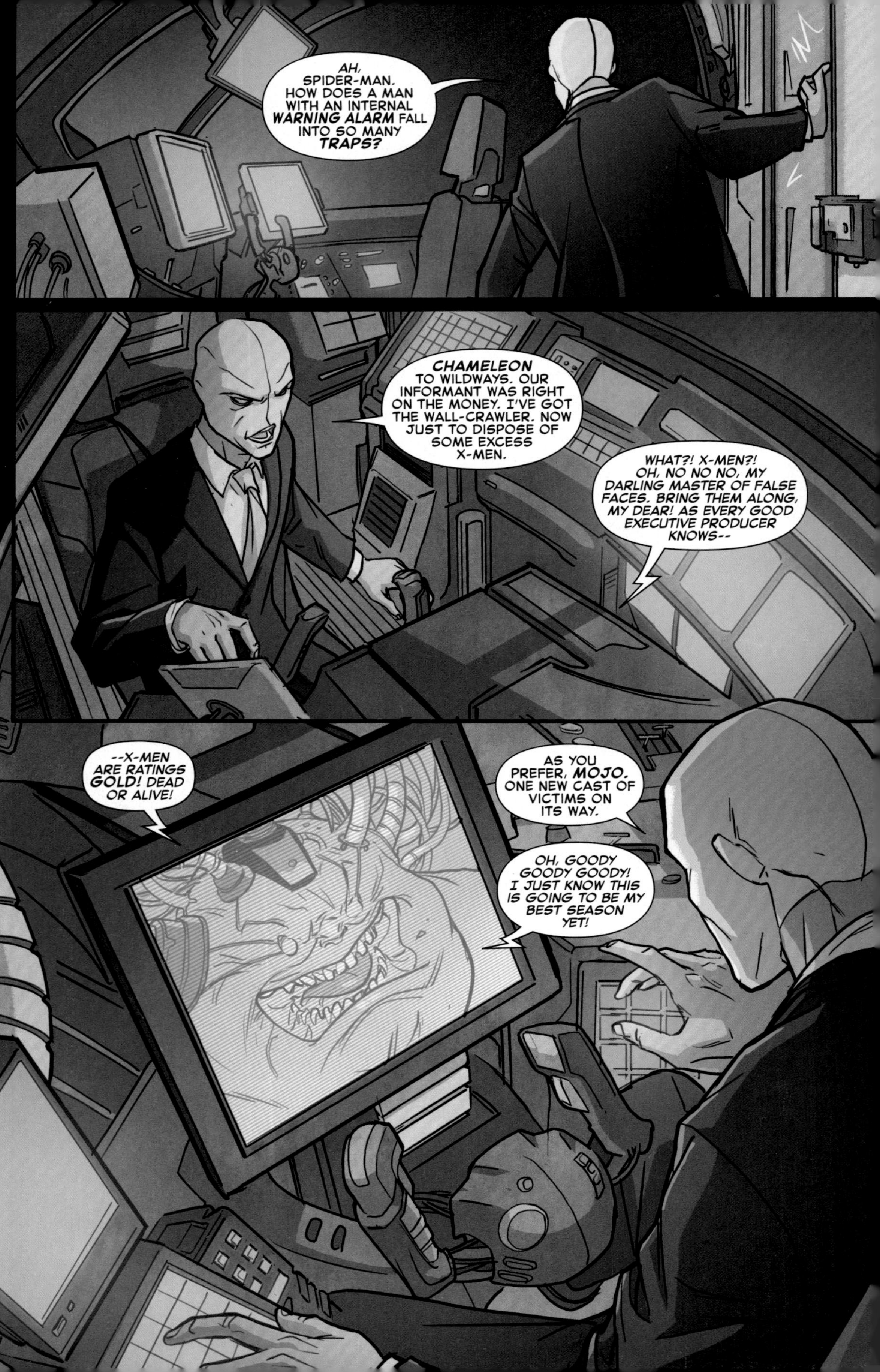
AH, SPIDER-MAN. HOW DOES A MAN WITH AN INTERNAL WARNING ALARM FALL INTO SO MANY TRAPS?
CHAMELEON TO WILDWAYS. OUR INFORMANT WAS RIGHT ON THE MONEY. I'VE GOT THE WALL-CRAWLER. NOW JUST TO DISPOSE OF SOME EXCESS X-MEN.
WHAT?! X-MEN?! OH, NO NO NO, MY DARLING MASTER OF FALSE FACES. BRING THEM ALONG, MY DEAR! AS EVERY GOOD EXECUTIVE PRODUCER KNOWS--
--X-MEN ARE RATINGS GOLD! DEAD OR ALIVE!
AS YOU PREFER, MOJO. ONE NEW CAST OF VICTIMS ON ITS WAY.
OH, GOODY GOODY GOODY! I JUST KNOW THIS IS GOING TO BE MY BEST SEASON YET!

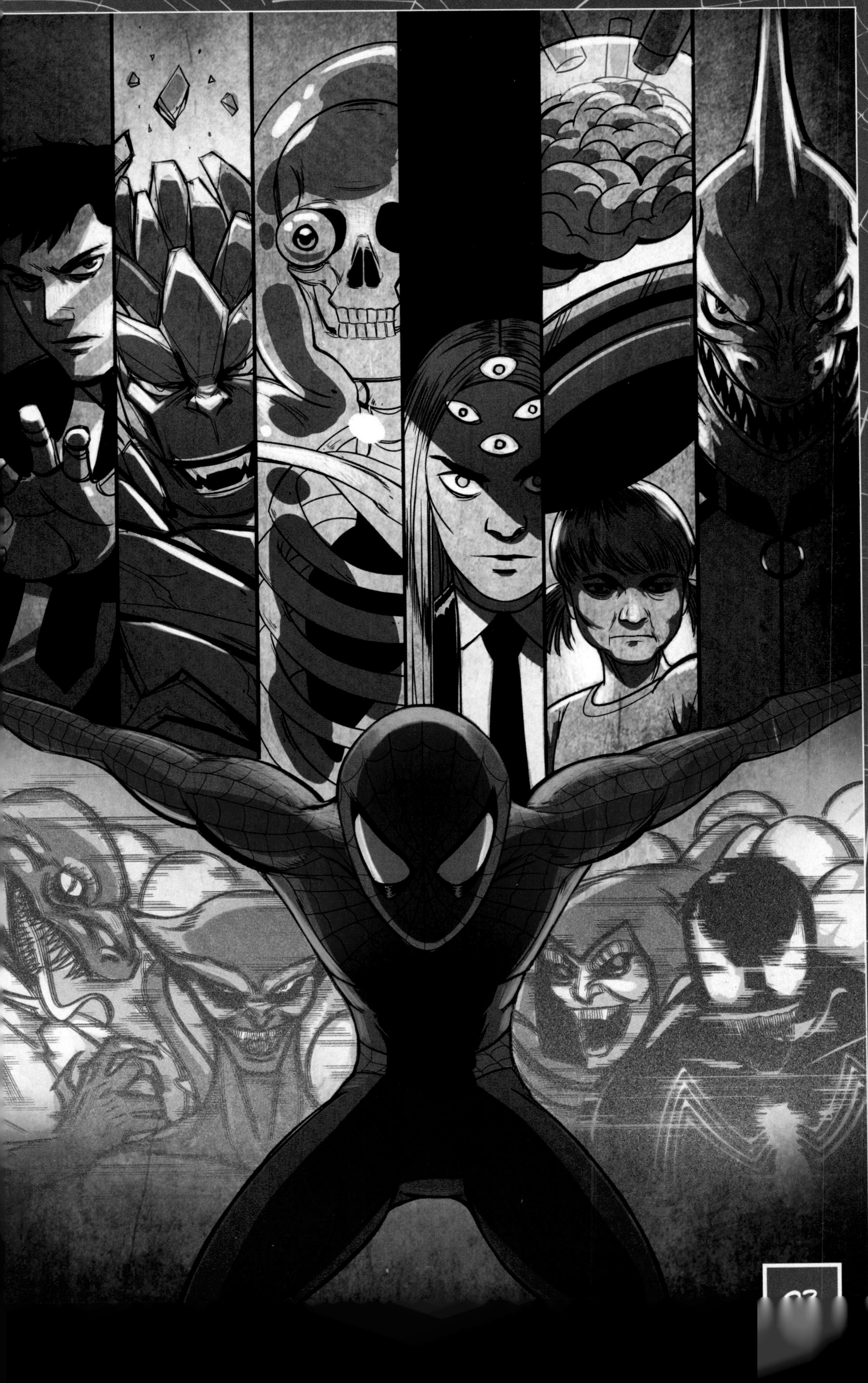

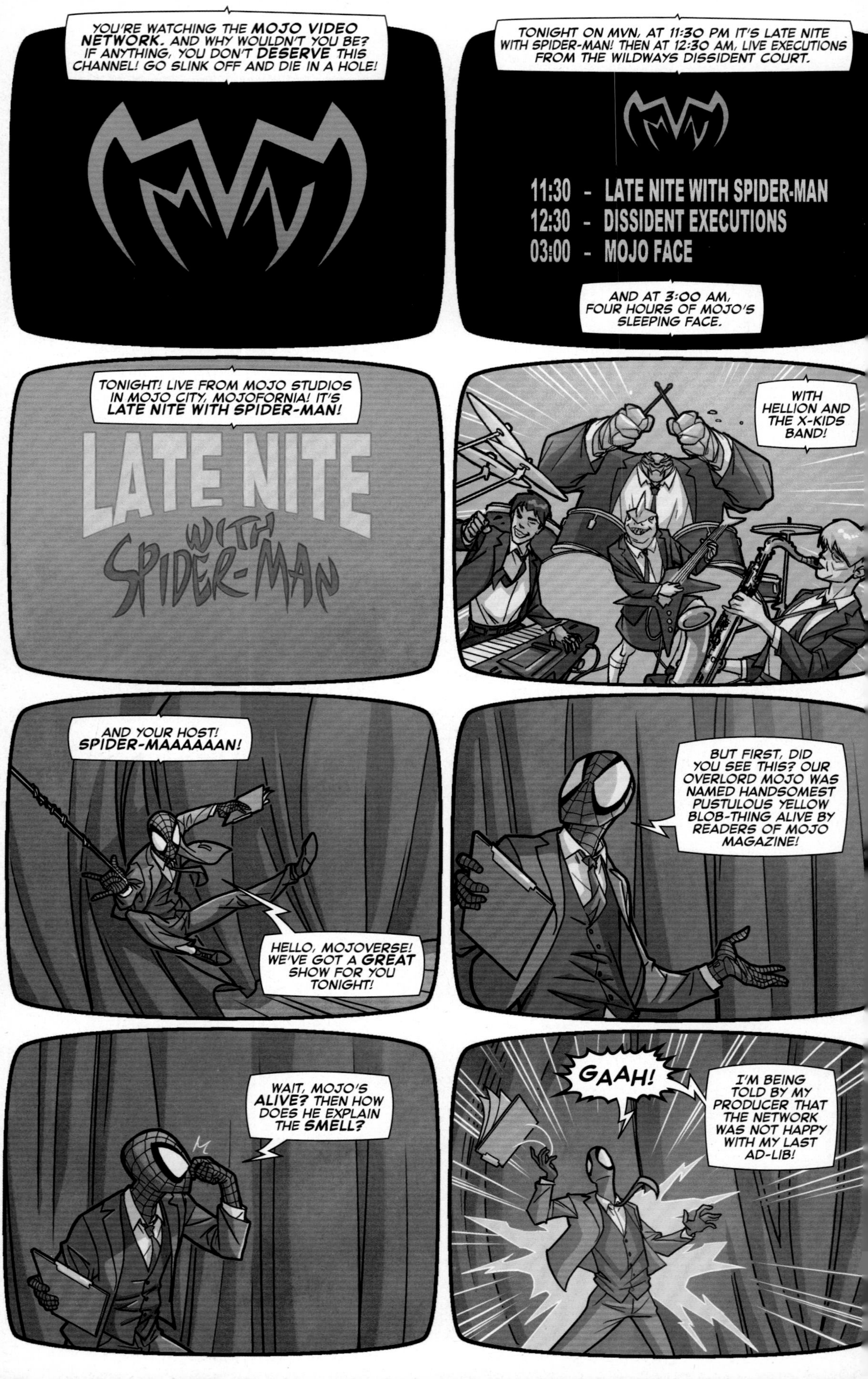
YOU'RE WATCHING THE MOJO VIDEO NETWORK. AND WHY WOULDN'T YOU BE? IF ANYTHING, YOU DON'T DESERVE THIS CHANNEL! GO SLINK OFF AND DIE IN A HOLE!
MVN
TONIGHT ON MVN, AT 11:30 PM IT'S LATE NITE WITH SPIDER-MAN! THEN AT 12:30 AM, LIVE EXECUTIONS FROM THE WILDWAYS DISSIDENT COURT.
MVN
11:30 - LATE NITE WITH SPIDER-MAN
12:30 - DISSIDENT EXECUTIONS
03:00 - MOJO FACE
AND AT 3:00 AM, FOUR HOURS OF MOJO'S SLEEPING FACE.
TONIGHT! LIVE FROM MOJO STUDIOS IN MOJO CITY, MOJOFORNIA! IT'S LATE NITE WITH SPIDER-MAN!
LATE NITE WITH SPIDER-MAN
WITH HELLION AND THE X-KIDS BAND!
AND YOUR HOST! SPIDER-MAAAAAAN!
HELLO, MOJOVERSE! WE'VE GOT A GREAT SHOW FOR YOU TONIGHT!
BUT FIRST, DID YOU SEE THIS? OUR OVERLORD MOJO WAS NAMED HANDSOMEST PUSTULOUS YELLOW BLOB-THING ALIVE BY READERS OF MOJO MAGAZINE!
WAIT, MOJO'S ALIVE? THEN HOW DOES HE EXPLAIN THE SMELL?
GAAH!
I'M BEING TOLD BY MY PRODUCER THAT THE NETWORK WAS NOT HAPPY WITH MY LAST AD-LIB!

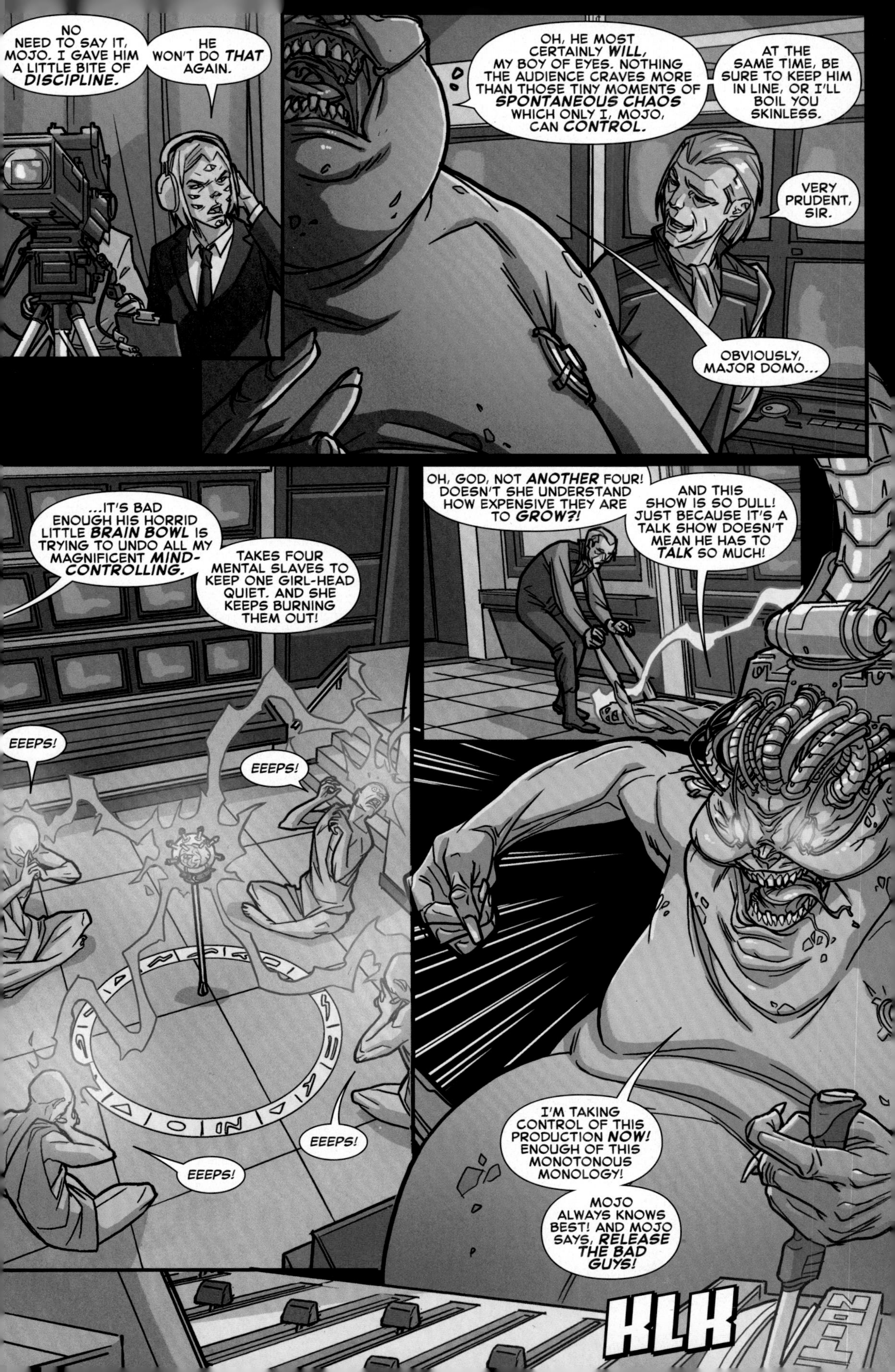
NO NEED TO SAY IT, MOJO. I GAVE HIM A LITTLE BITE OF DISCIPLINE.
HE WON'T DO THAT AGAIN.
OH, HE MOST CERTAINLY WILL, MY BOY OF EYES. NOTHING THE AUDIENCE CRAVES MORE THAN THOSE TINY MOMENTS OF SPONTANEOUS CHAOS WHICH ONLY I, MOJO, CAN CONTROL.
AT THE SAME TIME, BE SURE TO KEEP HIM IN LINE, OR I'LL BOIL YOU SKINLESS.
VERY PRUDENT, SIR.
OBVIOUSLY, MAJOR DOMO...
...IT'S BAD ENOUGH HIS HORRID LITTLE BRAIN BOWL IS TRYING TO UNDO ALL MY MAGNIFICENT MIND-CONTROLLING.
TAKES FOUR MENTAL SLAVES TO KEEP ONE GIRL-HEAD QUIET. AND SHE KEEPS BURNING THEM OUT!
EEEPS!
EEEPS!
EEEPS!
EEEPS!
OH, GOD, NOT ANOTHER FOUR! DOESN'T SHE UNDERSTAND HOW EXPENSIVE THEY ARE TO GROW?!
AND THIS SHOW IS SO DULL! JUST BECAUSE IT'S A TALK SHOW DOESN'T MEAN HE HAS TO TALK SO MUCH!
I'M TAKING CONTROL OF THIS PRODUCTION NOW! ENOUGH OF THIS MONOTONOUS MONOLOGY!
MOJO ALWAYS KNOWS BEST! AND MOJO SAYS, RELEASE THE BAD GUYS!
KLIK

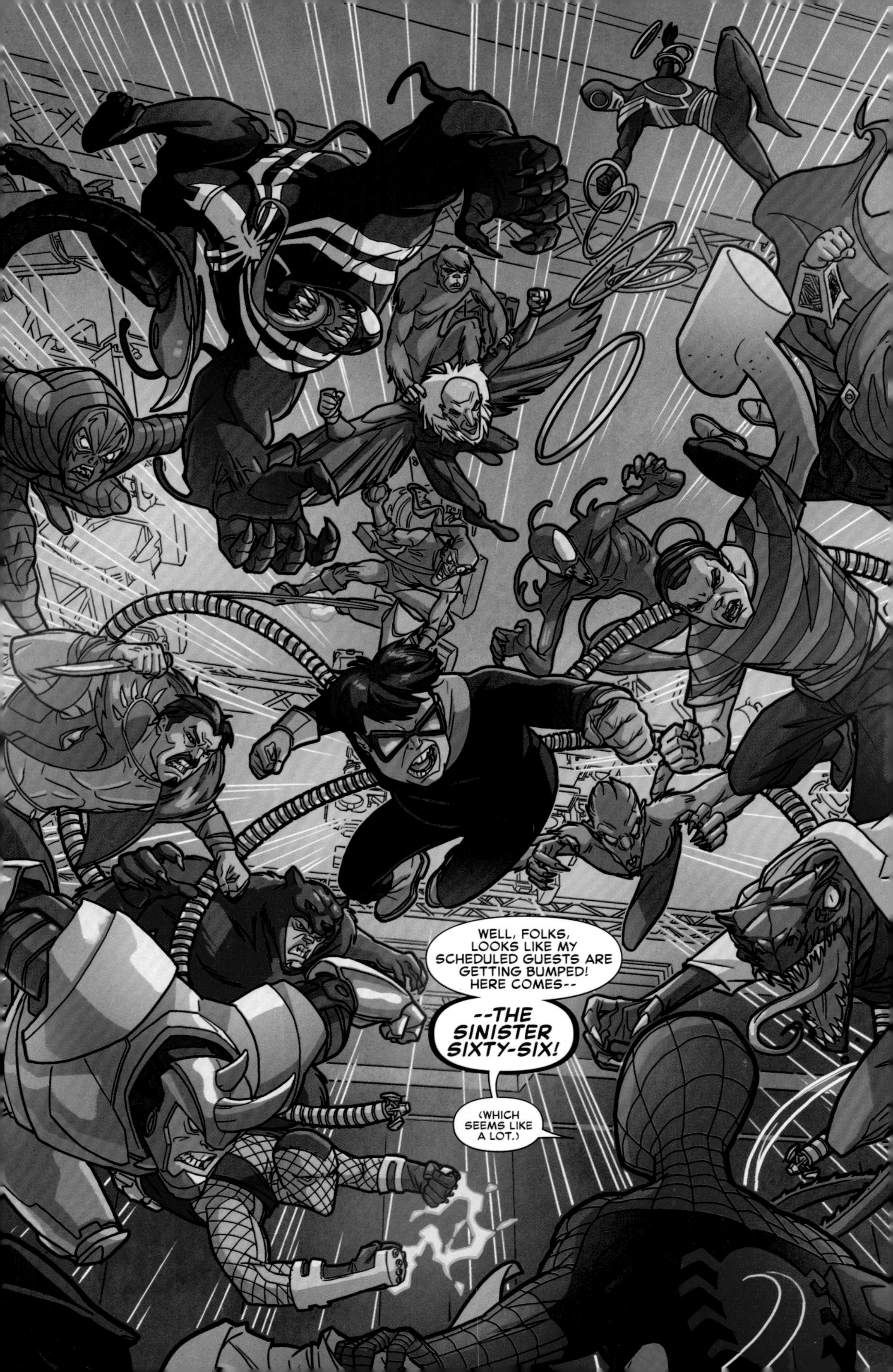
WELL, FOLKS, LOOKS LIKE MY SCHEDULED GUESTS ARE GETTING BUMPED! HERE COMES--
--THE SINISTER SIXTY-SIX!
(WHICH SEEMS LIKE A LOT.)

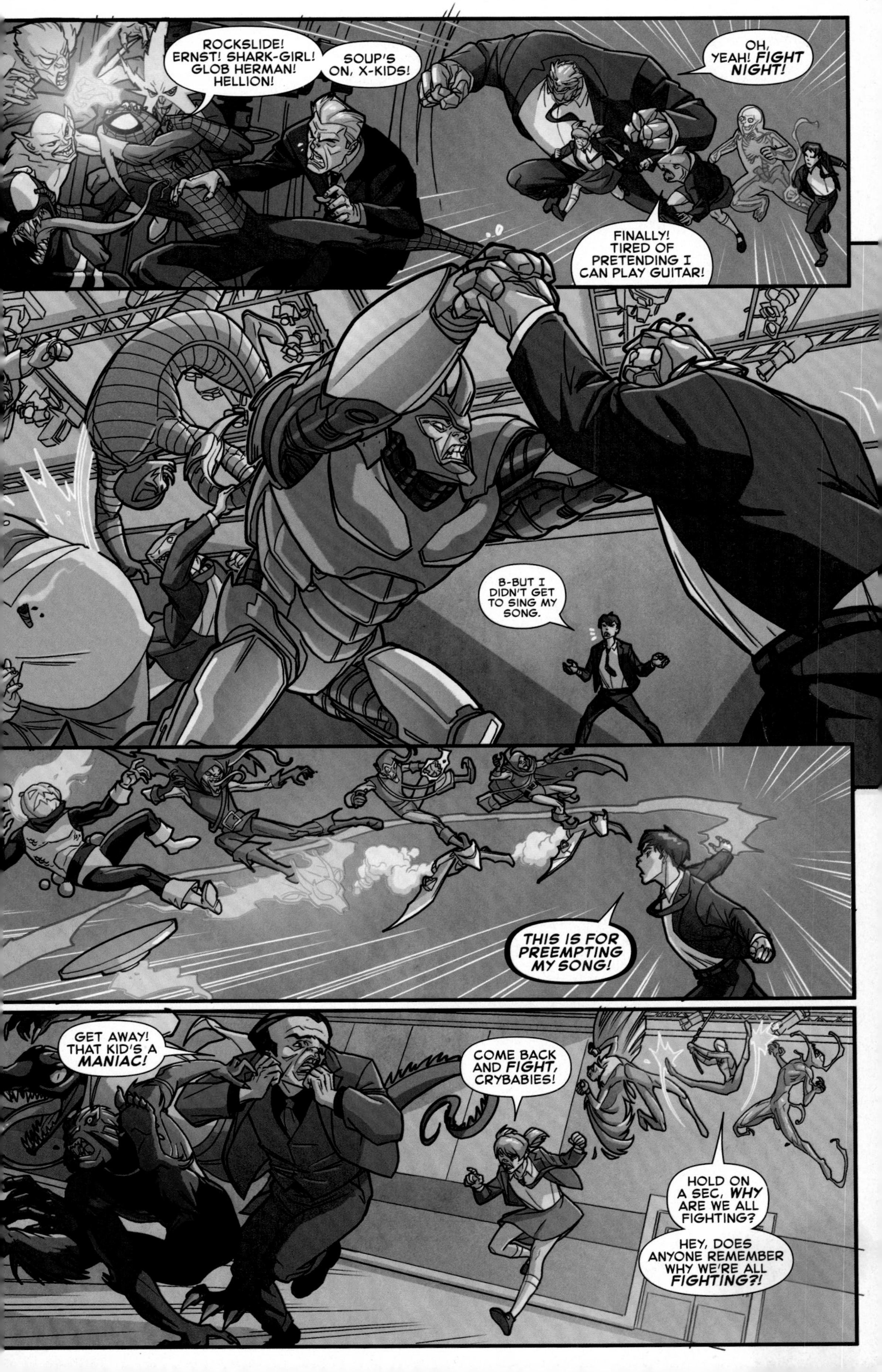
ROCKSLIDE! ERNST! SHARK-GIRL! GLOB HERMAN! HELLION!
SOUP'S ON, X-KIDS!
OH, YEAH! FIGHT NIGHT!
FINALLY! TIRED OF PRETENDING I CAN PLAY GUITAR!
B-BUT I DIDN'T GET TO SING MY SONG.
THIS IS FOR PREEMPTING MY SONG!
GET AWAY! THAT KID'S A MANIAC!
COME BACK AND FIGHT, CRYBABIES!
HOLD ON A SEC, WHY ARE WE ALL FIGHTING?
HEY, DOES ANYONE REMEMBER WHY WE'RE ALL FIGHTING?!

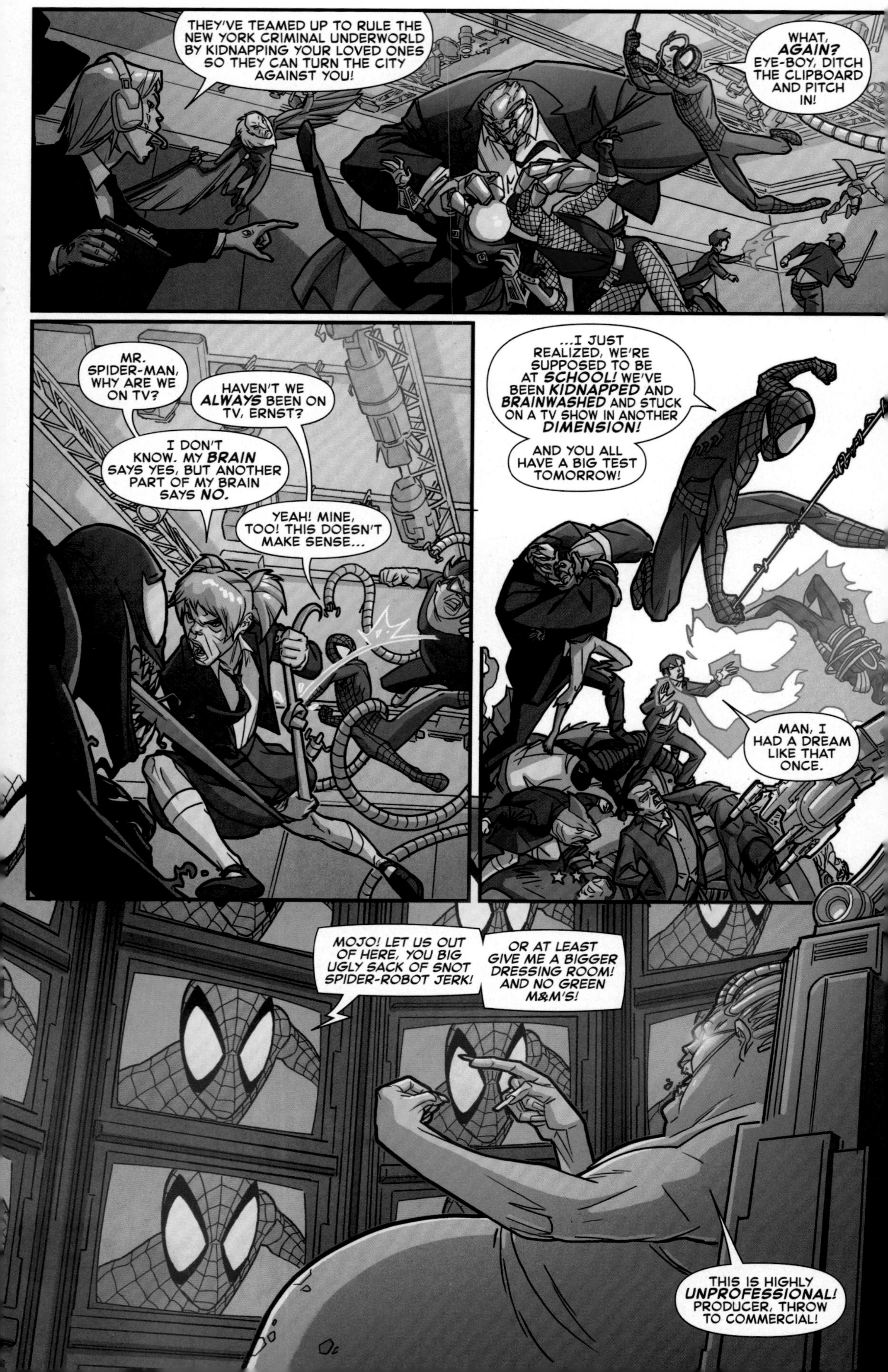
THEY'VE TEAMED UP TO RULE THE NEW YORK CRIMINAL UNDERWORLD BY KIDNAPPING YOUR LOVED ONES SO THEY CAN TURN THE CITY AGAINST YOU!
WHAT, AGAIN? EYE-BOY, DITCH THE CLIPBOARD AND PITCH IN!
MR. SPIDER-MAN, WHY ARE WE ON TV?
HAVEN'T WE ALWAYS BEEN ON TV, ERNST?
I DON'T KNOW. MY BRAIN SAYS YES, BUT ANOTHER PART OF MY BRAIN SAYS NO.
YEAH! MINE, TOO! THIS DOESN'T MAKE SENSE...
...I JUST REALIZED, WE'RE SUPPOSED TO BE AT SCHOOL! WE'VE BEEN KIDNAPPED AND BRAINWASHED AND STUCK ON A TV SHOW IN ANOTHER DIMENSION!
AND YOU ALL HAVE A BIG TEST TOMORROW!
MAN, I HAD A DREAM LIKE THAT ONCE.
MOJO! LET US OUT OF HERE, YOU BIG UGLY SACK OF SNOT SPIDER-ROBOT JERK!
OR AT LEAST GIVE ME A BIGGER DRESSING ROOM! AND NO GREEN M&M'S!
THIS IS HIGHLY UNPROFESSIONAL! PRODUCER, THROW TO COMMERCIAL!

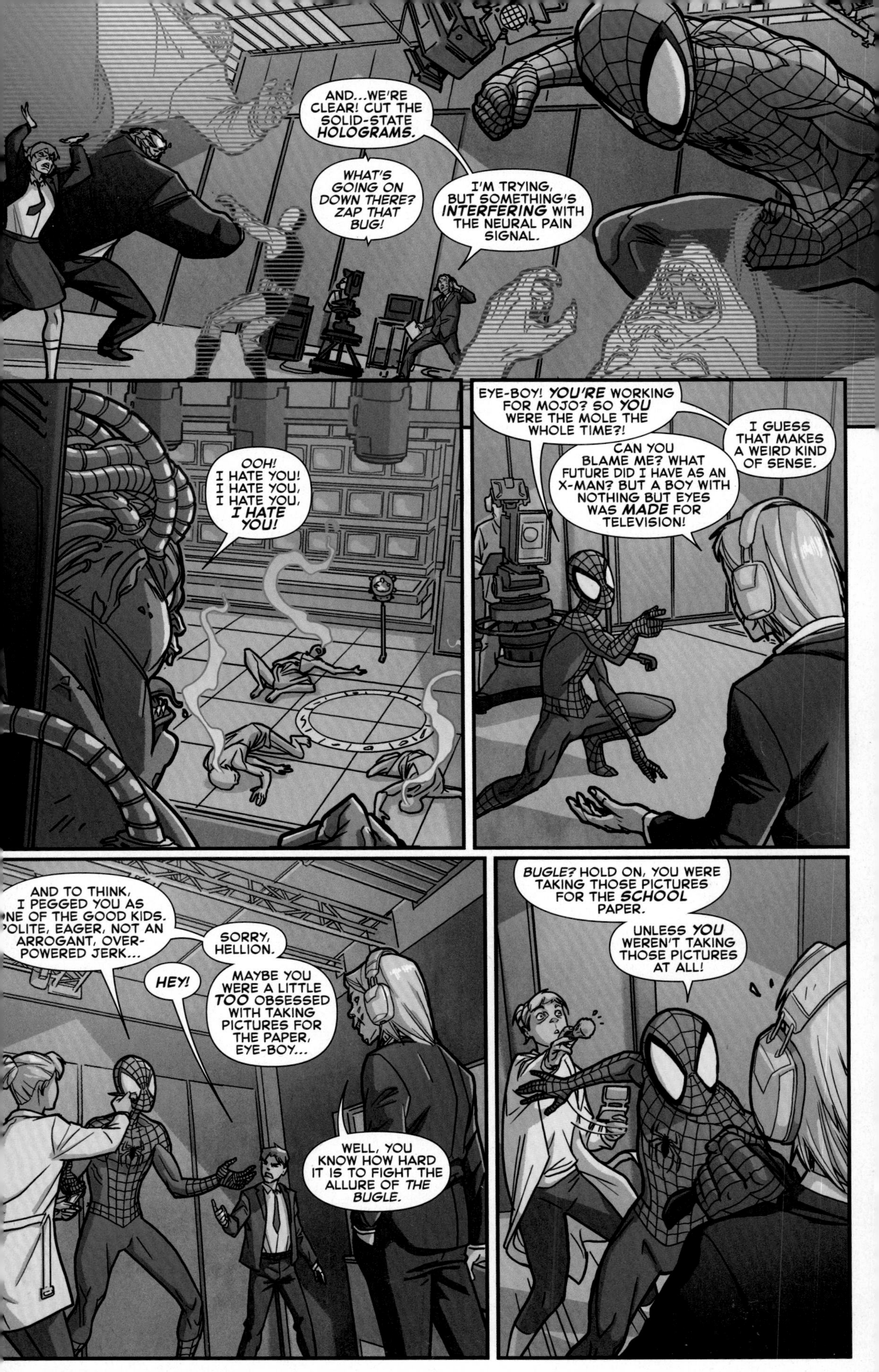
AND...WE'RE CLEAR! CUT THE SOLID-STATE HOLOGRAMS.
WHAT'S GOING ON DOWN THERE? ZAP THAT BUG!
I'M TRYING, BUT SOMETHING'S INTERFERING WITH THE NEURAL PAIN SIGNAL.
OOH! I HATE YOU! I HATE YOU, I HATE YOU, I HATE YOU!
EYE-BOY! YOU'RE WORKING FOR MOJO? SO YOU WERE THE MOLE THE WHOLE TIME?!
I GUESS THAT MAKES A WEIRD KIND OF SENSE.
CAN YOU BLAME ME? WHAT FUTURE DID I HAVE AS AN X-MAN? BUT A BOY WITH NOTHING BUT EYES WAS MADE FOR TELEVISION!
AND TO THINK, I PEGGED YOU AS ONE OF THE GOOD KIDS. POLITE, EAGER, NOT AN ARROGANT, OVER-POWERED JERK...
SORRY, HELLION.
HEY!
MAYBE YOU WERE A LITTLE TOO OBSESSED WITH TAKING PICTURES FOR THE PAPER, EYE-BOY...
WELL, YOU KNOW HOW HARD IT IS TO FIGHT THE ALLURE OF THE BUGLE.
BUGLE? HOLD ON, YOU WERE TAKING THOSE PICTURES FOR THE SCHOOL PAPER.
UNLESS YOU WEREN'T TAKING THOSE PICTURES AT ALL!

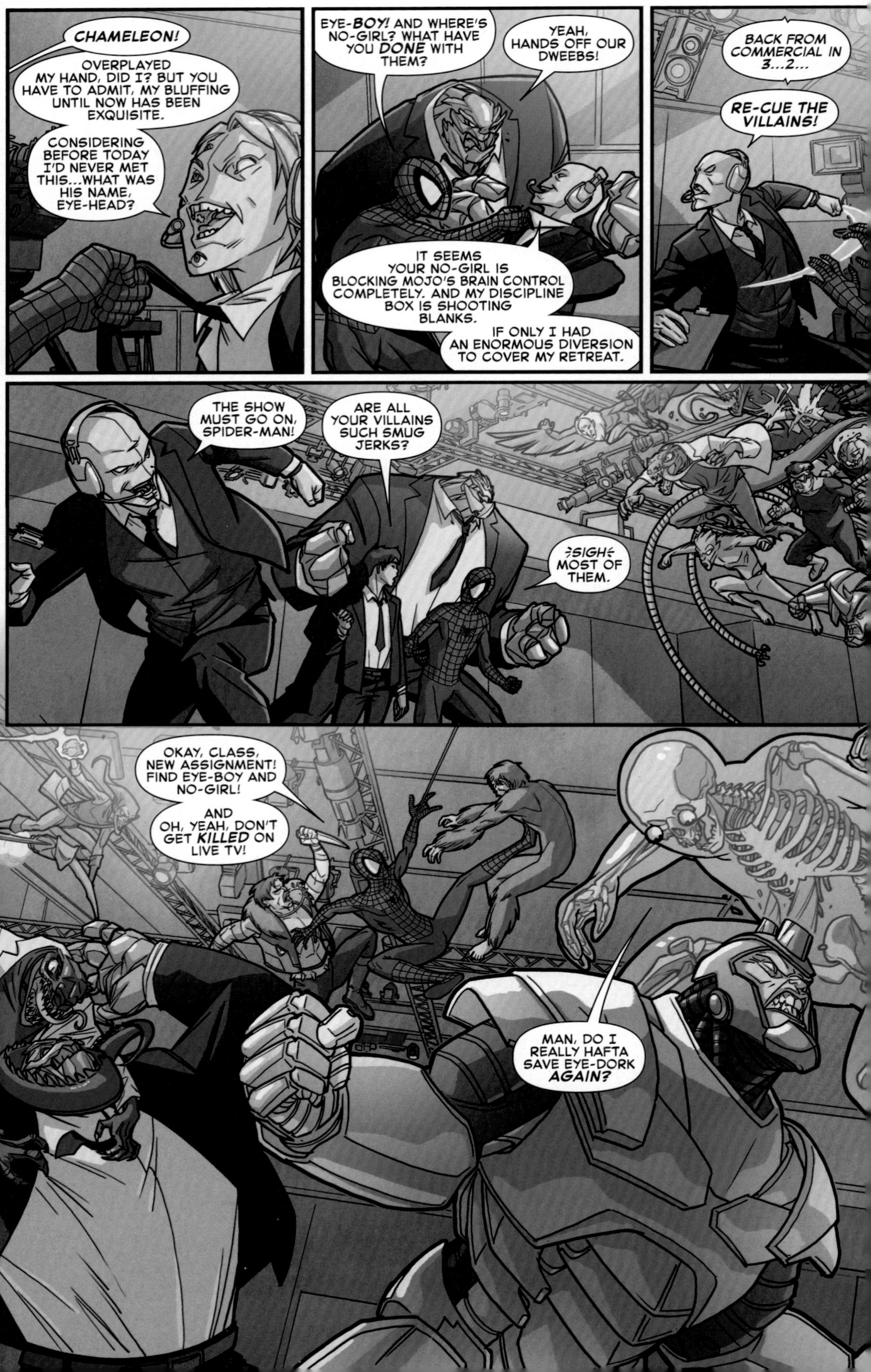
CHAMELEON!
OVERPLAYED MY HAND, DID I? BUT YOU HAVE TO ADMIT, MY BLUFFING UNTIL NOW HAS BEEN EXQUISITE.
CONSIDERING BEFORE TODAY I'D NEVER MET THIS...WHAT WAS HIS NAME, EYE-HEAD?
EYE-BOY! AND WHERE'S NO-GIRL? WHAT HAVE YOU DONE WITH THEM?
YEAH, HANDS OFF OUR DWEEBS!
IT SEEMS YOUR NO-GIRL IS BLOCKING MOJO'S BRAIN CONTROL COMPLETELY. AND MY DISCIPLINE BOX IS SHOOTING BLANKS.
IF ONLY I HAD AN ENORMOUS DIVERSION TO COVER MY RETREAT.
BACK FROM COMMERCIAL IN 3...2...
RE-CUE THE VILLAINS!
THE SHOW MUST GO ON, SPIDER-MAN!
ARE ALL YOUR VILLAINS SUCH SMUG JERKS?
SIGH MOST OF THEM.
OKAY, CLASS, NEW ASSIGNMENT! FIND EYE-BOY AND NO-GIRL!
AND OH, YEAH, DON'T GET KILLED ON LIVE TV!
MAN, DO I REALLY HAFTA SAVE EYE-DORK AGAIN?

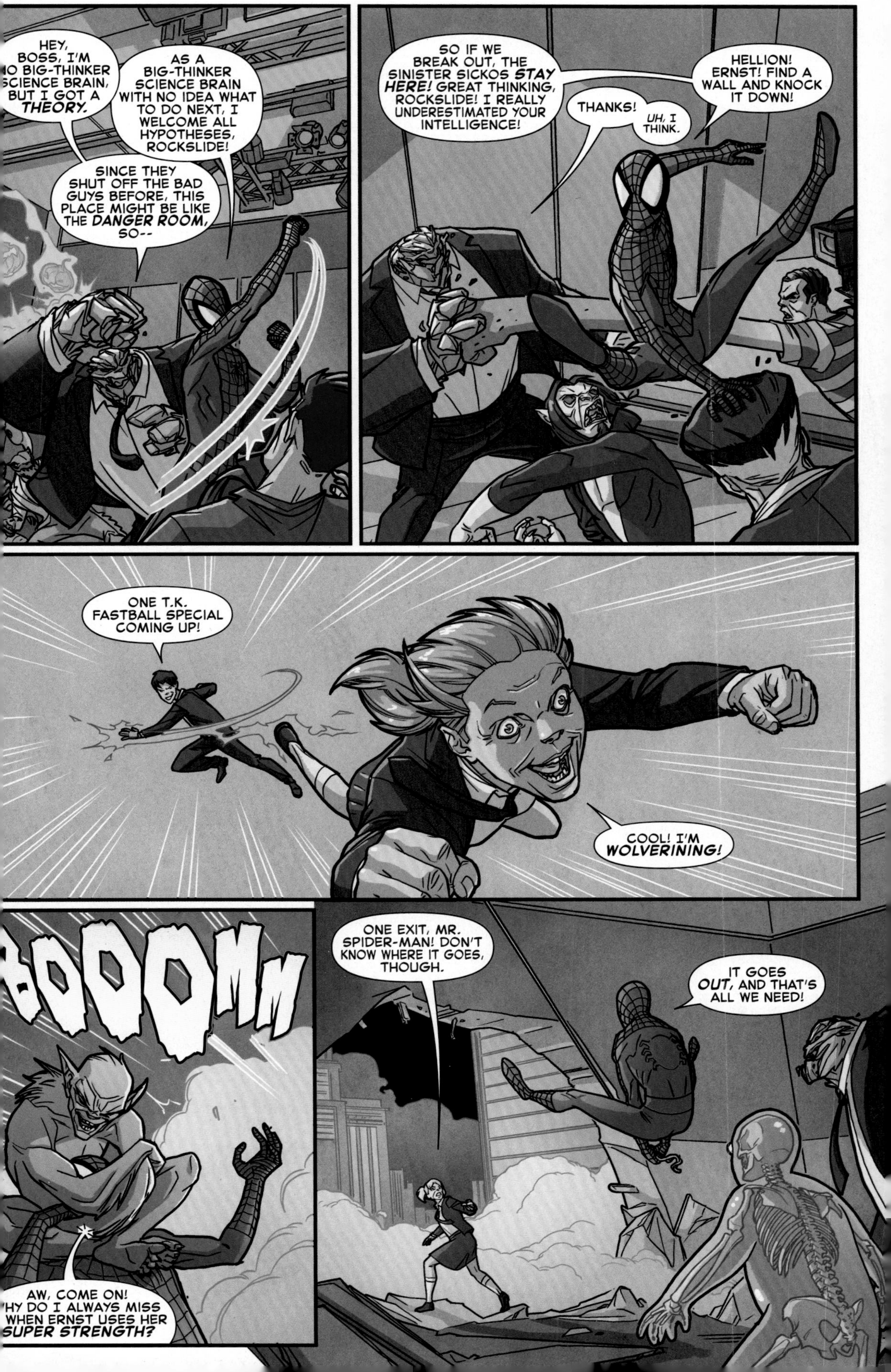
HEY, BOSS, I'M NO BIG-THINKER SCIENCE BRAIN, BUT I GOT A THEORY.
AS A BIG-THINKER SCIENCE BRAIN WITH NO IDEA WHAT TO DO NEXT, I WELCOME ALL HYPOTHESES, ROCKSLIDE!
SINCE THEY SHUT OFF THE BAD GUYS BEFORE, THIS PLACE MIGHT BE LIKE THE DANGER ROOM, SO--
SO IF WE BREAK OUT, THE SINISTER SICKOS STAY HERE! GREAT THINKING, ROCKSLIDE! I REALLY UNDERESTIMATED YOUR INTELLIGENCE!
THANKS!
UH, I THINK.
HELLION! ERNST! FIND A WALL AND KNOCK IT DOWN!
ONE T.K. FASTBALL SPECIAL COMING UP!
COOL! I'M WOLVERINING!
BOOOMM
AW, COME ON! WHY DO I ALWAYS MISS WHEN ERNST USES HER SUPER STRENGTH?
ONE EXIT, MR. SPIDER-MAN! DON'T KNOW WHERE IT GOES, THOUGH.
IT GOES OUT, AND THAT'S ALL WE NEED!

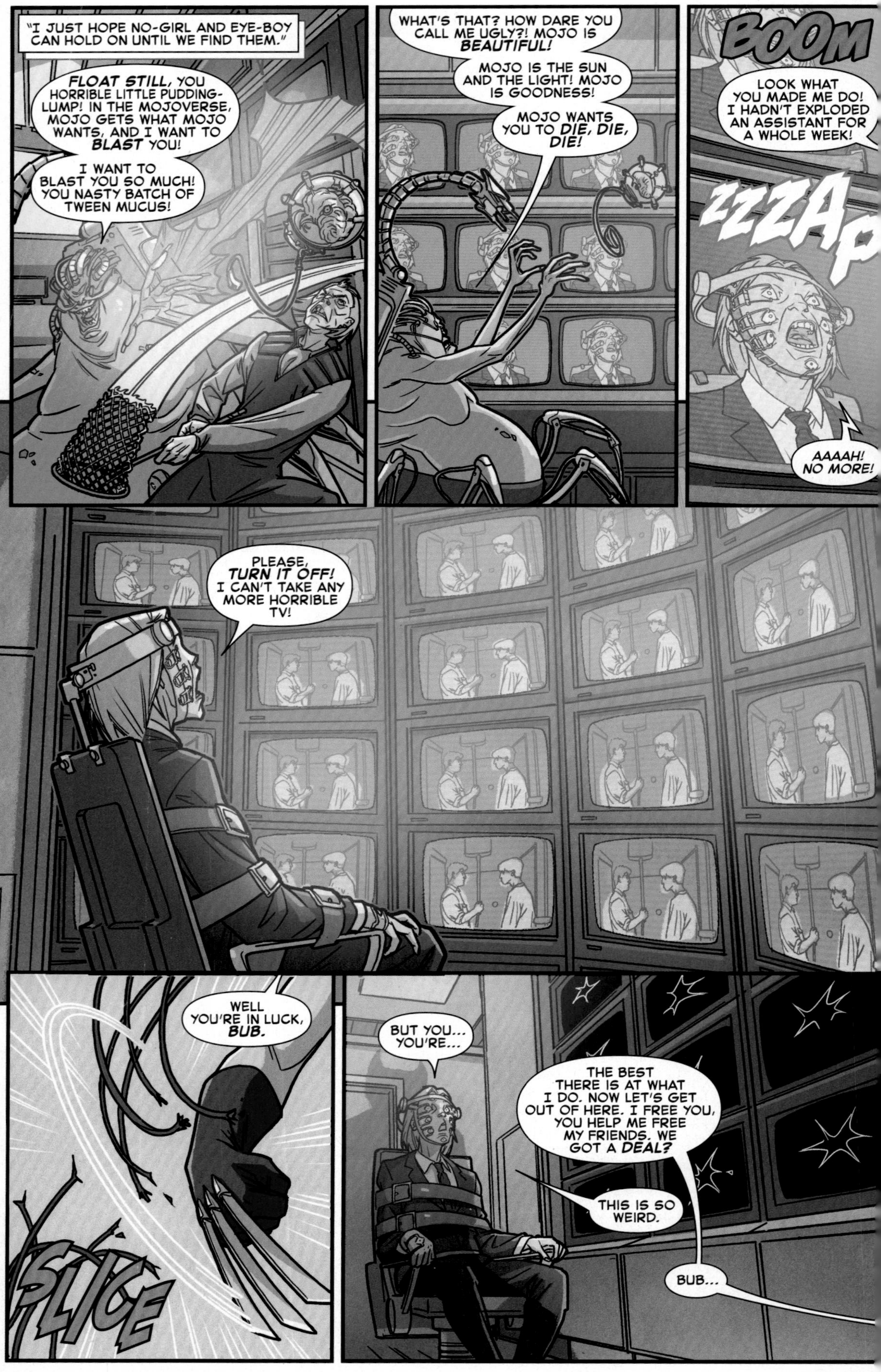
"I JUST HOPE NO-GIRL AND EYE-BOY CAN HOLD ON UNTIL WE FIND THEM."
FLOAT STILL, YOU HORRIBLE LITTLE PUDDING-LUMP! IN THE MOJOVERSE, MOJO GETS WHAT MOJO WANTS, AND I WANT TO BLAST YOU!
I WANT TO BLAST YOU SO MUCH! YOU NASTY BATCH OF TWEEN MUCUS!
WHAT'S THAT? HOW DARE YOU CALL ME UGLY?! MOJO IS BEAUTIFUL!
MOJO IS THE SUN AND THE LIGHT! MOJO IS GOODNESS!
MOJO WANTS YOU TO DIE, DIE, DIE!
BOOM
LOOK WHAT YOU MADE ME DO! I HADN'T EXPLODED AN ASSISTANT FOR A WHOLE WEEK!
ZZZAP
AAAAH! NO MORE!
PLEASE, TURN IT OFF! I CAN'T TAKE ANY MORE HORRIBLE TV!
WELL YOU'RE IN LUCK, BUB.
SLICE
BUT YOU... YOU'RE...
THE BEST THERE IS AT WHAT I DO. NOW LET'S GET OUT OF HERE. I FREE YOU, YOU HELP ME FREE MY FRIENDS. WE GOT A DEAL?
THIS IS SO WEIRD.
BUB...

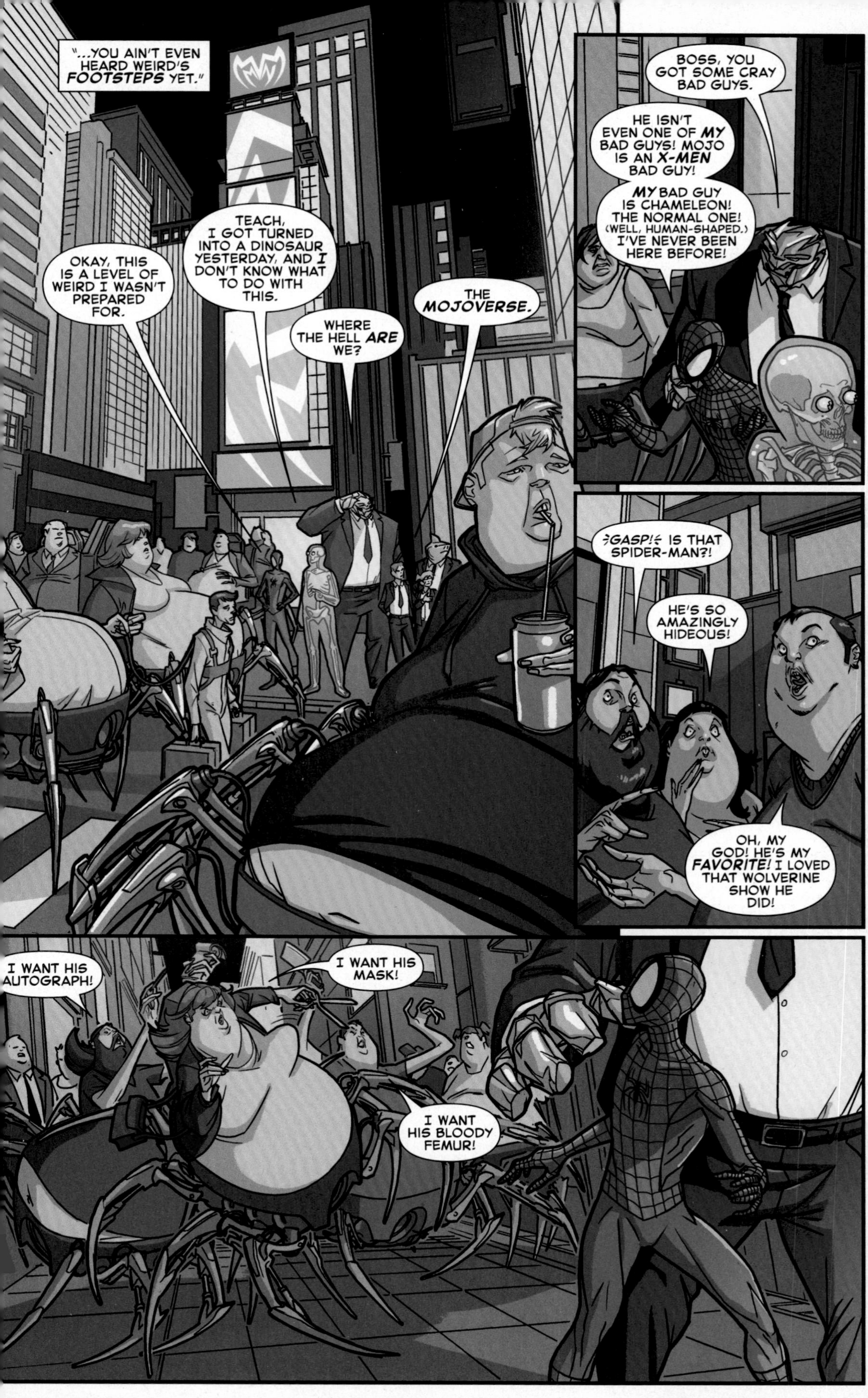
"...YOU AIN'T EVEN HEARD WEIRD'S FOOTSTEPS YET."
OKAY, THIS IS A LEVEL OF WEIRD I WASN'T PREPARED FOR.
TEACH, I GOT TURNED INTO A DINOSAUR YESTERDAY, AND I DON'T KNOW WHAT TO DO WITH THIS.
WHERE THE HELL ARE WE?
THE MOJOVERSE.
BOSS, YOU GOT SOME CRAY BAD GUYS.
HE ISN'T EVEN ONE OF MY BAD GUYS! MOJO IS AN X-MEN BAD GUY!
MY BAD GUY IS CHAMELEON! THE NORMAL ONE! (WELL, HUMAN-SHAPED.) I'VE NEVER BEEN HERE BEFORE!
GASP! IS THAT SPIDER-MAN?!
HE'S SO AMAZINGLY HIDEOUS!
OH, MY GOD! HE'S MY FAVORITE! I LOVED THAT WOLVERINE SHOW HE DID!
I WANT HIS AUTOGRAPH!
I WANT HIS MASK!
I WANT HIS BLOODY FEMUR!

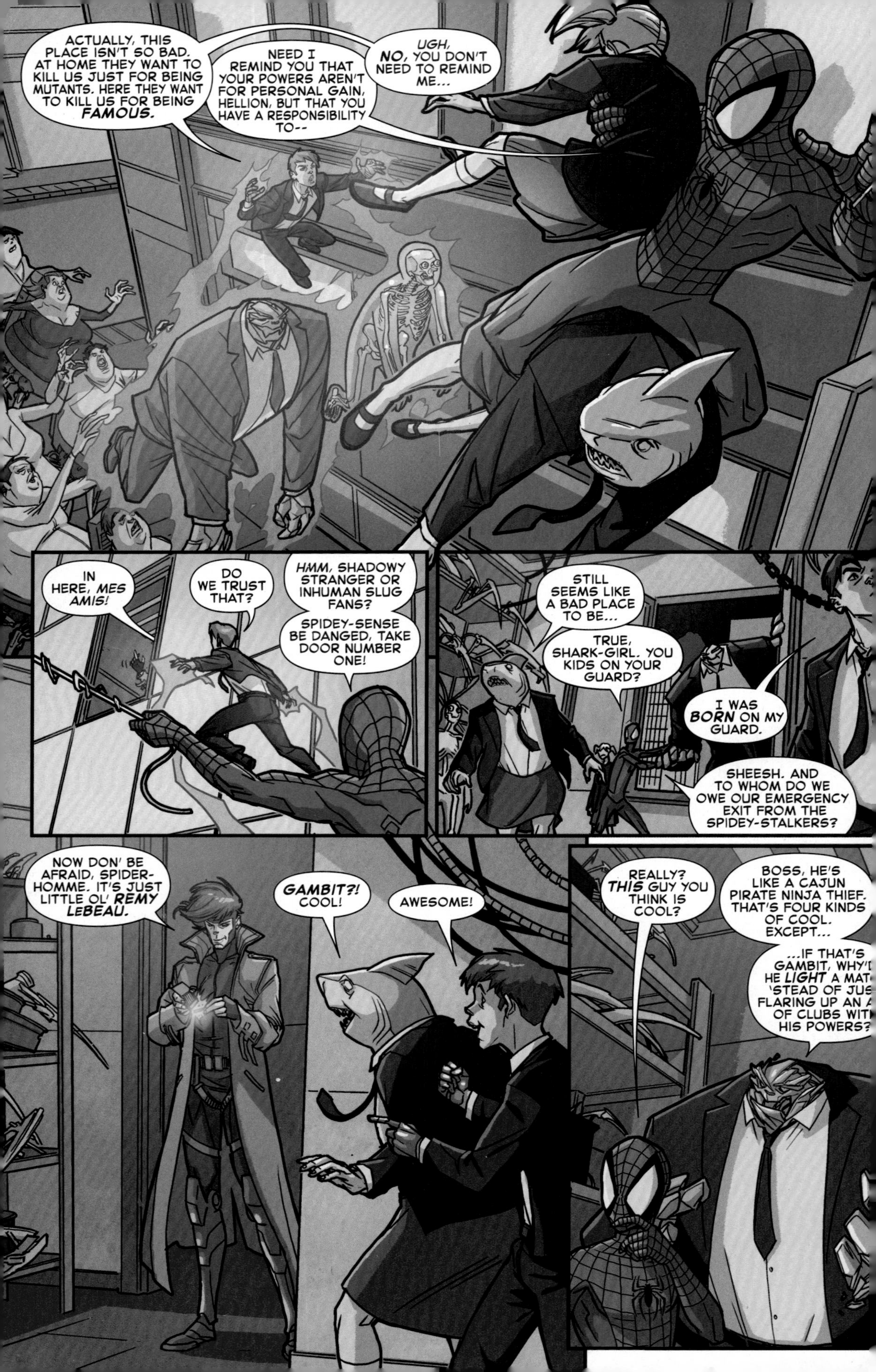
ACTUALLY, THIS PLACE ISN'T SO BAD. AT HOME THEY WANT TO KILL US JUST FOR BEING MUTANTS. HERE THEY WANT TO KILL US FOR BEING FAMOUS.
NEED I REMIND YOU THAT YOUR POWERS AREN'T FOR PERSONAL GAIN, HELLION, BUT THAT YOU HAVE A RESPONSIBILITY TO--
UGH, NO, YOU DON'T NEED TO REMIND ME...
IN HERE, MES AMIS!
DO WE TRUST THAT?
HMM, SHADOWY STRANGER OR INHUMAN SLUG FANS?
SPIDEY-SENSE BE DANGED, TAKE DOOR NUMBER ONE!
STILL SEEMS LIKE A BAD PLACE TO BE...
TRUE, SHARK-GIRL. YOU KIDS ON YOUR GUARD?
I WAS BORN ON MY GUARD.
SHEESH. AND TO WHOM DO WE OWE OUR EMERGENCY EXIT FROM THE SPIDEY-STALKERS?
NOW DON' BE AFRAID, SPIDER-HOMME. IT'S JUST LITTLE OL' REMY LEBEAU.
GAMBIT?! COOL!
AWESOME!
REALLY? THIS GUY YOU THINK IS COOL?
BOSS, HE'S LIKE A CAJUN PIRATE NINJA THIEF. THAT'S FOUR KINDS OF COOL. EXCEPT...
...IF THAT'S GAMBIT, WHY'D HE LIGHT A MAT 'STEAD OF JUS FLARING UP AN A OF CLUBS WIT HIS POWERS?

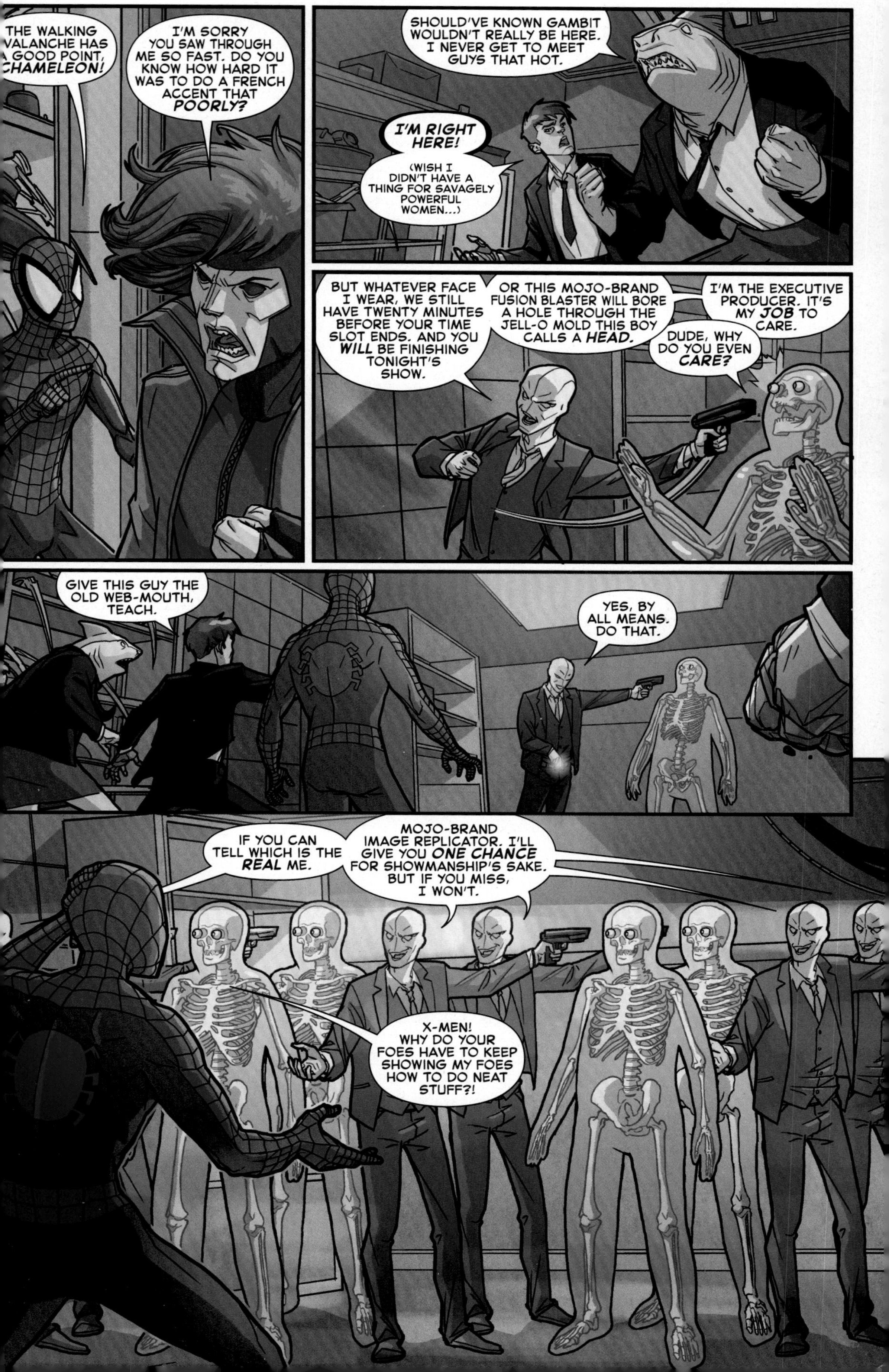
THE WALKING AVALANCHE HAS A GOOD POINT, CHAMELEON!
I'M SORRY YOU SAW THROUGH ME SO FAST. DO YOU KNOW HOW HARD IT WAS TO DO A FRENCH ACCENT THAT POORLY?
SHOULD'VE KNOWN GAMBIT WOULDN'T REALLY BE HERE. I NEVER GET TO MEET GUYS THAT HOT.
I'M RIGHT HERE!
(WISH I DIDN'T HAVE A THING FOR SAVAGELY POWERFUL WOMEN...)
BUT WHATEVER FACE I WEAR, WE STILL HAVE TWENTY MINUTES BEFORE YOUR TIME SLOT ENDS. AND YOU WILL BE FINISHING TONIGHT'S SHOW.
OR THIS MOJO-BRAND FUSION BLASTER WILL BORE A HOLE THROUGH THE JELL-O MOLD THIS BOY CALLS A HEAD.
DUDE, WHY DO YOU EVEN CARE?
I'M THE EXECUTIVE PRODUCER. IT'S MY JOB TO CARE.
GIVE THIS GUY THE OLD WEB-MOUTH, TEACH.
YES, BY ALL MEANS. DO THAT.
IF YOU CAN TELL WHICH IS THE REAL ME.
MOJO-BRAND IMAGE REPLICATOR. I'LL GIVE YOU ONE CHANCE FOR SHOWMANSHIP'S SAKE. BUT IF YOU MISS, I WON'T.
X-MEN! WHY DO YOUR FOES HAVE TO KEEP SHOWING MY FOES HOW TO DO NEAT STUFF?!

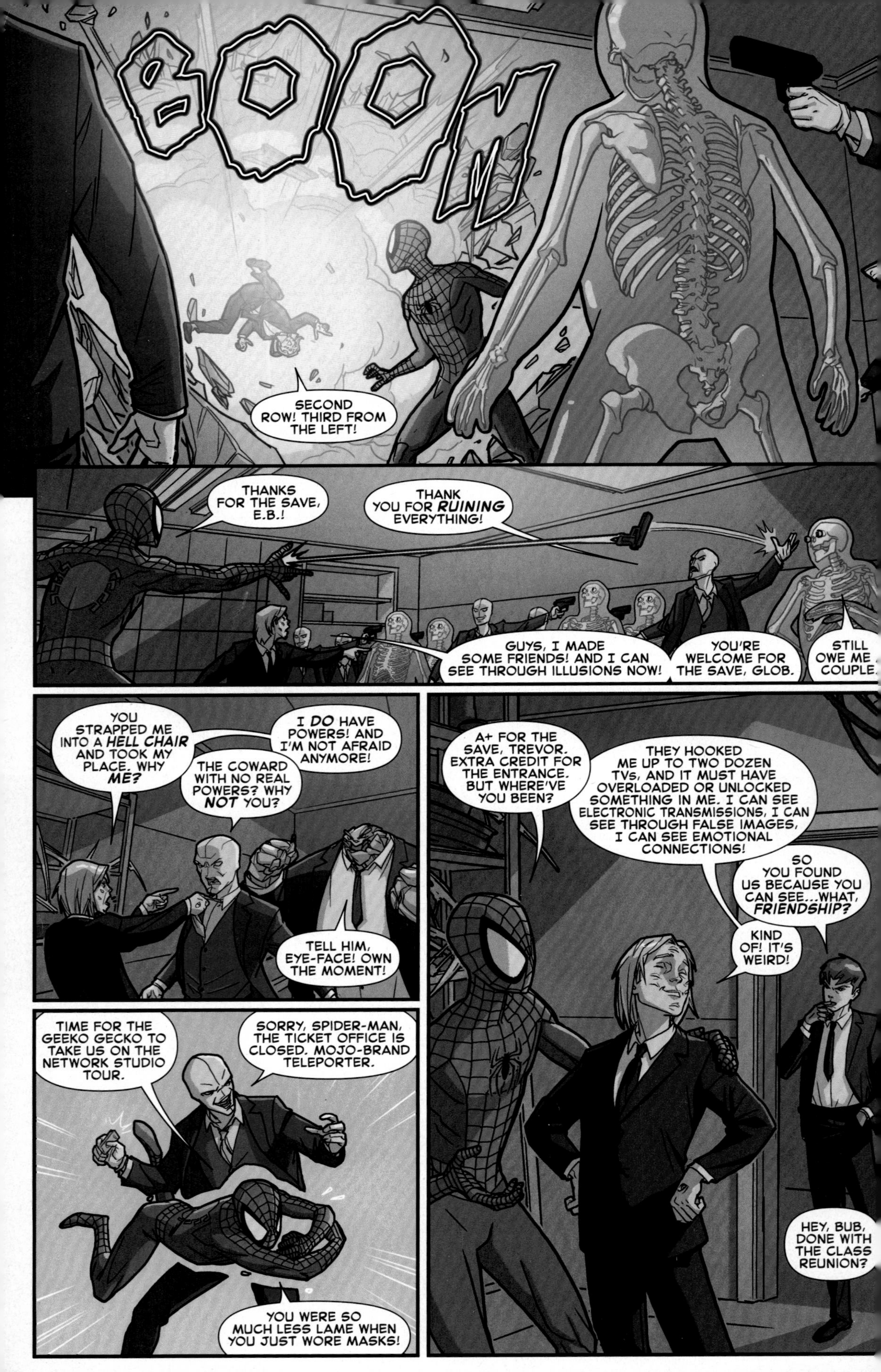
BOOM
SECOND ROW! THIRD FROM THE LEFT!
THANKS FOR THE SAVE, E.B.!
THANK YOU FOR RUINING EVERYTHING!
GUYS, I MADE SOME FRIENDS! AND I CAN SEE THROUGH ILLUSIONS NOW!
YOU'RE WELCOME FOR THE SAVE, GLOB.
STILL OWE ME COUPLE.
YOU STRAPPED ME INTO A HELL CHAIR AND TOOK MY PLACE. WHY ME?
I DO HAVE POWERS! AND I'M NOT AFRAID ANYMORE!
THE COWARD WITH NO REAL POWERS? WHY NOT YOU?
TELL HIM, EYE-FACE! OWN THE MOMENT!
TIME FOR THE GEEKO GECKO TO TAKE US ON THE NETWORK STUDIO TOUR.
SORRY, SPIDER-MAN, THE TICKET OFFICE IS CLOSED. MOJO-BRAND TELEPORTER.
YOU WERE SO MUCH LESS LAME WHEN YOU JUST WORE MASKS!
A+ FOR THE SAVE, TREVOR. EXTRA CREDIT FOR THE ENTRANCE. BUT WHERE'VE YOU BEEN?
THEY HOOKED ME UP TO TWO DOZEN TVs, AND IT MUST HAVE OVERLOADED OR UNLOCKED SOMETHING IN ME. I CAN SEE ELECTRONIC TRANSMISSIONS, I CAN SEE THROUGH FALSE IMAGES, I CAN SEE EMOTIONAL CONNECTIONS!
SO YOU FOUND US BECAUSE YOU CAN SEE...WHAT, FRIENDSHIP?
KIND OF! IT'S WEIRD!
HEY, BUB, DONE WITH THE CLASS REUNION?

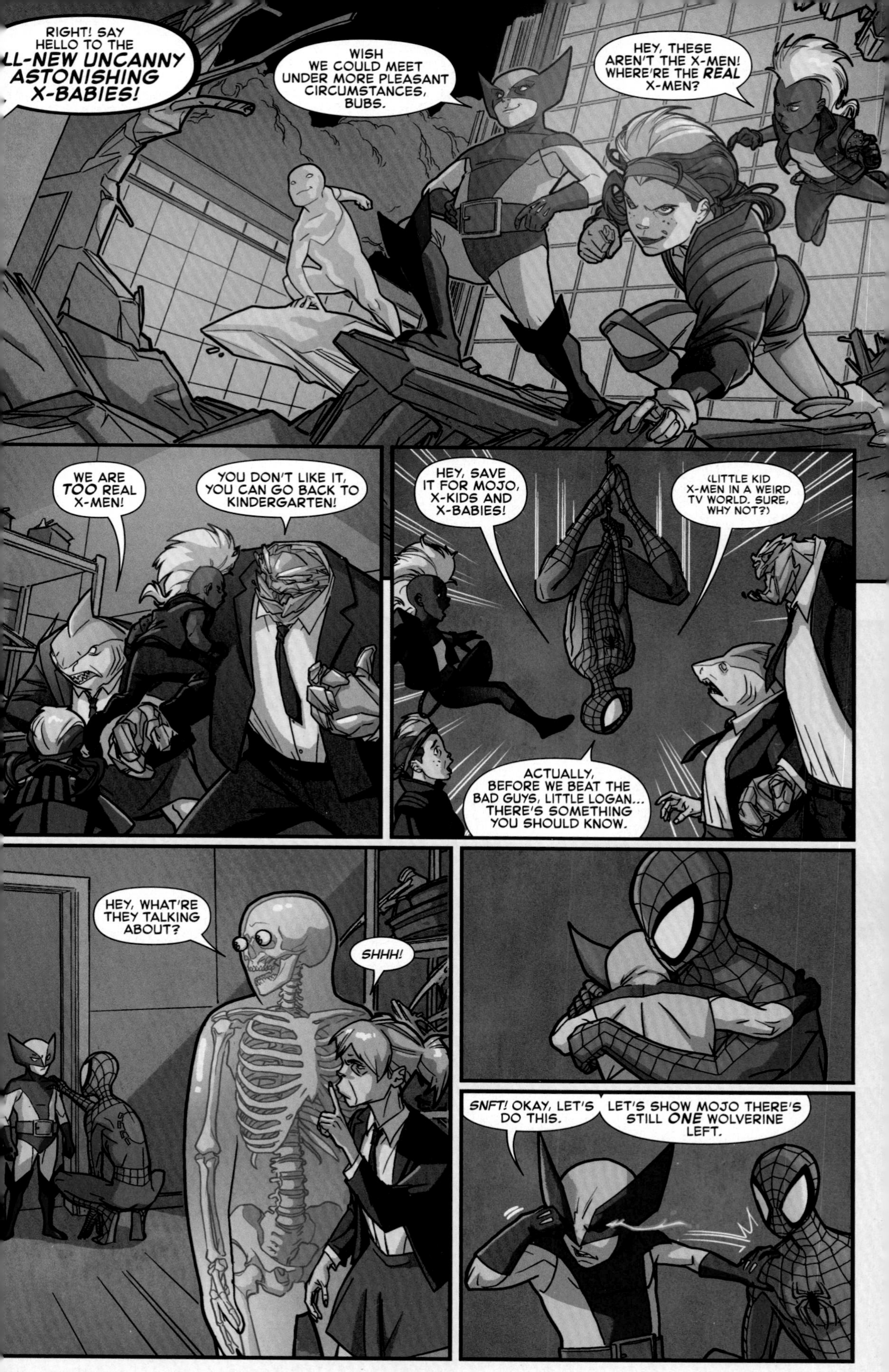

RIGHT! SAY HELLO TO THE ALL-NEW UNCANNY ASTONISHING X-BABIES!
WISH WE COULD MEET UNDER MORE PLEASANT CIRCUMSTANCES, BUBS.
HEY, THESE AREN'T THE X-MEN! WHERE'RE THE REAL X-MEN?
WE ARE TOO REAL X-MEN!
YOU DON'T LIKE IT, YOU CAN GO BACK TO KINDERGARTEN!
HEY, SAVE IT FOR MOJO, X-KIDS AND X-BABIES!
(LITTLE KID X-MEN IN A WEIRD TV WORLD. SURE, WHY NOT?)
ACTUALLY, BEFORE WE BEAT THE BAD GUYS, LITTLE LOGAN... THERE'S SOMETHING YOU SHOULD KNOW.
HEY, WHAT'RE THEY TALKING ABOUT?
SHHH!
SNFT! OKAY, LET'S DO THIS.
LET'S SHOW MOJO THERE'S STILL ONE WOLVERINE LEFT.

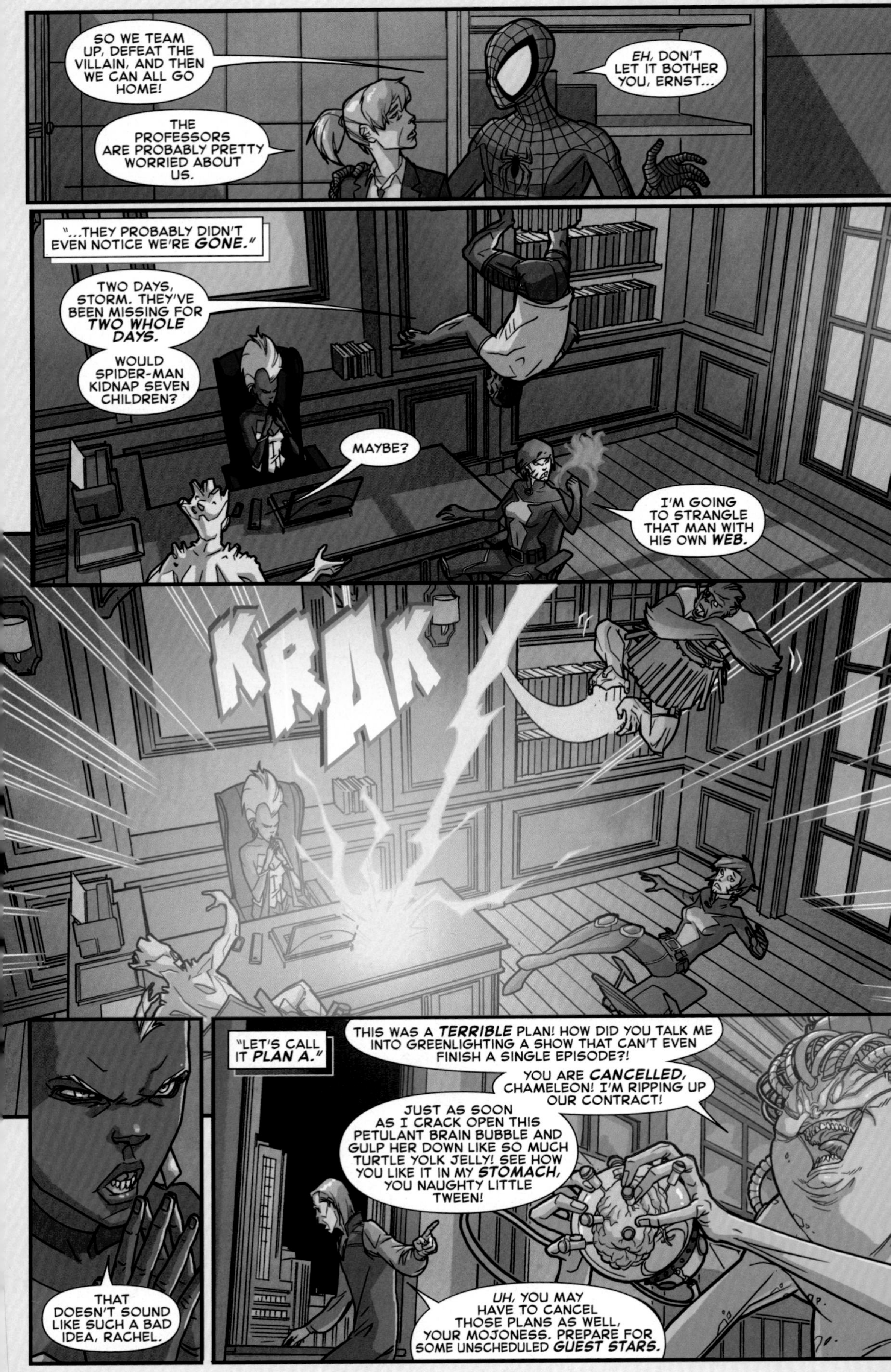
SO WE TEAM UP, DEFEAT THE VILLAIN, AND THEN WE CAN ALL GO HOME!
THE PROFESSORS ARE PROBABLY PRETTY WORRIED ABOUT US.
EH, DON'T LET IT BOTHER YOU, ERNST...
"...THEY PROBABLY DIDN'T EVEN NOTICE WE'RE GONE."
TWO DAYS, STORM. THEY'VE BEEN MISSING FOR TWO WHOLE DAYS.
WOULD SPIDER-MAN KIDNAP SEVEN CHILDREN?
MAYBE?
I'M GOING TO STRANGLE THAT MAN WITH HIS OWN WEB.
KRAK
THAT DOESN'T SOUND LIKE SUCH A BAD IDEA, RACHEL.
"LET'S CALL IT PLAN A."
THIS WAS A TERRIBLE PLAN! HOW DID YOU TALK ME INTO GREENLIGHTING A SHOW THAT CAN'T EVEN FINISH A SINGLE EPISODE?!
YOU ARE CANCELLED, CHAMELEON! I'M RIPPING UP OUR CONTRACT!
JUST AS SOON AS I CRACK OPEN THIS PETULANT BRAIN BUBBLE AND GULP HER DOWN LIKE SO MUCH TURTLE YOLK JELLY! SEE HOW YOU LIKE IT IN MY STOMACH, YOU NAUGHTY LITTLE TWEEN!
UH, YOU MAY HAVE TO CANCEL THOSE PLANS AS WELL, YOUR MOJONESS. PREPARE FOR SOME UNSCHEDULED GUEST STARS.

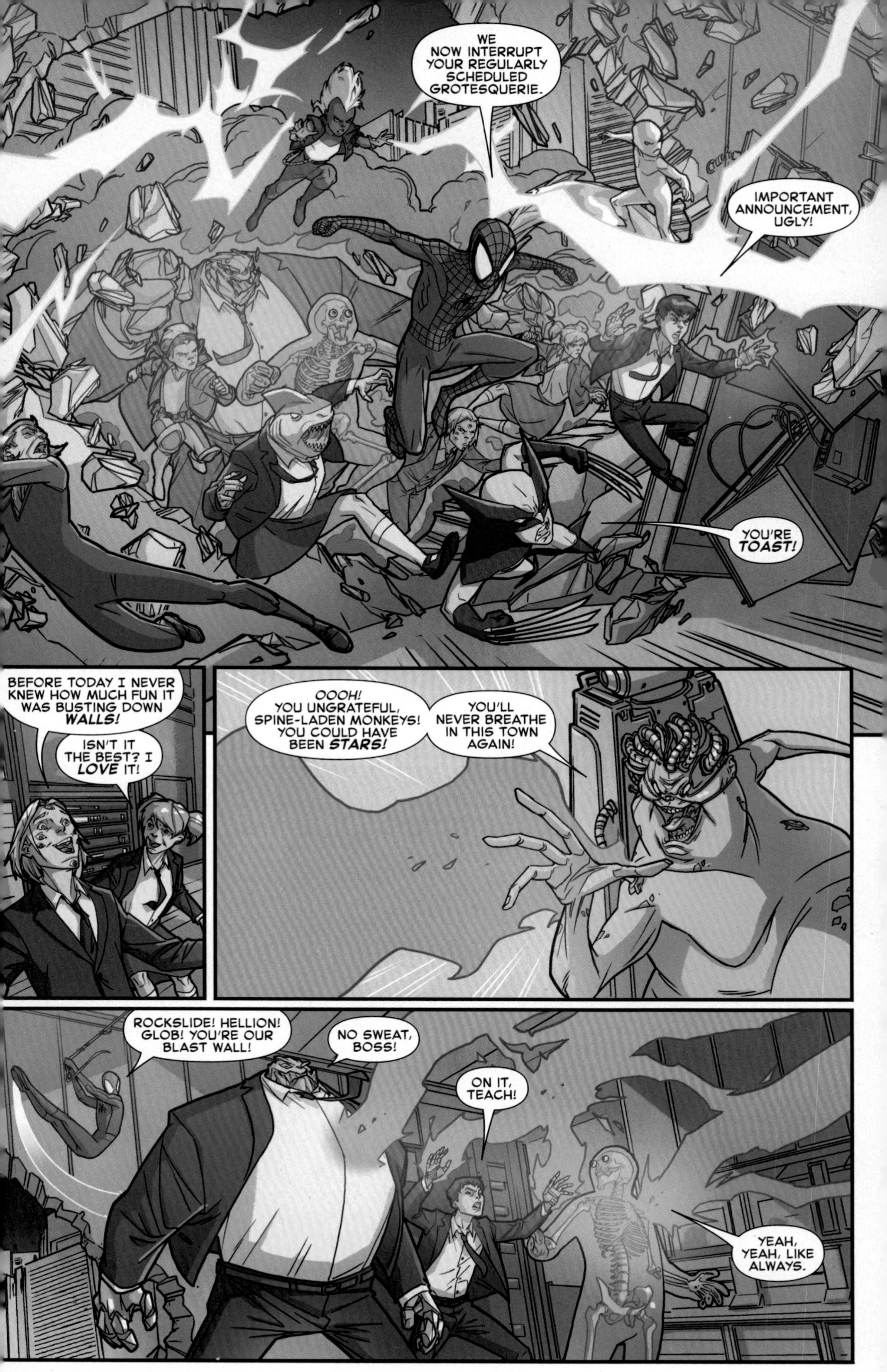
WE NOW INTERRUPT YOUR REGULARLY SCHEDULED GROTESQUERIE.
IMPORTANT ANNOUNCEMENT, UGLY!
YOU'RE *TOAST!*
BEFORE TODAY I NEVER KNEW HOW MUCH FUN IT WAS BUSTING DOWN *WALLS!*
ISN'T IT THE BEST? I *LOVE* IT!
OOOH! YOU UNGRATEFUL, SPINE-LADEN MONKEYS! YOU COULD HAVE BEEN *STARS!*
YOU'LL NEVER BREATHE IN THIS TOWN AGAIN!
ROCKSLIDE! HELLION! GLOB! YOU'RE OUR BLAST WALL!
NO SWEAT, BOSS!
ON IT, TEACH!
YEAH, YEAH, LIKE ALWAYS.

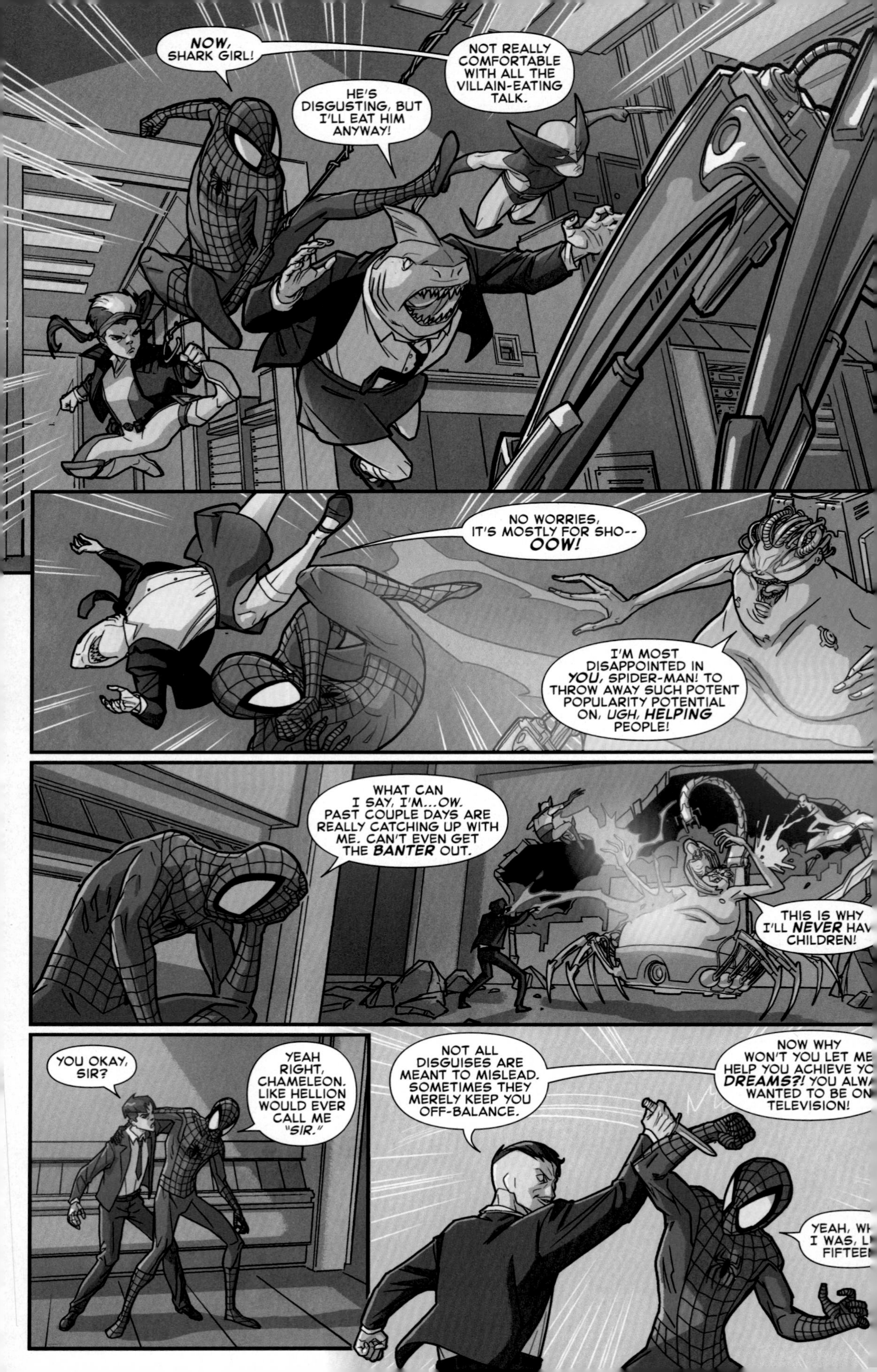
NOW, SHARK GIRL!
NOT REALLY COMFORTABLE WITH ALL THE VILLAIN-EATING TALK.
HE'S DISGUSTING, BUT I'LL EAT HIM ANYWAY!
NO WORRIES, IT'S MOSTLY FOR SHO-- OOW!
I'M MOST DISAPPOINTED IN YOU, SPIDER-MAN! TO THROW AWAY SUCH POTENT POPULARITY POTENTIAL ON, UGH, HELPING PEOPLE!
WHAT CAN I SAY, I'M...OW. PAST COUPLE DAYS ARE REALLY CATCHING UP WITH ME. CAN'T EVEN GET THE BANTER OUT.
THIS IS WHY I'LL NEVER HAV
CHILDREN!
YOU OKAY, SIR?
YEAH RIGHT, CHAMELEON. LIKE HELLION WOULD EVER CALL ME "SIR."
NOT ALL DISGUISES ARE MEANT TO MISLEAD. SOMETIMES THEY MERELY KEEP YOU OFF-BALANCE.
NOW WHY WON'T YOU LET ME HELP YOU ACHIEVE YO
DREAMS?! YOU ALWA
WANTED TO BE ON TELEVISION!
YEAH, WH
I WAS, LI
FIFTEEN

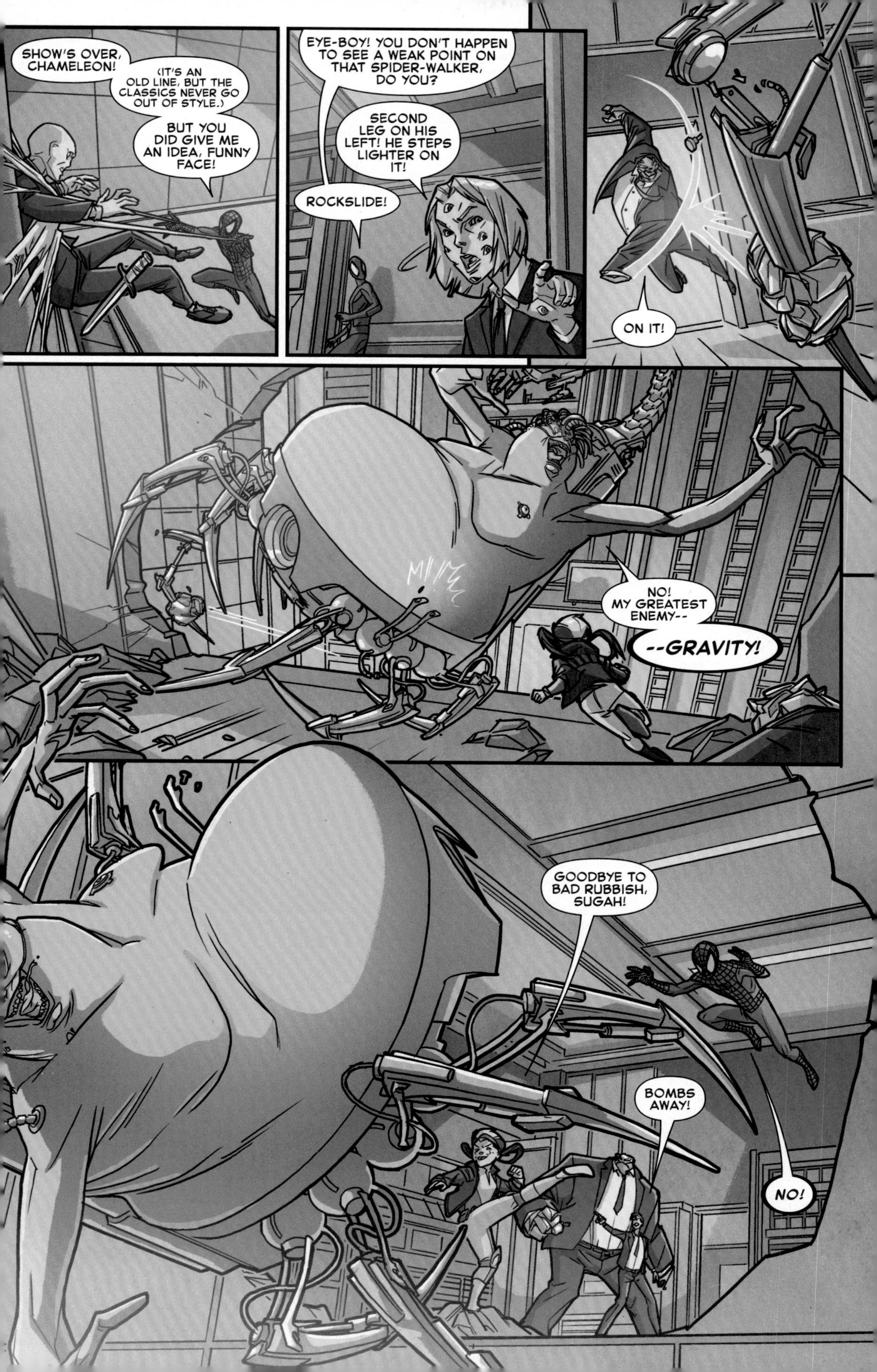
SHOW'S OVER, CHAMELEON!
(IT'S AN OLD LINE, BUT THE CLASSICS NEVER GO OUT OF STYLE.)
BUT YOU DID GIVE ME AN IDEA, FUNNY FACE!
EYE-BOY! YOU DON'T HAPPEN TO SEE A WEAK POINT ON THAT SPIDER-WALKER, DO YOU?
SECOND LEG ON HIS LEFT! HE STEPS LIGHTER ON IT!
ROCKSLIDE!
ON IT!
NO! MY GREATEST ENEMY--
--GRAVITY!
GOODBYE TO BAD RUBBISH, SUGAH!
BOMBS AWAY!
NO!

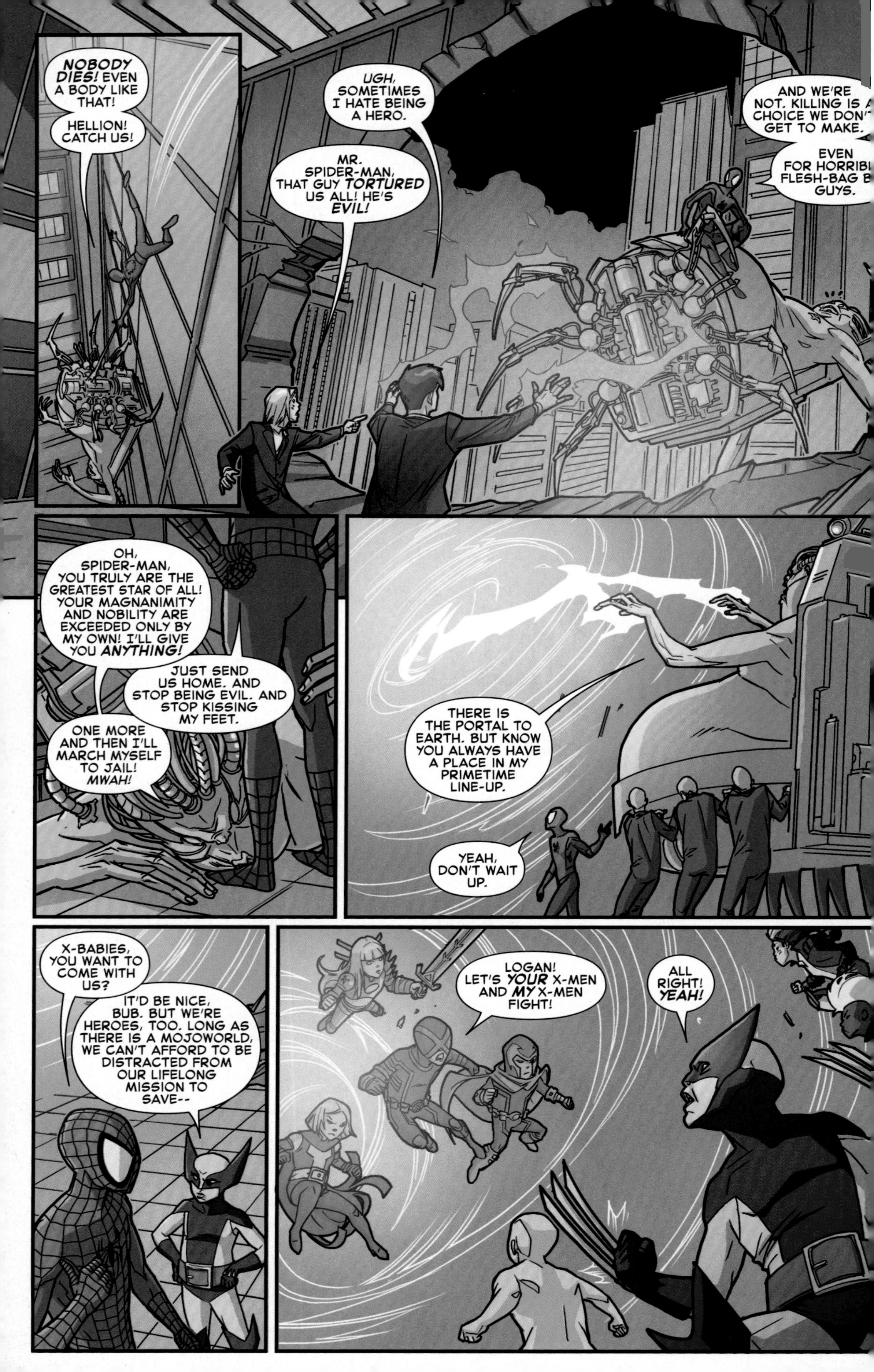
NOBODY DIES! EVEN A BODY LIKE THAT!
HELLION! CATCH US!
UGH, SOMETIMES I HATE BEING A HERO.
MR. SPIDER-MAN, THAT GUY TORTURED US ALL! HE'S EVIL!
AND WE'RE NOT. KILLING IS A CHOICE WE DON'T GET TO MAKE.
EVEN FOR HORRIBLE FLESH-BAG B GUYS.
OH, SPIDER-MAN, YOU TRULY ARE THE GREATEST STAR OF ALL! YOUR MAGNANIMITY AND NOBILITY ARE EXCEEDED ONLY BY MY OWN! I'LL GIVE YOU ANYTHING!
JUST SEND US HOME. AND STOP BEING EVIL. AND STOP KISSING MY FEET.
ONE MORE AND THEN I'LL MARCH MYSELF TO JAIL! MWAH!
THERE IS THE PORTAL TO EARTH. BUT KNOW YOU ALWAYS HAVE A PLACE IN MY PRIMETIME LINE-UP.
YEAH, DON'T WAIT UP.
X-BABIES, YOU WANT TO COME WITH US?
IT'D BE NICE, BUB. BUT WE'RE HEROES, TOO. LONG AS THERE IS A MOJOWORLD, WE CAN'T AFFORD TO BE DISTRACTED FROM OUR LIFELONG MISSION TO SAVE--
LOGAN! LET'S YOUR X-MEN AND MY X-MEN FIGHT!
ALL RIGHT! YEAH!

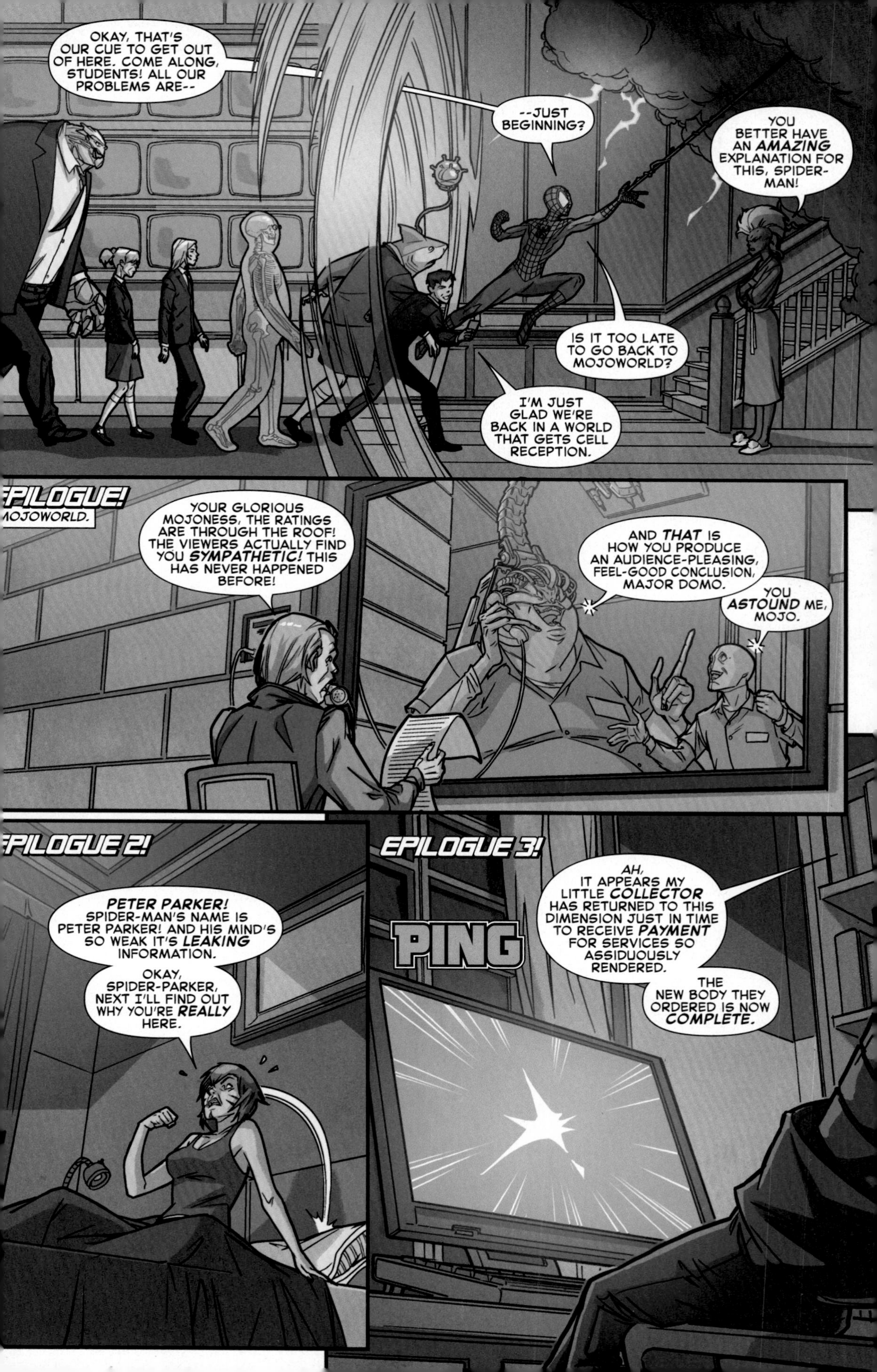
OKAY, THAT'S OUR CUE TO GET OUT OF HERE. COME ALONG, STUDENTS! ALL OUR PROBLEMS ARE--
--JUST BEGINNING?
YOU BETTER HAVE AN AMAZING EXPLANATION FOR THIS, SPIDER-MAN!
IS IT TOO LATE TO GO BACK TO MOJOWORLD?
I'M JUST GLAD WE'RE BACK IN A WORLD THAT GETS CELL RECEPTION.
EPILOGUE!
MOJOWORLD.
YOUR GLORIOUS MOJONESS, THE RATINGS ARE THROUGH THE ROOF! THE VIEWERS ACTUALLY FIND YOU SYMPATHETIC! THIS HAS NEVER HAPPENED BEFORE!
AND THAT IS HOW YOU PRODUCE AN AUDIENCE-PLEASING, FEEL-GOOD CONCLUSION, MAJOR DOMO.
YOU ASTOUND ME, MOJO.
EPILOGUE 2!
PETER PARKER! SPIDER-MAN'S NAME IS PETER PARKER! AND HIS MIND'S SO WEAK IT'S LEAKING INFORMATION.
OKAY, SPIDER-PARKER, NEXT I'LL FIND OUT WHY YOU'RE REALLY HERE.
EPILOGUE 3!
PING
AH, IT APPEARS MY LITTLE COLLECTOR HAS RETURNED TO THIS DIMENSION JUST IN TIME TO RECEIVE PAYMENT FOR SERVICES SO ASSIDUOUSLY RENDERED.
THE NEW BODY THEY ORDERED IS NOW COMPLETE.

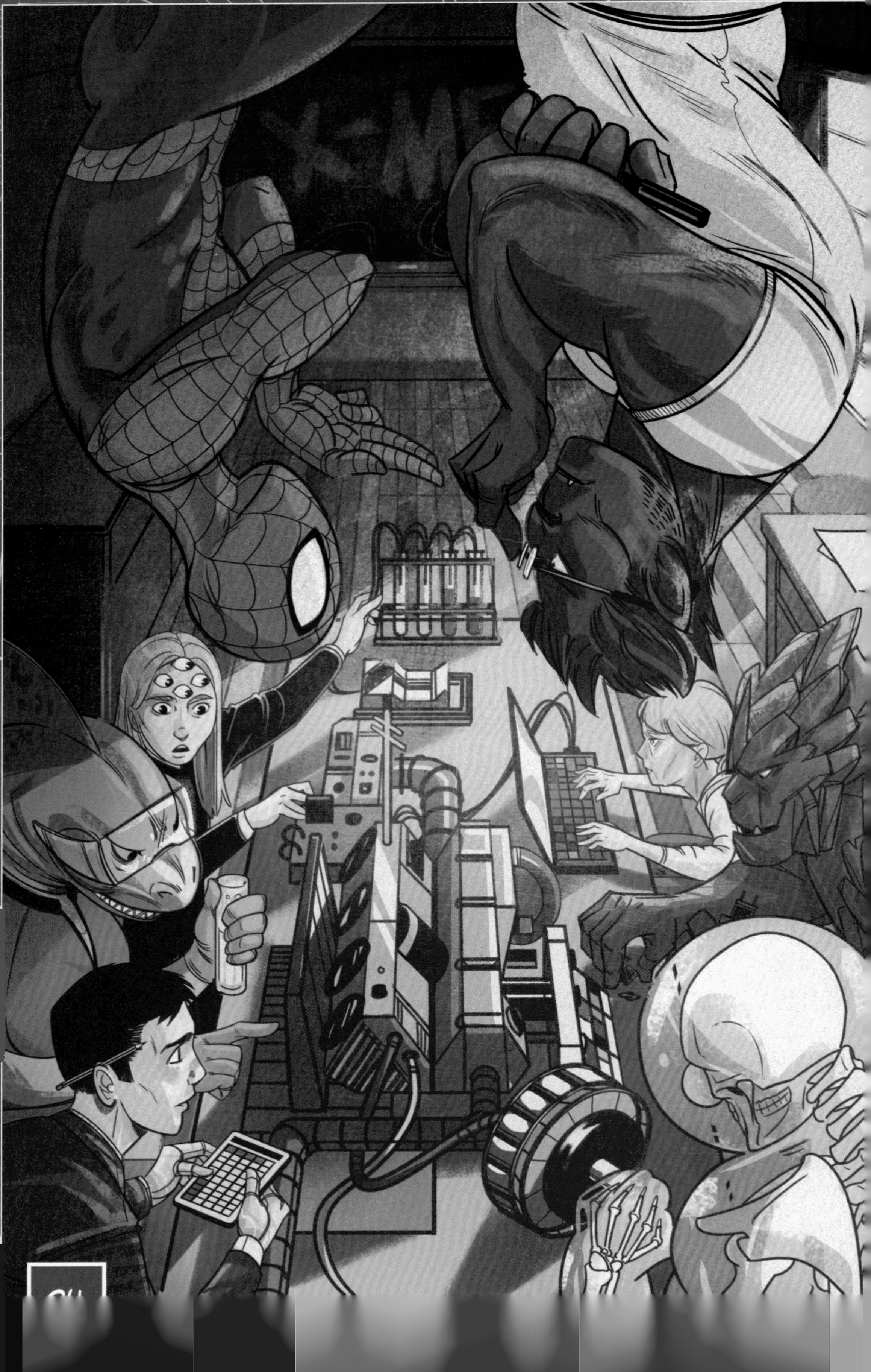

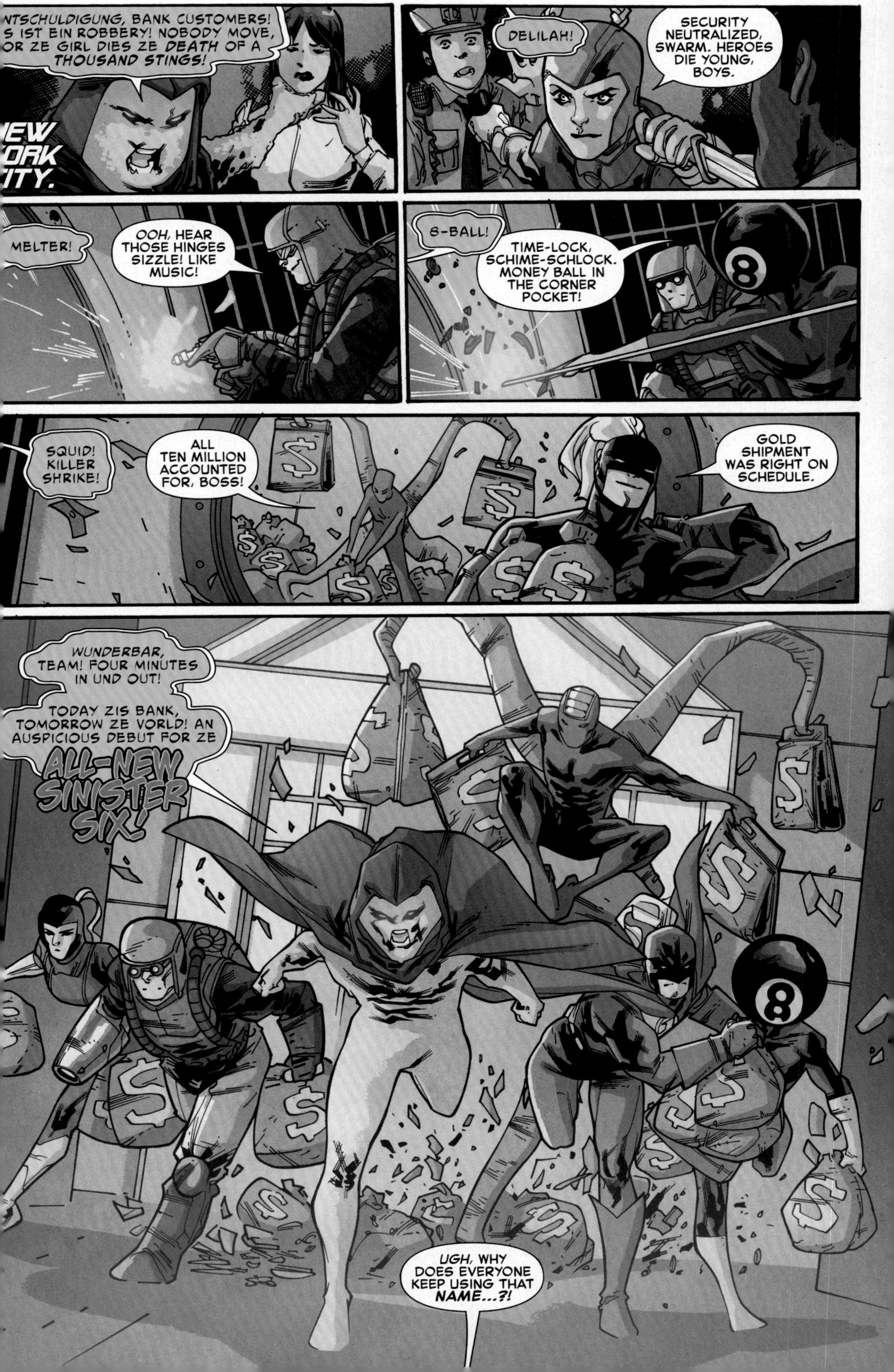

NTSCHULDIGUNG, BANK CUSTOMERS! S IST EIN ROBBERY! NOBODY MOVE, OR ZE GIRL DIES ZE DEATH OF A THOUSAND STINGS!
NEW YORK CITY.
DELILAH!
SECURITY NEUTRALIZED, SWARM. HEROES DIE YOUNG, BOYS.
MELTER!
OOH, HEAR THOSE HINGES SIZZLE! LIKE MUSIC!
8-BALL!
TIME-LOCK, SCHIME-SCHLOCK. MONEY BALL IN THE CORNER POCKET!
SQUID! KILLER SHRIKE!
ALL TEN MILLION ACCOUNTED FOR, BOSS!
GOLD SHIPMENT WAS RIGHT ON SCHEDULE.
WUNDERBAR, TEAM! FOUR MINUTES IN UND OUT!
TODAY ZIS BANK, TOMORROW ZE VORLD! AN AUSPICIOUS DEBUT FOR ZE
ALL-NEW SINISTER SIX!
UGH, WHY DOES EVERYONE KEEP USING THAT NAME...?!

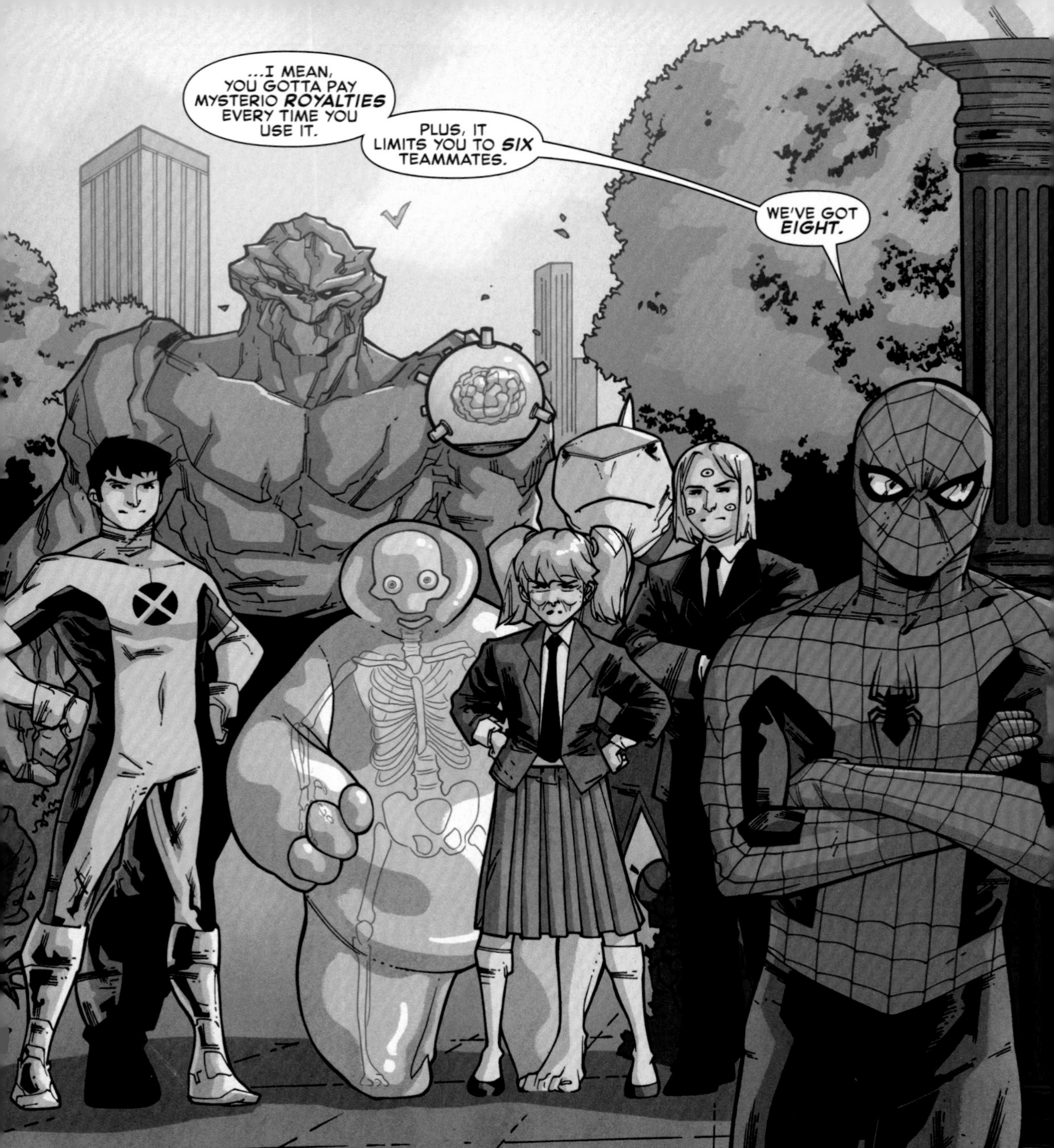
...I MEAN, YOU GOTTA PAY MYSTERIO ROYALTIES EVERY TIME YOU USE IT.
PLUS, IT LIMITS YOU TO SIX TEAMMATES.
WE'VE GOT EIGHT.

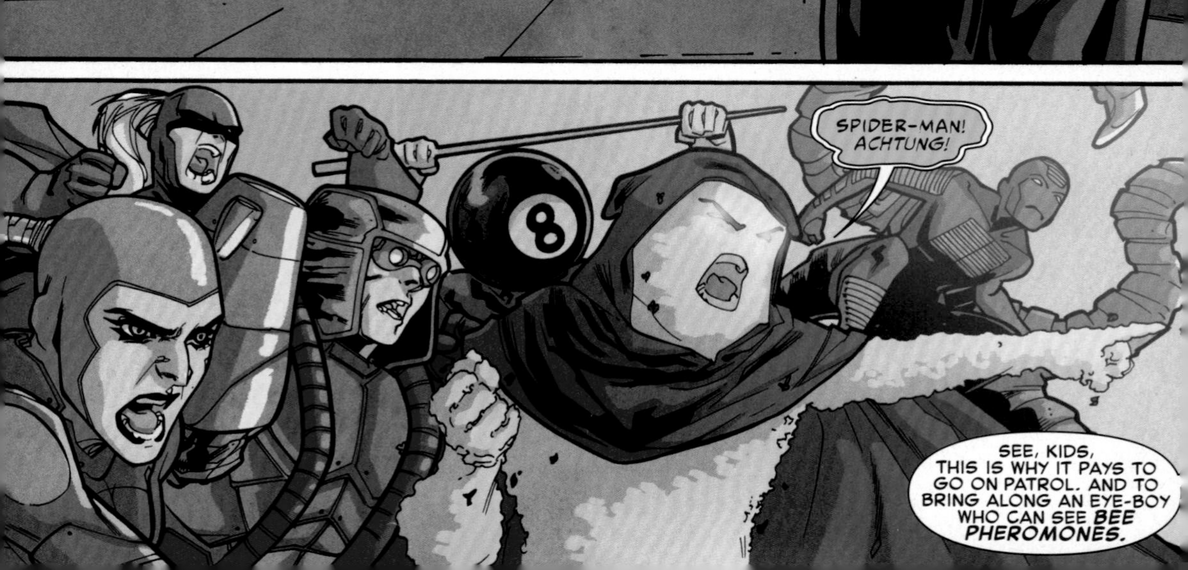
SPIDER-MAN! ACHTUNG!
SEE, KIDS, THIS IS WHY IT PAYS TO GO ON PATROL. AND TO BRING ALONG AN EYE-BOY WHO CAN SEE BEE PHEROMONES.

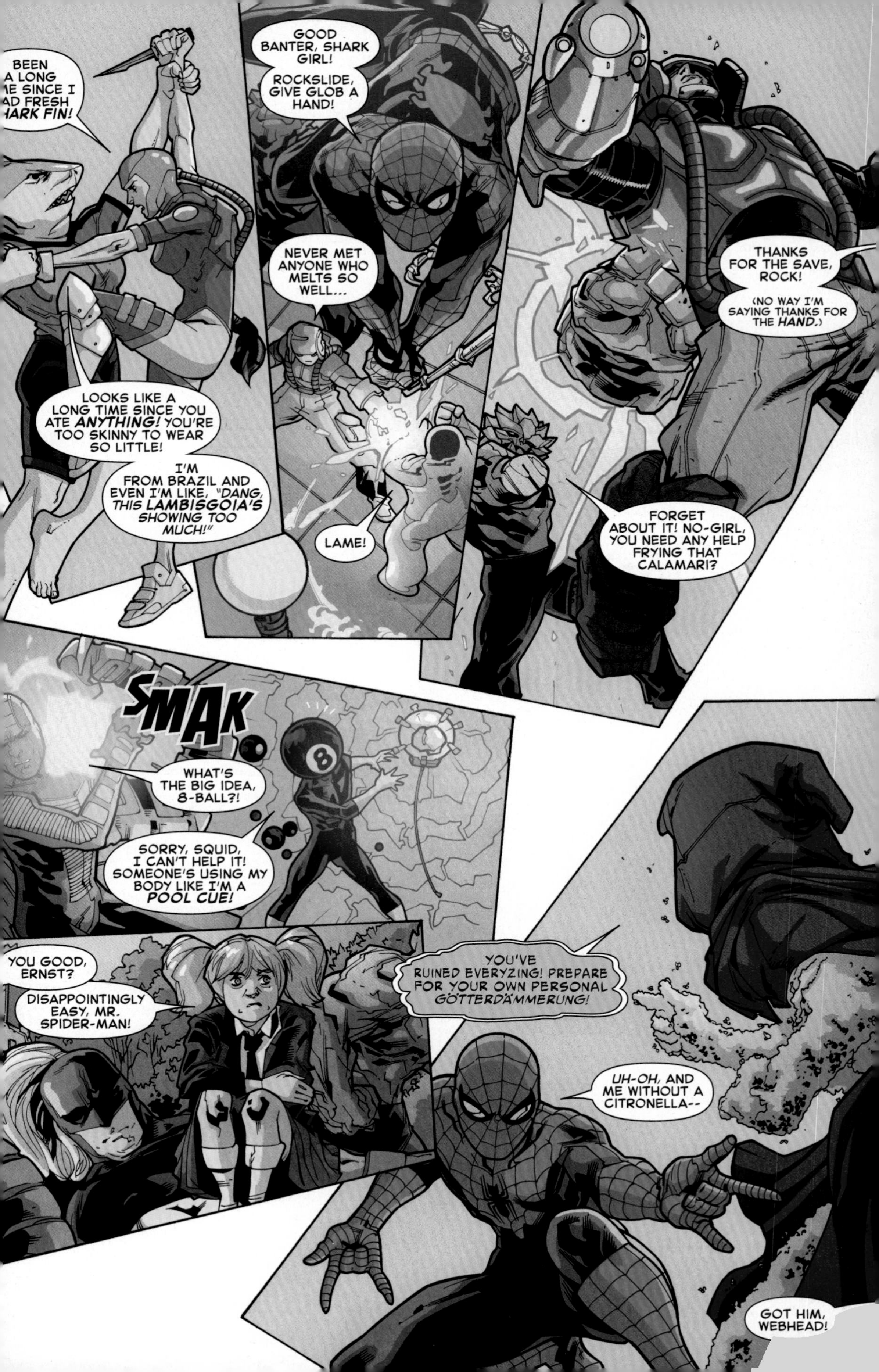
BEEN A LONG ME SINCE I AD FRESH HARK FIN!
LOOKS LIKE A LONG TIME SINCE YOU ATE ANYTHING! YOU'RE TOO SKINNY TO WEAR SO LITTLE!
I'M FROM BRAZIL AND EVEN I'M LIKE, "DANG, THIS LAMBISGOIA'S SHOWING TOO MUCH!"
GOOD BANTER, SHARK GIRL!
ROCKSLIDE, GIVE GLOB A HAND!
NEVER MET ANYONE WHO MELTS SO WELL...
LAME!
THANKS FOR THE SAVE, ROCK!
(NO WAY I'M SAYING THANKS FOR THE HAND.)
FORGET ABOUT IT! NO-GIRL, YOU NEED ANY HELP FRYING THAT CALAMARI?
SMAK
WHAT'S THE BIG IDEA, 8-BALL?!
SORRY, SQUID, I CAN'T HELP IT! SOMEONE'S USING MY BODY LIKE I'M A POOL CUE!
YOU GOOD, ERNST?
DISAPPOINTINGLY EASY, MR. SPIDER-MAN!
YOU'VE RUINED EVERYZING! PREPARE FOR YOUR OWN PERSONAL GÖTTERDÄMMERUNG!
UH-OH, AND ME WITHOUT A CITRONELLA--
GOT HIM, WEBHEAD!

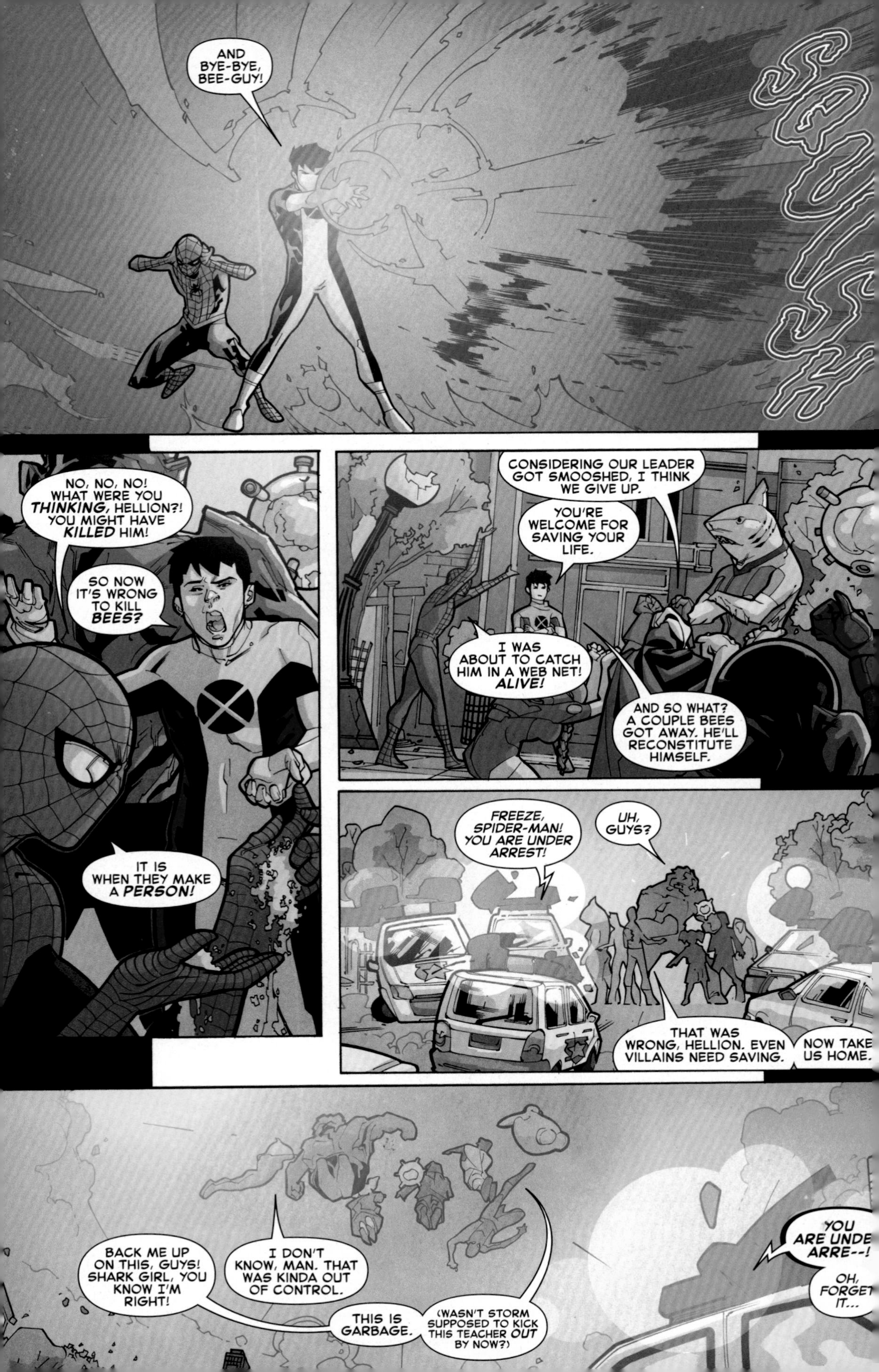

AND BYE-BYE, BEE-GUY!
NO, NO, NO! WHAT WERE YOU *THINKING,* HELLION?! YOU MIGHT HAVE *KILLED* HIM!
SO NOW IT'S WRONG TO KILL *BEES?*
IT IS WHEN THEY MAKE A *PERSON!*
CONSIDERING OUR LEADER GOT SMOOSHED, I THINK WE GIVE UP.
YOU'RE WELCOME FOR SAVING YOUR LIFE.
I WAS ABOUT TO CATCH HIM IN A WEB NET! *ALIVE!*
AND SO WHAT? A COUPLE BEES GOT AWAY. HE'LL RECONSTITUTE HIMSELF.
FREEZE, SPIDER-MAN! YOU ARE UNDER ARREST!
UH, GUYS?
THAT WAS WRONG, HELLION. EVEN VILLAINS NEED SAVING.
NOW TAKE US HOME.
BACK ME UP ON THIS, GUYS! SHARK GIRL, YOU KNOW I'M RIGHT!
I DON'T KNOW, MAN. THAT WAS KINDA OUT OF CONTROL.
THIS IS GARBAGE.
(WASN'T STORM SUPPOSED TO KICK THIS TEACHER *OUT* BY NOW?)
YOU ARE UNDE ARRE--!
OH, FORGET IT...

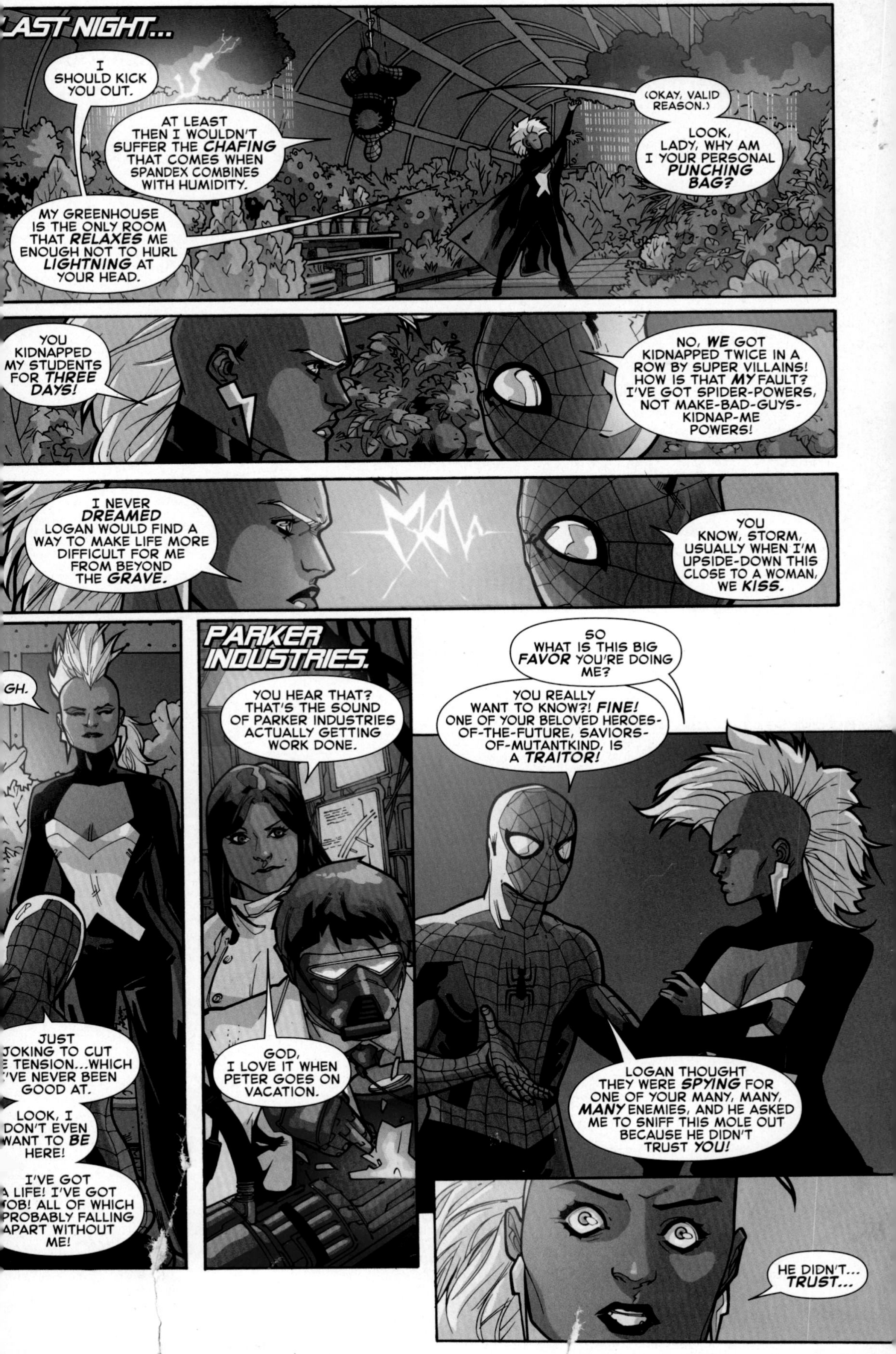
LAST NIGHT...
I SHOULD KICK YOU OUT.
AT LEAST THEN I WOULDN'T SUFFER THE CHAFING THAT COMES WHEN SPANDEX COMBINES WITH HUMIDITY.
MY GREENHOUSE IS THE ONLY ROOM THAT RELAXES ME ENOUGH NOT TO HURL LIGHTNING AT YOUR HEAD.
(OKAY, VALID REASON.)
LOOK, LADY, WHY AM I YOUR PERSONAL PUNCHING BAG?
YOU KIDNAPPED MY STUDENTS FOR THREE DAYS!
NO, WE GOT KIDNAPPED TWICE IN A ROW BY SUPER VILLAINS! HOW IS THAT MY FAULT? I'VE GOT SPIDER-POWERS, NOT MAKE-BAD-GUYS-KIDNAP-ME POWERS!
I NEVER DREAMED LOGAN WOULD FIND A WAY TO MAKE LIFE MORE DIFFICULT FOR ME FROM BEYOND THE GRAVE.
YOU KNOW, STORM, USUALLY WHEN I'M UPSIDE-DOWN THIS CLOSE TO A WOMAN, WE KISS.
GH.
JUST JOKING TO CUT E TENSION...WHICH 'VE NEVER BEEN GOOD AT.
LOOK, I DON'T EVEN WANT TO BE HERE!
I'VE GOT A LIFE! I'VE GOT JOB! ALL OF WHICH PROBABLY FALLING APART WITHOUT ME!
PARKER INDUSTRIES.
YOU HEAR THAT? THAT'S THE SOUND OF PARKER INDUSTRIES ACTUALLY GETTING WORK DONE.
GOD, I LOVE IT WHEN PETER GOES ON VACATION.
SO WHAT IS THIS BIG FAVOR YOU'RE DOING ME?
YOU REALLY WANT TO KNOW?! FINE! ONE OF YOUR BELOVED HEROES-OF-THE-FUTURE, SAVIORS-OF-MUTANTKIND, IS A TRAITOR!
LOGAN THOUGHT THEY WERE SPYING FOR ONE OF YOUR MANY, MANY, MANY ENEMIES, AND HE ASKED ME TO SNIFF THIS MOLE OUT BECAUSE HE DIDN'T TRUST YOU!
HE DIDN'T... TRUST...

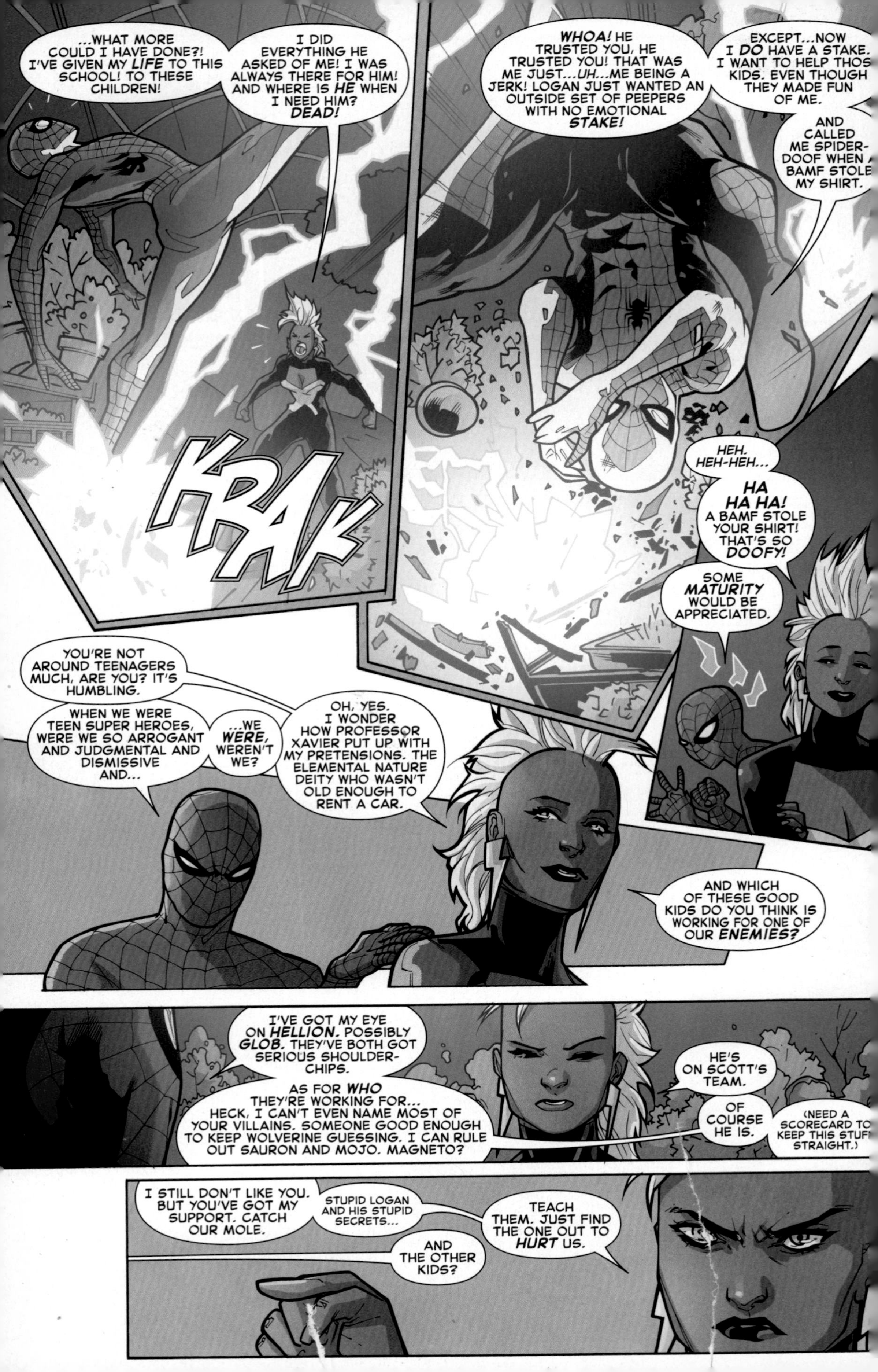

...WHAT MORE COULD I HAVE DONE?! I'VE GIVEN MY LIFE TO THIS SCHOOL! TO THESE CHILDREN!
I DID EVERYTHING HE ASKED OF ME! I WAS ALWAYS THERE FOR HIM! AND WHERE IS HE WHEN I NEED HIM? DEAD!
KRAK
WHOA! HE TRUSTED YOU, HE TRUSTED YOU! THAT WAS ME JUST...UH...ME BEING A JERK! LOGAN JUST WANTED AN OUTSIDE SET OF PEEPERS WITH NO EMOTIONAL STAKE!
EXCEPT...NOW I DO HAVE A STAKE. I WANT TO HELP THOS KIDS. EVEN THOUGH THEY MADE FUN OF ME.
AND CALLED ME SPIDER-DOOF WHEN A BAMF STOLE MY SHIRT.
HEH. HEH-HEH...
HA HA HA! A BAMF STOLE YOUR SHIRT! THAT'S SO DOOFY!
SOME MATURITY WOULD BE APPRECIATED.
YOU'RE NOT AROUND TEENAGERS MUCH, ARE YOU? IT'S HUMBLING.
WHEN WE WERE TEEN SUPER HEROES, WERE WE SO ARROGANT AND JUDGMENTAL AND DISMISSIVE AND...
...WE WERE, WEREN'T WE?
OH, YES. I WONDER HOW PROFESSOR XAVIER PUT UP WITH MY PRETENSIONS. THE ELEMENTAL NATURE DEITY WHO WASN'T OLD ENOUGH TO RENT A CAR.
AND WHICH OF THESE GOOD KIDS DO YOU THINK IS WORKING FOR ONE OF OUR ENEMIES?
I'VE GOT MY EYE ON HELLION. POSSIBLY GLOB. THEY'VE BOTH GOT SERIOUS SHOULDER-CHIPS.
AS FOR WHO THEY'RE WORKING FOR... HECK, I CAN'T EVEN NAME MOST OF YOUR VILLAINS. SOMEONE GOOD ENOUGH TO KEEP WOLVERINE GUESSING. I CAN RULE OUT SAURON AND MOJO. MAGNETO?
HE'S ON SCOTT'S TEAM.
OF COURSE HE IS.
(NEED A SCORECARD TO KEEP THIS STUFF STRAIGHT.)
I STILL DON'T LIKE YOU. BUT YOU'VE GOT MY SUPPORT. CATCH OUR MOLE.
STUPID LOGAN AND HIS STUPID SECRETS...
AND THE OTHER KIDS?
TEACH THEM. JUST FIND THE ONE OUT TO HURT US.

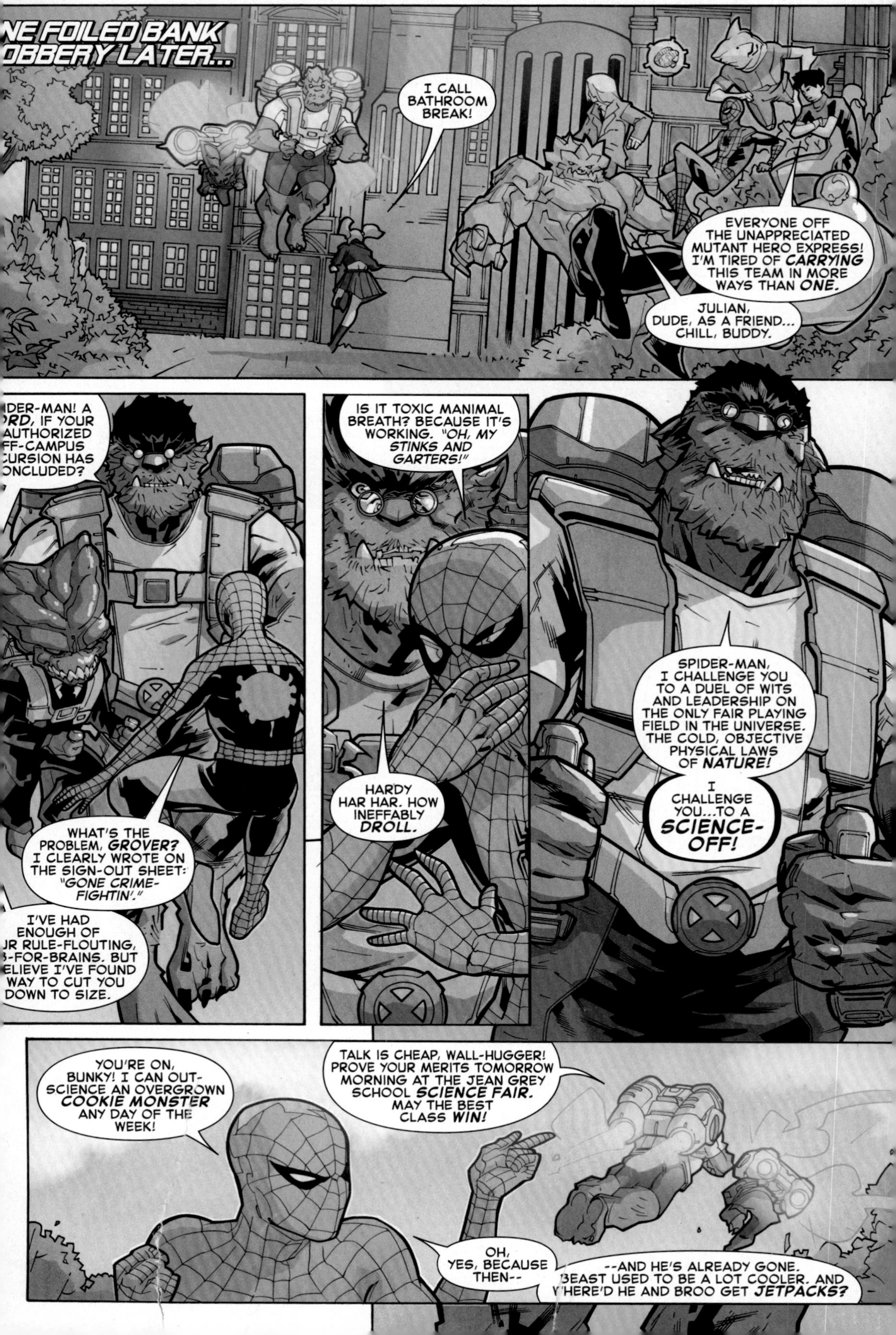
NE FOILED BANK
OBBERY LATER...
I CALL BATHROOM BREAK!
EVERYONE OFF THE UNAPPRECIATED MUTANT HERO EXPRESS! I'M TIRED OF CARRYING THIS TEAM IN MORE WAYS THAN ONE.
JULIAN, DUDE, AS A FRIEND... CHILL, BUDDY.
IDER-MAN! A ORD, IF YOUR AUTHORIZED FF-CAMPUS CURSION HAS ONCLUDED?
WHAT'S THE PROBLEM, GROVER? I CLEARLY WROTE ON THE SIGN-OUT SHEET: "GONE CRIME-FIGHTIN'."
I'VE HAD ENOUGH OF UR RULE-FLOUTING, -FOR-BRAINS. BUT ELIEVE I'VE FOUND WAY TO CUT YOU DOWN TO SIZE.
IS IT TOXIC MANIMAL BREATH? BECAUSE IT'S WORKING. "OH, MY STINKS AND GARTERS!"
HARDY HAR HAR. HOW INEFFABLY DROLL.
SPIDER-MAN, I CHALLENGE YOU TO A DUEL OF WITS AND LEADERSHIP ON THE ONLY FAIR PLAYING FIELD IN THE UNIVERSE. THE COLD, OBJECTIVE PHYSICAL LAWS OF NATURE!
I CHALLENGE YOU...TO A SCIENCE-OFF!
YOU'RE ON, BUNKY! I CAN OUT-SCIENCE AN OVERGROWN COOKIE MONSTER ANY DAY OF THE WEEK!
TALK IS CHEAP, WALL-HUGGER! PROVE YOUR MERITS TOMORROW MORNING AT THE JEAN GREY SCHOOL SCIENCE FAIR. MAY THE BEST CLASS WIN!
OH, YES, BECAUSE THEN--
--AND HE'S ALREADY GONE. BEAST USED TO BE A LOT COOLER. AND WHERE'D HE AND BROO GET JETPACKS?

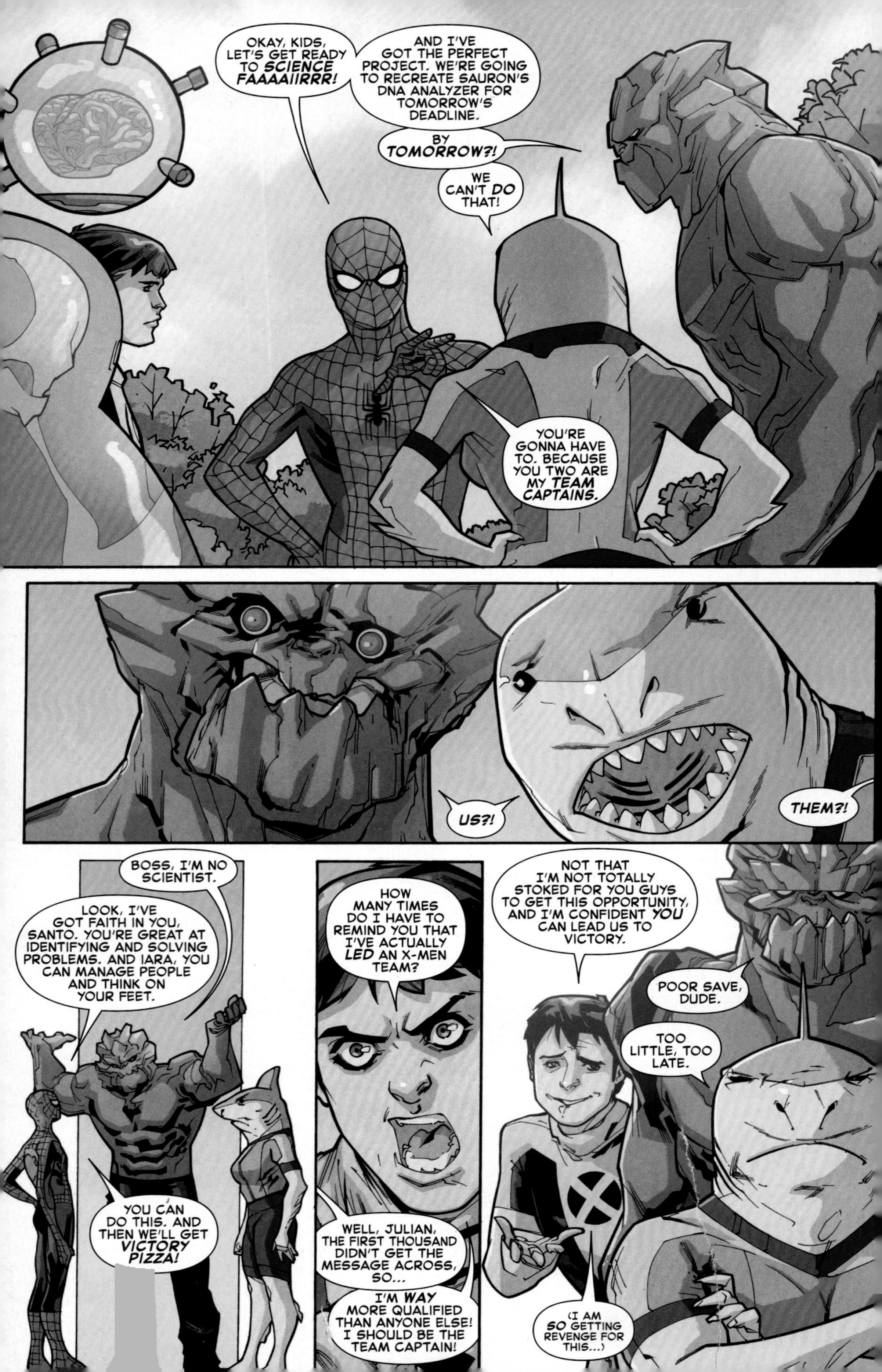
OKAY, KIDS, LET'S GET READY TO SCIENCE FAAAAIIRRR!
AND I'VE GOT THE PERFECT PROJECT. WE'RE GOING TO RECREATE SAURON'S DNA ANALYZER FOR TOMORROW'S DEADLINE.
BY TOMORROW?!
WE CAN'T DO THAT!
YOU'RE GONNA HAVE TO. BECAUSE YOU TWO ARE MY TEAM CAPTAINS.
US?!
THEM?!
BOSS, I'M NO SCIENTIST.
LOOK, I'VE GOT FAITH IN YOU, SANTO. YOU'RE GREAT AT IDENTIFYING AND SOLVING PROBLEMS. AND IARA, YOU CAN MANAGE PEOPLE AND THINK ON YOUR FEET.
YOU CAN DO THIS. AND THEN WE'LL GET VICTORY PIZZA!
HOW MANY TIMES DO I HAVE TO REMIND YOU THAT I'VE ACTUALLY LED AN X-MEN TEAM?
WELL, JULIAN, THE FIRST THOUSAND DIDN'T GET THE MESSAGE ACROSS, SO...
I'M WAY MORE QUALIFIED THAN ANYONE ELSE! I SHOULD BE THE TEAM CAPTAIN!
NOT THAT I'M NOT TOTALLY STOKED FOR YOU GUYS TO GET THIS OPPORTUNITY, AND I'M CONFIDENT YOU CAN LEAD US TO VICTORY.
POOR SAVE, DUDE.
TOO LITTLE, TOO LATE.
(I AM SO GETTING REVENGE FOR THIS...)

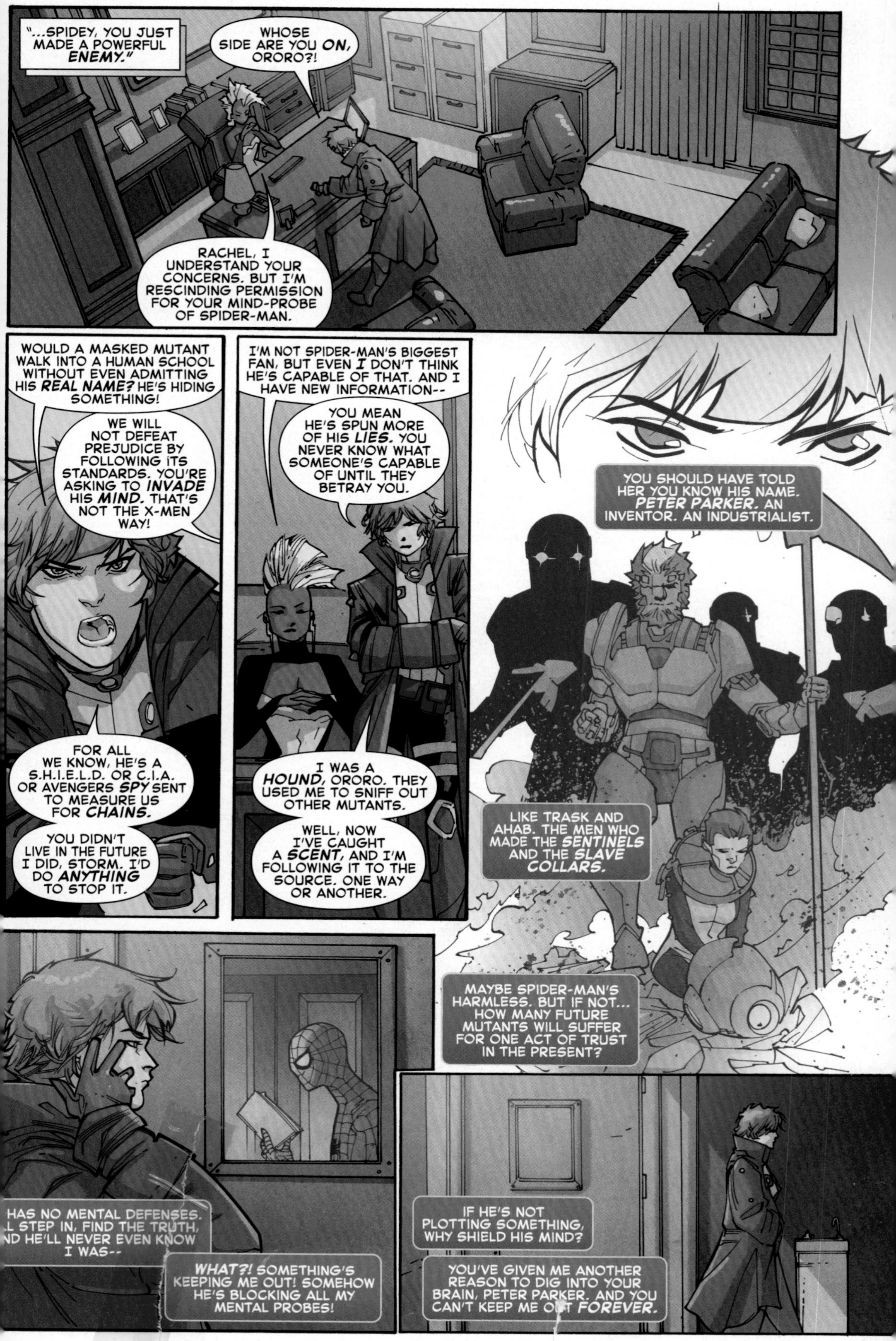
"...SPIDEY, YOU JUST MADE A POWERFUL ENEMY."
WHOSE SIDE ARE YOU ON, ORORO?!
RACHEL, I UNDERSTAND YOUR CONCERNS. BUT I'M RESCINDING PERMISSION FOR YOUR MIND-PROBE OF SPIDER-MAN.
WOULD A MASKED MUTANT WALK INTO A HUMAN SCHOOL WITHOUT EVEN ADMITTING HIS REAL NAME? HE'S HIDING SOMETHING!
WE WILL NOT DEFEAT PREJUDICE BY FOLLOWING ITS STANDARDS. YOU'RE ASKING TO INVADE HIS MIND. THAT'S NOT THE X-MEN WAY!
FOR ALL WE KNOW, HE'S A S.H.I.E.L.D. OR C.I.A. OR AVENGERS SPY SENT TO MEASURE US FOR CHAINS.
YOU DIDN'T LIVE IN THE FUTURE I DID, STORM. I'D DO ANYTHING TO STOP IT.
I'M NOT SPIDER-MAN'S BIGGEST FAN, BUT EVEN I DON'T THINK HE'S CAPABLE OF THAT. AND I HAVE NEW INFORMATION--
YOU MEAN HE'S SPUN MORE OF HIS LIES. YOU NEVER KNOW WHAT SOMEONE'S CAPABLE OF UNTIL THEY BETRAY YOU.
I WAS A HOUND, ORORO. THEY USED ME TO SNIFF OUT OTHER MUTANTS.
WELL, NOW I'VE CAUGHT A SCENT, AND I'M FOLLOWING IT TO THE SOURCE. ONE WAY OR ANOTHER.
YOU SHOULD HAVE TOLD HER YOU KNOW HIS NAME. PETER PARKER. AN INVENTOR. AN INDUSTRIALIST.
LIKE TRASK AND AHAB. THE MEN WHO MADE THE SENTINELS AND THE SLAVE COLLARS.
MAYBE SPIDER-MAN'S HARMLESS. BUT IF NOT... HOW MANY FUTURE MUTANTS WILL SUFFER FOR ONE ACT OF TRUST IN THE PRESENT?
HAS NO MENTAL DEFENSES. L STEP IN, FIND THE TRUTH, ND HE'LL NEVER EVEN KNOW I WAS--
WHAT?! SOMETHING'S KEEPING ME OUT! SOMEHOW HE'S BLOCKING ALL MY MENTAL PROBES!
IF HE'S NOT PLOTTING SOMETHING, WHY SHIELD HIS MIND?
YOU'VE GIVEN ME ANOTHER REASON TO DIG INTO YOUR BRAIN, PETER PARKER. AND YOU CAN'T KEEP ME OUT FOREVER.

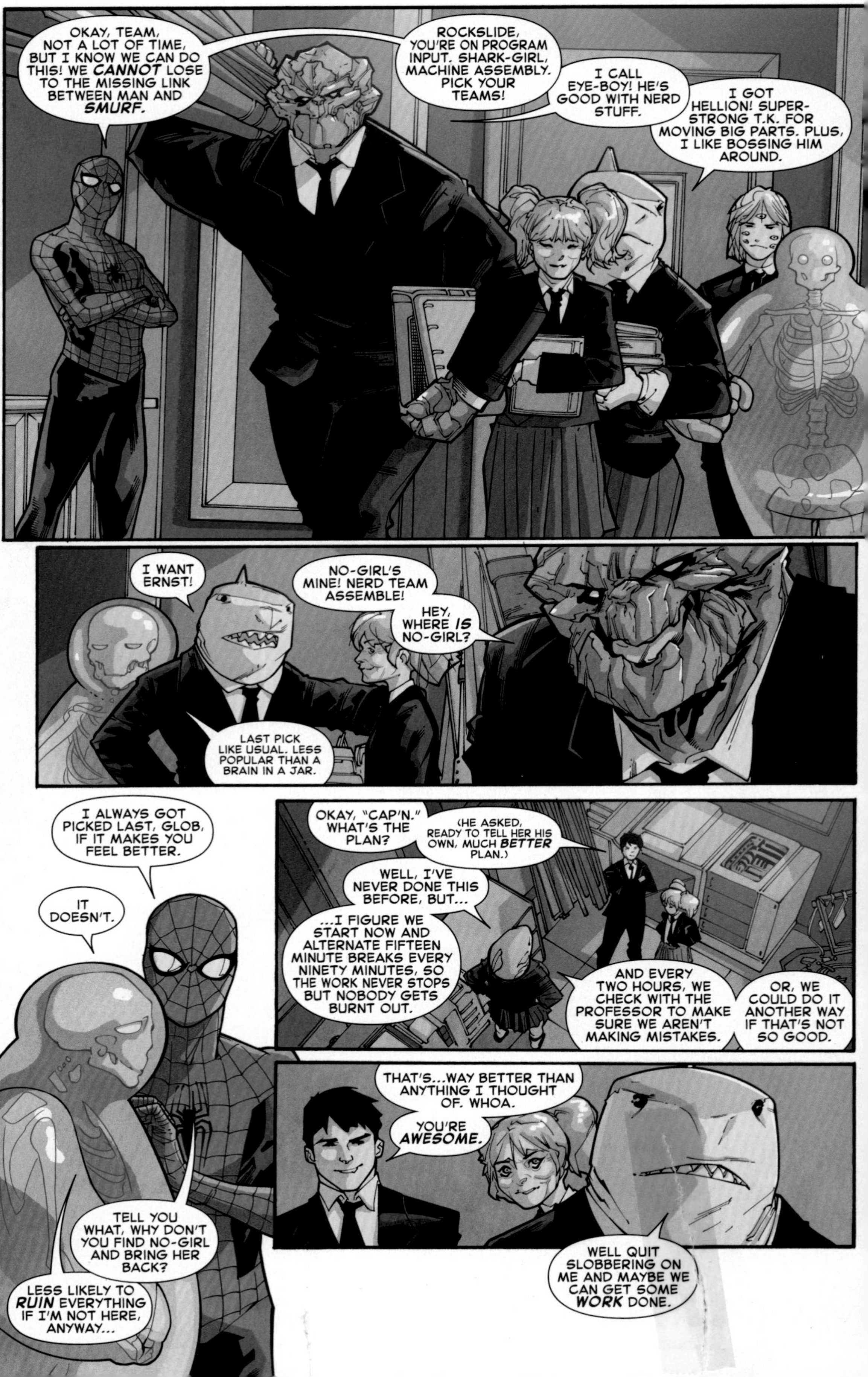
OKAY, TEAM, NOT A LOT OF TIME, BUT I KNOW WE CAN DO THIS! WE CANNOT LOSE TO THE MISSING LINK BETWEEN MAN AND SMURF.
ROCKSLIDE, YOU'RE ON PROGRAM INPUT. SHARK-GIRL, MACHINE ASSEMBLY. PICK YOUR TEAMS!
I CALL EYE-BOY! HE'S GOOD WITH NERD STUFF.
I GOT HELLION! SUPER-STRONG T.K. FOR MOVING BIG PARTS. PLUS, I LIKE BOSSING HIM AROUND.
I WANT ERNST!
NO-GIRL'S MINE! NERD TEAM ASSEMBLE!
HEY, WHERE IS NO-GIRL?
LAST PICK LIKE USUAL. LESS POPULAR THAN A BRAIN IN A JAR.
I ALWAYS GOT PICKED LAST, GLOB, IF IT MAKES YOU FEEL BETTER.
IT DOESN'T.
TELL YOU WHAT, WHY DON'T YOU FIND NO-GIRL AND BRING HER BACK?
LESS LIKELY TO RUIN EVERYTHING IF I'M NOT HERE, ANYWAY...
OKAY, "CAP'N." WHAT'S THE PLAN?
(HE ASKED, READY TO TELL HER HIS OWN, MUCH BETTER PLAN.)
WELL, I'VE NEVER DONE THIS BEFORE, BUT...
...I FIGURE WE START NOW AND ALTERNATE FIFTEEN MINUTE BREAKS EVERY NINETY MINUTES, SO THE WORK NEVER STOPS BUT NOBODY GETS BURNT OUT.
AND EVERY TWO HOURS, WE CHECK WITH THE PROFESSOR TO MAKE SURE WE AREN'T MAKING MISTAKES.
OR, WE COULD DO IT ANOTHER WAY IF THAT'S NOT SO GOOD.
THAT'S...WAY BETTER THAN ANYTHING I THOUGHT OF. WHOA.
YOU'RE AWESOME.
WELL QUIT SLOBBERING ON ME AND MAYBE WE CAN GET SOME WORK DONE.

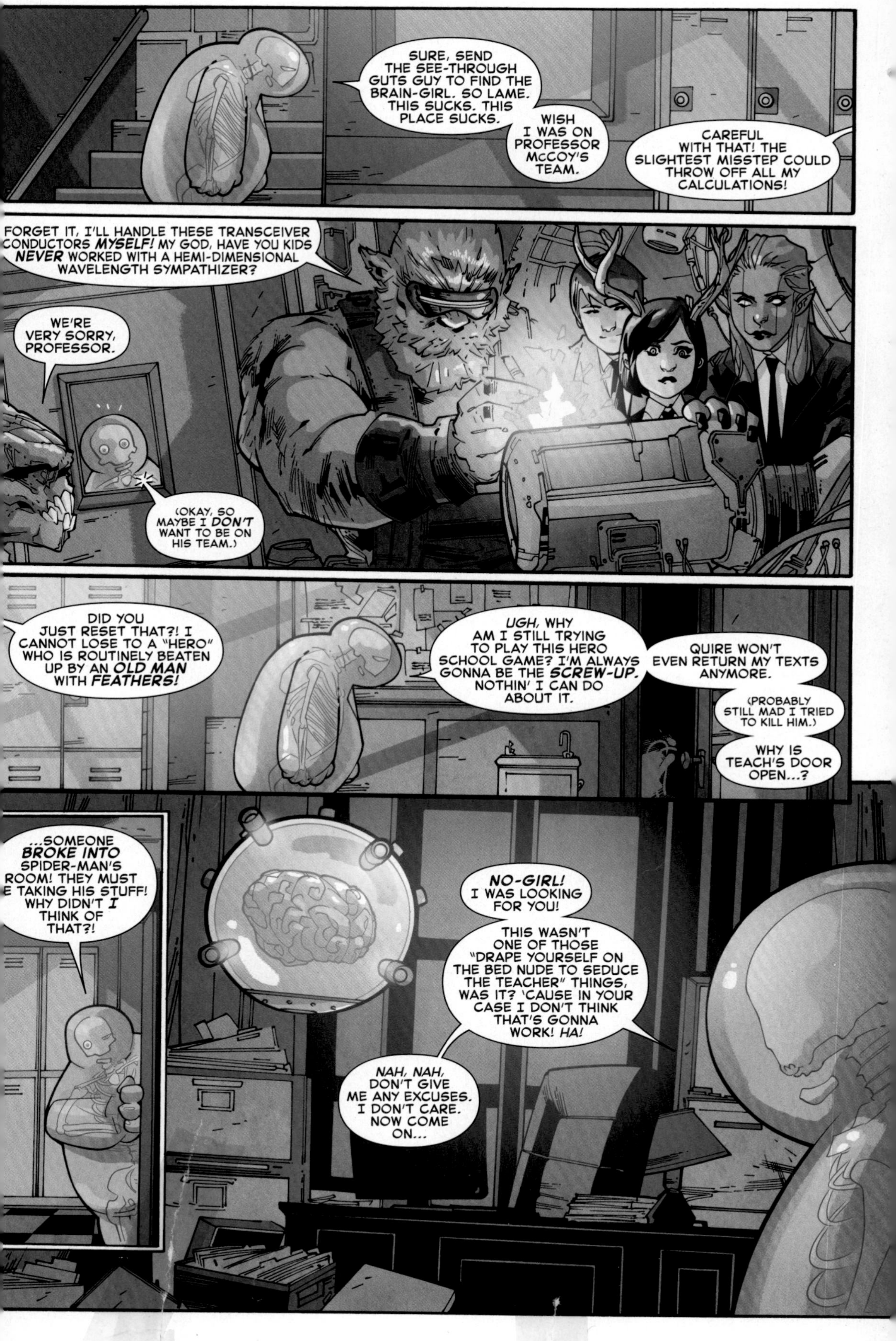
SURE, SEND THE SEE-THROUGH GUTS GUY TO FIND THE BRAIN-GIRL. SO LAME. THIS SUCKS. THIS PLACE SUCKS.
WISH I WAS ON PROFESSOR McCOY'S TEAM.
CAREFUL WITH THAT! THE SLIGHTEST MISSTEP COULD THROW OFF ALL MY CALCULATIONS!
FORGET IT, I'LL HANDLE THESE TRANSCEIVER CONDUCTORS MYSELF! MY GOD, HAVE YOU KIDS NEVER WORKED WITH A HEMI-DIMENSIONAL WAVELENGTH SYMPATHIZER?
WE'RE VERY SORRY, PROFESSOR.
(OKAY, SO MAYBE I DON'T WANT TO BE ON HIS TEAM.)
DID YOU JUST RESET THAT?! I CANNOT LOSE TO A "HERO" WHO IS ROUTINELY BEATEN UP BY AN OLD MAN WITH FEATHERS!
UGH, WHY AM I STILL TRYING TO PLAY THIS HERO SCHOOL GAME? I'M ALWAYS GONNA BE THE SCREW-UP. NOTHIN' I CAN DO ABOUT IT.
QUIRE WON'T EVEN RETURN MY TEXTS ANYMORE.
(PROBABLY STILL MAD I TRIED TO KILL HIM.)
WHY IS TEACH'S DOOR OPEN...?
...SOMEONE BROKE INTO SPIDER-MAN'S ROOM! THEY MUST E TAKING HIS STUFF! WHY DIDN'T I THINK OF THAT?!
NO-GIRL! I WAS LOOKING FOR YOU!
THIS WASN'T ONE OF THOSE "DRAPE YOURSELF ON THE BED NUDE TO SEDUCE THE TEACHER" THINGS, WAS IT? 'CAUSE IN YOUR CASE I DON'T THINK THAT'S GONNA WORK! HA!
NAH, NAH, DON'T GIVE ME ANY EXCUSES. I DON'T CARE. NOW COME ON...

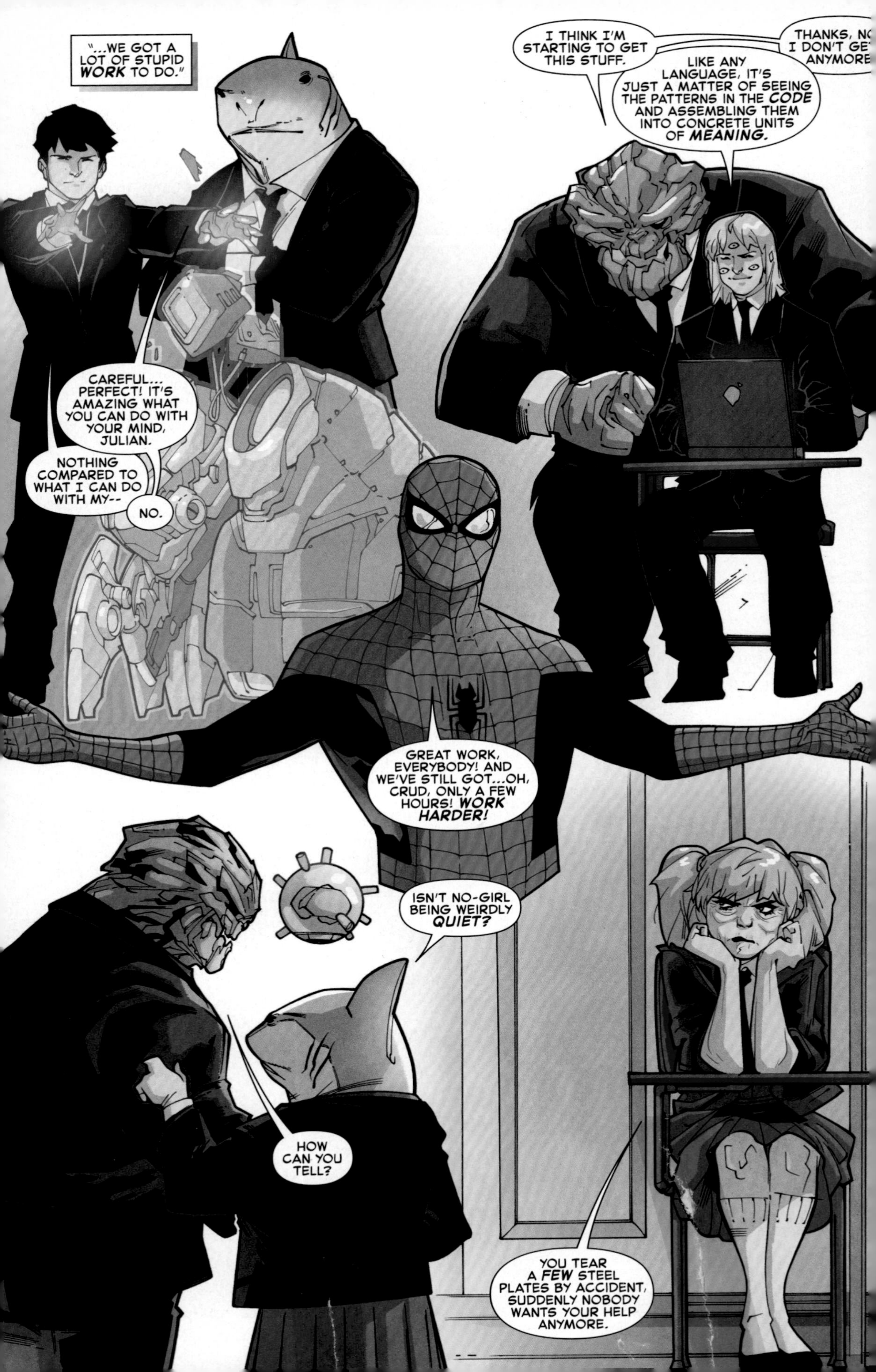
"...WE GOT A LOT OF STUPID *WORK* TO DO."
CAREFUL... PERFECT! IT'S AMAZING WHAT YOU CAN DO WITH YOUR MIND, JULIAN.
NOTHING COMPARED TO WHAT I CAN DO WITH MY--
NO.
I THINK I'M STARTING TO GET THIS STUFF.
THANKS, N
I DON'T GE
ANYMORE
LIKE ANY LANGUAGE, IT'S JUST A MATTER OF SEEING THE PATTERNS IN THE *CODE* AND ASSEMBLING THEM INTO CONCRETE UNITS OF *MEANING.*
GREAT WORK, EVERYBODY! AND WE'VE STILL GOT...OH, CRUD, ONLY A FEW HOURS! *WORK HARDER!*
ISN'T NO-GIRL BEING WEIRDLY *QUIET?*
HOW CAN YOU TELL?
YOU TEAR A *FEW* STEEL PLATES BY ACCIDENT, SUDDENLY NOBODY WANTS YOUR HELP ANYMORE.

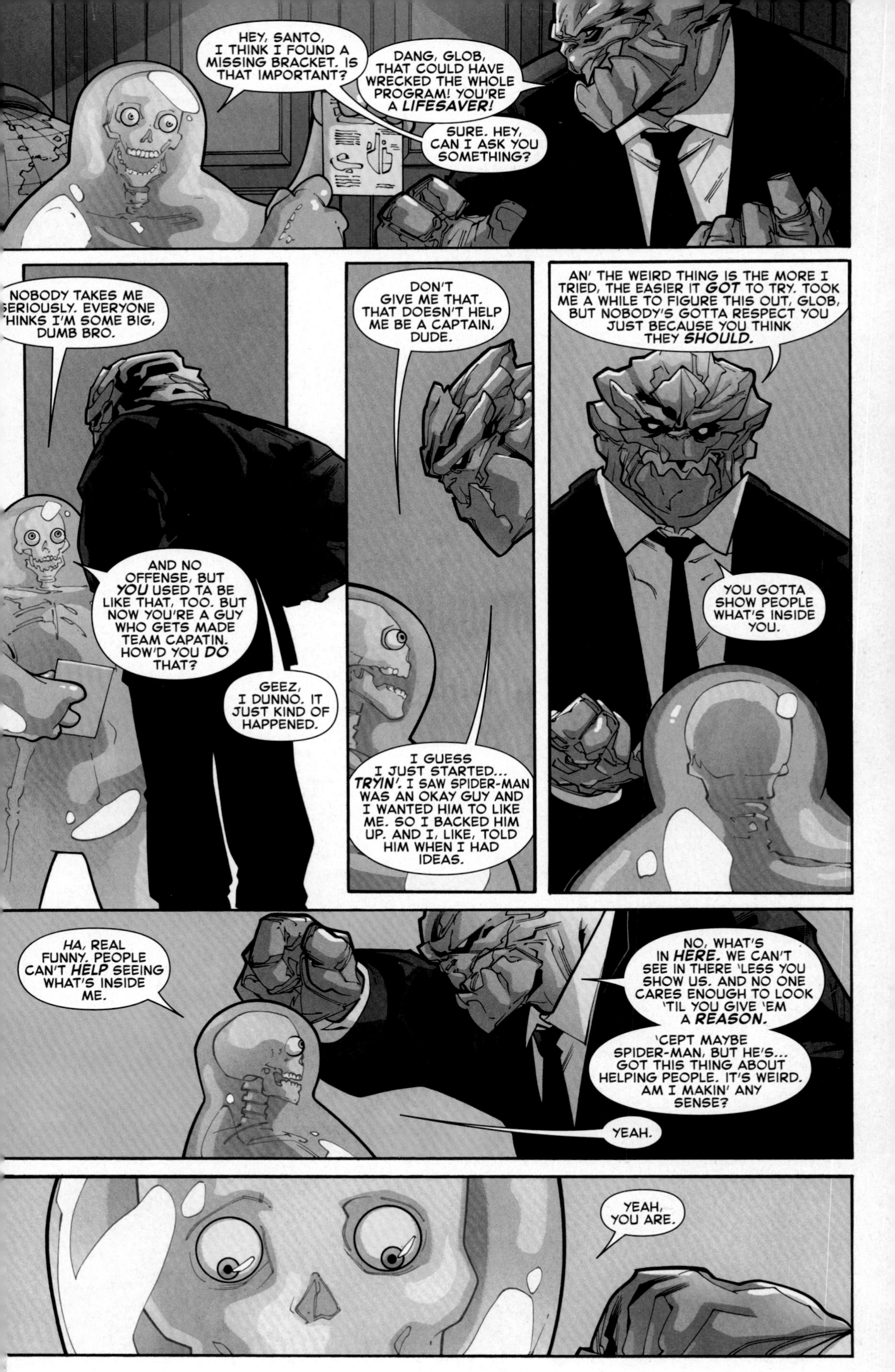
HEY, SANTO, I THINK I FOUND A MISSING BRACKET. IS THAT IMPORTANT?
DANG, GLOB, THAT COULD HAVE WRECKED THE WHOLE PROGRAM! YOU'RE A LIFESAVER!
SURE. HEY, CAN I ASK YOU SOMETHING?
NOBODY TAKES ME SERIOUSLY. EVERYONE THINKS I'M SOME BIG, DUMB BRO.
AND NO OFFENSE, BUT YOU USED TA BE LIKE THAT, TOO. BUT NOW YOU'RE A GUY WHO GETS MADE TEAM CAPATIN. HOW'D YOU DO THAT?
GEEZ, I DUNNO. IT JUST KIND OF HAPPENED.
DON'T GIVE ME THAT. THAT DOESN'T HELP ME BE A CAPTAIN, DUDE.
I GUESS I JUST STARTED... TRYIN'. I SAW SPIDER-MAN WAS AN OKAY GUY AND I WANTED HIM TO LIKE ME. SO I BACKED HIM UP. AND I, LIKE, TOLD HIM WHEN I HAD IDEAS.
AN' THE WEIRD THING IS THE MORE I TRIED, THE EASIER IT GOT TO TRY. TOOK ME A WHILE TO FIGURE THIS OUT, GLOB, BUT NOBODY'S GOTTA RESPECT YOU JUST BECAUSE YOU THINK THEY SHOULD.
YOU GOTTA SHOW PEOPLE WHAT'S INSIDE YOU.
HA, REAL FUNNY. PEOPLE CAN'T HELP SEEING WHAT'S INSIDE ME.
NO, WHAT'S IN HERE. WE CAN'T SEE IN THERE 'LESS YOU SHOW US. AND NO ONE CARES ENOUGH TO LOOK 'TIL YOU GIVE 'EM A REASON.
'CEPT MAYBE SPIDER-MAN, BUT HE'S... GOT THIS THING ABOUT HELPING PEOPLE. IT'S WEIRD. AM I MAKIN' ANY SENSE?
YEAH.
YEAH, YOU ARE.

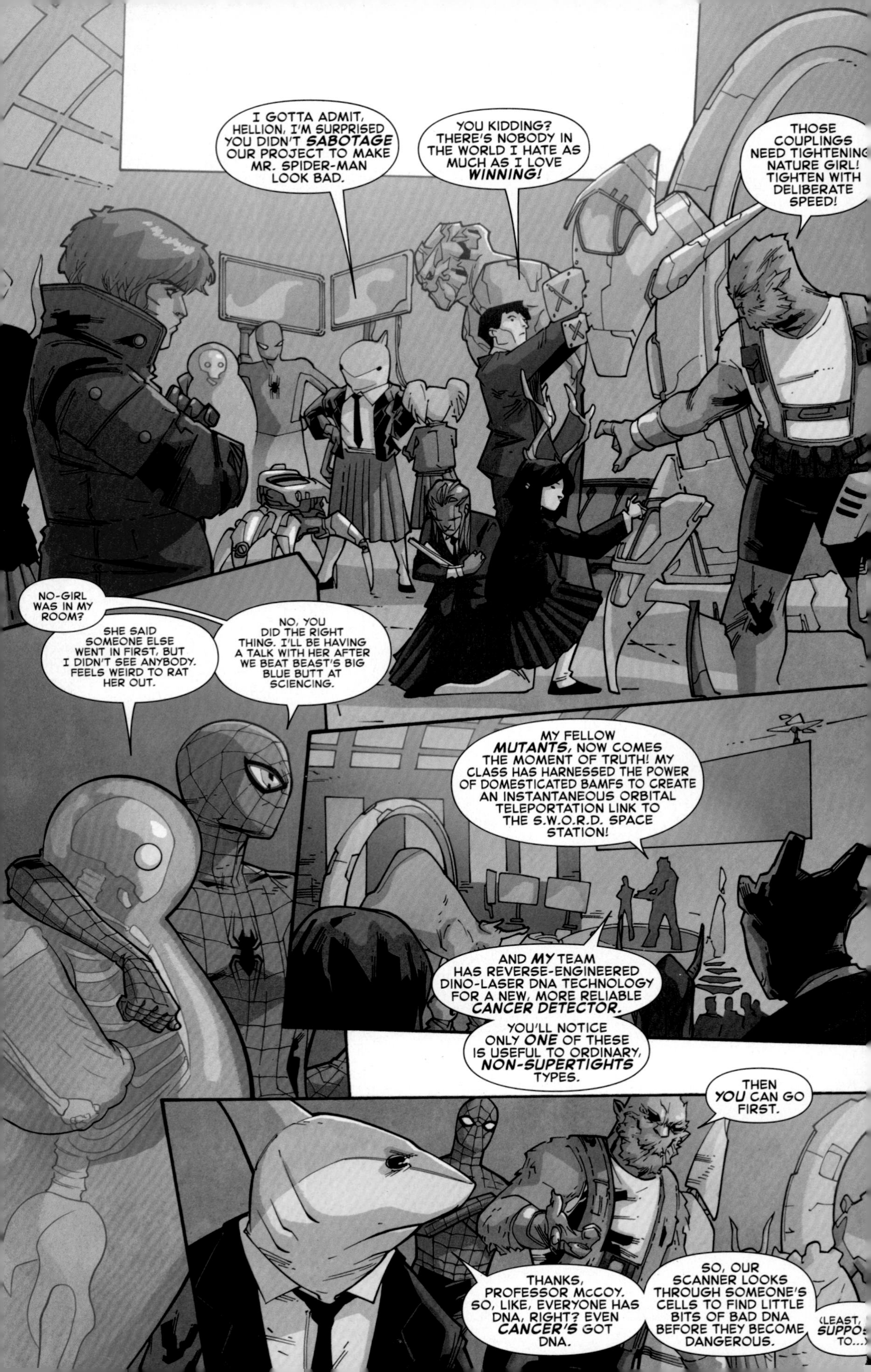
I GOTTA ADMIT, HELLION, I'M SURPRISED YOU DIDN'T SABOTAGE OUR PROJECT TO MAKE MR. SPIDER-MAN LOOK BAD.
YOU KIDDING? THERE'S NOBODY IN THE WORLD I HATE AS MUCH AS I LOVE WINNING!
THOSE COUPLINGS NEED TIGHTENING NATURE GIRL! TIGHTEN WITH DELIBERATE SPEED!
NO-GIRL WAS IN MY ROOM?
SHE SAID SOMEONE ELSE WENT IN FIRST, BUT I DIDN'T SEE ANYBODY. FEELS WEIRD TO RAT HER OUT.
NO, YOU DID THE RIGHT THING. I'LL BE HAVING A TALK WITH HER AFTER WE BEAT BEAST'S BIG BLUE BUTT AT SCIENCING.
MY FELLOW MUTANTS, NOW COMES THE MOMENT OF TRUTH! MY CLASS HAS HARNESSED THE POWER OF DOMESTICATED BAMFS TO CREATE AN INSTANTANEOUS ORBITAL TELEPORTATION LINK TO THE S.W.O.R.D. SPACE STATION!
AND MY TEAM HAS REVERSE-ENGINEERED DINO-LASER DNA TECHNOLOGY FOR A NEW, MORE RELIABLE CANCER DETECTOR.
YOU'LL NOTICE ONLY ONE OF THESE IS USEFUL TO ORDINARY, NON-SUPERTIGHTS TYPES.
THEN YOU CAN GO FIRST.
THANKS, PROFESSOR McCOY. SO, LIKE, EVERYONE HAS DNA, RIGHT? EVEN CANCER'S GOT DNA.
SO, OUR SCANNER LOOKS THROUGH SOMEONE'S CELLS TO FIND LITTLE BITS OF BAD DNA BEFORE THEY BECOME DANGEROUS.
(LEAST, SUPPO TO...)

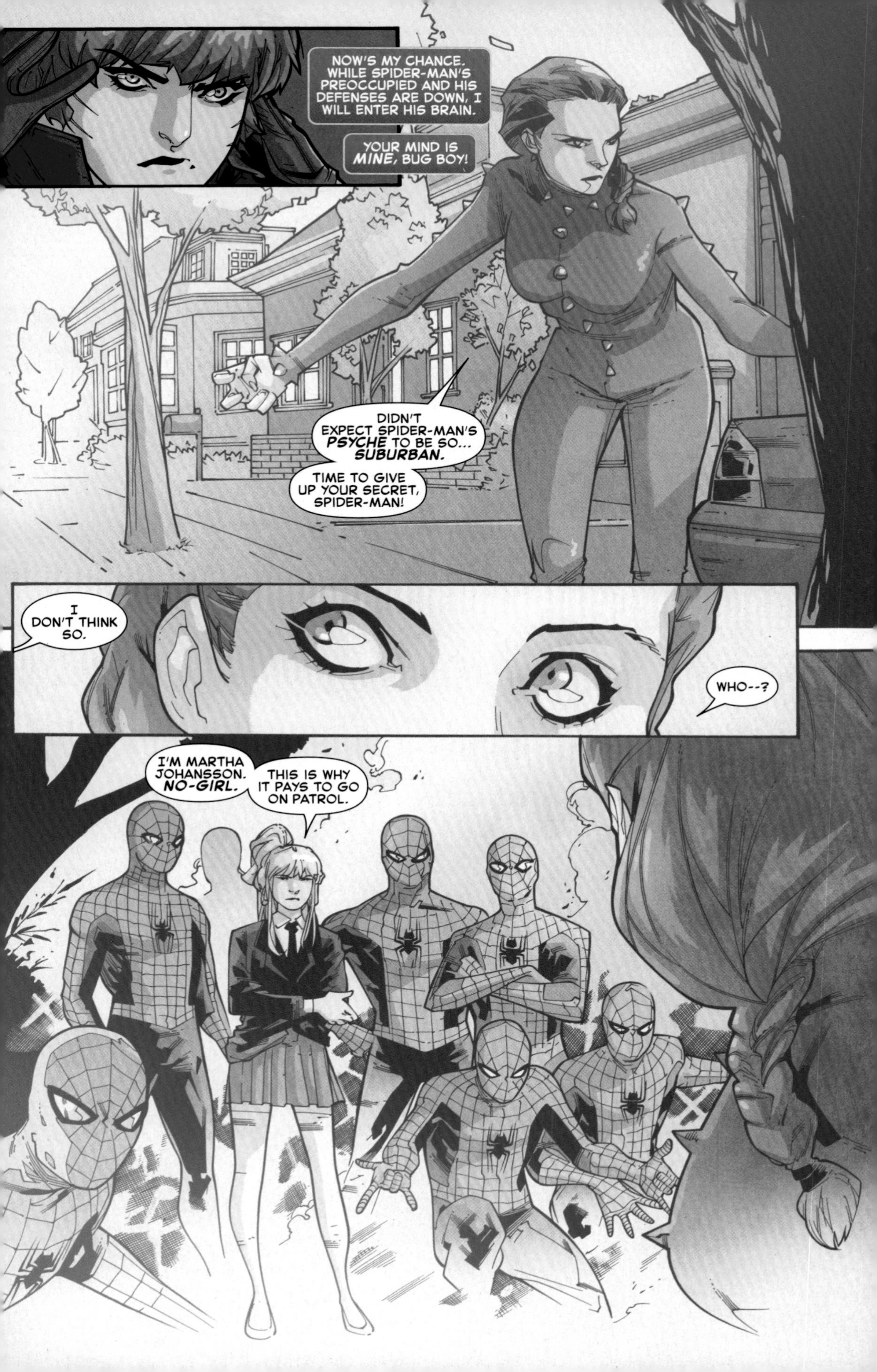
NOW'S MY CHANCE. WHILE SPIDER-MAN'S PREOCCUPIED AND HIS DEFENSES ARE DOWN, I WILL ENTER HIS BRAIN.
YOUR MIND IS MINE, BUG BOY!
DIDN'T EXPECT SPIDER-MAN'S PSYCHE TO BE SO... SUBURBAN.
TIME TO GIVE UP YOUR SECRET, SPIDER-MAN!
I DON'T THINK SO.
WHO--?
I'M MARTHA JOHANSSON. NO-GIRL.
THIS IS WHY IT PAYS TO GO ON PATROL.

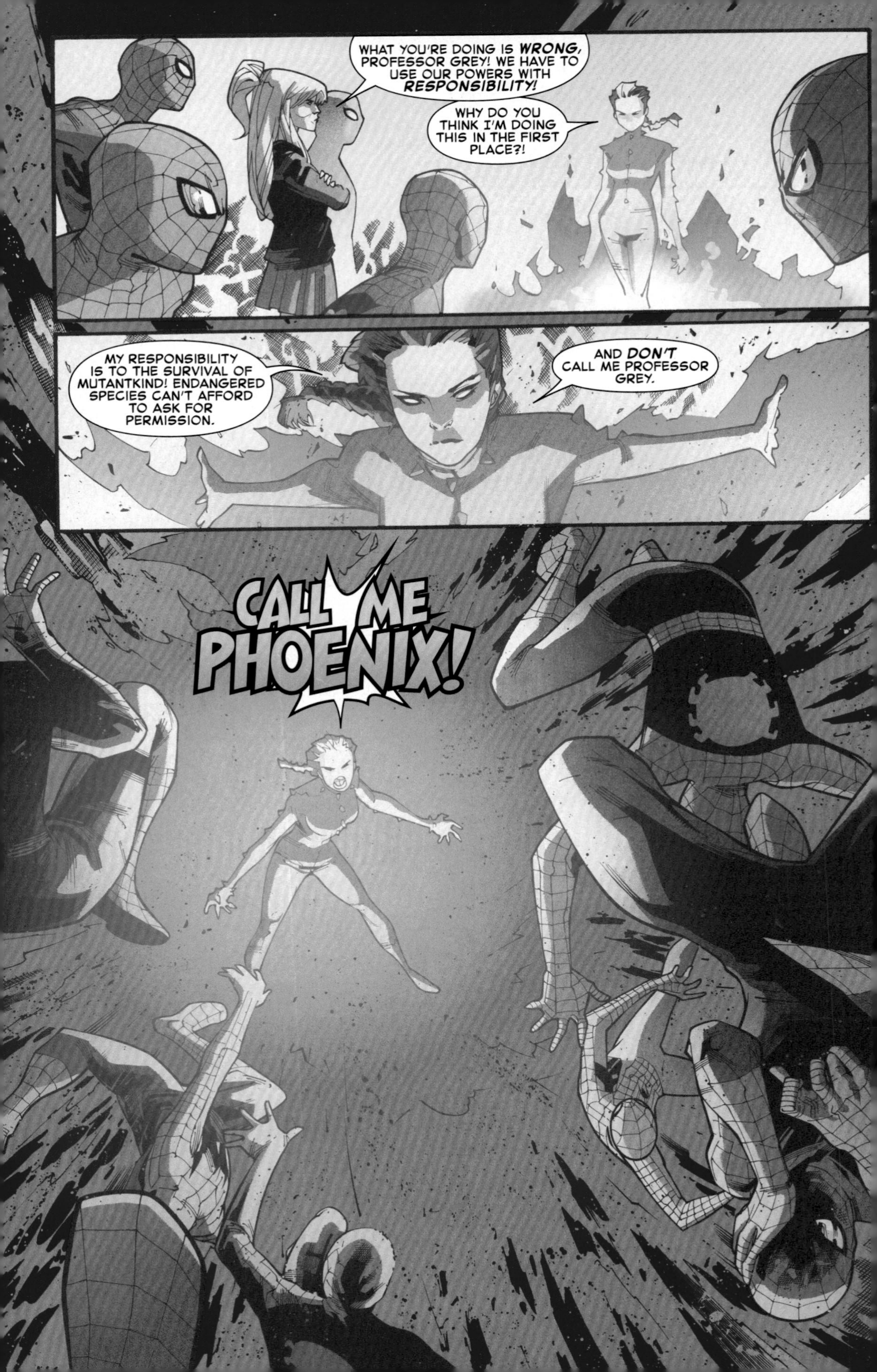
WHAT YOU'RE DOING IS WRONG, PROFESSOR GREY! WE HAVE TO USE OUR POWERS WITH RESPONSIBILITY!
WHY DO YOU THINK I'M DOING THIS IN THE FIRST PLACE?!
MY RESPONSIBILITY IS TO THE SURVIVAL OF MUTANTKIND! ENDANGERED SPECIES CAN'T AFFORD TO ASK FOR PERMISSION.
AND DON'T CALL ME PROFESSOR GREY.
CALL ME PHOENIX!

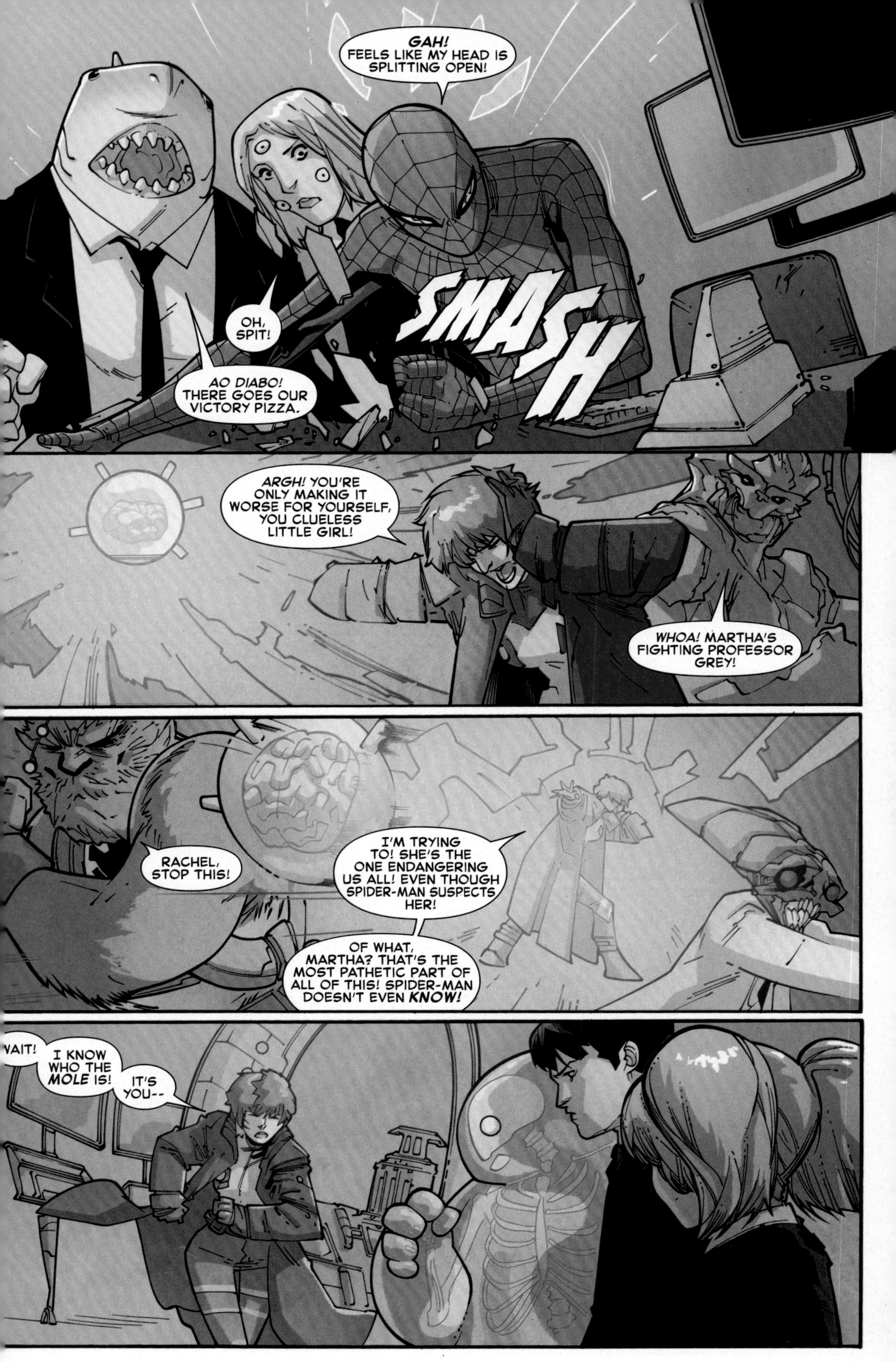
GAH! FEELS LIKE MY HEAD IS SPLITTING OPEN!
OH, SPIT!
AO DIABO! THERE GOES OUR VICTORY PIZZA.
SMASH
ARGH! YOU'RE ONLY MAKING IT WORSE FOR YOURSELF, YOU CLUELESS LITTLE GIRL!
WHOA! MARTHA'S FIGHTING PROFESSOR GREY!
RACHEL, STOP THIS!
I'M TRYING TO! SHE'S THE ONE ENDANGERING US ALL! EVEN THOUGH SPIDER-MAN SUSPECTS HER!
OF WHAT, MARTHA? THAT'S THE MOST PATHETIC PART OF ALL OF THIS! SPIDER-MAN DOESN'T EVEN KNOW!
WAIT!
I KNOW WHO THE MOLE IS!
IT'S YOU--

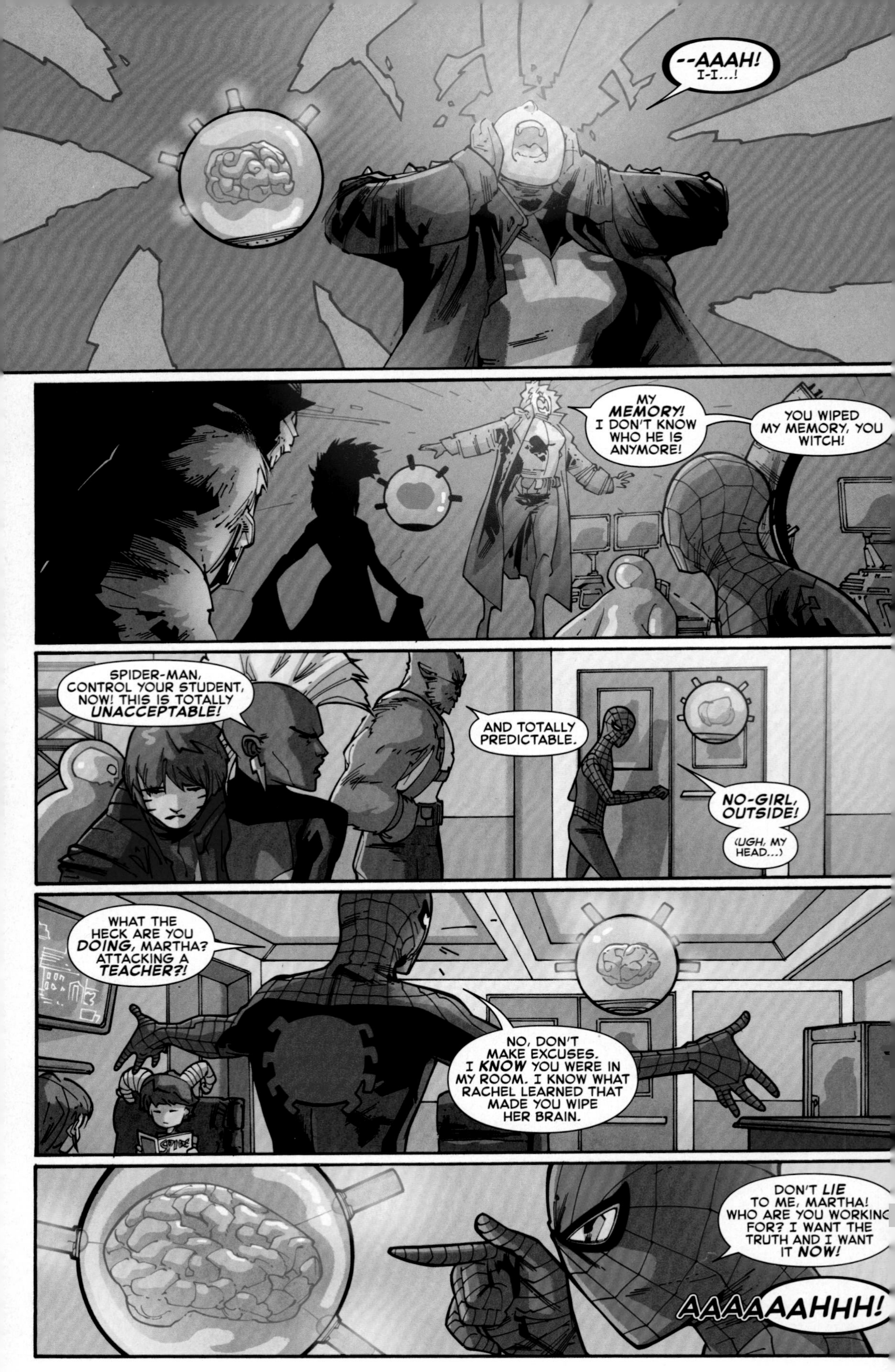
--AAAH! I-I...!
MY MEMORY! I DON'T KNOW WHO HE IS ANYMORE!
YOU WIPED MY MEMORY, YOU WITCH!
SPIDER-MAN, CONTROL YOUR STUDENT, NOW! THIS IS TOTALLY UNACCEPTABLE!
AND TOTALLY PREDICTABLE.
NO-GIRL, OUTSIDE!
(UGH, MY HEAD...)
WHAT THE HECK ARE YOU DOING, MARTHA? ATTACKING A TEACHER?!
NO, DON'T MAKE EXCUSES. I KNOW YOU WERE IN MY ROOM. I KNOW WHAT RACHEL LEARNED THAT MADE YOU WIPE HER BRAIN.
DON'T LIE TO ME, MARTHA! WHO ARE YOU WORKING FOR? I WANT THE TRUTH AND I WANT IT NOW!
AAAAAAHHH!

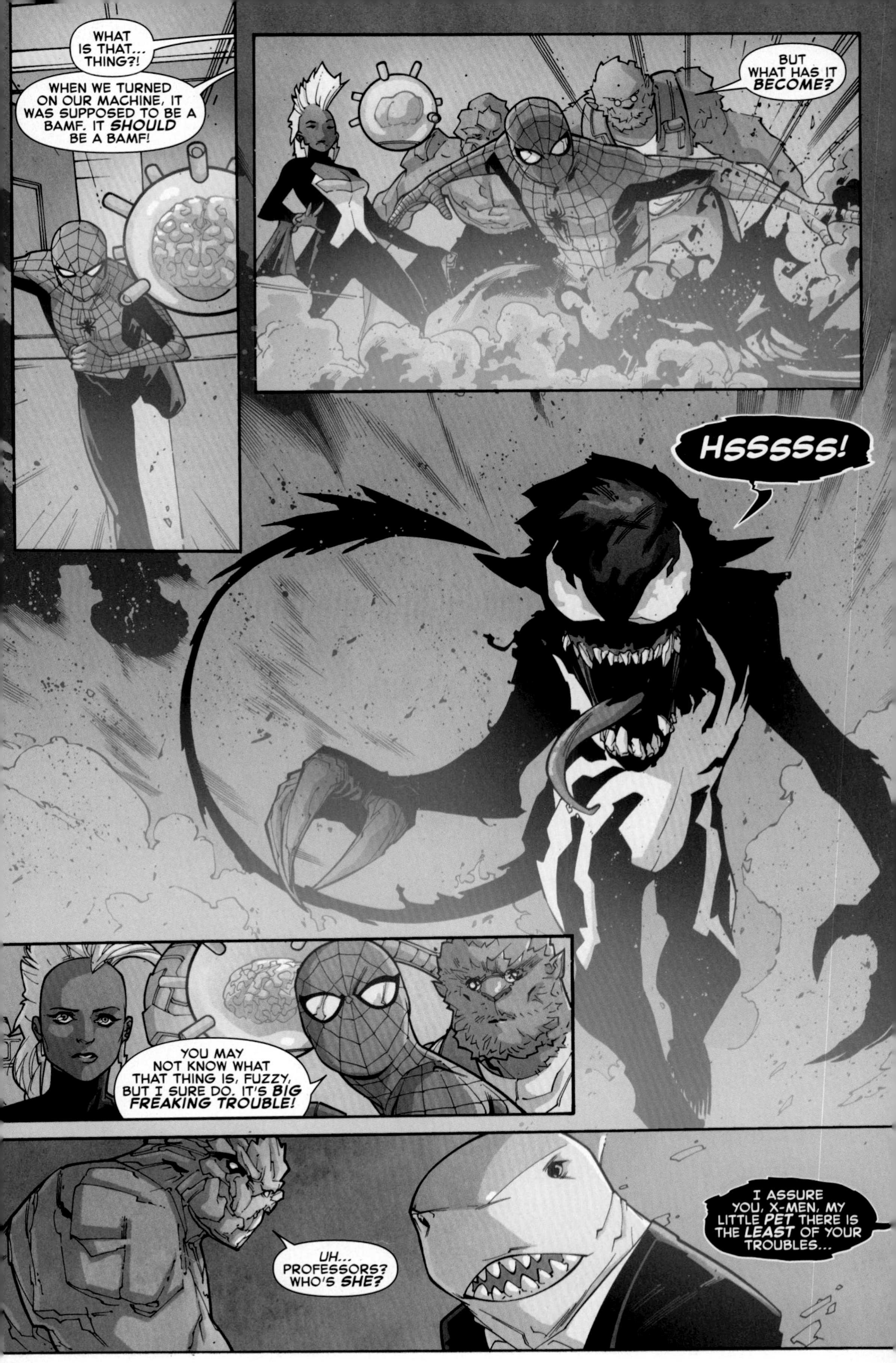

WHAT IS THAT... THING?!
WHEN WE TURNED ON OUR MACHINE, IT WAS SUPPOSED TO BE A BAMF. IT SHOULD BE A BAMF!
BUT WHAT HAS IT BECOME?
HSSSSS!
YOU MAY NOT KNOW WHAT THAT THING IS, FUZZY, BUT I SURE DO. IT'S BIG FREAKING TROUBLE!
UH... PROFESSORS? WHO'S SHE?
I ASSURE YOU, X-MEN, MY LITTLE PET THERE IS THE LEAST OF YOUR TROUBLES...

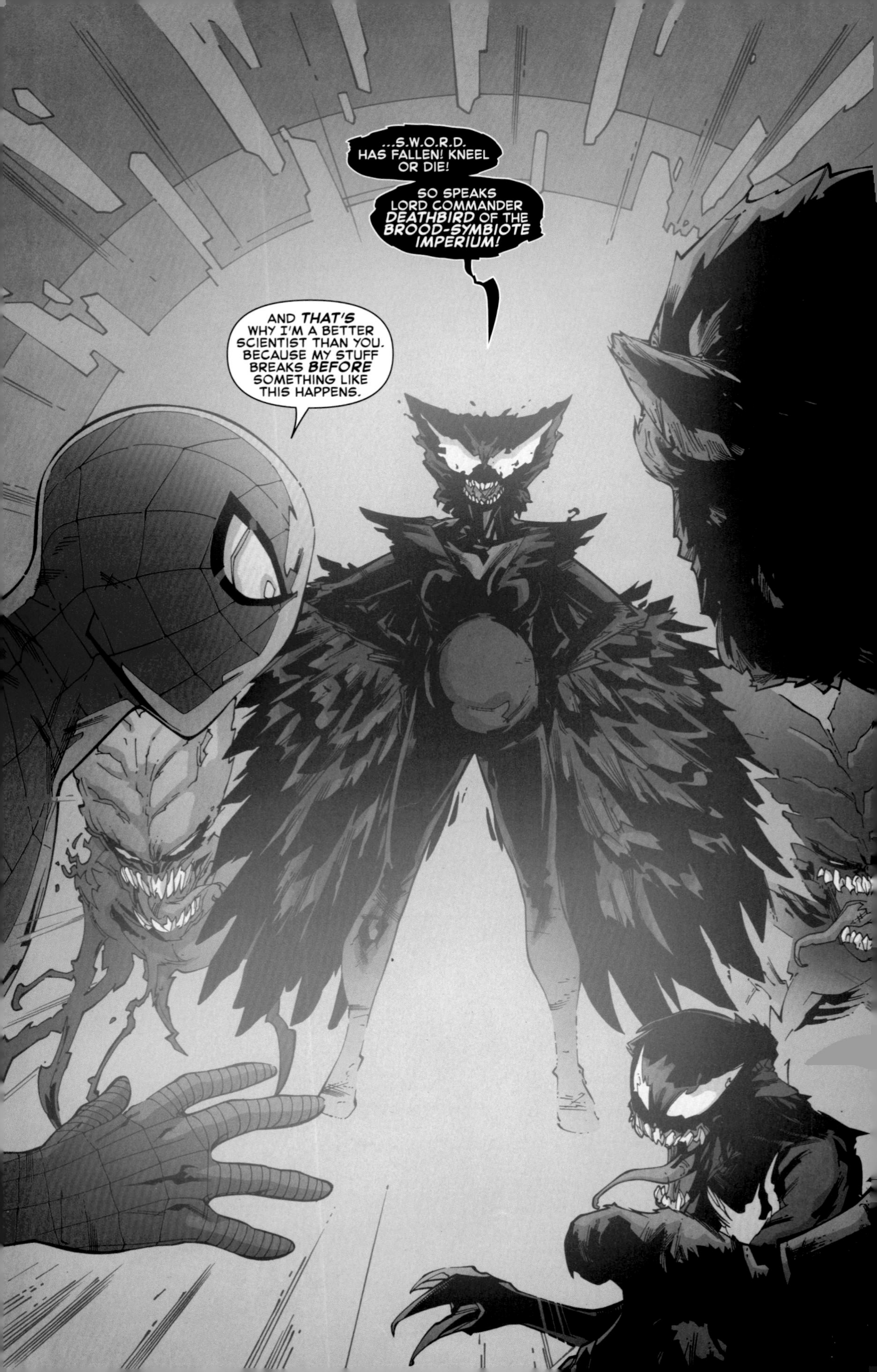
...S.W.O.R.D. HAS FALLEN! KNEEL OR DIE!
SO SPEAKS LORD COMMANDER DEATHBIRD OF THE BROOD-SYMBIOTE IMPERIUM!
AND THAT'S WHY I'M A BETTER SCIENTIST THAN YOU. BECAUSE MY STUFF BREAKS BEFORE SOMETHING LIKE THIS HAPPENS.

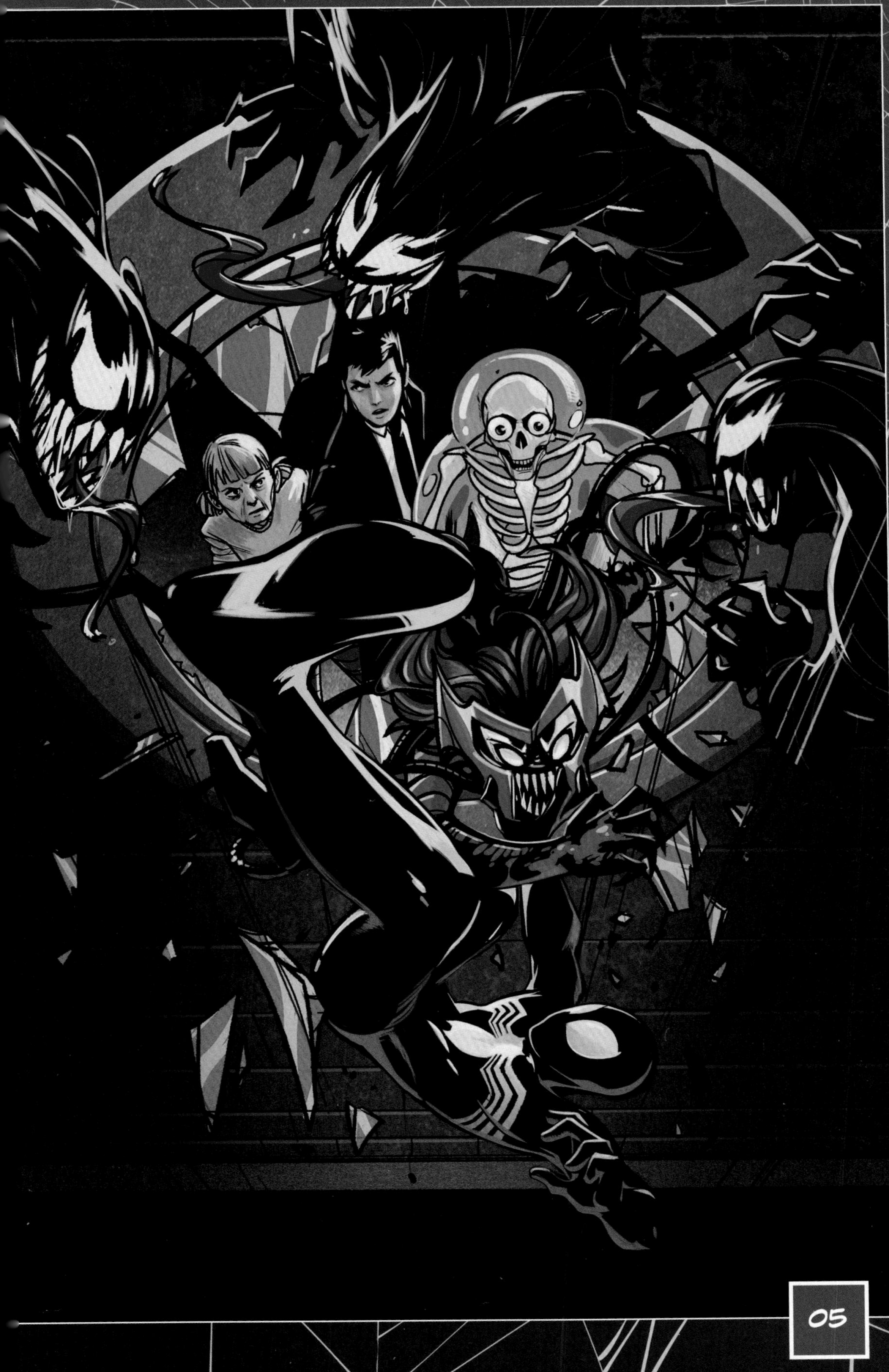

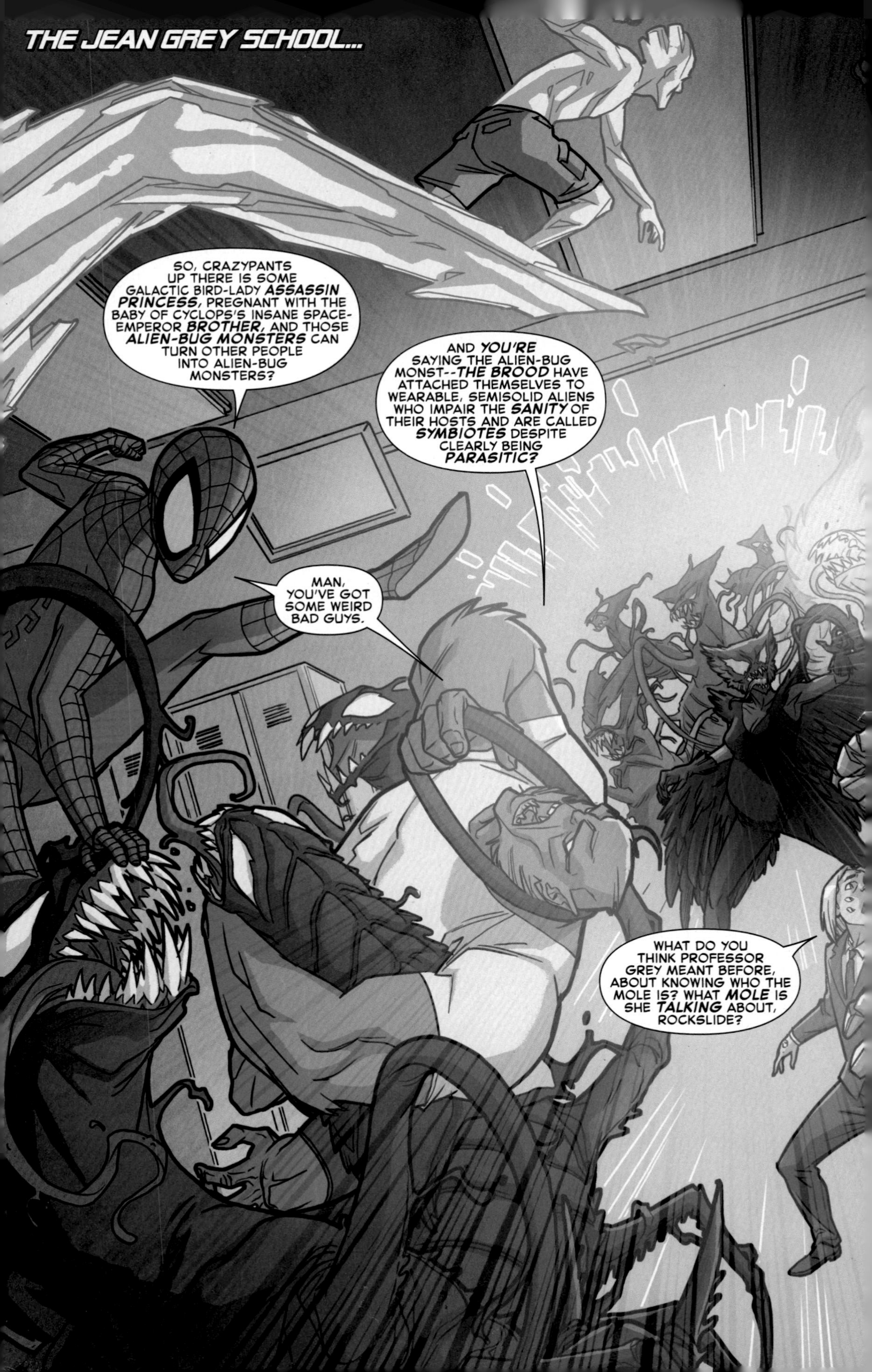
THE JEAN GREY SCHOOL...
SO, CRAZYPANTS UP THERE IS SOME GALACTIC BIRD-LADY ASSASSIN PRINCESS, PREGNANT WITH THE BABY OF CYCLOPS'S INSANE SPACE-EMPEROR BROTHER, AND THOSE ALIEN-BUG MONSTERS CAN TURN OTHER PEOPLE INTO ALIEN-BUG MONSTERS?
AND YOU'RE SAYING THE ALIEN-BUG MONST--THE BROOD HAVE ATTACHED THEMSELVES TO WEARABLE, SEMISOLID ALIENS WHO IMPAIR THE SANITY OF THEIR HOSTS AND ARE CALLED SYMBIOTES DESPITE CLEARLY BEING PARASITIC?
MAN, YOU'VE GOT SOME WEIRD BAD GUYS.
WHAT DO YOU THINK PROFESSOR GREY MEANT BEFORE, ABOUT KNOWING WHO THE MOLE IS? WHAT MOLE IS SHE TALKING ABOUT, ROCKSLIDE?

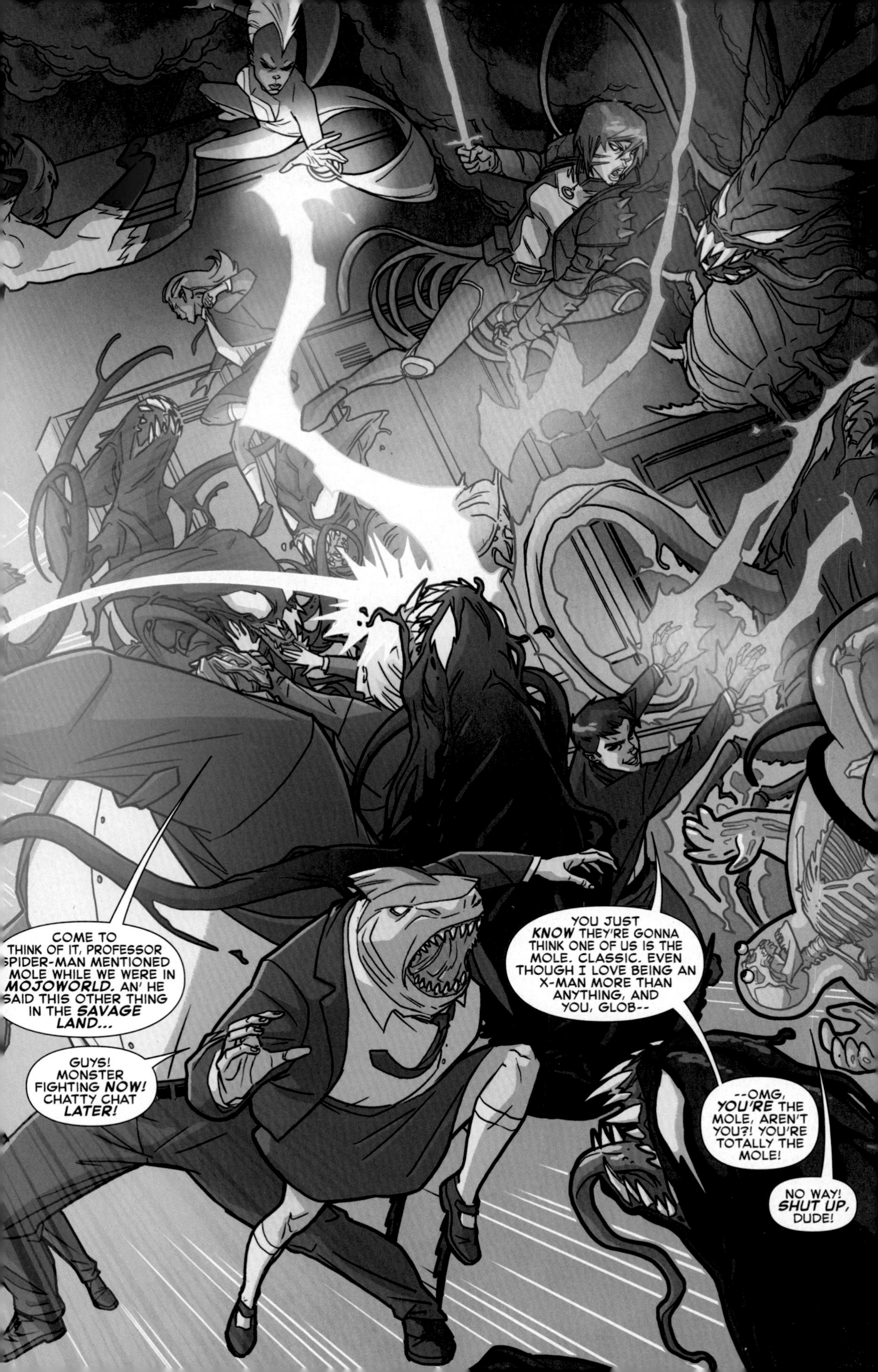
COME TO THINK OF IT, PROFESSOR SPIDER-MAN MENTIONED MOLE WHILE WE WERE IN MOJOWORLD. AN' HE SAID THIS OTHER THING IN THE SAVAGE LAND...
GUYS! MONSTER FIGHTING NOW! CHATTY CHAT LATER!
YOU JUST KNOW THEY'RE GONNA THINK ONE OF US IS THE MOLE. CLASSIC. EVEN THOUGH I LOVE BEING AN X-MAN MORE THAN ANYTHING, AND YOU, GLOB--
--OMG, YOU'RE THE MOLE, AREN'T YOU?! YOU'RE TOTALLY THE MOLE!
NO WAY! SHUT UP, DUDE!

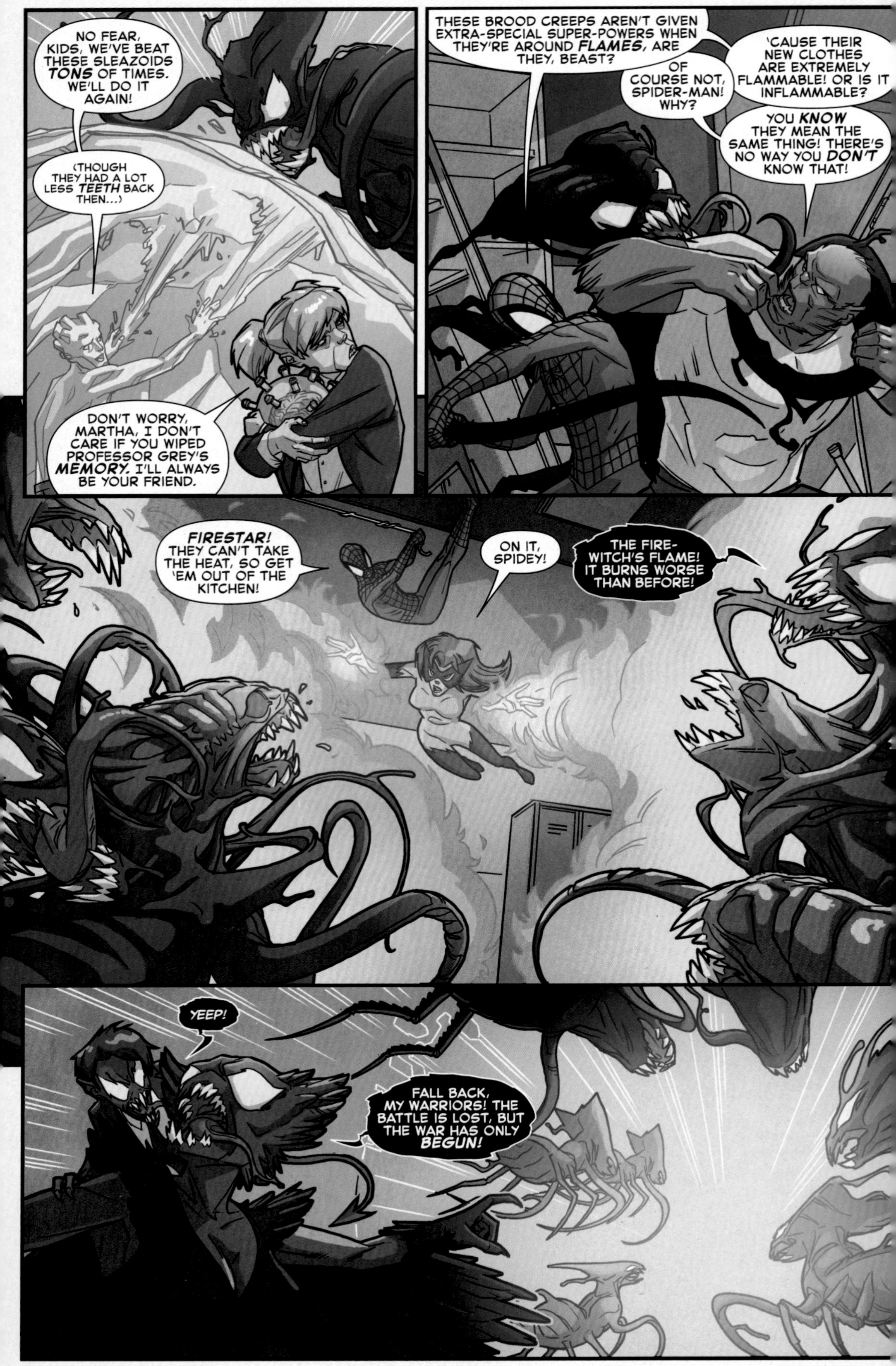
NO FEAR, KIDS, WE'VE BEAT THESE SLEAZOIDS TONS OF TIMES. WE'LL DO IT AGAIN!
(THOUGH THEY HAD A LOT LESS TEETH BACK THEN...)
DON'T WORRY, MARTHA, I DON'T CARE IF YOU WIPED PROFESSOR GREY'S MEMORY. I'LL ALWAYS BE YOUR FRIEND.
THESE BROOD CREEPS AREN'T GIVEN EXTRA-SPECIAL SUPER-POWERS WHEN THEY'RE AROUND FLAMES, ARE THEY, BEAST?
OF COURSE NOT, SPIDER-MAN! WHY?
'CAUSE THEIR NEW CLOTHES ARE EXTREMELY FLAMMABLE! OR IS IT INFLAMMABLE?
YOU KNOW THEY MEAN THE SAME THING! THERE'S NO WAY YOU DON'T KNOW THAT!
FIRESTAR! THEY CAN'T TAKE THE HEAT, SO GET 'EM OUT OF THE KITCHEN!
ON IT, SPIDEY!
THE FIRE-WITCH'S FLAME! IT BURNS WORSE THAN BEFORE!
YEEP!
FALL BACK, MY WARRIORS! THE BATTLE IS LOST, BUT THE WAR HAS ONLY BEGUN!

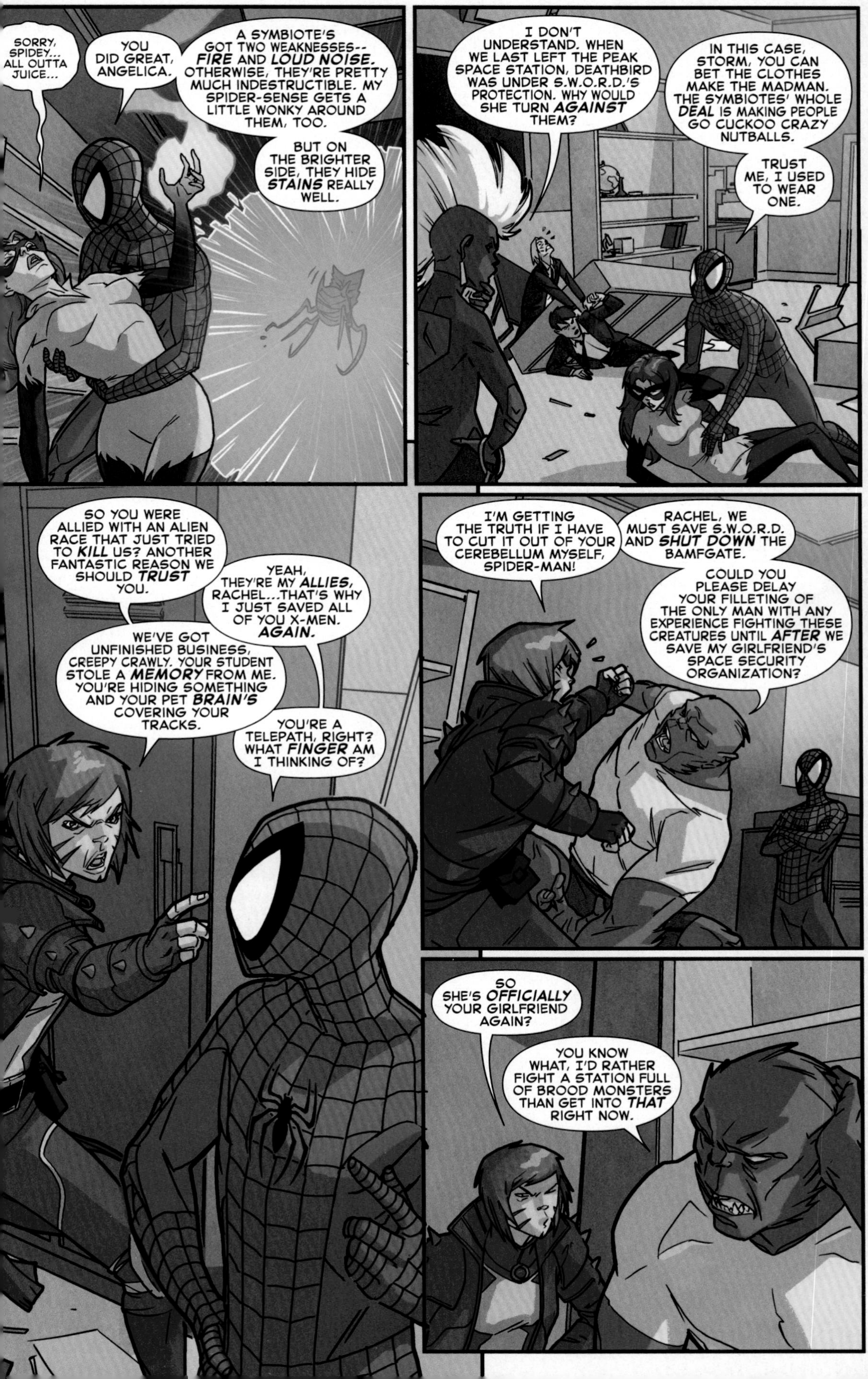
SORRY, SPIDEY... ALL OUTTA JUICE...
YOU DID GREAT, ANGELICA.
A SYMBIOTE'S GOT TWO WEAKNESSES-- FIRE AND LOUD NOISE. OTHERWISE, THEY'RE PRETTY MUCH INDESTRUCTIBLE. MY SPIDER-SENSE GETS A LITTLE WONKY AROUND THEM, TOO.
BUT ON THE BRIGHTER SIDE, THEY HIDE STAINS REALLY WELL.
I DON'T UNDERSTAND. WHEN WE LAST LEFT THE PEAK SPACE STATION, DEATHBIRD WAS UNDER S.W.O.R.D.'S PROTECTION. WHY WOULD SHE TURN AGAINST THEM?
IN THIS CASE, STORM, YOU CAN BET THE CLOTHES MAKE THE MADMAN. THE SYMBIOTES' WHOLE DEAL IS MAKING PEOPLE GO CUCKOO CRAZY NUTBALLS.
TRUST ME, I USED TO WEAR ONE.
SO YOU WERE ALLIED WITH AN ALIEN RACE THAT JUST TRIED TO KILL US? ANOTHER FANTASTIC REASON WE SHOULD TRUST YOU.
YEAH, THEY'RE MY ALLIES, RACHEL...THAT'S WHY I JUST SAVED ALL OF YOU X-MEN. AGAIN.
WE'VE GOT UNFINISHED BUSINESS, CREEPY CRAWLY. YOUR STUDENT STOLE A MEMORY FROM ME. YOU'RE HIDING SOMETHING AND YOUR PET BRAIN'S COVERING YOUR TRACKS.
YOU'RE A TELEPATH, RIGHT? WHAT FINGER AM I THINKING OF?
I'M GETTING THE TRUTH IF I HAVE TO CUT IT OUT OF YOUR CEREBELLUM MYSELF, SPIDER-MAN!
RACHEL, WE MUST SAVE S.W.O.R.D. AND SHUT DOWN THE BAMFGATE.
COULD YOU PLEASE DELAY YOUR FILLETING OF THE ONLY MAN WITH ANY EXPERIENCE FIGHTING THESE CREATURES UNTIL AFTER WE SAVE MY GIRLFRIEND'S SPACE SECURITY ORGANIZATION?
SO SHE'S OFFICIALLY YOUR GIRLFRIEND AGAIN?
YOU KNOW WHAT, I'D RATHER FIGHT A STATION FULL OF BROOD MONSTERS THAN GET INTO THAT RIGHT NOW.

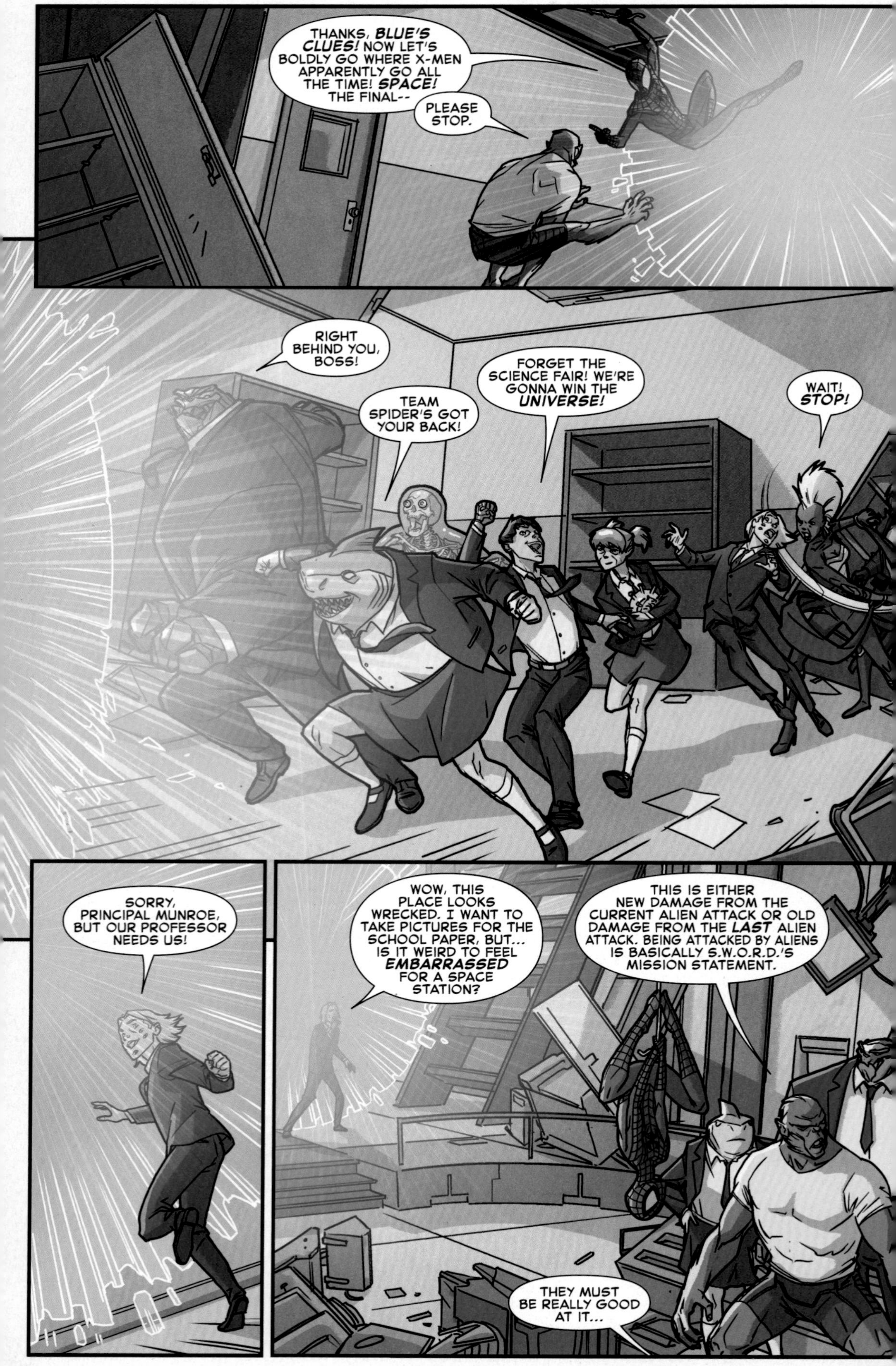
THANKS, BLUE'S CLUES! NOW LET'S BOLDLY GO WHERE X-MEN APPARENTLY GO ALL THE TIME! SPACE! THE FINAL--
PLEASE STOP.
RIGHT BEHIND YOU, BOSS!
TEAM SPIDER'S GOT YOUR BACK!
FORGET THE SCIENCE FAIR! WE'RE GONNA WIN THE UNIVERSE!
WAIT! STOP!
SORRY, PRINCIPAL MUNROE, BUT OUR PROFESSOR NEEDS US!
WOW, THIS PLACE LOOKS WRECKED. I WANT TO TAKE PICTURES FOR THE SCHOOL PAPER, BUT... IS IT WEIRD TO FEEL EMBARRASSED FOR A SPACE STATION?
THIS IS EITHER NEW DAMAGE FROM THE CURRENT ALIEN ATTACK OR OLD DAMAGE FROM THE LAST ALIEN ATTACK. BEING ATTACKED BY ALIENS IS BASICALLY S.W.O.R.D.'S MISSION STATEMENT.
THEY MUST BE REALLY GOOD AT IT...

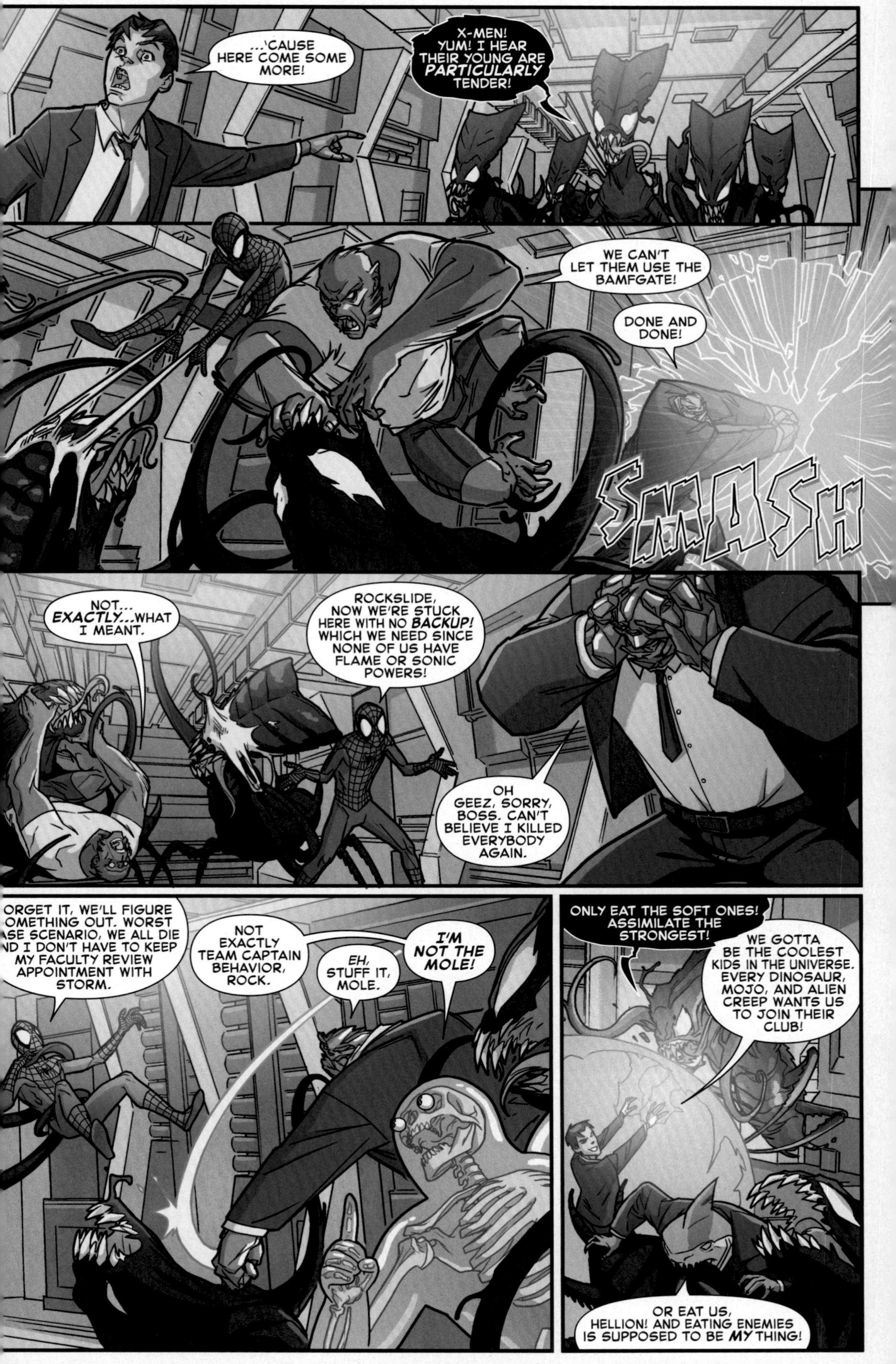

...'CAUSE HERE COME SOME MORE!
X-MEN! YUM! I HEAR THEIR YOUNG ARE *PARTICULARLY* TENDER!
WE CAN'T LET THEM USE THE BAMFGATE!
DONE AND DONE!
SMASH
NOT... *EXACTLY*...WHAT I MEANT.
ROCKSLIDE, NOW WE'RE STUCK HERE WITH NO *BACKUP!* WHICH WE NEED SINCE NONE OF US HAVE FLAME OR SONIC POWERS!
OH GEEZ, SORRY, BOSS. CAN'T BELIEVE I KILLED EVERYBODY AGAIN.
ORGET IT, WE'LL FIGURE OMETHING OUT. WORST ASE SCENARIO, WE ALL DIE ND I DON'T HAVE TO KEEP MY FACULTY REVIEW APPOINTMENT WITH STORM.
NOT EXACTLY TEAM CAPTAIN BEHAVIOR, ROCK.
I'M NOT THE MOLE!
EH, STUFF IT, MOLE.
ONLY EAT THE SOFT ONES! ASSIMILATE THE STRONGEST!
WE GOTTA BE THE COOLEST KIDS IN THE UNIVERSE. EVERY DINOSAUR, MOJO, AND ALIEN CREEP WANTS US TO JOIN THEIR CLUB!
OR EAT US, HELLION! AND EATING ENEMIES IS SUPPOSED TO BE *MY* THING!

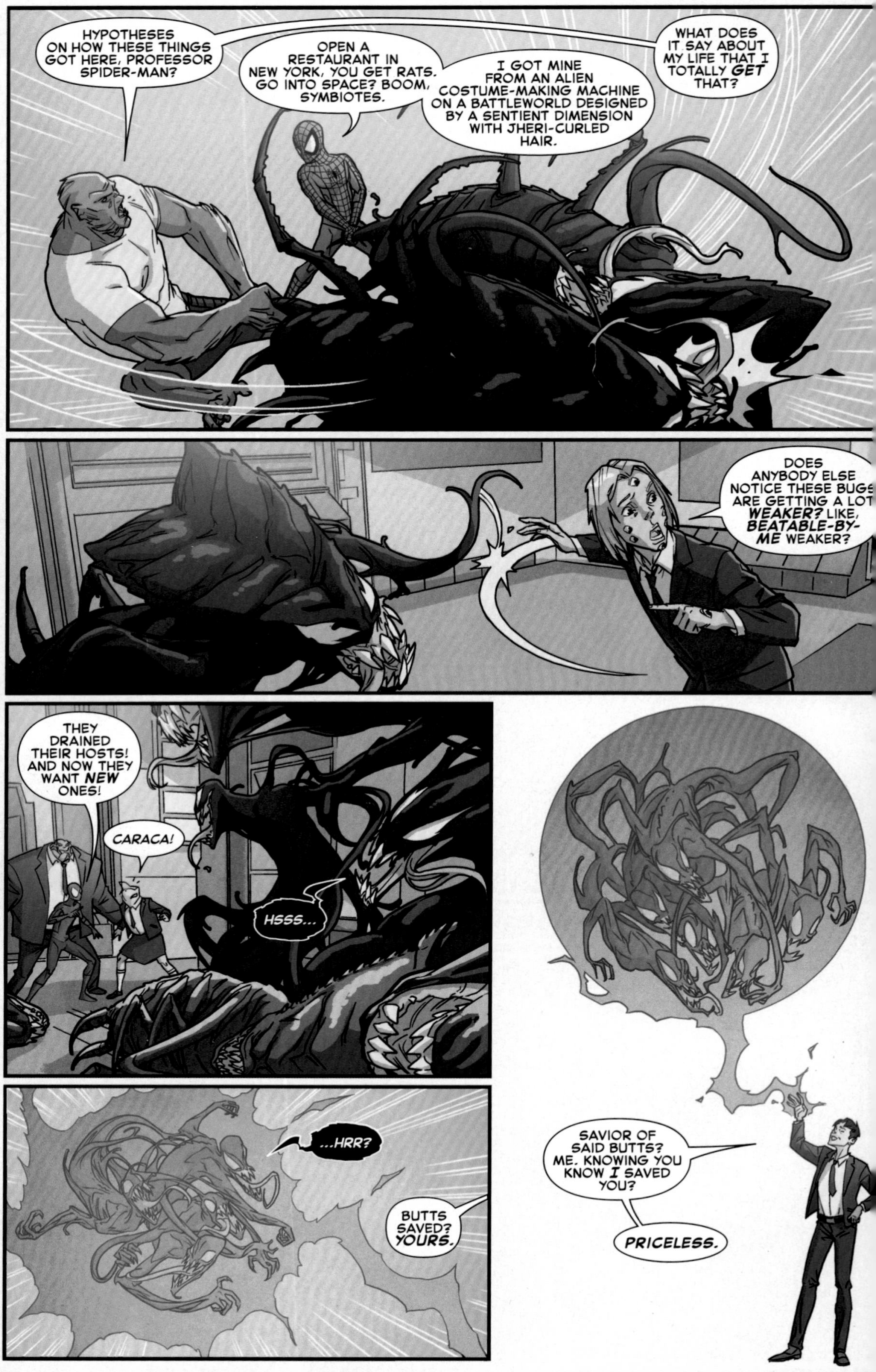
HYPOTHESES ON HOW THESE THINGS GOT HERE, PROFESSOR SPIDER-MAN?
OPEN A RESTAURANT IN NEW YORK, YOU GET RATS. GO INTO SPACE? BOOM, SYMBIOTES.
I GOT MINE FROM AN ALIEN COSTUME-MAKING MACHINE ON A BATTLEWORLD DESIGNED BY A SENTIENT DIMENSION WITH JHERI-CURLED HAIR.
WHAT DOES IT SAY ABOUT MY LIFE THAT I TOTALLY GET THAT?
DOES ANYBODY ELSE NOTICE THESE BUGS ARE GETTING A LOT WEAKER? LIKE, BEATABLE-BY-ME WEAKER?
THEY DRAINED THEIR HOSTS! AND NOW THEY WANT NEW ONES!
CARACA!
HSSS...
...HRR?
BUTTS SAVED? YOURS.
SAVIOR OF SAID BUTTS? ME. KNOWING YOU KNOW I SAVED YOU?
PRICELESS.

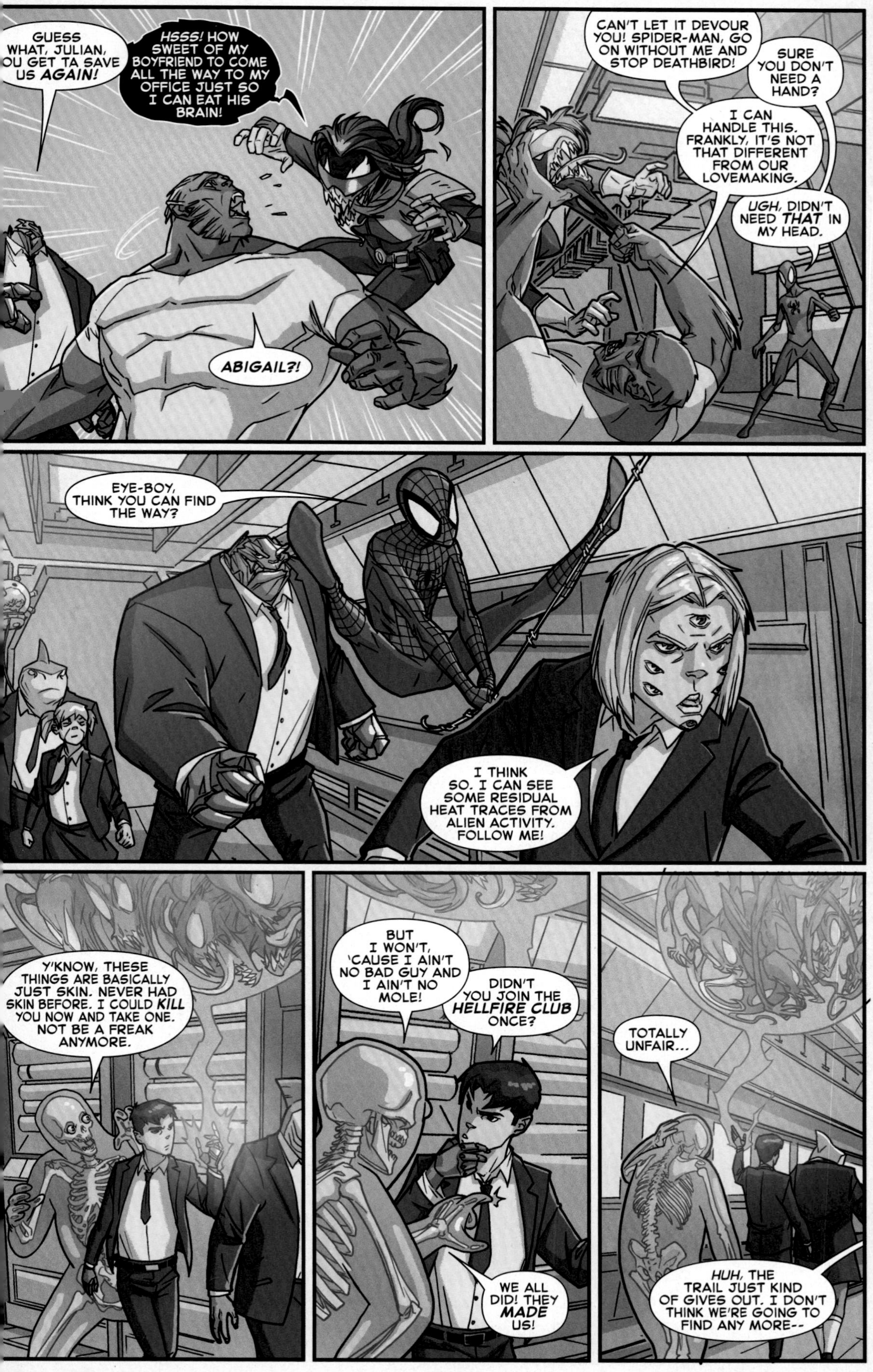
GUESS WHAT, JULIAN, YOU GET TA SAVE US *AGAIN!*
HSSS! HOW SWEET OF MY BOYFRIEND TO COME ALL THE WAY TO MY OFFICE JUST SO I CAN EAT HIS BRAIN!
ABIGAIL?!
CAN'T LET IT DEVOUR YOU! SPIDER-MAN, GO ON WITHOUT ME AND STOP DEATHBIRD!
SURE YOU DON'T NEED A HAND?
I CAN HANDLE THIS. FRANKLY, IT'S NOT THAT DIFFERENT FROM OUR LOVEMAKING.
UGH, DIDN'T NEED ***THAT*** IN MY HEAD.
EYE-BOY, THINK YOU CAN FIND THE WAY?
I THINK SO. I CAN SEE SOME RESIDUAL HEAT TRACES FROM ALIEN ACTIVITY. FOLLOW ME!
Y'KNOW, THESE THINGS ARE BASICALLY JUST SKIN. NEVER HAD SKIN BEFORE. I COULD *KILL* YOU NOW AND TAKE ONE. NOT BE A FREAK ANYMORE.
BUT I WON'T, 'CAUSE I AIN'T NO BAD GUY AND I AIN'T NO MOLE!
DIDN'T YOU JOIN THE ***HELLFIRE CLUB*** ONCE?
WE ALL DID! THEY ***MADE*** US!
TOTALLY UNFAIR...
HUH, THE TRAIL JUST KIND OF GIVES OUT. I DON'T THINK WE'RE GOING TO FIND ANY MORE--

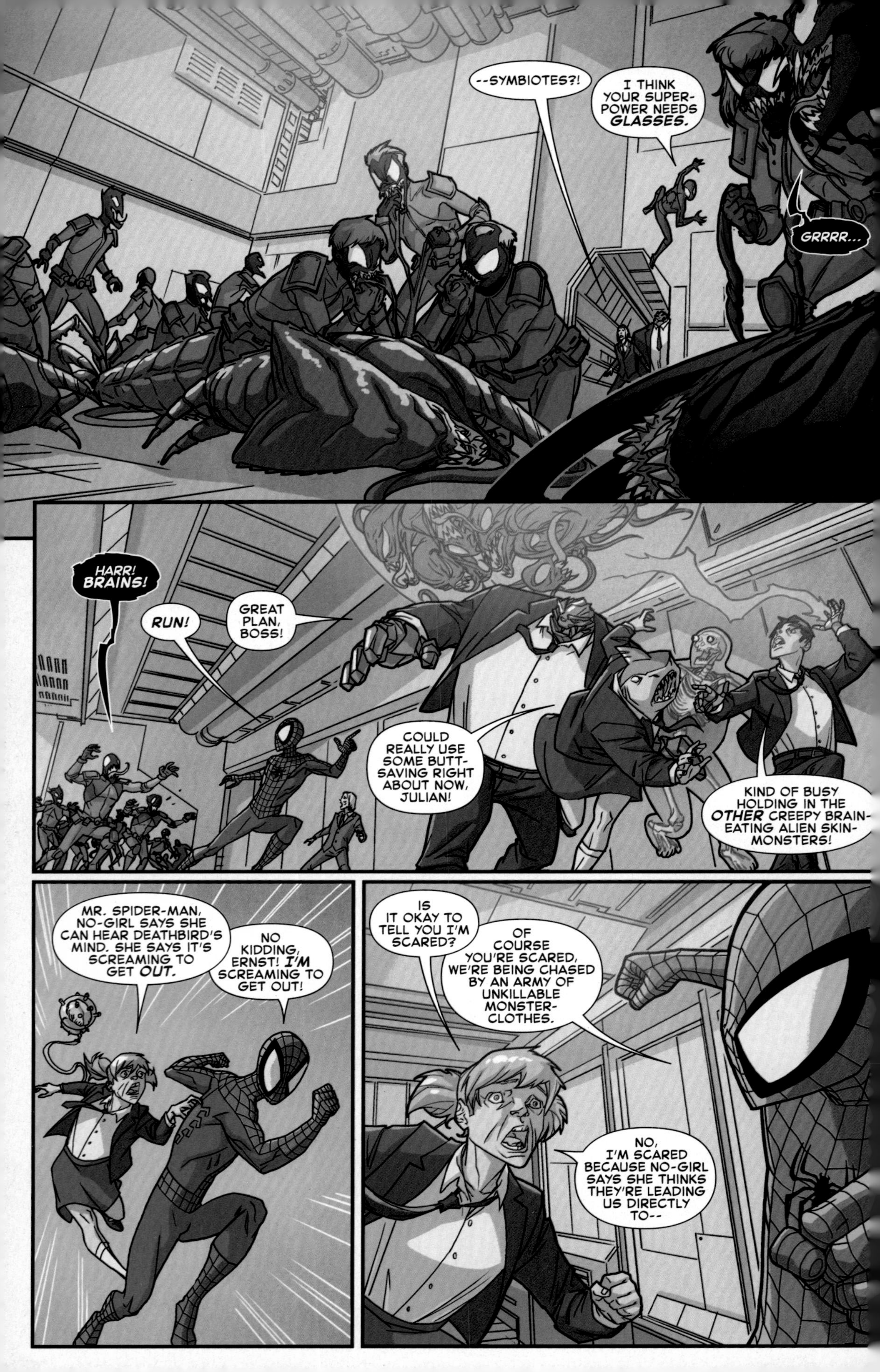
--SYMBIOTES?!
I THINK YOUR SUPER-POWER NEEDS GLASSES.
GRRRR...
HARR! BRAINS!
RUN!
GREAT PLAN, BOSS!
COULD REALLY USE SOME BUTT-SAVING RIGHT ABOUT NOW, JULIAN!
KIND OF BUSY HOLDING IN THE OTHER CREEPY BRAIN-EATING ALIEN SKIN-MONSTERS!
MR. SPIDER-MAN, NO-GIRL SAYS SHE CAN HEAR DEATHBIRD'S MIND. SHE SAYS IT'S SCREAMING TO GET OUT.
NO KIDDING, ERNST! I'M SCREAMING TO GET OUT!
IS IT OKAY TO TELL YOU I'M SCARED?
OF COURSE YOU'RE SCARED, WE'RE BEING CHASED BY AN ARMY OF UNKILLABLE MONSTER-CLOTHES.
NO, I'M SCARED BECAUSE NO-GIRL SAYS SHE THINKS THEY'RE LEADING US DIRECTLY TO--

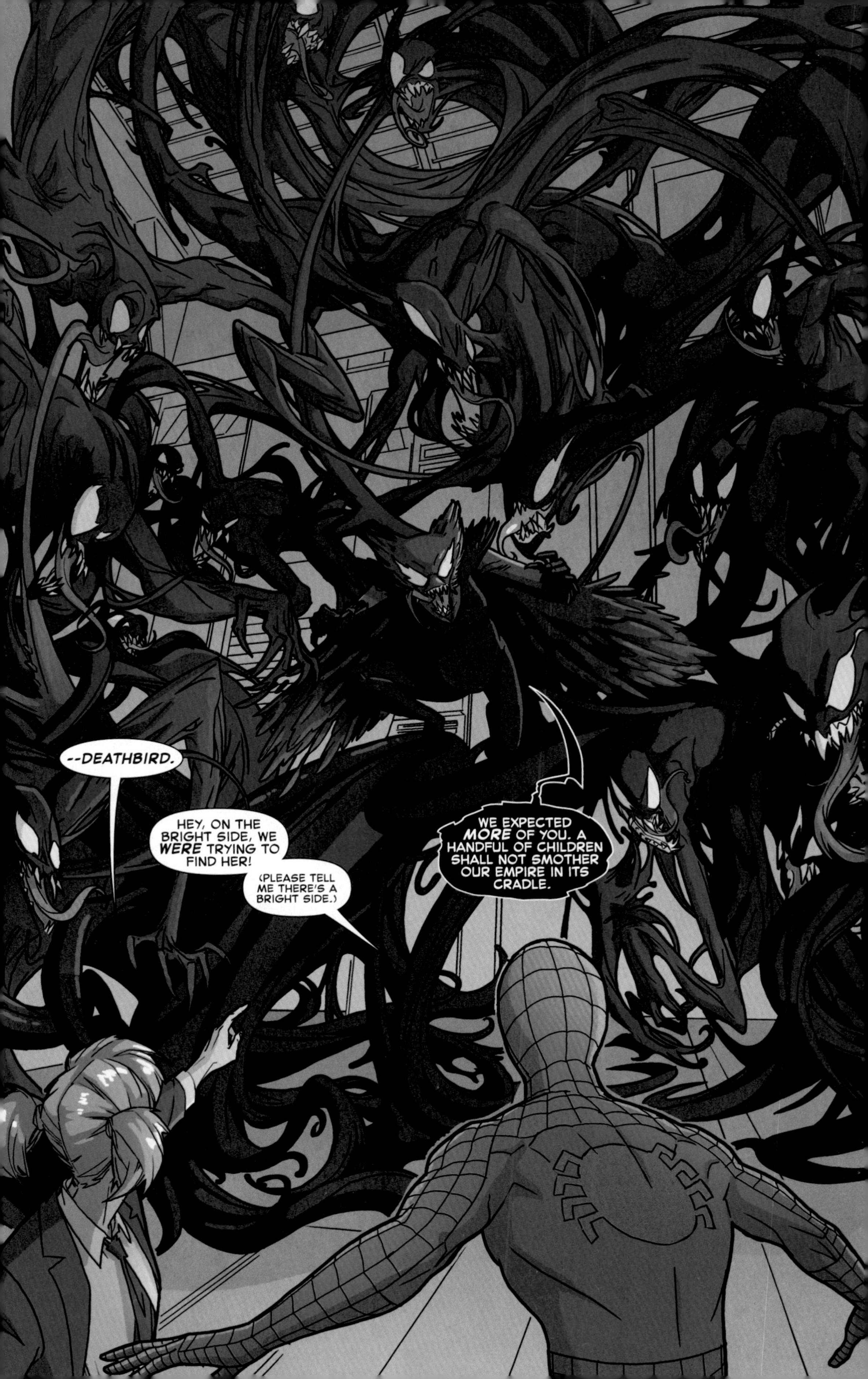
--DEATHBIRD.
HEY, ON THE BRIGHT SIDE, WE WERE TRYING TO FIND HER!
(PLEASE TELL ME THERE'S A BRIGHT SIDE.)
WE EXPECTED MORE OF YOU. A HANDFUL OF CHILDREN SHALL NOT SMOTHER OUR EMPIRE IN ITS CRADLE.

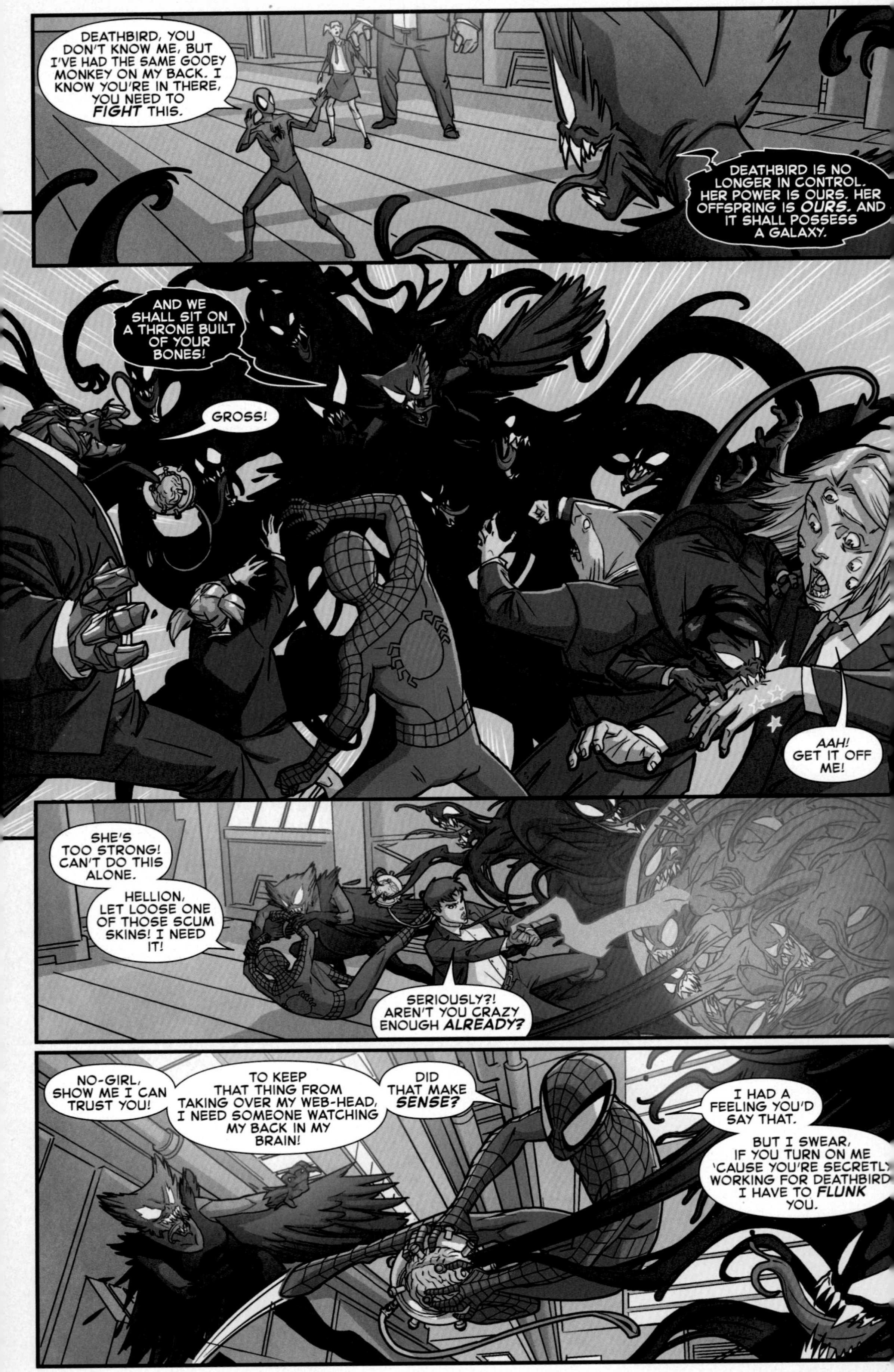
DEATHBIRD, YOU DON'T KNOW ME, BUT I'VE HAD THE SAME GOOEY MONKEY ON MY BACK. I KNOW YOU'RE IN THERE, YOU NEED TO FIGHT THIS.
DEATHBIRD IS NO LONGER IN CONTROL. HER POWER IS OURS. HER OFFSPRING IS OURS. AND IT SHALL POSSESS A GALAXY.
AND WE SHALL SIT ON A THRONE BUILT OF YOUR BONES!
GROSS!
AAH! GET IT OFF ME!
SHE'S TOO STRONG! CAN'T DO THIS ALONE.
HELLION, LET LOOSE ONE OF THOSE SCUM SKINS! I NEED IT!
SERIOUSLY?! AREN'T YOU CRAZY ENOUGH ALREADY?
NO-GIRL, SHOW ME I CAN TRUST YOU!
TO KEEP THAT THING FROM TAKING OVER MY WEB-HEAD, I NEED SOMEONE WATCHING MY BACK IN MY BRAIN!
DID THAT MAKE SENSE?
I HAD A FEELING YOU'D SAY THAT.
BUT I SWEAR, IF YOU TURN ON ME 'CAUSE YOU'RE SECRETLY WORKING FOR DEATHBIRD I HAVE TO FLUNK YOU.

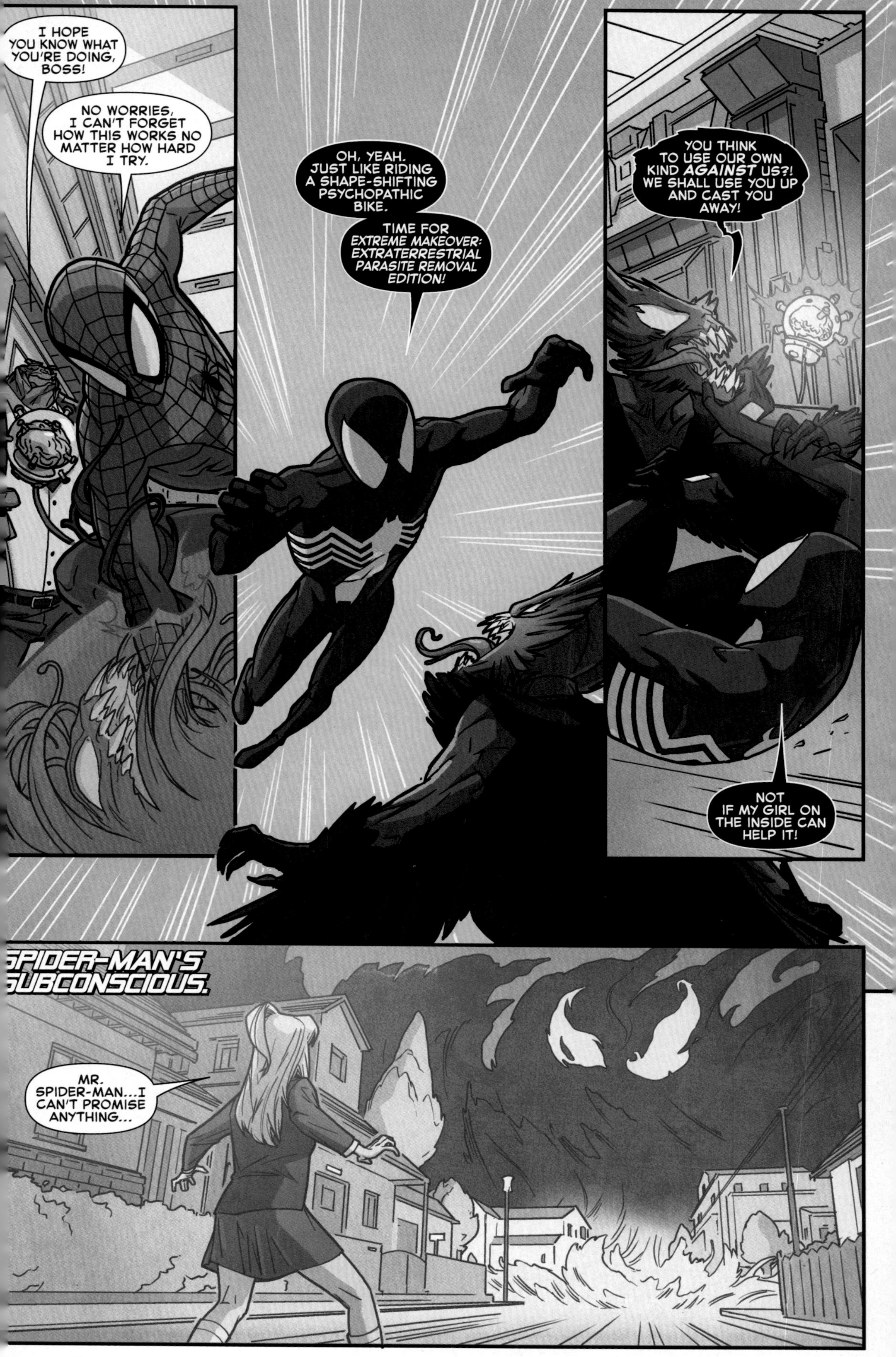
I HOPE YOU KNOW WHAT YOU'RE DOING, BOSS!
NO WORRIES, I CAN'T FORGET HOW THIS WORKS NO MATTER HOW HARD I TRY.
OH, YEAH. JUST LIKE RIDING A SHAPE-SHIFTING PSYCHOPATHIC BIKE.
TIME FOR EXTREME MAKEOVER: EXTRATERRESTRIAL PARASITE REMOVAL EDITION!
YOU THINK TO USE OUR OWN KIND AGAINST US?! WE SHALL USE YOU UP AND CAST YOU AWAY!
NOT IF MY GIRL ON THE INSIDE CAN HELP IT!
SPIDER-MAN'S SUBCONSCIOUS.
MR. SPIDER-MAN...I CAN'T PROMISE ANYTHING...

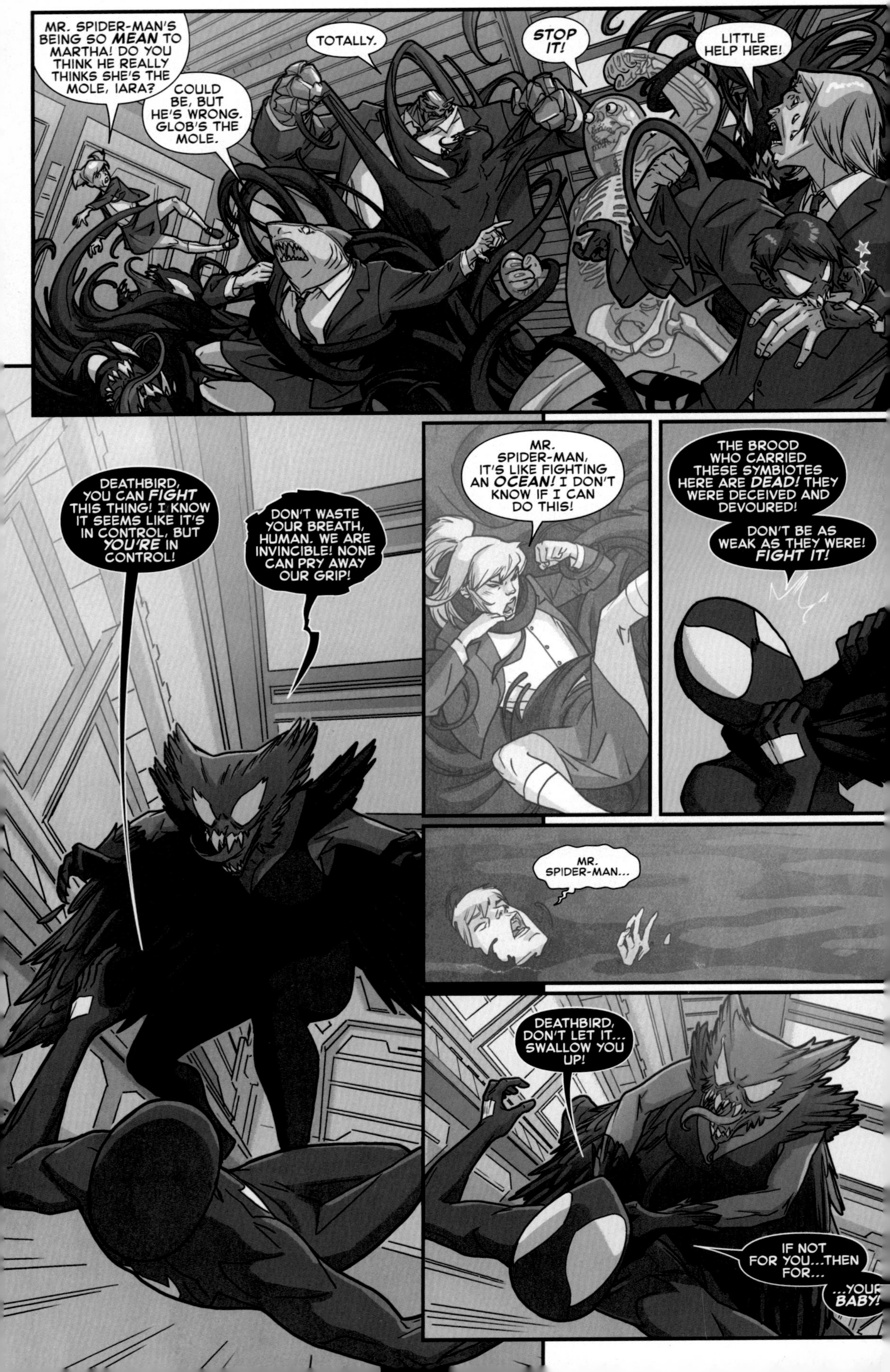
MR. SPIDER-MAN'S BEING SO MEAN TO MARTHA! DO YOU THINK HE REALLY THINKS SHE'S THE MOLE, IARA?
COULD BE, BUT HE'S WRONG. GLOB'S THE MOLE.
TOTALLY.
STOP IT!
LITTLE HELP HERE!
DEATHBIRD, YOU CAN FIGHT THIS THING! I KNOW IT SEEMS LIKE IT'S IN CONTROL, BUT YOU'RE IN CONTROL!
DON'T WASTE YOUR BREATH, HUMAN. WE ARE INVINCIBLE! NONE CAN PRY AWAY OUR GRIP!
MR. SPIDER-MAN, IT'S LIKE FIGHTING AN OCEAN! I DON'T KNOW IF I CAN DO THIS!
THE BROOD WHO CARRIED THESE SYMBIOTES HERE ARE DEAD! THEY WERE DECEIVED AND DEVOURED!
DON'T BE AS WEAK AS THEY WERE! FIGHT IT!
MR. SPIDER-MAN...
DEATHBIRD, DON'T LET IT... SWALLOW YOU UP!
IF NOT FOR YOU...THEN FOR...
...YOUR BABY!

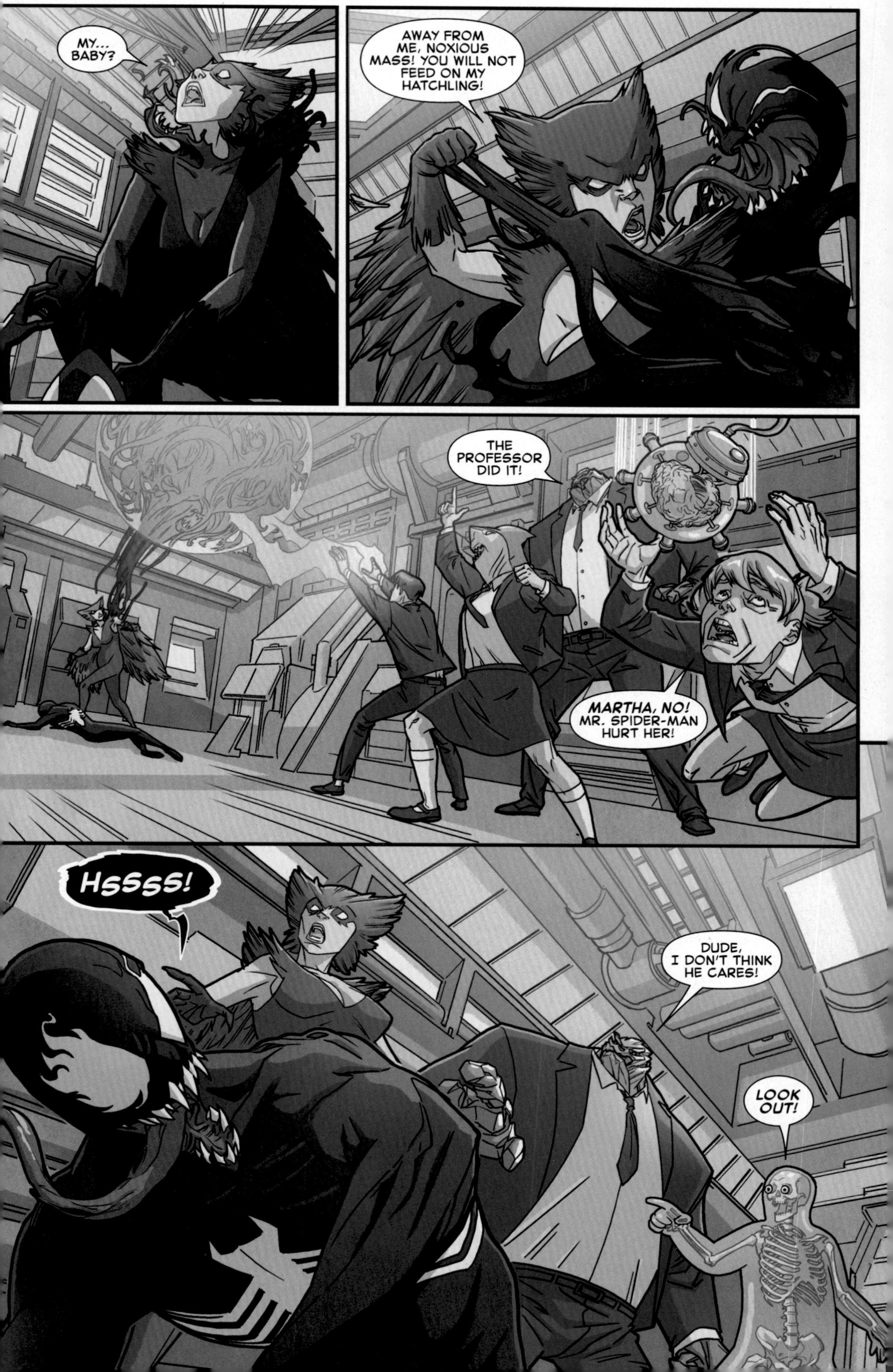
MY... BABY?
AWAY FROM ME, NOXIOUS MASS! YOU WILL NOT FEED ON MY HATCHLING!
THE PROFESSOR DID IT!
MARTHA, NO! MR. SPIDER-MAN HURT HER!
HSSSS!
DUDE, I DON'T THINK HE CARES!
LOOK OUT!

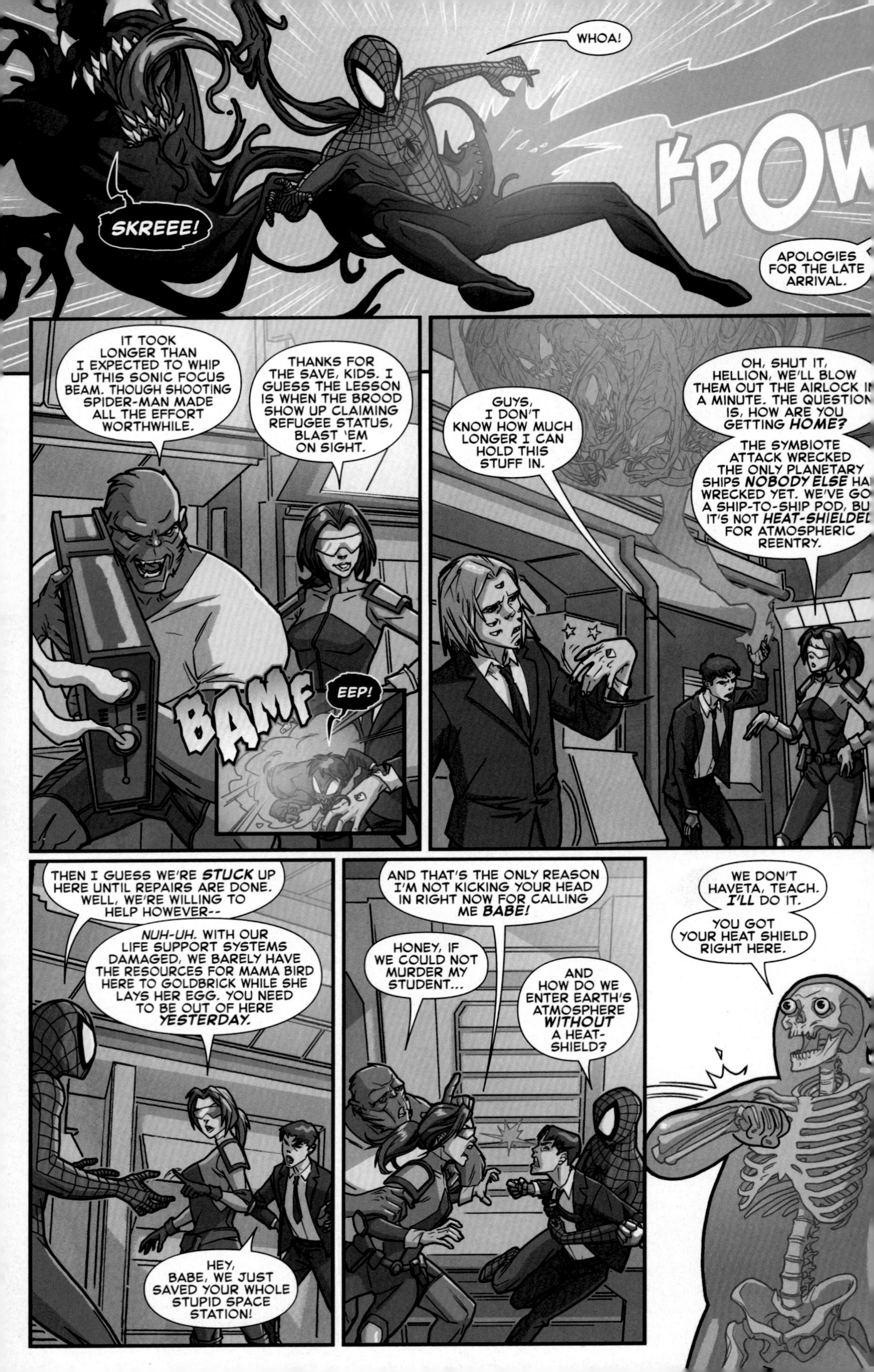
WHOA!
SKREEE!
KPOW
APOLOGIES FOR THE LATE ARRIVAL.
IT TOOK LONGER THAN I EXPECTED TO WHIP UP THIS SONIC FOCUS BEAM. THOUGH SHOOTING SPIDER-MAN MADE ALL THE EFFORT WORTHWHILE.
THANKS FOR THE SAVE, KIDS. I GUESS THE LESSON IS WHEN THE BROOD SHOW UP CLAIMING REFUGEE STATUS, BLAST 'EM ON SIGHT.
BAMF
EEP!
GUYS, I DON'T KNOW HOW MUCH LONGER I CAN HOLD THIS STUFF IN.
OH, SHUT IT, HELLION, WE'LL BLOW THEM OUT THE AIRLOCK IN A MINUTE. THE QUESTION IS, HOW ARE YOU GETTING HOME?
THE SYMBIOTE ATTACK WRECKED THE ONLY PLANETARY SHIPS NOBODY ELSE HAD WRECKED YET. WE'VE GOT A SHIP-TO-SHIP POD, BUT IT'S NOT HEAT-SHIELDED FOR ATMOSPHERIC REENTRY.
THEN I GUESS WE'RE STUCK UP HERE UNTIL REPAIRS ARE DONE. WELL, WE'RE WILLING TO HELP HOWEVER--
NUH-UH. WITH OUR LIFE SUPPORT SYSTEMS DAMAGED, WE BARELY HAVE THE RESOURCES FOR MAMA BIRD HERE TO GOLDBRICK WHILE SHE LAYS HER EGG. YOU NEED TO BE OUT OF HERE YESTERDAY.
HEY, BABE, WE JUST SAVED YOUR WHOLE STUPID SPACE STATION!
AND THAT'S THE ONLY REASON I'M NOT KICKING YOUR HEAD IN RIGHT NOW FOR CALLING ME BABE!
HONEY, IF WE COULD NOT MURDER MY STUDENT...
AND HOW DO WE ENTER EARTH'S ATMOSPHERE WITHOUT A HEAT-SHIELD?
WE DON'T HAVETA, TEACH. I'LL DO IT.
YOU GOT YOUR HEAT SHIELD RIGHT HERE.

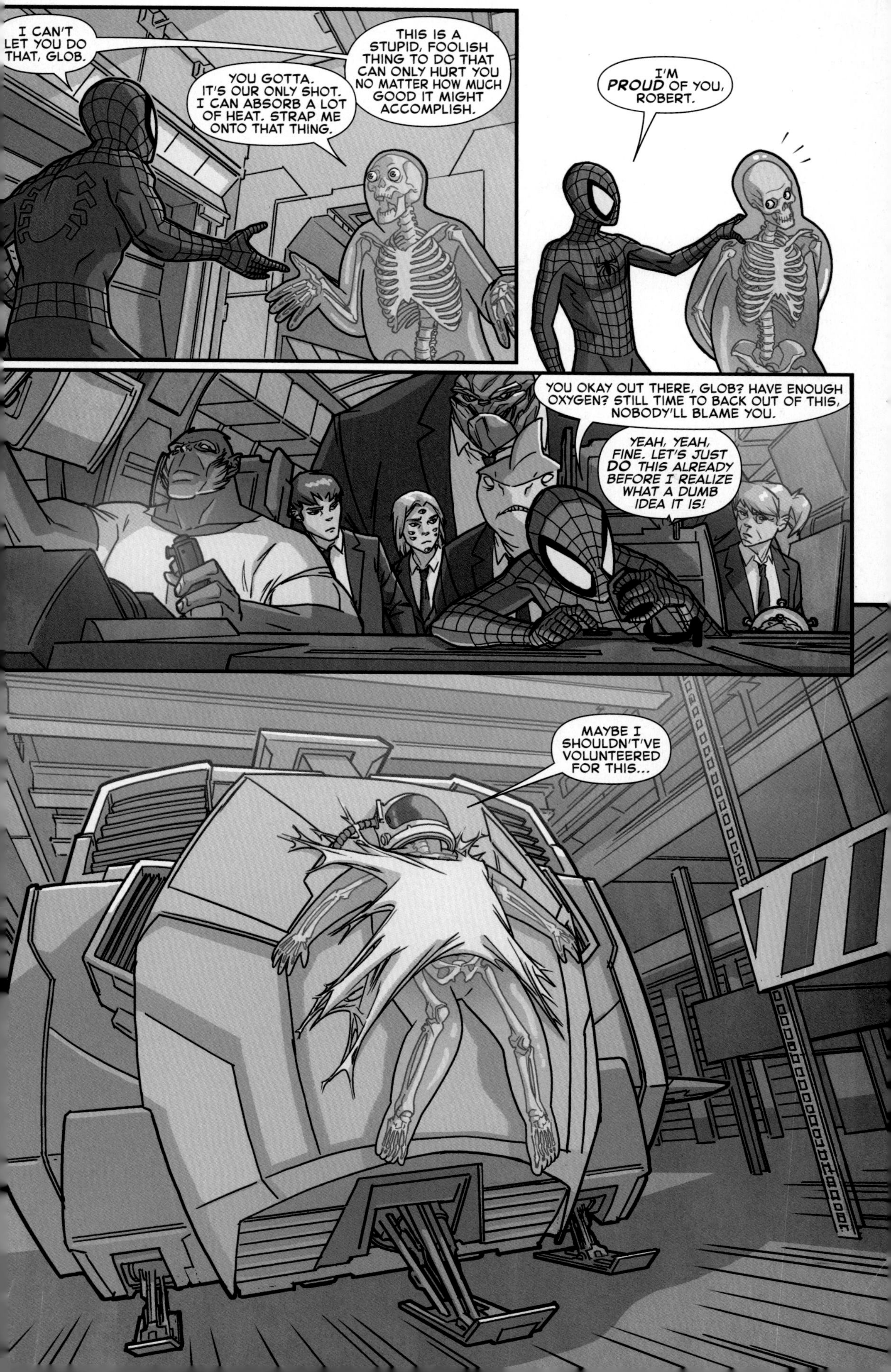
I CAN'T LET YOU DO THAT, GLOB.
YOU GOTTA. IT'S OUR ONLY SHOT. I CAN ABSORB A LOT OF HEAT. STRAP ME ONTO THAT THING.
THIS IS A STUPID, FOOLISH THING TO DO THAT CAN ONLY HURT YOU NO MATTER HOW MUCH GOOD IT MIGHT ACCOMPLISH.
I'M PROUD OF YOU, ROBERT.
YOU OKAY OUT THERE, GLOB? HAVE ENOUGH OXYGEN? STILL TIME TO BACK OUT OF THIS, NOBODY'LL BLAME YOU.
YEAH, YEAH, FINE. LET'S JUST DO THIS ALREADY BEFORE I REALIZE WHAT A DUMB IDEA IT IS!
MAYBE I SHOULDN'T'VE VOLUNTEERED FOR THIS...

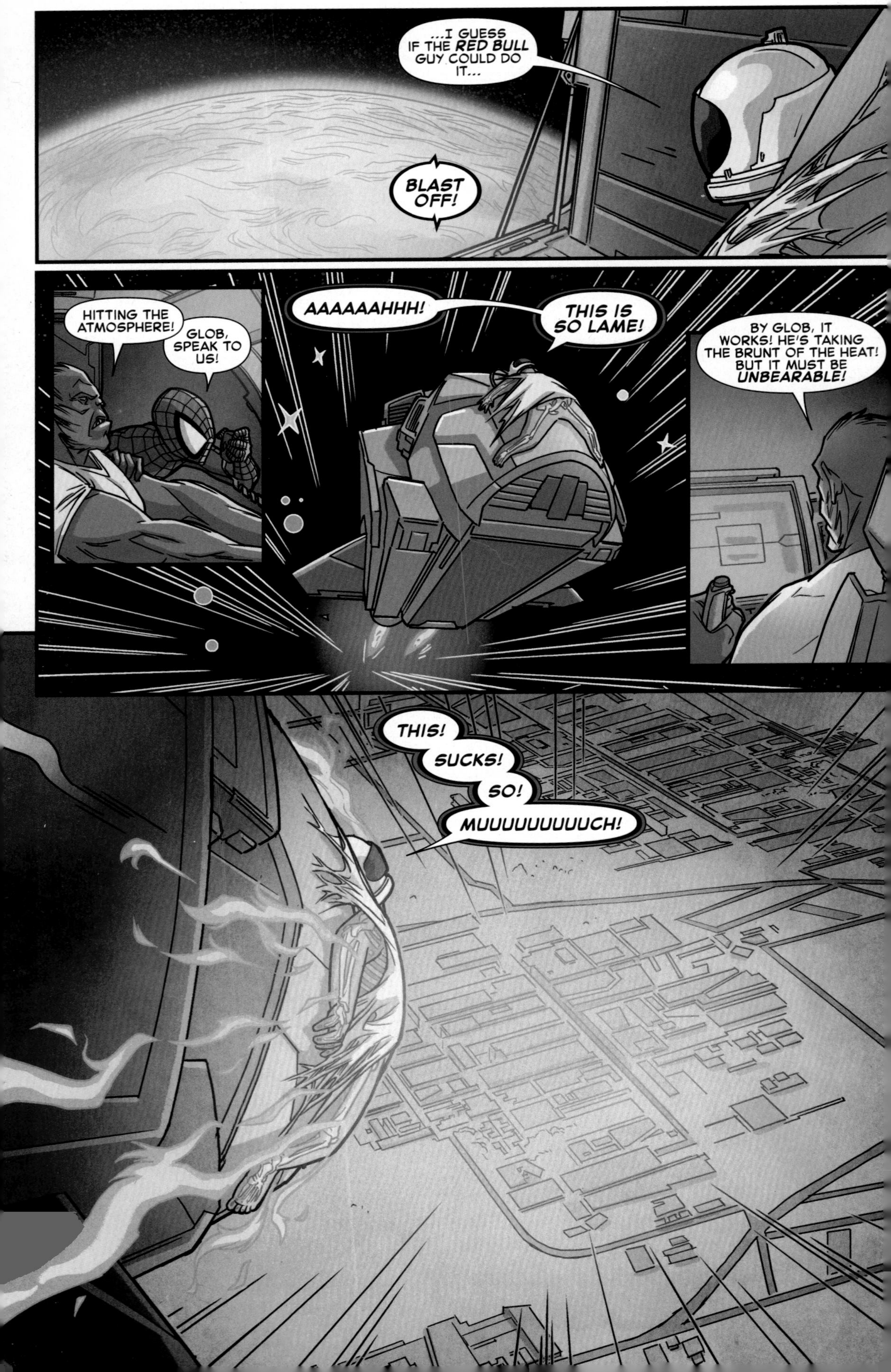
...I GUESS IF THE RED BULL GUY COULD DO IT...
BLAST OFF!
HITTING THE ATMOSPHERE!
GLOB, SPEAK TO US!
AAAAAAHHH!
THIS IS SO LAME!
BY GLOB, IT WORKS! HE'S TAKING THE BRUNT OF THE HEAT! BUT IT MUST BE UNBEARABLE!
THIS!
SUCKS!
SO!
MUUUUUUUUUCH!

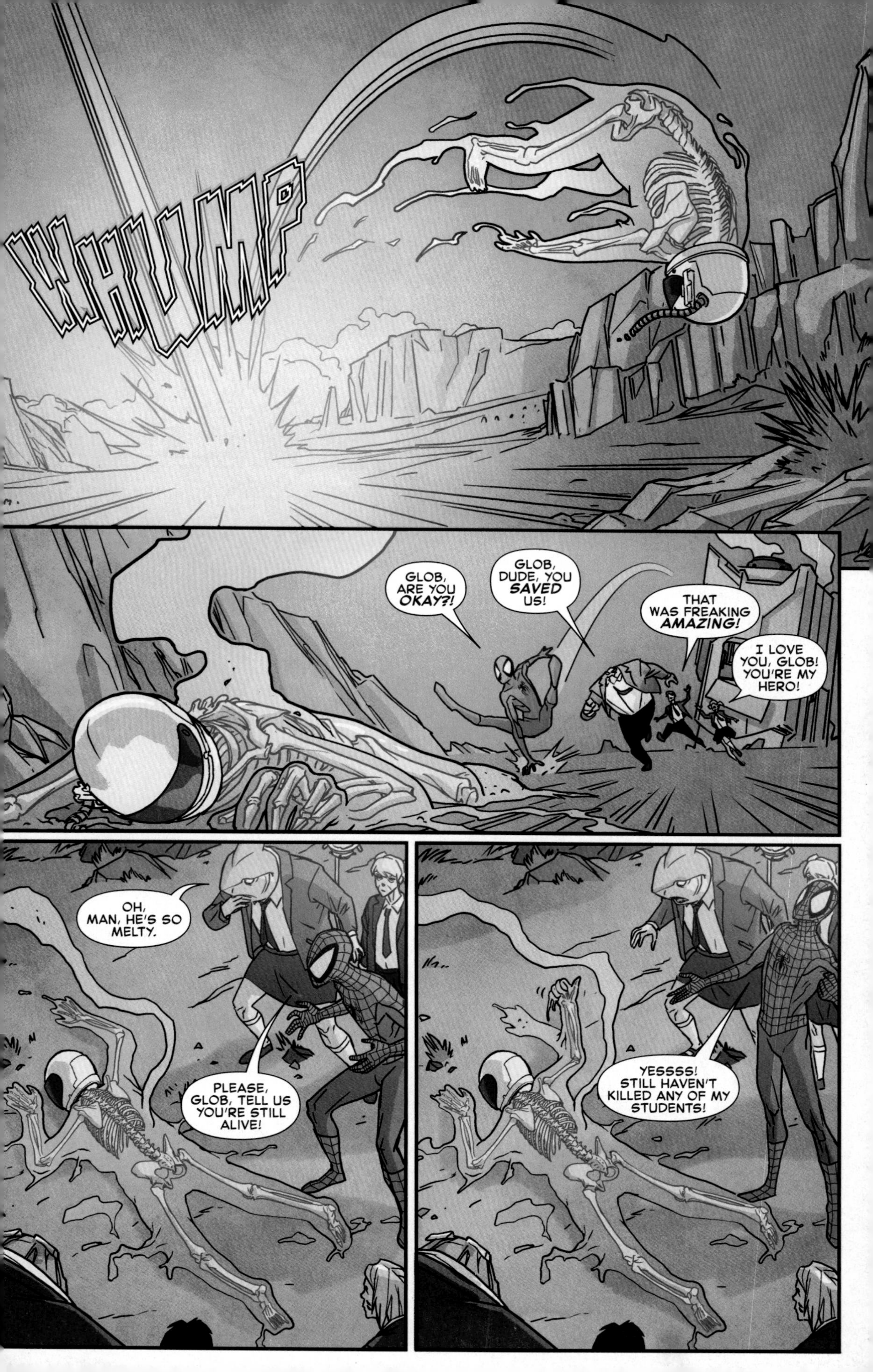
WHUMP
GLOB, ARE YOU OKAY?!
GLOB, DUDE, YOU SAVED US!
THAT WAS FREAKING AMAZING!
I LOVE YOU, GLOB! YOU'RE MY HERO!
OH, MAN, HE'S SO MELTY.
PLEASE, GLOB, TELL US YOU'RE STILL ALIVE!
YESSSS! STILL HAVEN'T KILLED ANY OF MY STUDENTS!

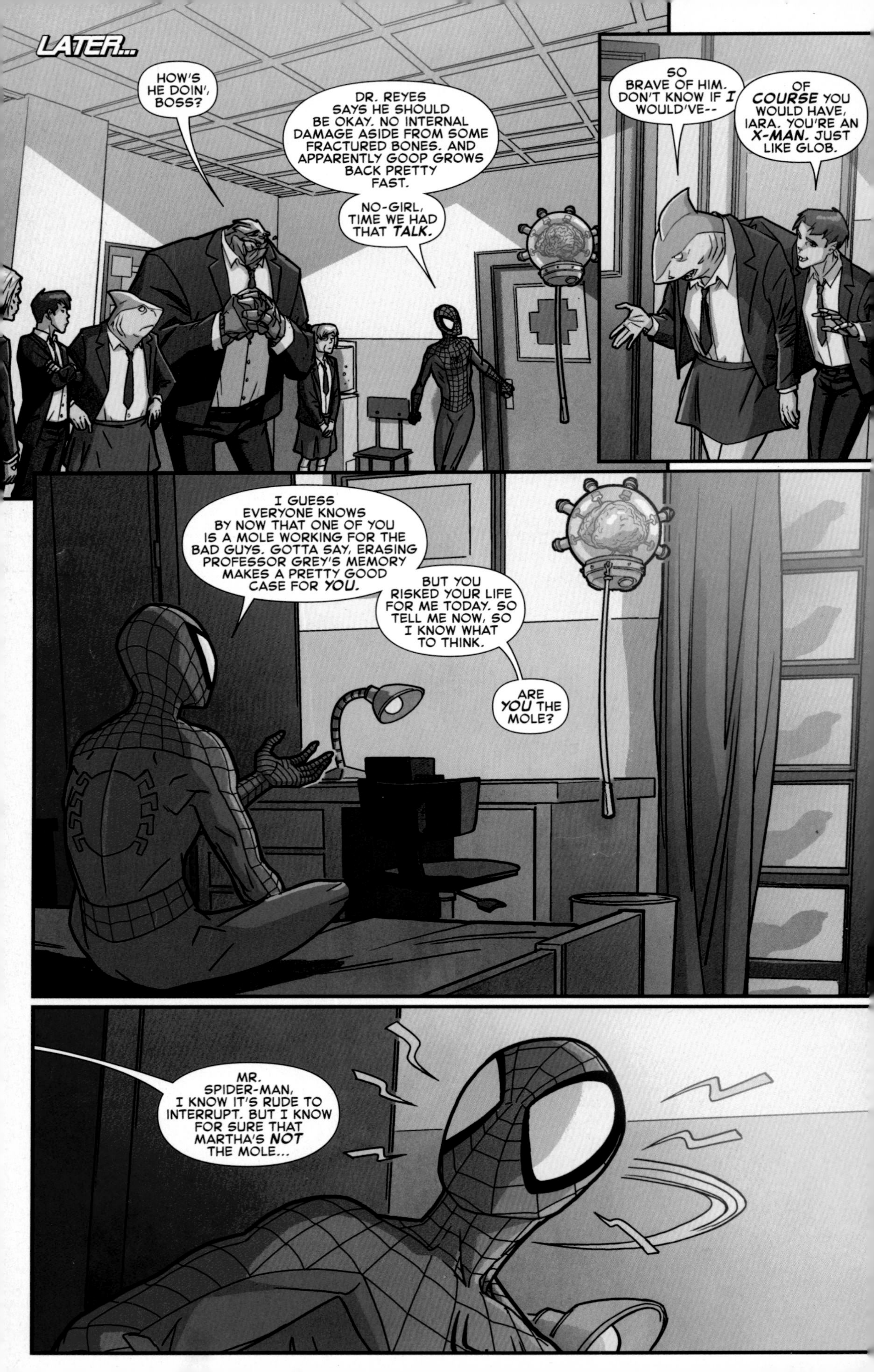
LATER...
HOW'S HE DOIN', BOSS?
DR. REYES SAYS HE SHOULD BE OKAY. NO INTERNAL DAMAGE ASIDE FROM SOME FRACTURED BONES. AND APPARENTLY GOOP GROWS BACK PRETTY FAST.
NO-GIRL, TIME WE HAD THAT TALK.
SO BRAVE OF HIM. DON'T KNOW IF I WOULD'VE--
OF COURSE YOU WOULD HAVE, IARA. YOU'RE AN X-MAN. JUST LIKE GLOB.
I GUESS EVERYONE KNOWS BY NOW THAT ONE OF YOU IS A MOLE WORKING FOR THE BAD GUYS. GOTTA SAY, ERASING PROFESSOR GREY'S MEMORY MAKES A PRETTY GOOD CASE FOR YOU.
BUT YOU RISKED YOUR LIFE FOR ME TODAY. SO TELL ME NOW, SO I KNOW WHAT TO THINK.
ARE YOU THE MOLE?
MR. SPIDER-MAN, I KNOW IT'S RUDE TO INTERRUPT. BUT I KNOW FOR SURE THAT MARTHA'S NOT THE MOLE...

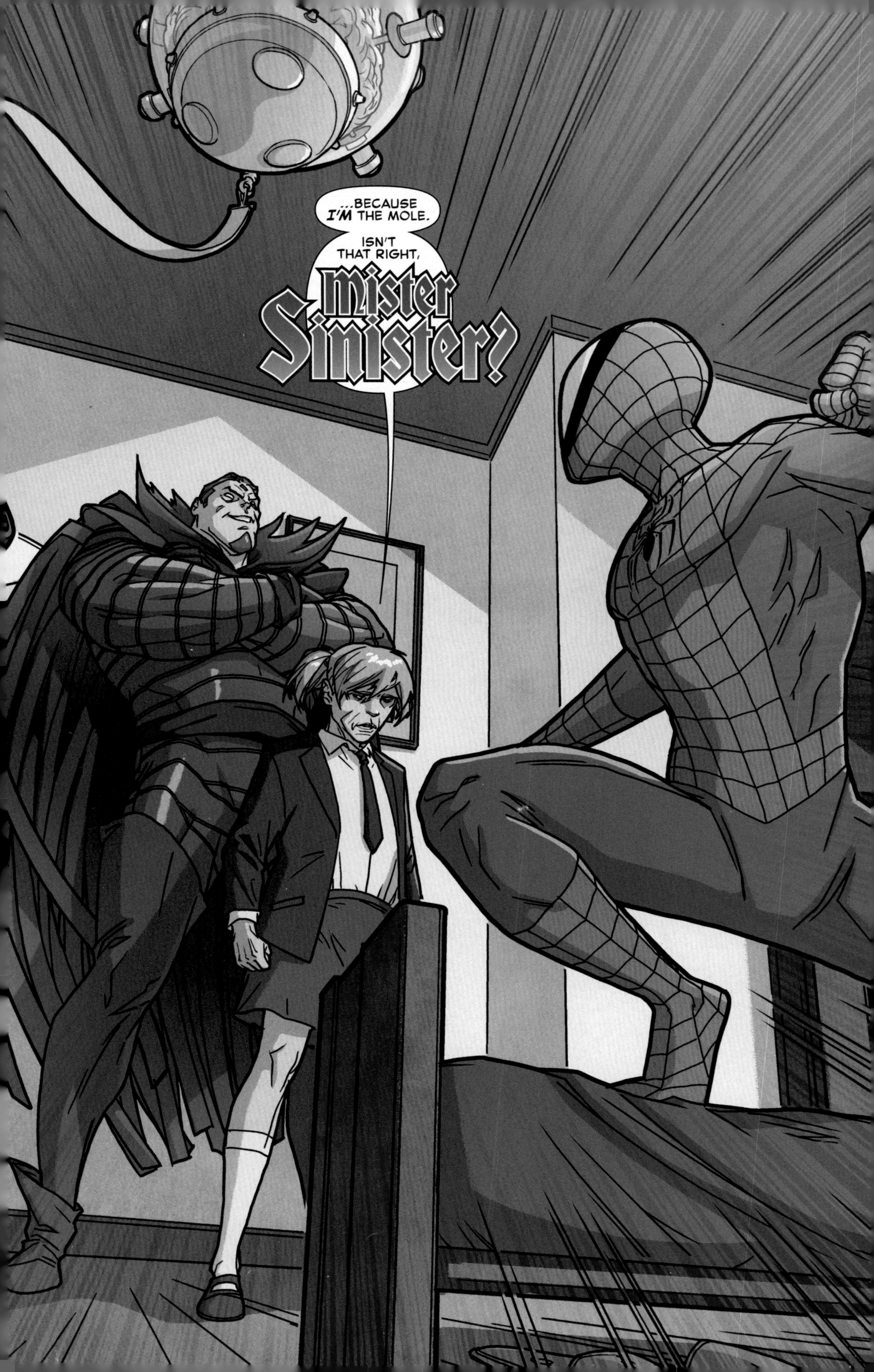
...BECAUSE I'M THE MOLE.
ISN'T THAT RIGHT,
MISTER SINISTER?

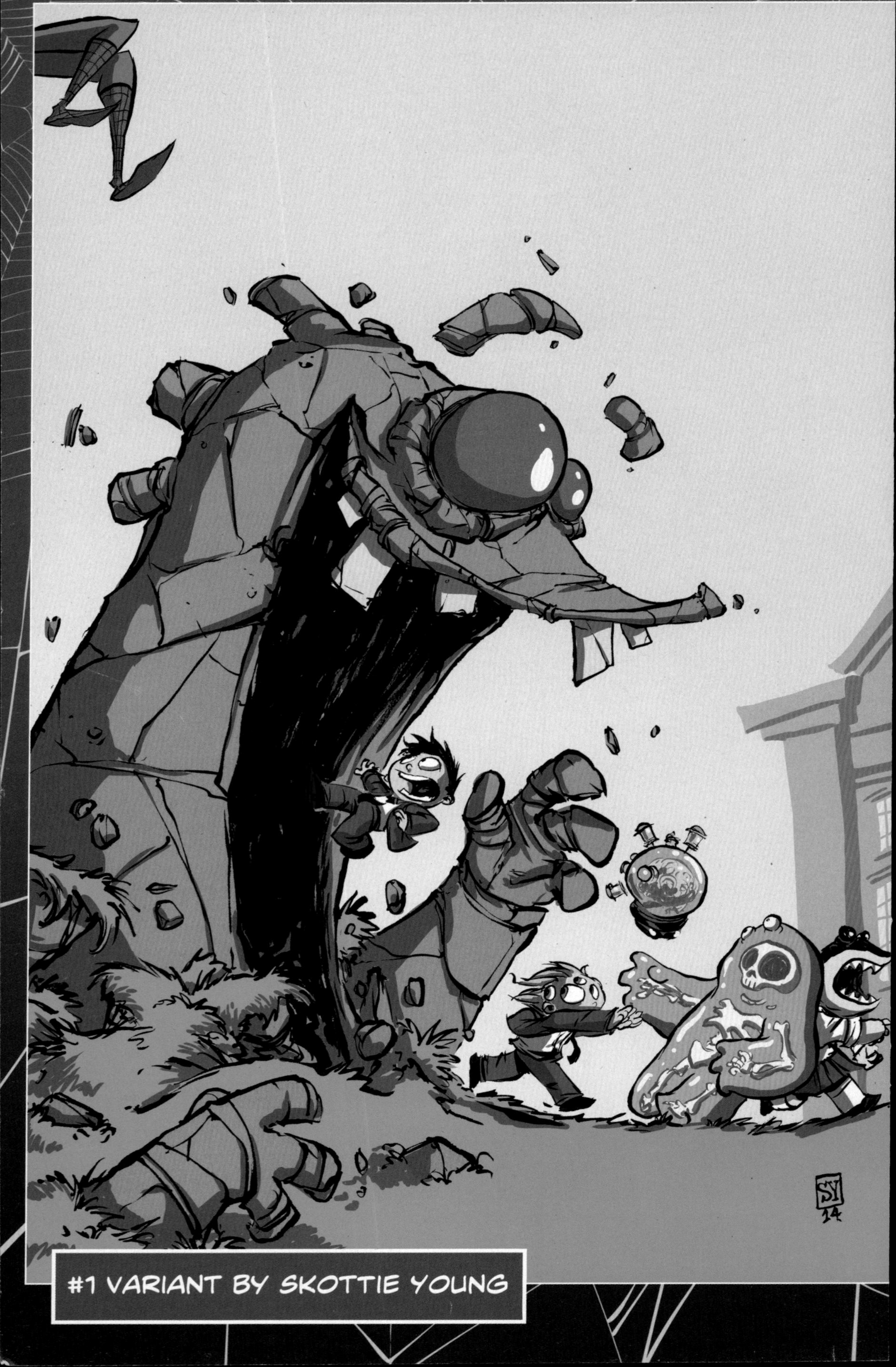

#1 VARIANT BY SKOTTIE YOUNG

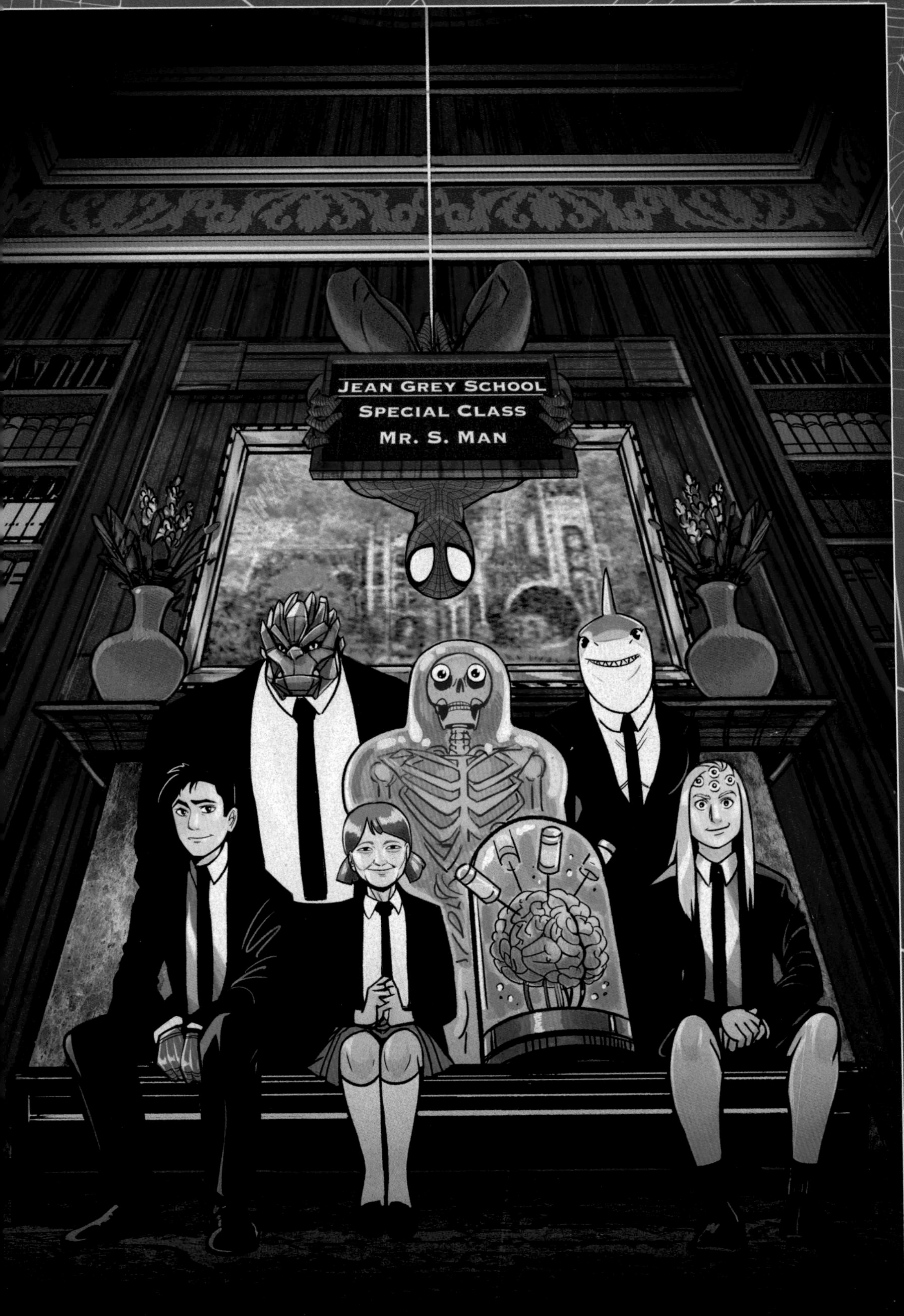
JEAN GREY SCHOOL
SPECIAL CLASS
MR. S. MAN

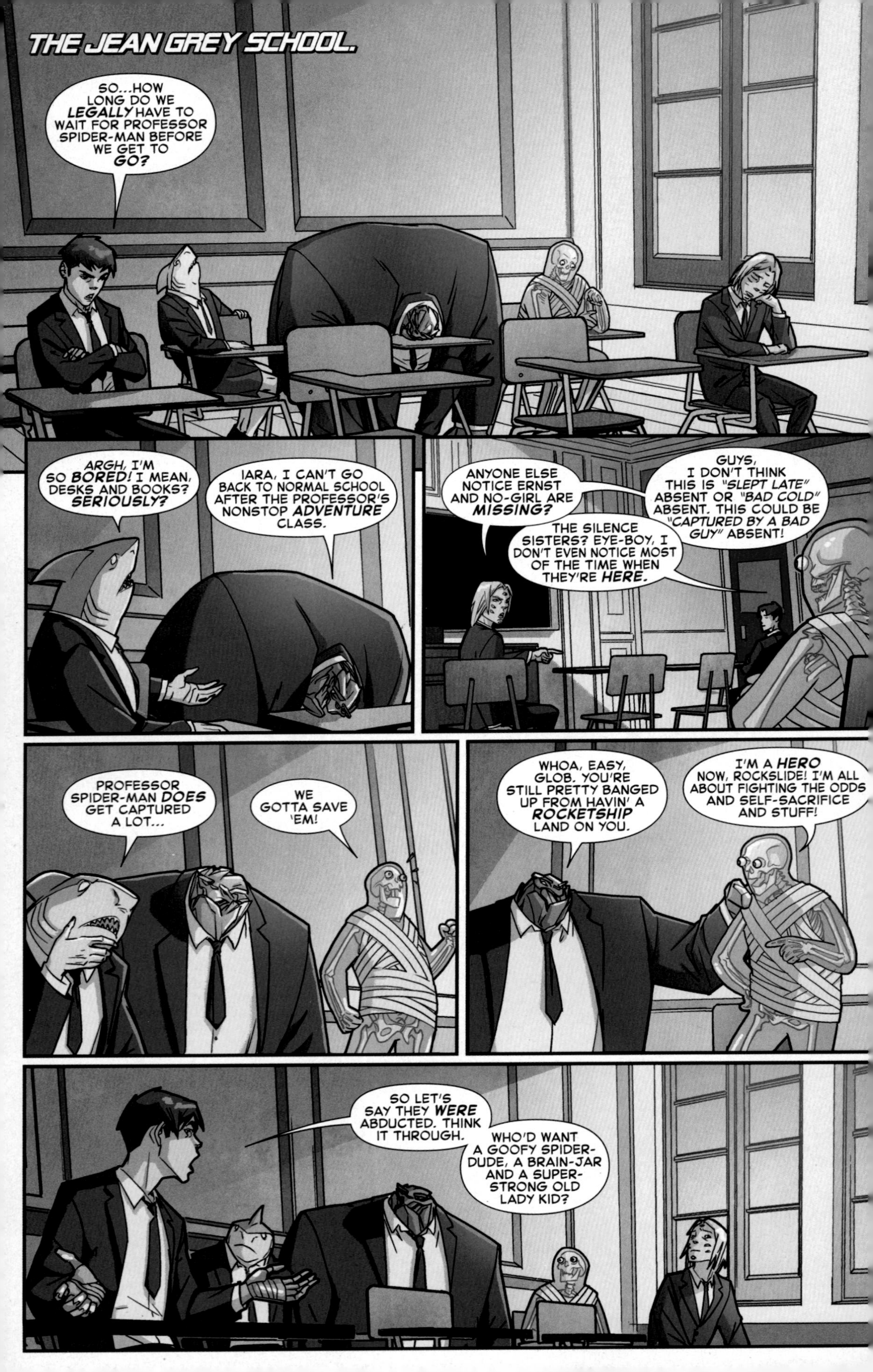
THE JEAN GREY SCHOOL.
SO...HOW LONG DO WE LEGALLY HAVE TO WAIT FOR PROFESSOR SPIDER-MAN BEFORE WE GET TO GO?
ARGH, I'M SO BORED! I MEAN, DESKS AND BOOKS? SERIOUSLY?
IARA, I CAN'T GO BACK TO NORMAL SCHOOL AFTER THE PROFESSOR'S NONSTOP ADVENTURE CLASS.
ANYONE ELSE NOTICE ERNST AND NO-GIRL ARE MISSING?
THE SILENCE SISTERS? EYE-BOY, I DON'T EVEN NOTICE MOST OF THE TIME WHEN THEY'RE HERE.
GUYS, I DON'T THINK THIS IS "SLEPT LATE" ABSENT OR "BAD COLD" ABSENT. THIS COULD BE "CAPTURED BY A BAD GUY" ABSENT!
PROFESSOR SPIDER-MAN DOES GET CAPTURED A LOT...
WE GOTTA SAVE 'EM!
WHOA, EASY, GLOB. YOU'RE STILL PRETTY BANGED UP FROM HAVIN' A ROCKETSHIP LAND ON YOU.
I'M A HERO NOW, ROCKSLIDE! I'M ALL ABOUT FIGHTING THE ODDS AND SELF-SACRIFICE AND STUFF!
SO LET'S SAY THEY WERE ABDUCTED. THINK IT THROUGH.
WHO'D WANT A GOOFY SPIDER-DUDE, A BRAIN-JAR AND A SUPER-STRONG OLD LADY KID?

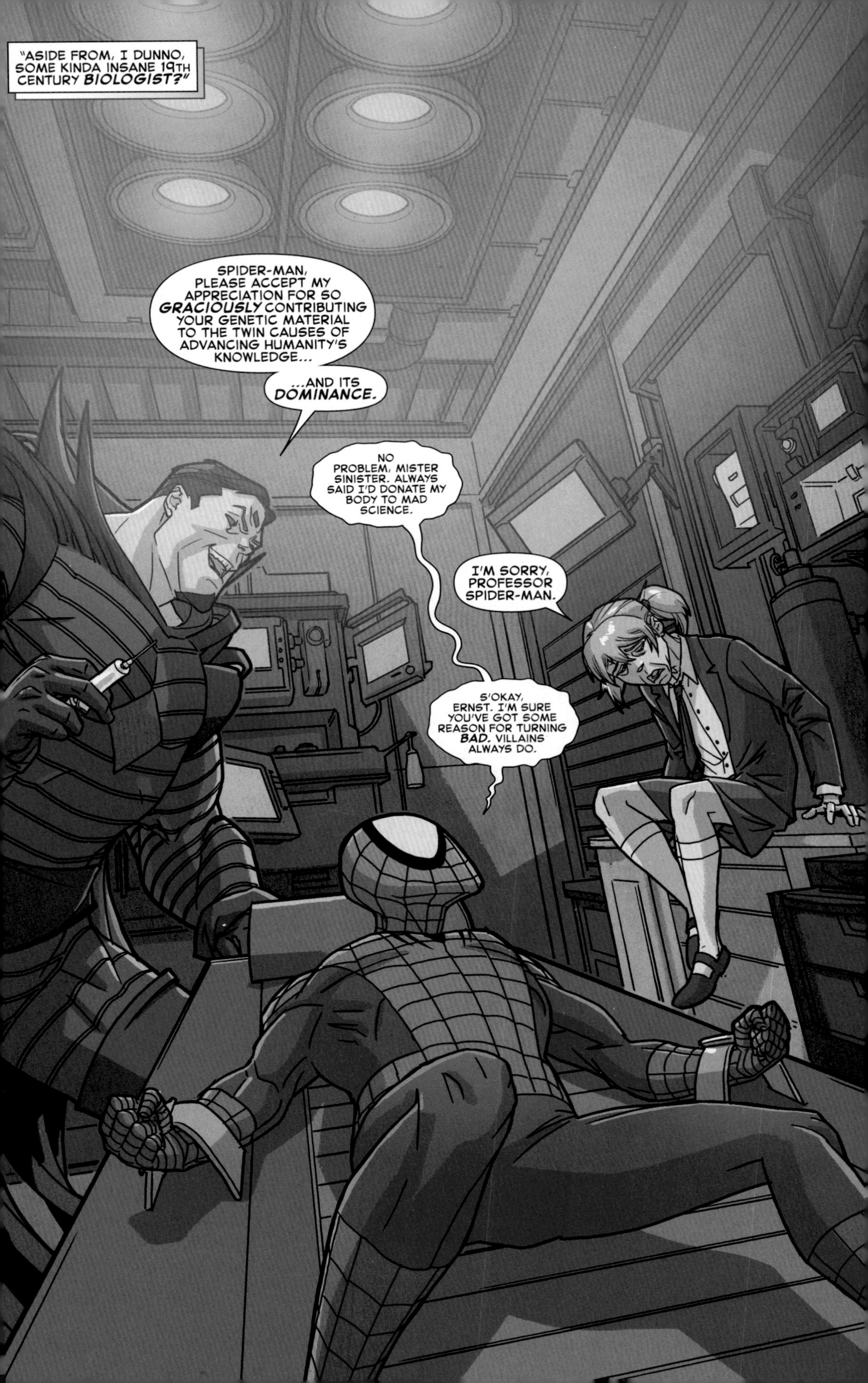
"ASIDE FROM, I DUNNO, SOME KINDA INSANE 19TH CENTURY BIOLOGIST?"
SPIDER-MAN, PLEASE ACCEPT MY APPRECIATION FOR SO GRACIOUSLY CONTRIBUTING YOUR GENETIC MATERIAL TO THE TWIN CAUSES OF ADVANCING HUMANITY'S KNOWLEDGE...
...AND ITS DOMINANCE.
NO PROBLEM, MISTER SINISTER. ALWAYS SAID I'D DONATE MY BODY TO MAD SCIENCE.
I'M SORRY, PROFESSOR SPIDER-MAN.
S'OKAY, ERNST. I'M SURE YOU'VE GOT SOME REASON FOR TURNING BAD. VILLAINS ALWAYS DO.

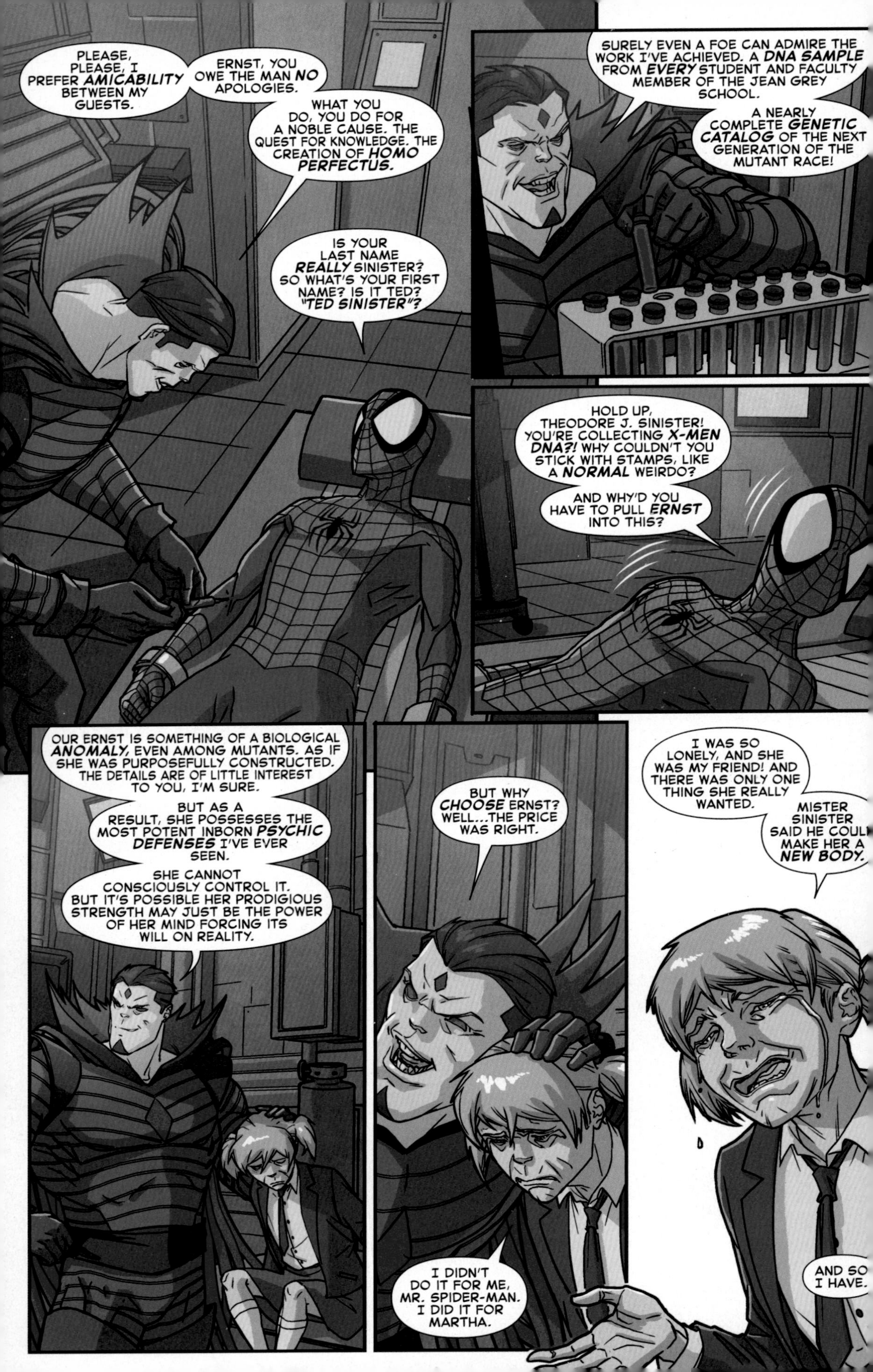
PLEASE, PLEASE, I PREFER AMICABILITY BETWEEN MY GUESTS.
ERNST, YOU OWE THE MAN NO APOLOGIES.
WHAT YOU DO, YOU DO FOR A NOBLE CAUSE. THE QUEST FOR KNOWLEDGE. THE CREATION OF HOMO PERFECTUS.
IS YOUR LAST NAME REALLY SINISTER? SO WHAT'S YOUR FIRST NAME? IS IT TED? "TED SINISTER"?
SURELY EVEN A FOE CAN ADMIRE THE WORK I'VE ACHIEVED. A DNA SAMPLE FROM EVERY STUDENT AND FACULTY MEMBER OF THE JEAN GREY SCHOOL.
A NEARLY COMPLETE GENETIC CATALOG OF THE NEXT GENERATION OF THE MUTANT RACE!
HOLD UP, THEODORE J. SINISTER! YOU'RE COLLECTING X-MEN DNA?! WHY COULDN'T YOU STICK WITH STAMPS, LIKE A NORMAL WEIRDO?
AND WHY'D YOU HAVE TO PULL ERNST INTO THIS?
OUR ERNST IS SOMETHING OF A BIOLOGICAL ANOMALY, EVEN AMONG MUTANTS. AS IF SHE WAS PURPOSEFULLY CONSTRUCTED. THE DETAILS ARE OF LITTLE INTEREST TO YOU, I'M SURE.
BUT AS A RESULT, SHE POSSESSES THE MOST POTENT INBORN PSYCHIC DEFENSES I'VE EVER SEEN.
SHE CANNOT CONSCIOUSLY CONTROL IT. BUT IT'S POSSIBLE HER PRODIGIOUS STRENGTH MAY JUST BE THE POWER OF HER MIND FORCING ITS WILL ON REALITY.
BUT WHY CHOOSE ERNST? WELL... THE PRICE WAS RIGHT.
I DIDN'T DO IT FOR ME, MR. SPIDER-MAN. I DID IT FOR MARTHA.
I WAS SO LONELY, AND SHE WAS MY FRIEND! AND THERE WAS ONLY ONE THING SHE REALLY WANTED.
MISTER SINISTER SAID HE COUL MAKE HER A NEW BODY.
AND SO I HAVE.

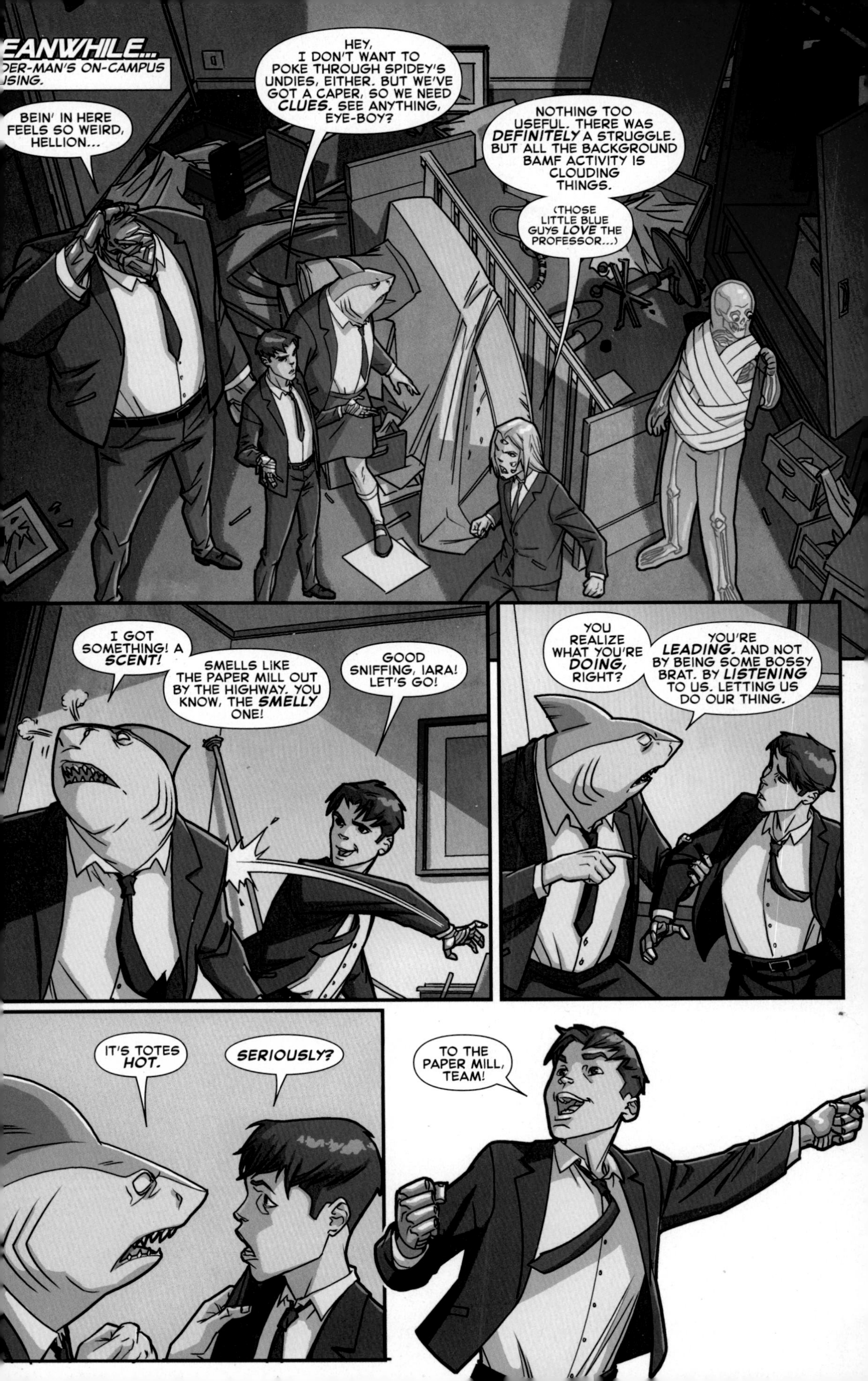
EANWHILE...
DER-MAN'S ON-CAMPUS
USING.
BEIN' IN HERE FEELS SO WEIRD, HELLION...
HEY, I DON'T WANT TO POKE THROUGH SPIDEY'S UNDIES, EITHER. BUT WE'VE GOT A CAPER, SO WE NEED CLUES. SEE ANYTHING, EYE-BOY?
NOTHING TOO USEFUL. THERE WAS DEFINITELY A STRUGGLE. BUT ALL THE BACKGROUND BAMF ACTIVITY IS CLOUDING THINGS.
(THOSE LITTLE BLUE GUYS LOVE THE PROFESSOR...)
I GOT SOMETHING! A SCENT!
SMELLS LIKE THE PAPER MILL OUT BY THE HIGHWAY. YOU KNOW, THE SMELLY ONE!
GOOD SNIFFING, IARA! LET'S GO!
YOU REALIZE WHAT YOU'RE DOING, RIGHT?
YOU'RE LEADING. AND NOT BY BEING SOME BOSSY BRAT. BY LISTENING TO US. LETTING US DO OUR THING.
IT'S TOTES HOT.
SERIOUSLY?
TO THE PAPER MILL, TEAM!

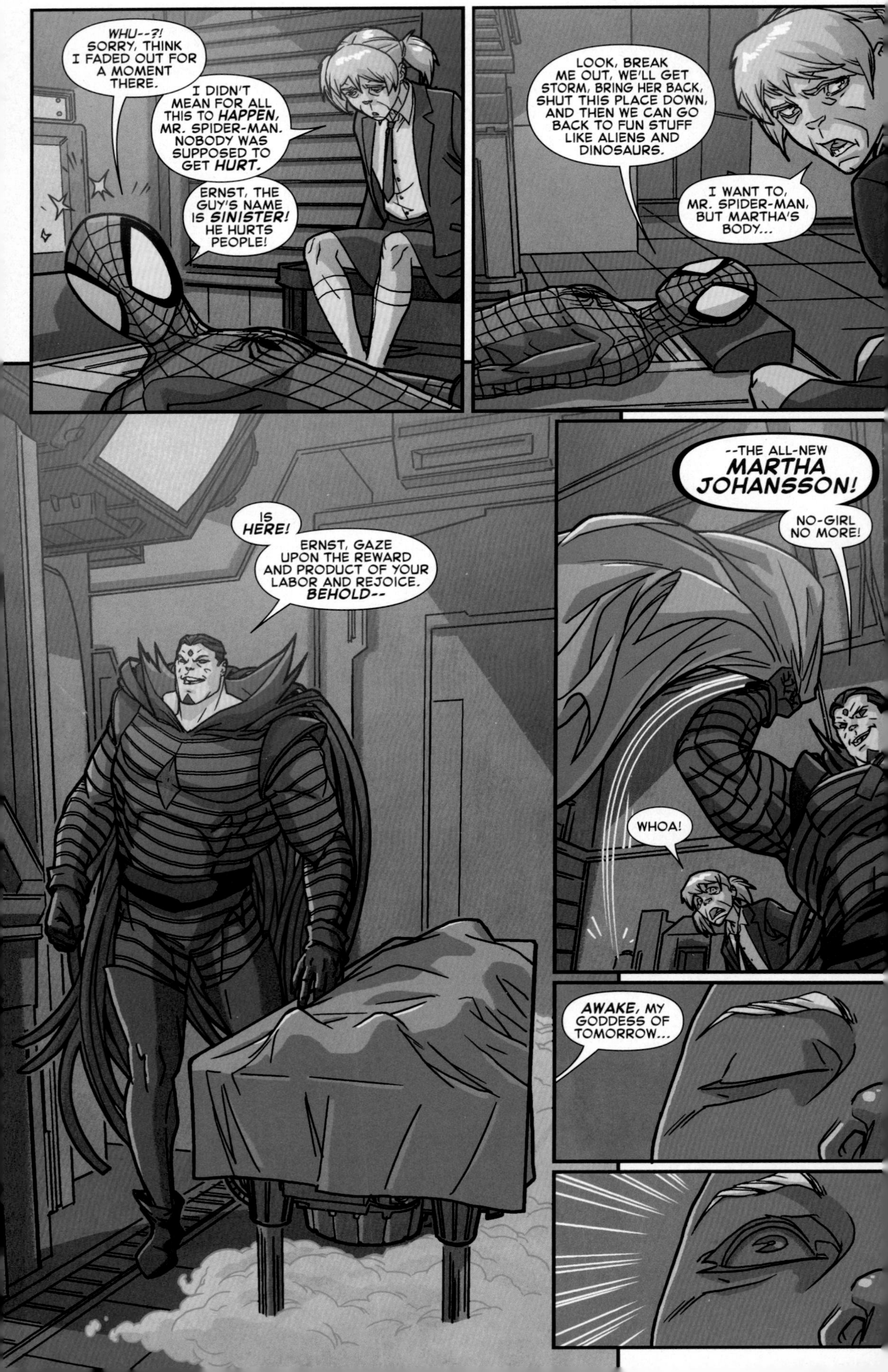
WHU--?! SORRY, THINK I FADED OUT FOR A MOMENT THERE.
I DIDN'T MEAN FOR ALL THIS TO HAPPEN, MR. SPIDER-MAN. NOBODY WAS SUPPOSED TO GET HURT.
ERNST, THE GUY'S NAME IS SINISTER! HE HURTS PEOPLE!
LOOK, BREAK ME OUT, WE'LL GET STORM, BRING HER BACK, SHUT THIS PLACE DOWN, AND THEN WE CAN GO BACK TO FUN STUFF LIKE ALIENS AND DINOSAURS.
I WANT TO, MR. SPIDER-MAN, BUT MARTHA'S BODY...
IS HERE!
ERNST, GAZE UPON THE REWARD AND PRODUCT OF YOUR LABOR AND REJOICE. BEHOLD--
--THE ALL-NEW MARTHA JOHANSSON!
NO-GIRL NO MORE!
WHOA!
AWAKE, MY GODDESS OF TOMORROW...

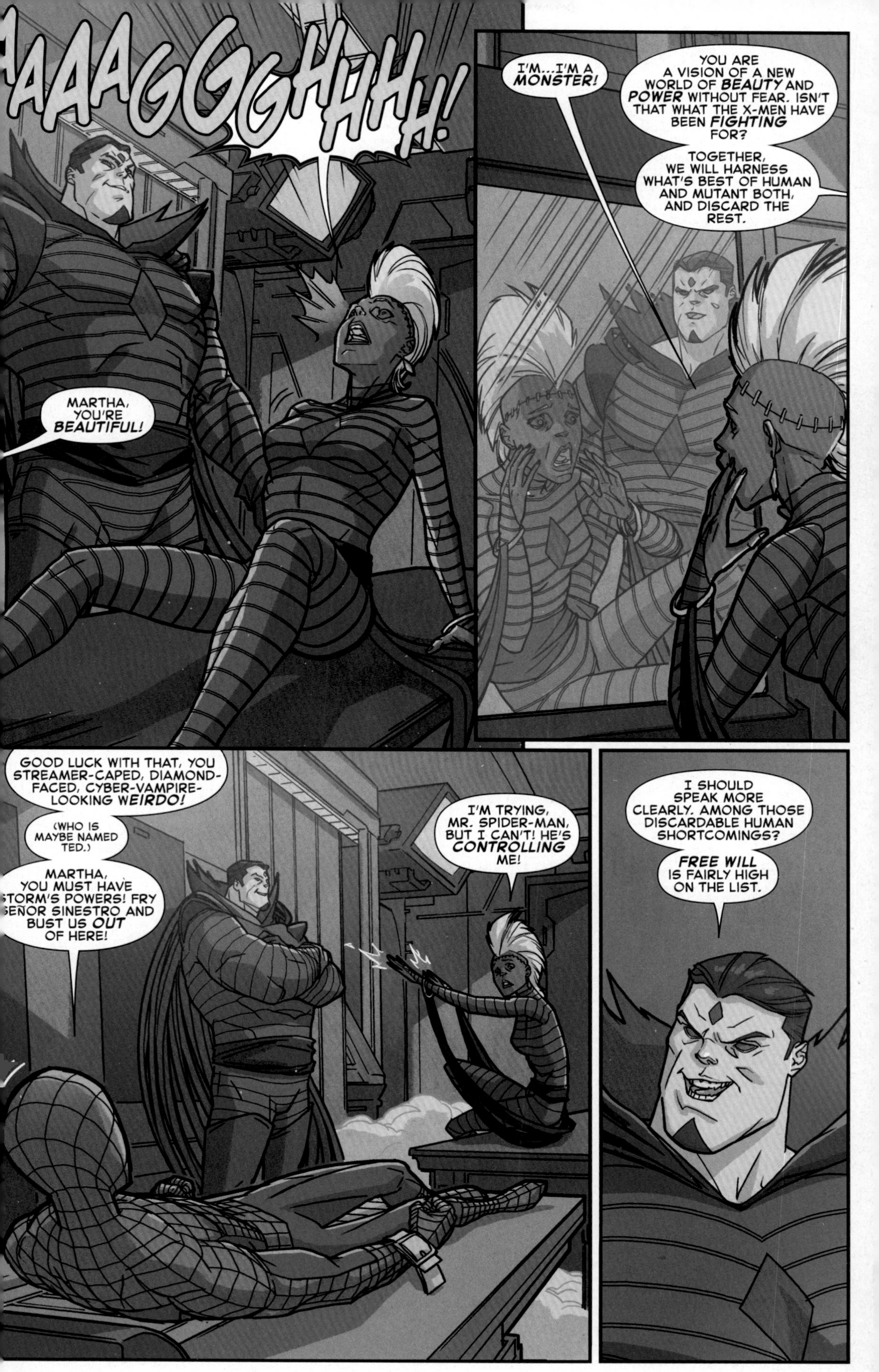
AAAGGGHHHH!
MARTHA, YOU'RE BEAUTIFUL!
I'M...I'M A MONSTER!
YOU ARE A VISION OF A NEW WORLD OF BEAUTY AND POWER WITHOUT FEAR. ISN'T THAT WHAT THE X-MEN HAVE BEEN FIGHTING FOR?
TOGETHER, WE WILL HARNESS WHAT'S BEST OF HUMAN AND MUTANT BOTH, AND DISCARD THE REST.
GOOD LUCK WITH THAT, YOU STREAMER-CAPED, DIAMOND-FACED, CYBER-VAMPIRE-LOOKING WEIRDO!
(WHO IS MAYBE NAMED TED.)
MARTHA, YOU MUST HAVE STORM'S POWERS! FRY SEÑOR SINESTRO AND BUST US OUT OF HERE!
I'M TRYING, MR. SPIDER-MAN, BUT I CAN'T! HE'S CONTROLLING ME!
I SHOULD SPEAK MORE CLEARLY. AMONG THOSE DISCARDABLE HUMAN SHORTCOMINGS?
FREE WILL IS FAIRLY HIGH ON THE LIST.

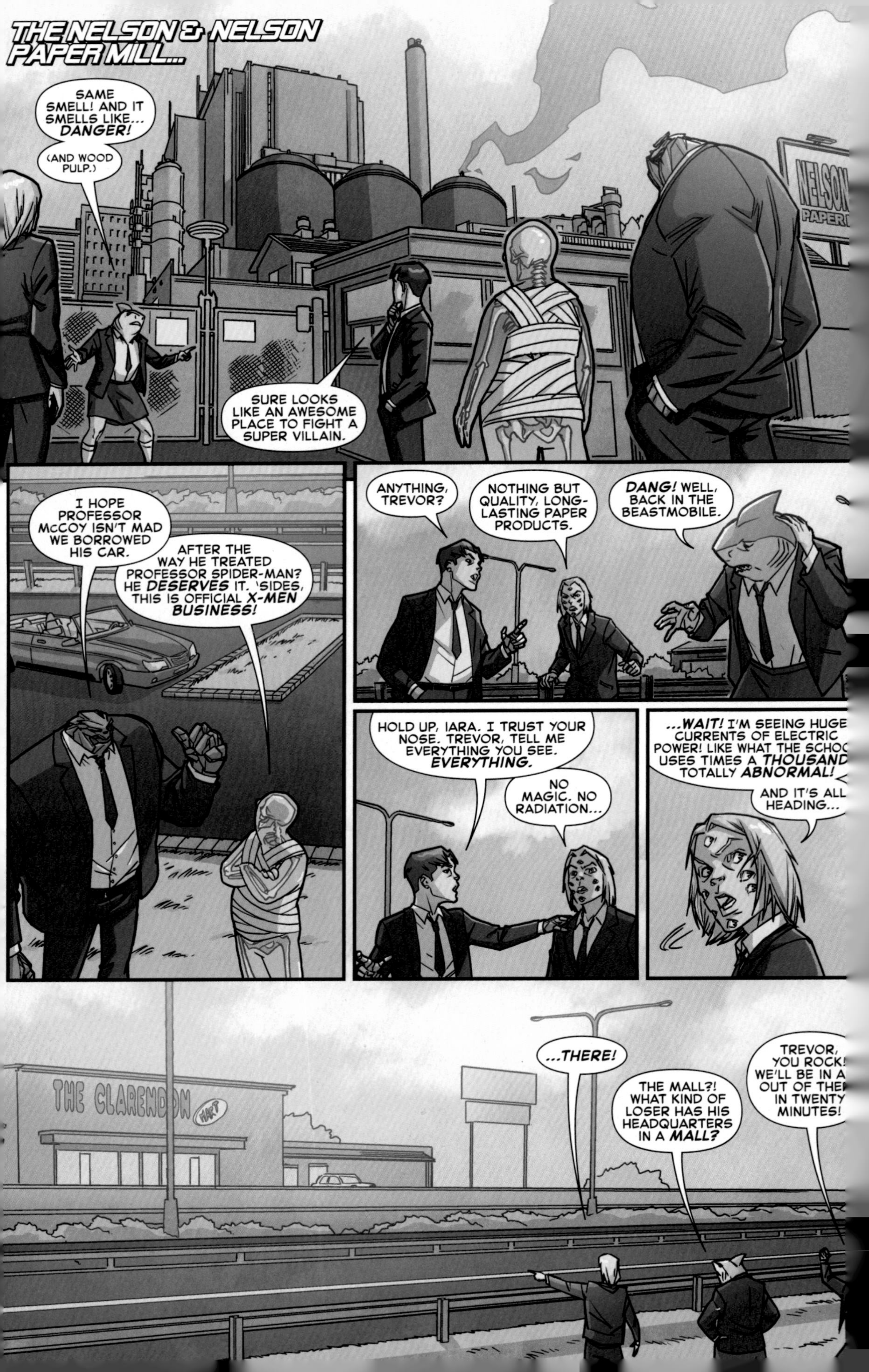
THE NELSON & NELSON PAPER MILL...
SAME SMELL! AND IT SMELLS LIKE... DANGER!
(AND WOOD PULP.)
SURE LOOKS LIKE AN AWESOME PLACE TO FIGHT A SUPER VILLAIN.
NELSON
PAPER
I HOPE PROFESSOR McCOY ISN'T MAD WE BORROWED HIS CAR.
AFTER THE WAY HE TREATED PROFESSOR SPIDER-MAN? HE DESERVES IT. 'SIDES, THIS IS OFFICIAL X-MEN BUSINESS!
ANYTHING, TREVOR?
NOTHING BUT QUALITY, LONG-LASTING PAPER PRODUCTS.
DANG! WELL, BACK IN THE BEASTMOBILE.
HOLD UP, IARA. I TRUST YOUR NOSE. TREVOR, TELL ME EVERYTHING YOU SEE. EVERYTHING.
NO MAGIC. NO RADIATION...
...WAIT! I'M SEEING HUGE CURRENTS OF ELECTRIC POWER! LIKE WHAT THE SCHOO USES TIMES A THOUSAND TOTALLY ABNORMAL!
AND IT'S ALL HEADING...
THE CLARENDON
...THERE!
THE MALL?! WHAT KIND OF LOSER HAS HIS HEADQUARTERS IN A MALL?
TREVOR, YOU ROCK! WE'LL BE IN A OUT OF THE IN TWENTY MINUTES!

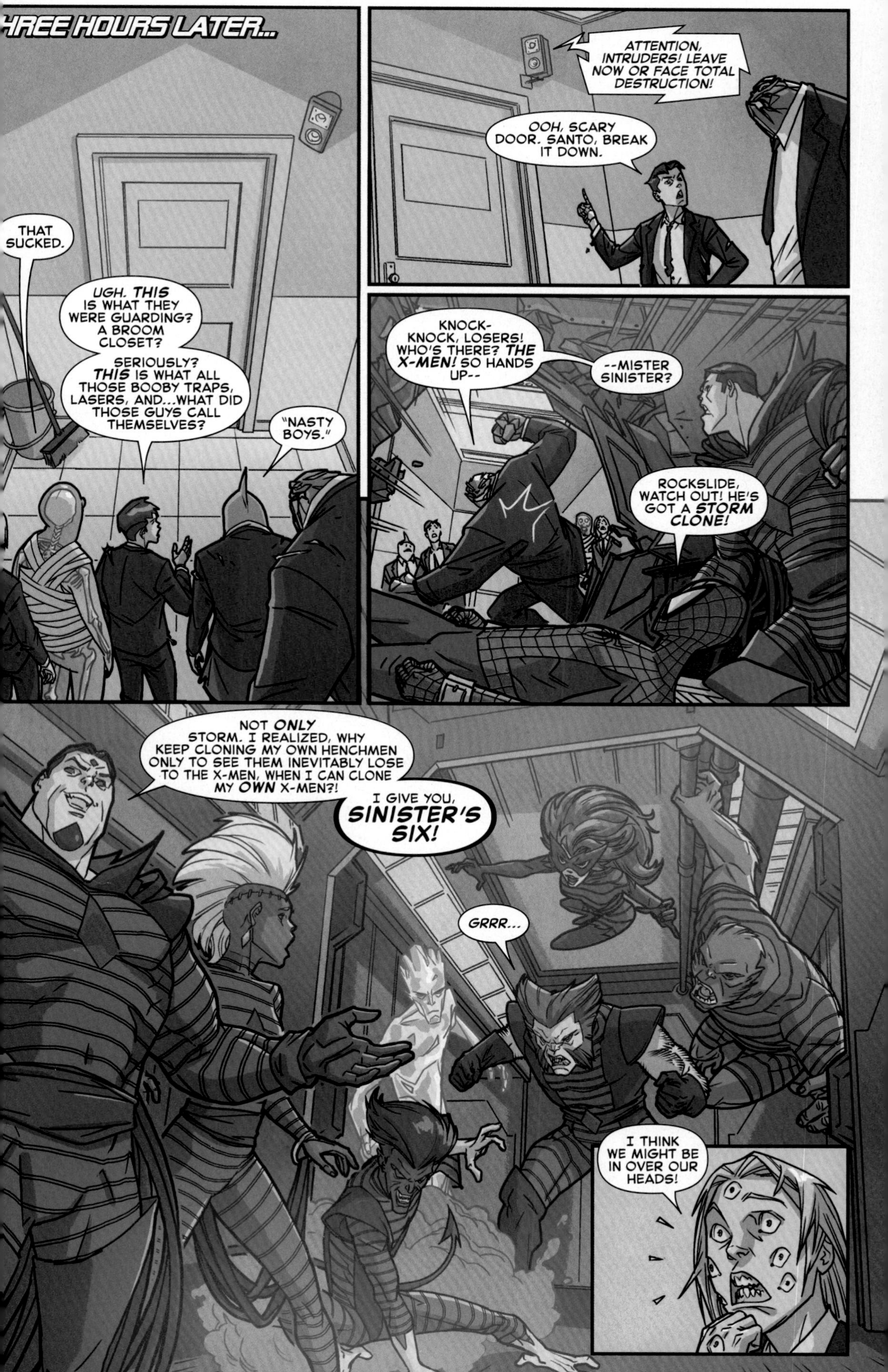

THREE HOURS LATER...
THAT SUCKED.
UGH. THIS IS WHAT THEY WERE GUARDING? A BROOM CLOSET?
SERIOUSLY? THIS IS WHAT ALL THOSE BOOBY TRAPS, LASERS, AND...WHAT DID THOSE GUYS CALL THEMSELVES?
"NASTY BOYS."
ATTENTION, INTRUDERS! LEAVE NOW OR FACE TOTAL DESTRUCTION!
OOH, SCARY DOOR. SANTO, BREAK IT DOWN.
KNOCK-KNOCK, LOSERS! WHO'S THERE? THE X-MEN! SO HANDS UP--
--MISTER SINISTER?
ROCKSLIDE, WATCH OUT! HE'S GOT A STORM CLONE!
NOT ONLY STORM. I REALIZED, WHY KEEP CLONING MY OWN HENCHMEN ONLY TO SEE THEM INEVITABLY LOSE TO THE X-MEN, WHEN I CAN CLONE MY OWN X-MEN?!
I GIVE YOU, SINISTER'S SIX!
GRRR...
I THINK WE MIGHT BE IN OVER OUR HEADS!

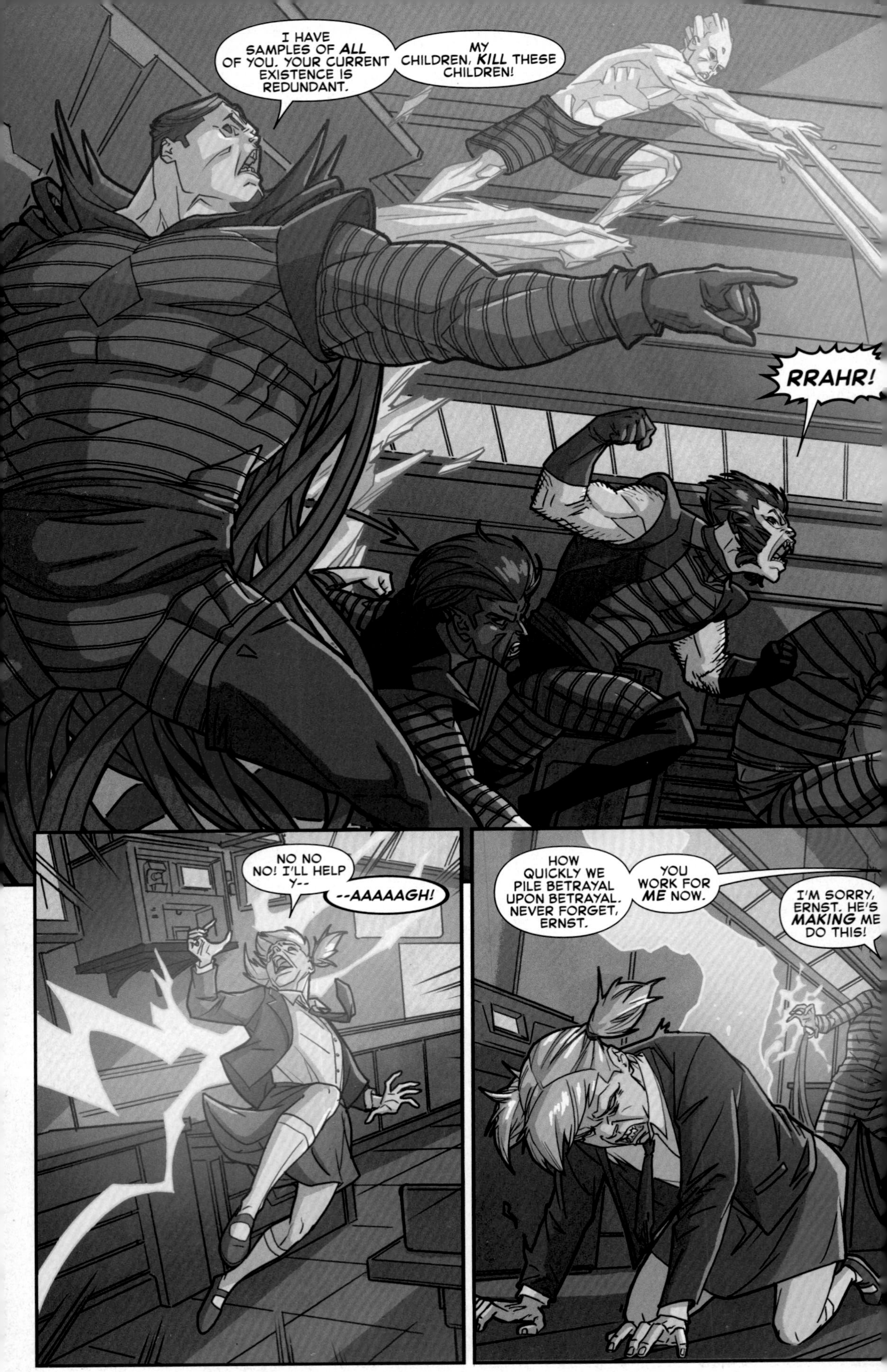
I HAVE SAMPLES OF ALL OF YOU. YOUR CURRENT EXISTENCE IS REDUNDANT.
MY CHILDREN, KILL THESE CHILDREN!
RRAHR!
NO NO NO! I'LL HELP Y--
--AAAAAGH!
HOW QUICKLY WE PILE BETRAYAL UPON BETRAYAL. NEVER FORGET, ERNST.
YOU WORK FOR ME NOW.
I'M SORRY, ERNST. HE'S MAKING ME DO THIS!

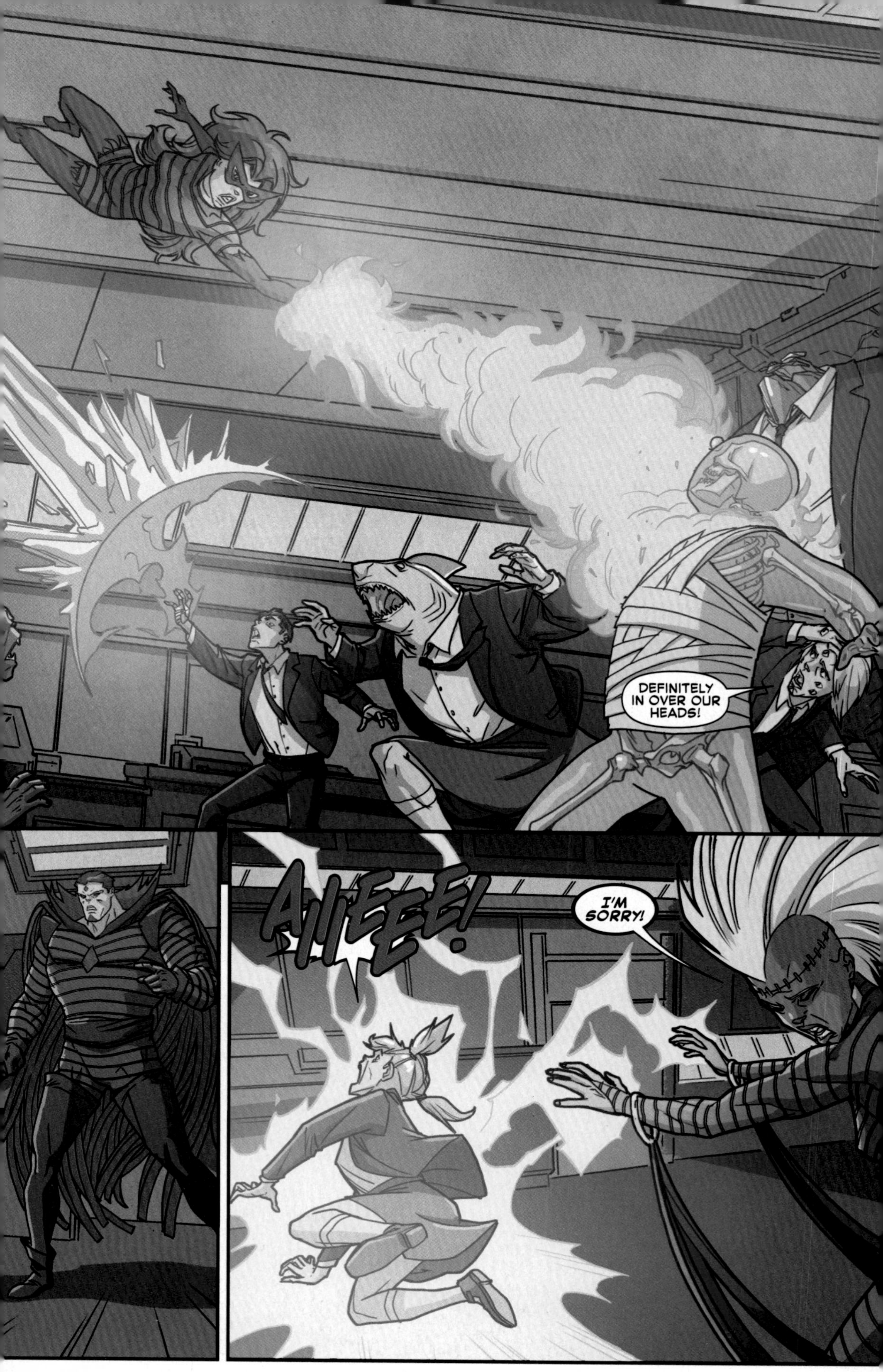

DEFINITELY IN OVER OUR HEADS!
AIIEEE!
I'M SORRY!

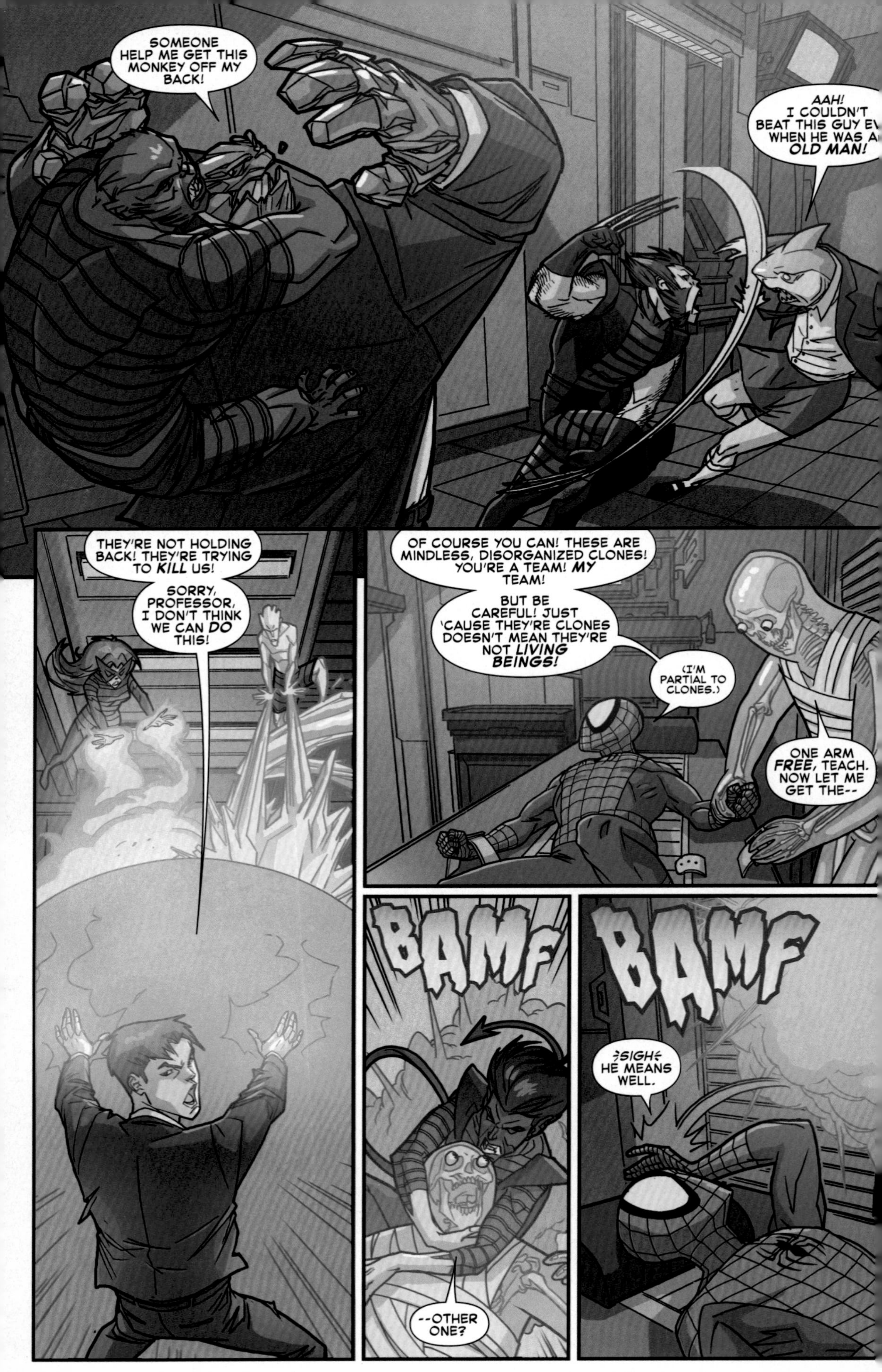
SOMEONE HELP ME GET THIS MONKEY OFF MY BACK!
AAH! I COULDN'T BEAT THIS GUY EV WHEN HE WAS A OLD MAN!
THEY'RE NOT HOLDING BACK! THEY'RE TRYING TO KILL US!
SORRY, PROFESSOR, I DON'T THINK WE CAN DO THIS!
OF COURSE YOU CAN! THESE ARE MINDLESS, DISORGANIZED CLONES! YOU'RE A TEAM! MY TEAM!
BUT BE CAREFUL! JUST 'CAUSE THEY'RE CLONES DOESN'T MEAN THEY'RE NOT LIVING BEINGS!
(I'M PARTIAL TO CLONES.)
ONE ARM FREE, TEACH. NOW LET ME GET THE--
BAMF
BAMF
--OTHER ONE?
SIGH HE MEANS WELL.

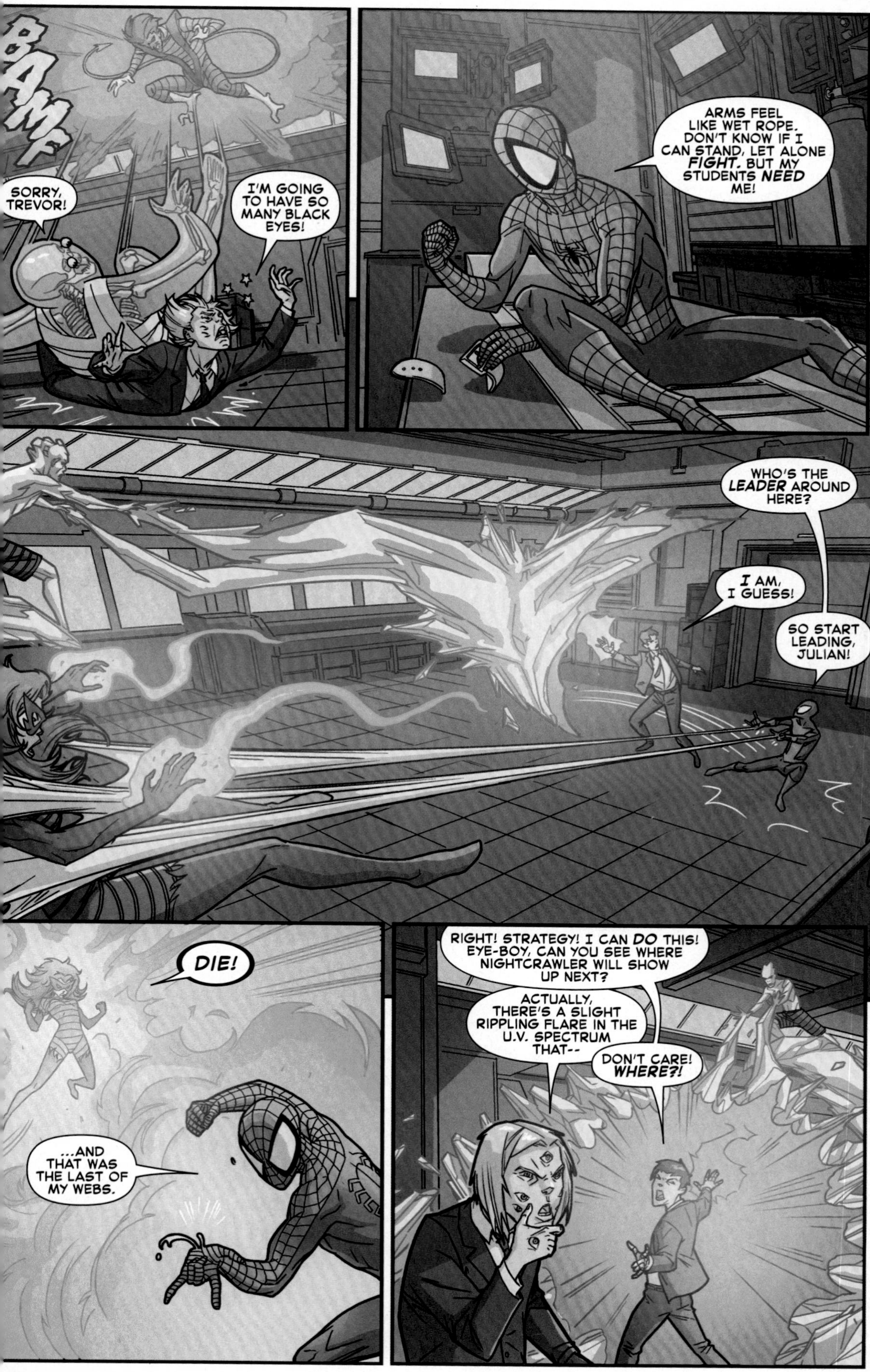
BAMF
SORRY, TREVOR!
I'M GOING TO HAVE SO MANY BLACK EYES!
ARMS FEEL LIKE WET ROPE. DON'T KNOW IF I CAN STAND, LET ALONE FIGHT. BUT MY STUDENTS NEED ME!
WHO'S THE LEADER AROUND HERE?
I AM, I GUESS!
SO START LEADING, JULIAN!
DIE!
...AND THAT WAS THE LAST OF MY WEBS.
RIGHT! STRATEGY! I CAN DO THIS! EYE-BOY, CAN YOU SEE WHERE NIGHTCRAWLER WILL SHOW UP NEXT?
ACTUALLY, THERE'S A SLIGHT RIPPLING FLARE IN THE U.V. SPECTRUM THAT--
DON'T CARE! WHERE?!

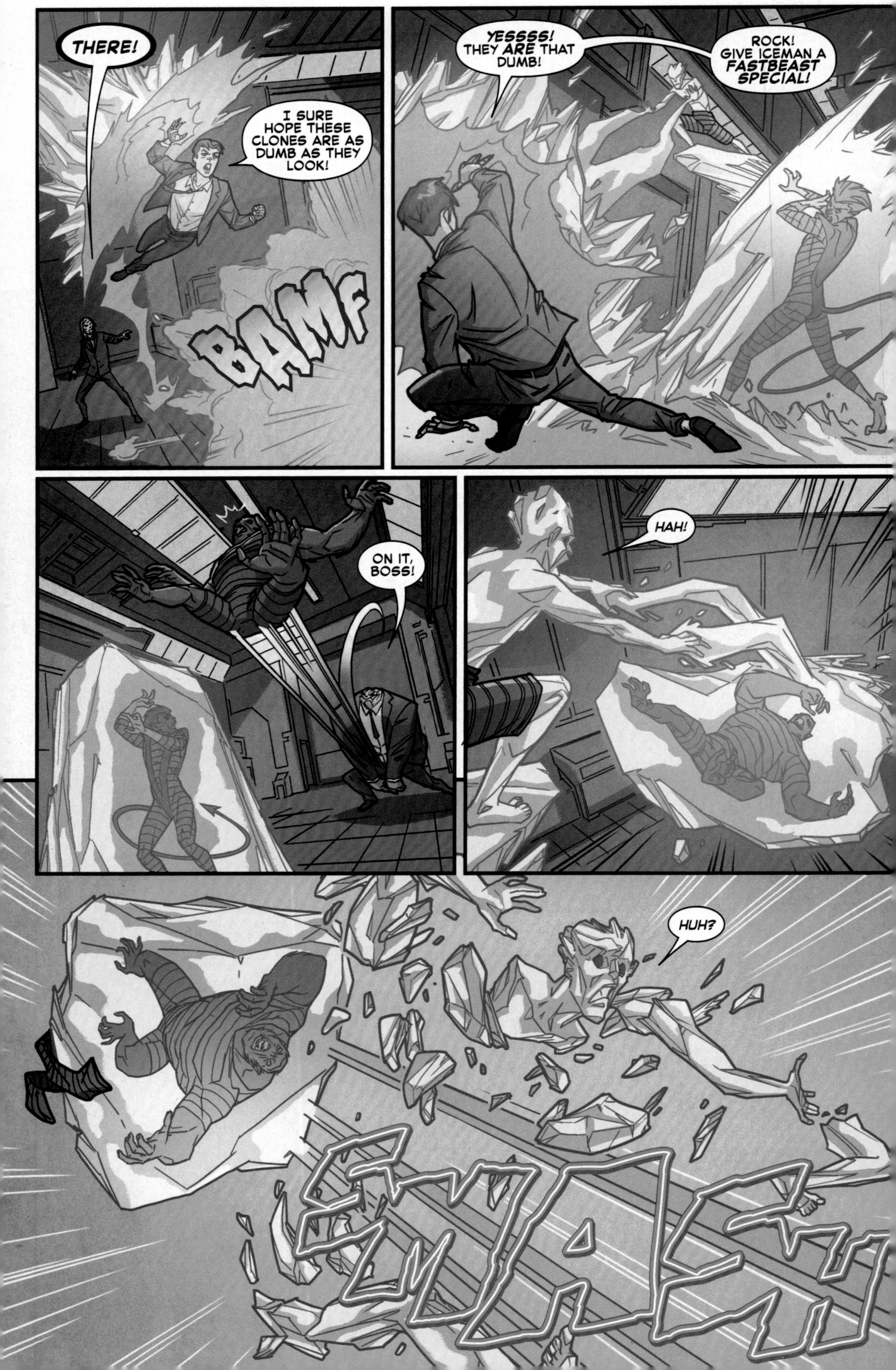
THERE!
I SURE HOPE THESE CLONES ARE AS DUMB AS THEY LOOK!
BAMF
YESSSS! THEY ARE THAT DUMB!
ROCK! GIVE ICEMAN A FASTBEAST SPECIAL!
ON IT, BOSS!
HAH!
HUH?

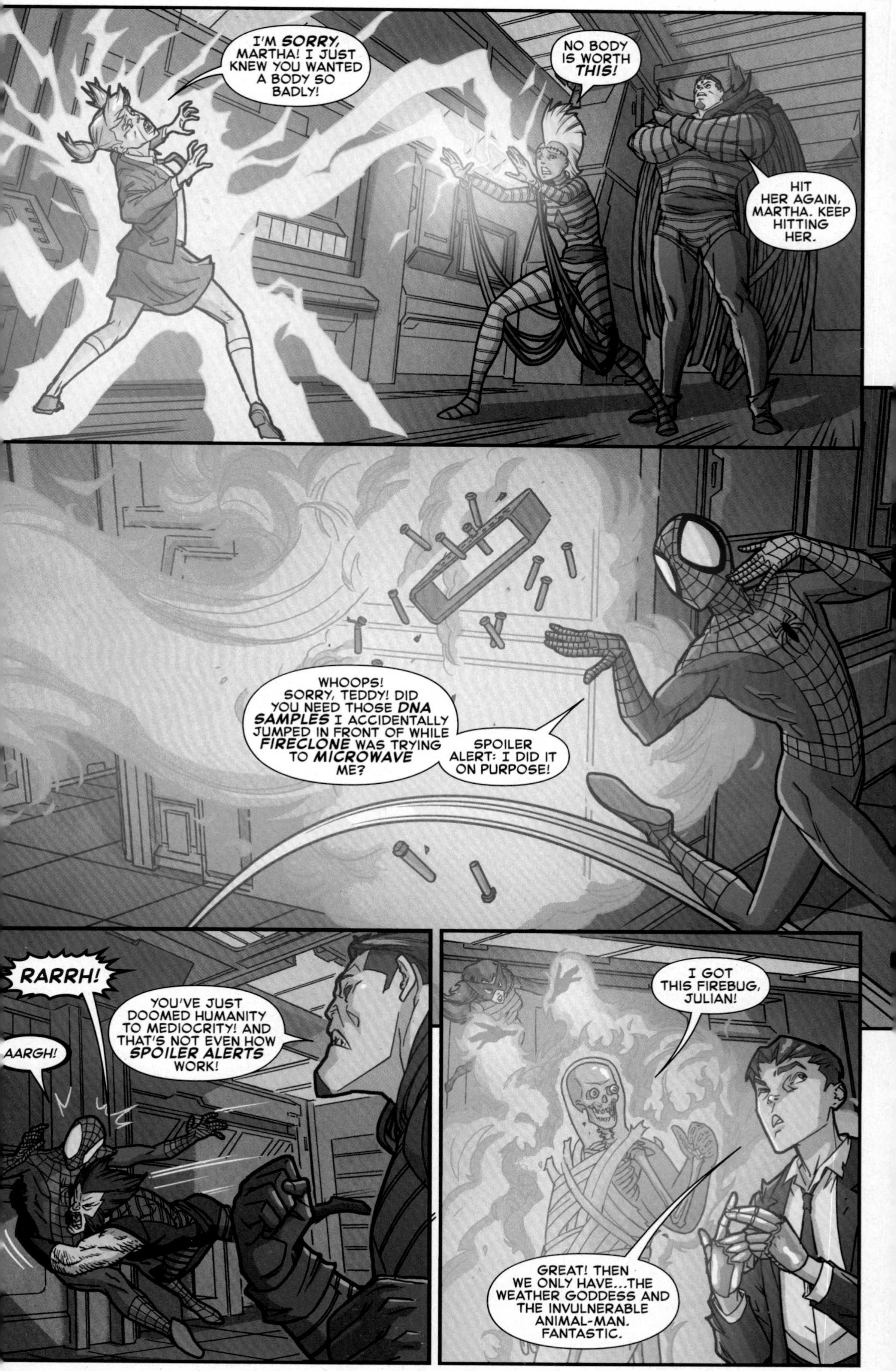
I'M SORRY, MARTHA! I JUST KNEW YOU WANTED A BODY SO BADLY!
NO BODY IS WORTH THIS!
HIT HER AGAIN, MARTHA. KEEP HITTING HER.
WHOOPS! SORRY, TEDDY! DID YOU NEED THOSE DNA SAMPLES I ACCIDENTALLY JUMPED IN FRONT OF WHILE FIRECLONE WAS TRYING TO MICROWAVE ME?
SPOILER ALERT: I DID IT ON PURPOSE!
RARRH!
YOU'VE JUST DOOMED HUMANITY TO MEDIOCRITY! AND THAT'S NOT EVEN HOW SPOILER ALERTS WORK!
AARGH!
I GOT THIS FIREBUG, JULIAN!
GREAT! THEN WE ONLY HAVE...THE WEATHER GODDESS AND THE INVULNERABLE ANIMAL-MAN. FANTASTIC.

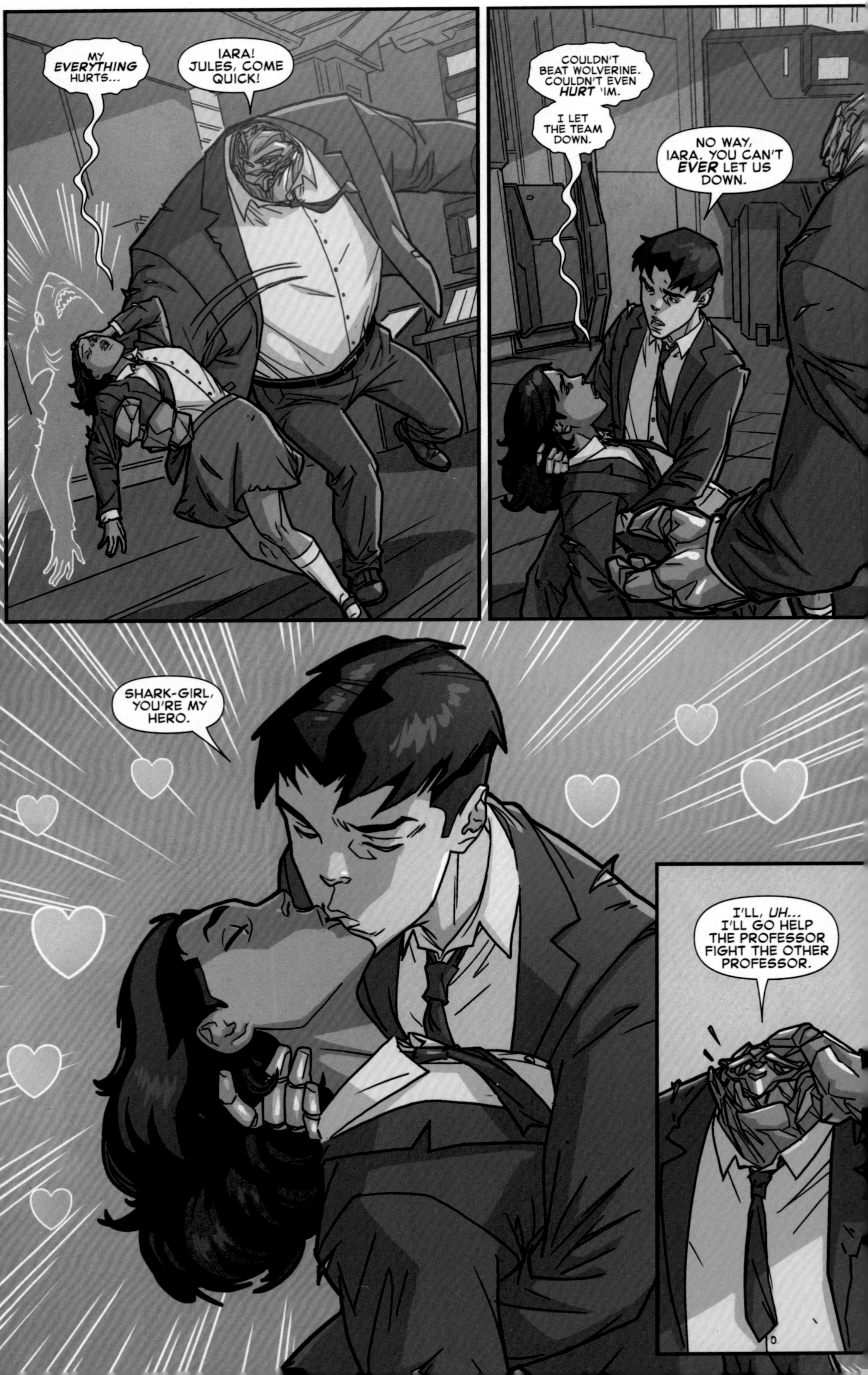
MY *EVERYTHING* HURTS...
IARA! JULES, COME QUICK!
COULDN'T BEAT WOLVERINE. COULDN'T EVEN *HURT* 'IM.
I LET THE TEAM DOWN.
NO WAY, IARA. YOU CAN'T *EVER* LET US DOWN.
SHARK-GIRL, YOU'RE MY HERO.
I'LL, *UH...* I'LL GO HELP THE PROFESSOR FIGHT THE OTHER PROFESSOR.

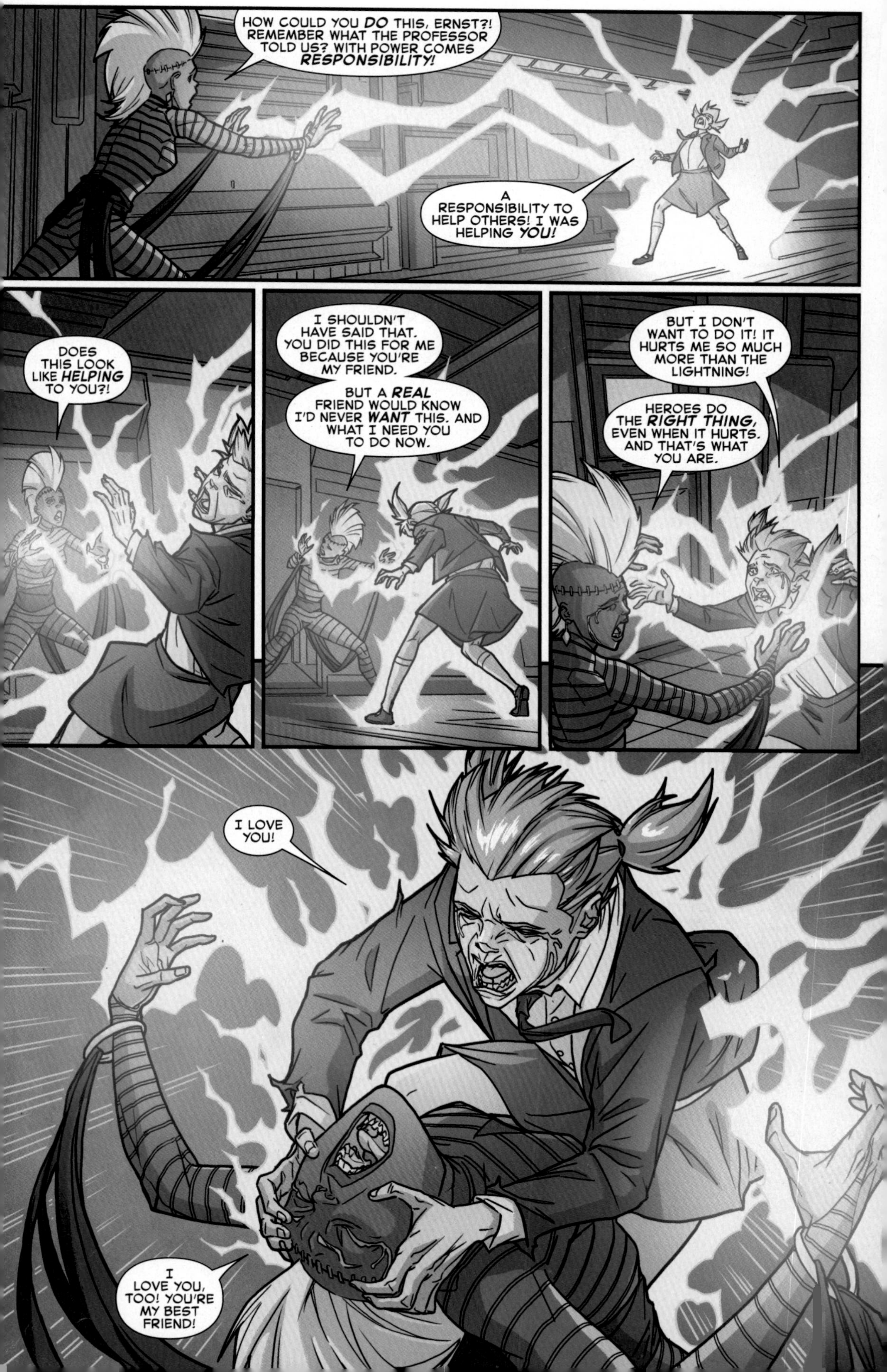
HOW COULD YOU DO THIS, ERNST?! REMEMBER WHAT THE PROFESSOR TOLD US? WITH POWER COMES RESPONSIBILITY!
A RESPONSIBILITY TO HELP OTHERS! I WAS HELPING YOU!
DOES THIS LOOK LIKE HELPING TO YOU?!
I SHOULDN'T HAVE SAID THAT. YOU DID THIS FOR ME BECAUSE YOU'RE MY FRIEND.
BUT A REAL FRIEND WOULD KNOW I'D NEVER WANT THIS. AND WHAT I NEED YOU TO DO NOW.
BUT I DON'T WANT TO DO IT! IT HURTS ME SO MUCH MORE THAN THE LIGHTNING!
HEROES DO THE RIGHT THING, EVEN WHEN IT HURTS. AND THAT'S WHAT YOU ARE.
I LOVE YOU!
I LOVE YOU, TOO! YOU'RE MY BEST FRIEND!

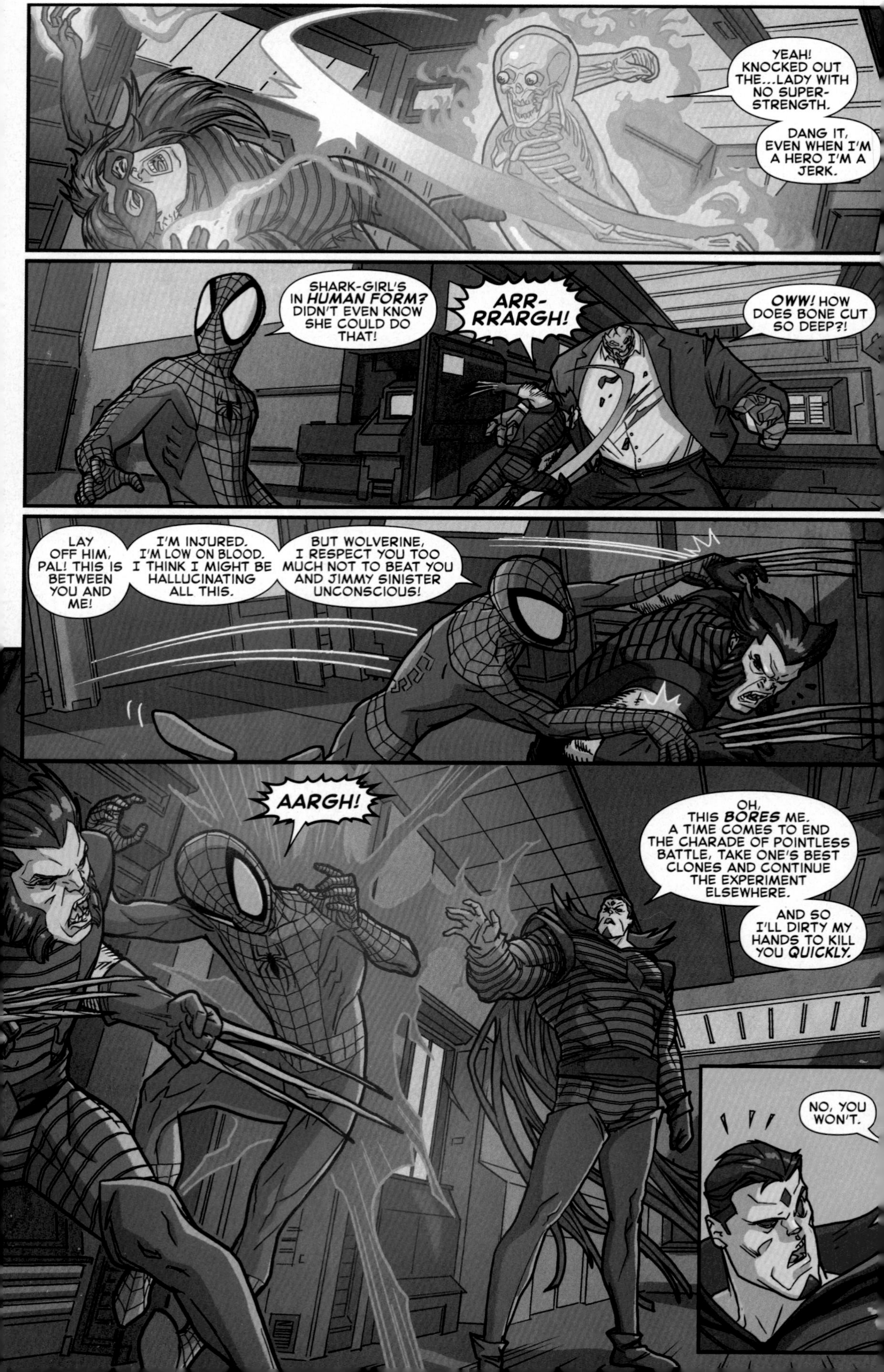
YEAH! KNOCKED OUT THE...LADY WITH NO SUPER-STRENGTH.
DANG IT, EVEN WHEN I'M A HERO I'M A JERK.
SHARK-GIRL'S IN HUMAN FORM? DIDN'T EVEN KNOW SHE COULD DO THAT!
ARR-RRARGH!
OWW! HOW DOES BONE CUT SO DEEP?!
LAY OFF HIM, PAL! THIS IS BETWEEN YOU AND ME!
I'M INJURED. I'M LOW ON BLOOD. I THINK I MIGHT BE HALLUCINATING ALL THIS.
BUT WOLVERINE, I RESPECT YOU TOO MUCH NOT TO BEAT YOU AND JIMMY SINISTER UNCONSCIOUS!
AARGH!
OH, THIS BORES ME. A TIME COMES TO END THE CHARADE OF POINTLESS BATTLE, TAKE ONE'S BEST CLONES AND CONTINUE THE EXPERIMENT ELSEWHERE.
AND SO I'LL DIRTY MY HANDS TO KILL YOU QUICKLY.
NO, YOU WON'T.

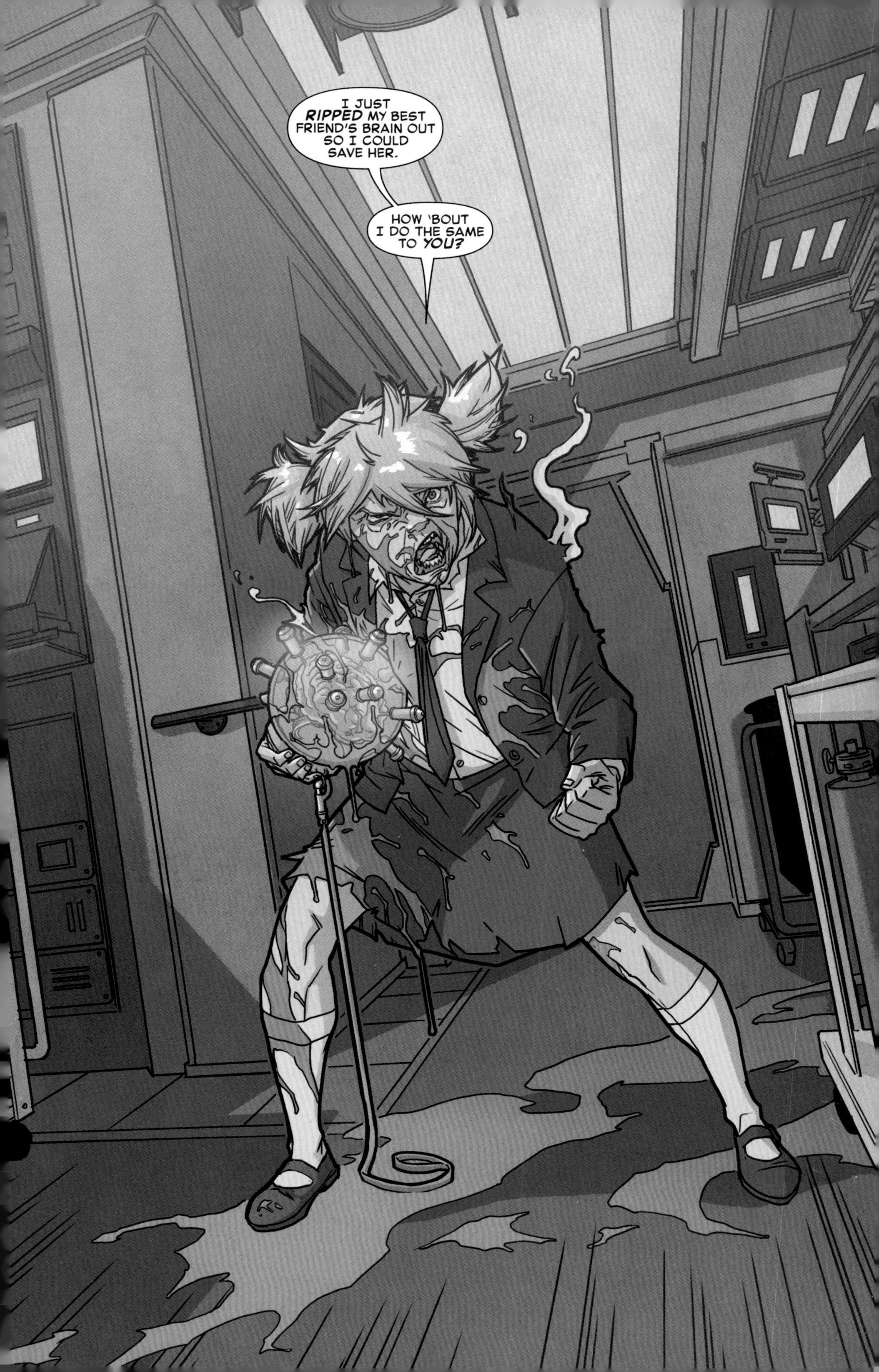
I JUST RIPPED MY BEST FRIEND'S BRAIN OUT SO I COULD SAVE HER.
HOW 'BOUT I DO THE SAME TO YOU?

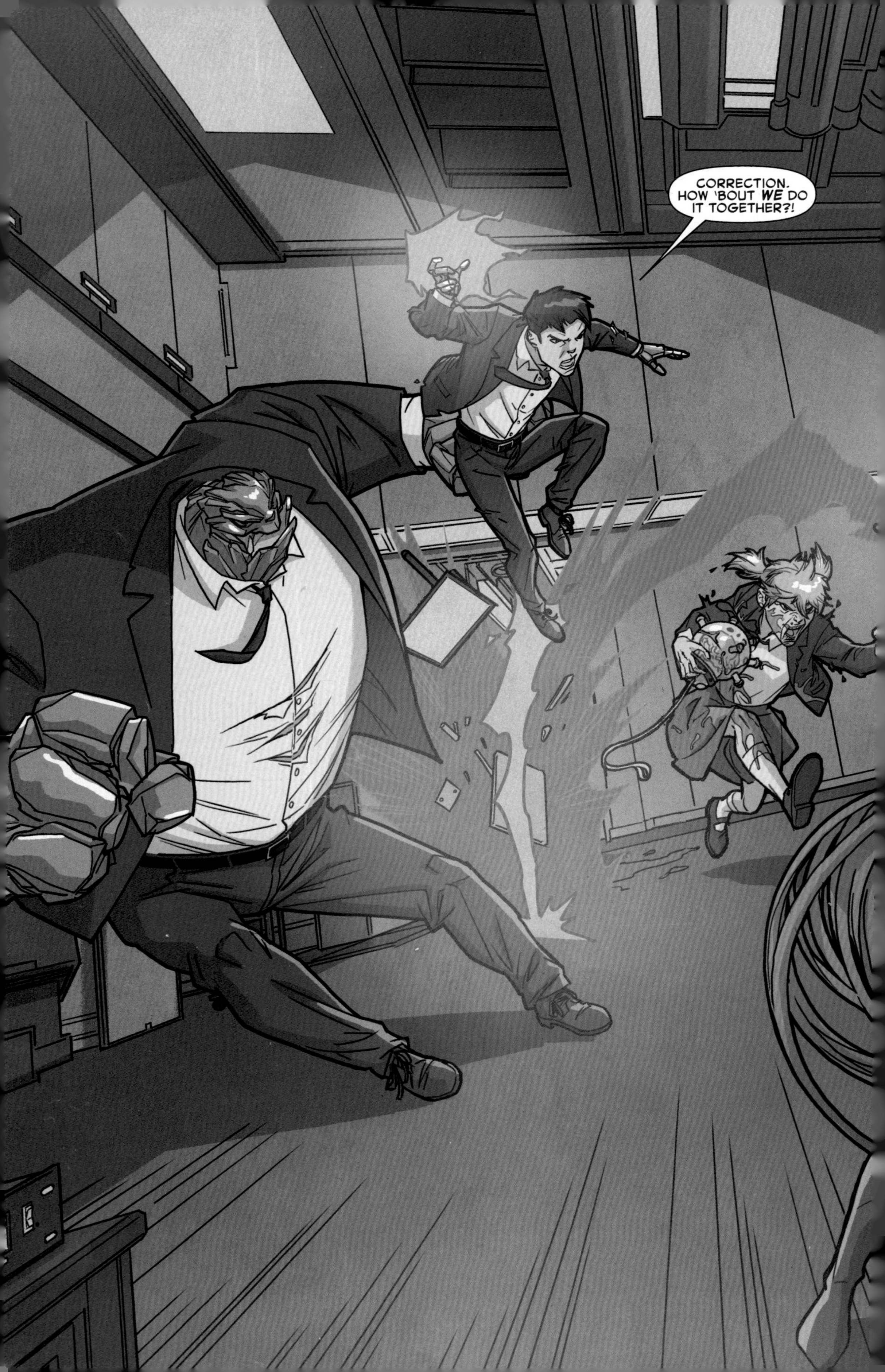
CORRECTION. HOW 'BOUT WE DO IT TOGETHER?!

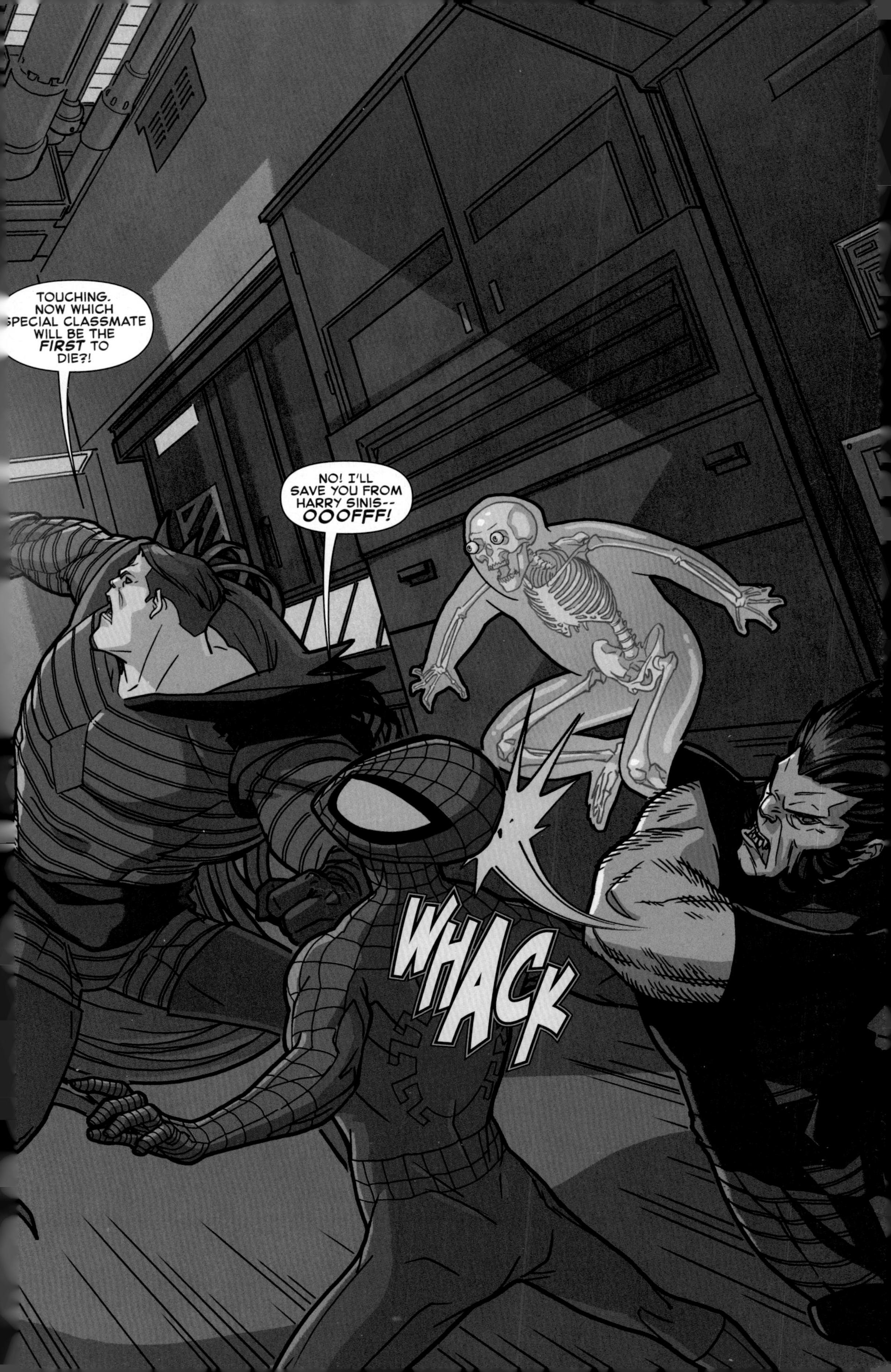
TOUCHING. NOW WHICH SPECIAL CLASSMATE WILL BE THE *FIRST* TO DIE?!
NO! I'LL SAVE YOU FROM HARRY SINIS-- *OOOFFF!*
WHACK

FOR A WHILE I THINK I'M DEAD. THAT WOLVERINE HAD ME JOIN HIS SCHOOL JUST SO HE COULD COME BACK FROM THE GRAVE AND KILL ME.

BUT THEN I WAKE UP.

AND I ONLY *WISH* I WAS DEAD.

I HAVE A FEW THINGS TO SAY TO YOU, SPIDER-MAN.

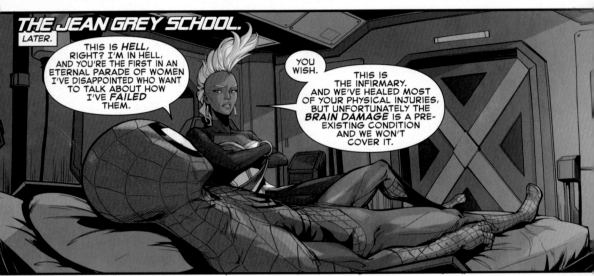

THE JEAN GREY SCHOOL.
LATER.

THIS IS *HELL*, RIGHT? I'M IN HELL, AND YOU'RE THE FIRST IN AN ETERNAL PARADE OF WOMEN I'VE DISAPPOINTED WHO WANT TO TALK ABOUT HOW I'VE *FAILED* THEM.

YOU WISH.

THIS IS THE INFIRMARY. AND WE'VE HEALED MOST OF YOUR PHYSICAL INJURIES, BUT UNFORTUNATELY THE *BRAIN DAMAGE* IS A PRE-EXISTING CONDITION AND WE WON'T COVER IT.

HEY! WAS THAT AN ACTUAL *JOKE?*

SMART LADY.

I'VE DECIDED TO TURN OFF MY HUMORLESS-HEADMASTER-BURDENED-WITH-RESPONSIBILITY-SUPERTEAM-LEADER ACT FOR THE MOMENT.

IT GETS TIRING. AND I'M STARTING TO THINK MY BEING SILLY IS THE ONLY WAY TO GET YOU TO TAKE ANYTHING *SERIOUSLY.*

WHY DON'T WE CONTINUE THIS CONVERSATION SOMEWHERE MORE *COMFORTABLE?*

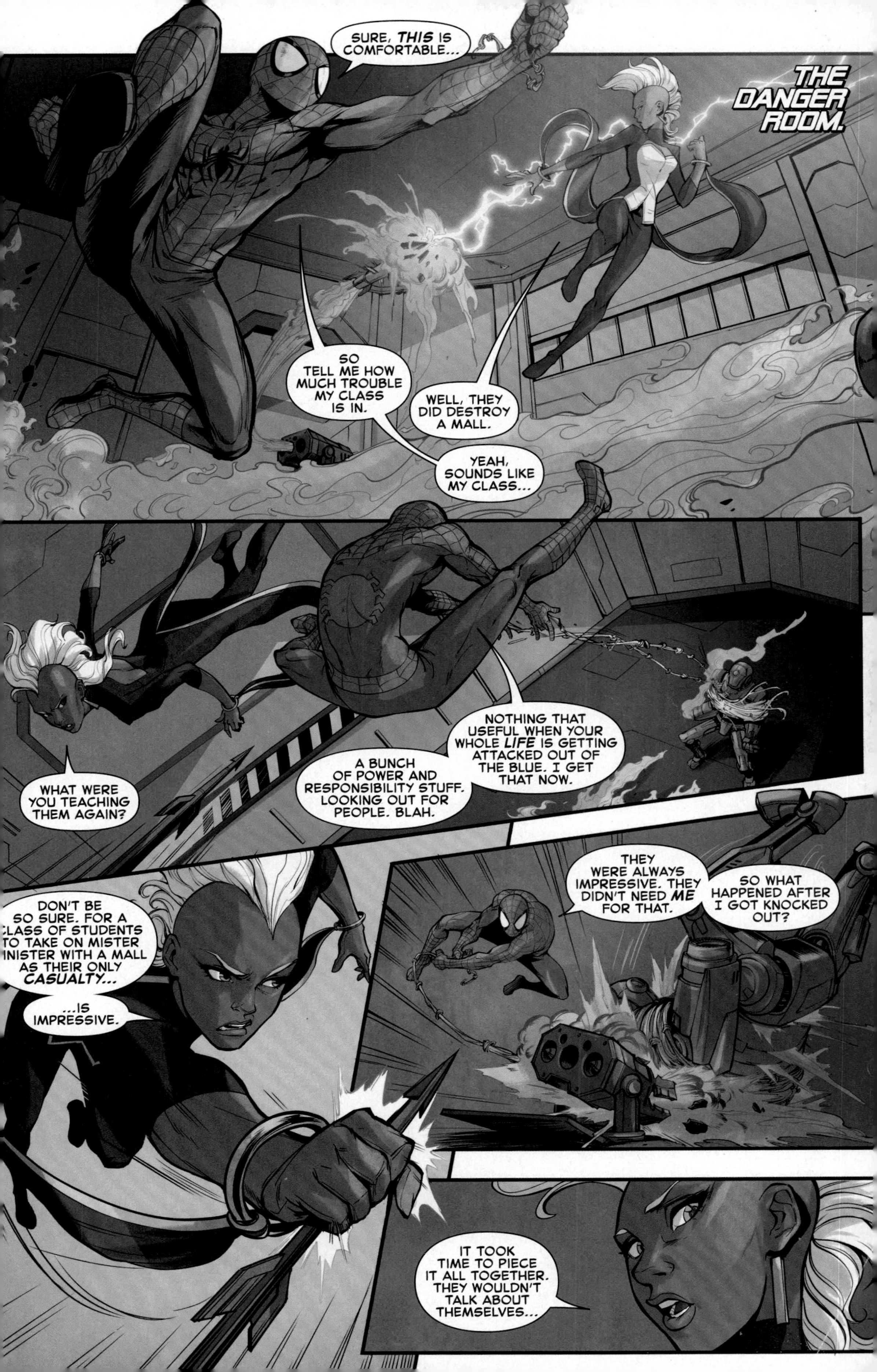
SURE, THIS IS COMFORTABLE...
THE DANGER ROOM.
SO TELL ME HOW MUCH TROUBLE MY CLASS IS IN.
WELL, THEY DID DESTROY A MALL.
YEAH, SOUNDS LIKE MY CLASS...
WHAT WERE YOU TEACHING THEM AGAIN?
A BUNCH OF POWER AND RESPONSIBILITY STUFF. LOOKING OUT FOR PEOPLE. BLAH.
NOTHING THAT USEFUL WHEN YOUR WHOLE LIFE IS GETTING ATTACKED OUT OF THE BLUE. I GET THAT NOW.
DON'T BE SO SURE. FOR A CLASS OF STUDENTS TO TAKE ON MISTER SINISTER WITH A MALL AS THEIR ONLY CASUALTY...
...IS IMPRESSIVE.
THEY WERE ALWAYS IMPRESSIVE. THEY DIDN'T NEED ME FOR THAT.
SO WHAT HAPPENED AFTER I GOT KNOCKED OUT?
IT TOOK TIME TO PIECE IT ALL TOGETHER. THEY WOULDN'T TALK ABOUT THEMSELVES...

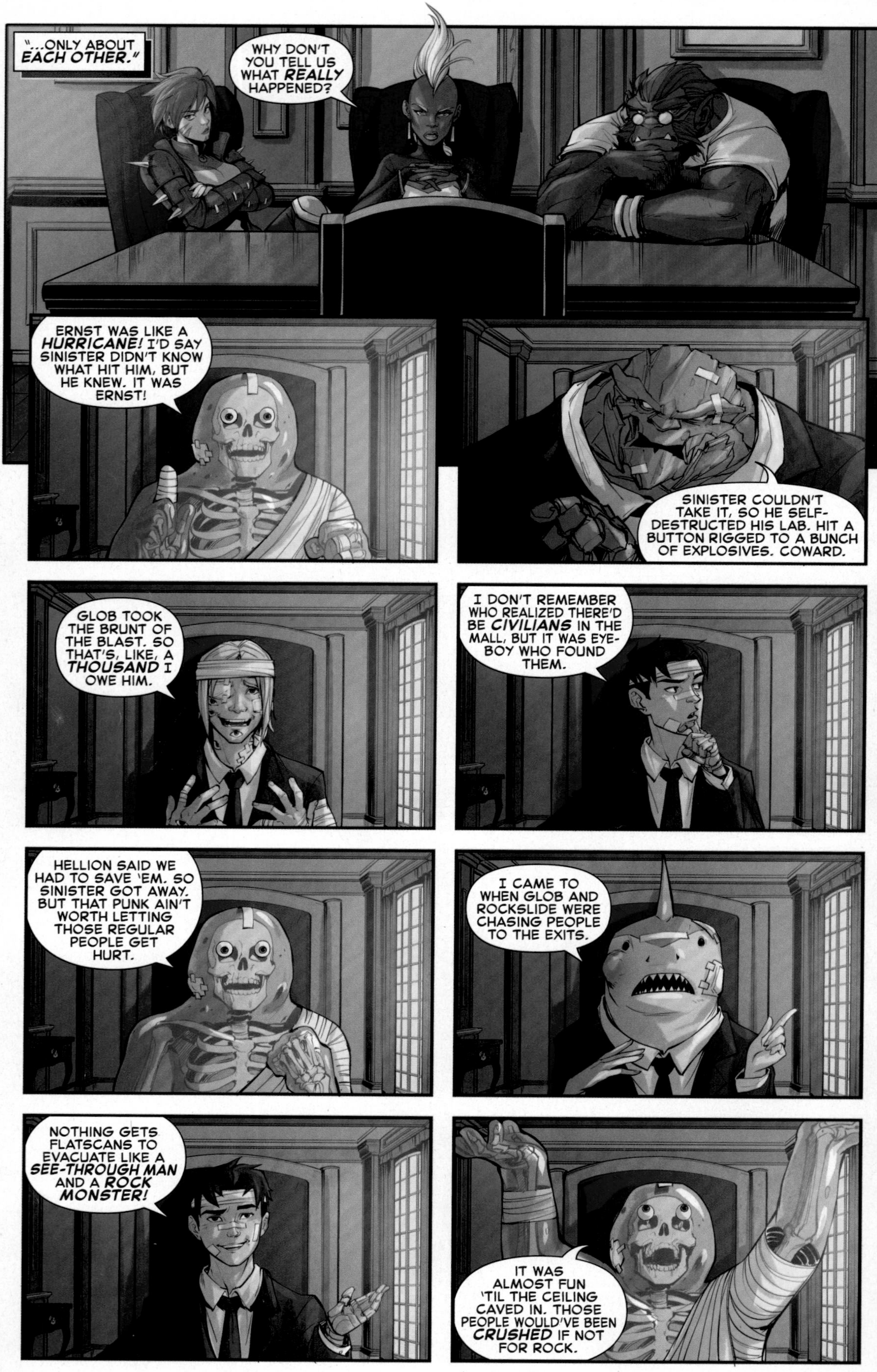
"...ONLY ABOUT EACH OTHER."
WHY DON'T YOU TELL US WHAT REALLY HAPPENED?
ERNST WAS LIKE A HURRICANE! I'D SAY SINISTER DIDN'T KNOW WHAT HIT HIM, BUT HE KNEW. IT WAS ERNST!
SINISTER COULDN'T TAKE IT, SO HE SELF-DESTRUCTED HIS LAB. HIT A BUTTON RIGGED TO A BUNCH OF EXPLOSIVES. COWARD.
GLOB TOOK THE BRUNT OF THE BLAST. SO THAT'S, LIKE, A THOUSAND I OWE HIM.
I DON'T REMEMBER WHO REALIZED THERE'D BE CIVILIANS IN THE MALL, BUT IT WAS EYE-BOY WHO FOUND THEM.
HELLION SAID WE HAD TO SAVE 'EM. SO SINISTER GOT AWAY. BUT THAT PUNK AIN'T WORTH LETTING THOSE REGULAR PEOPLE GET HURT.
I CAME TO WHEN GLOB AND ROCKSLIDE WERE CHASING PEOPLE TO THE EXITS.
NOTHING GETS FLATSCANS TO EVACUATE LIKE A SEE-THROUGH MAN AND A ROCK MONSTER!
IT WAS ALMOST FUN 'TIL THE CEILING CAVED IN. THOSE PEOPLE WOULD'VE BEEN CRUSHED IF NOT FOR ROCK.

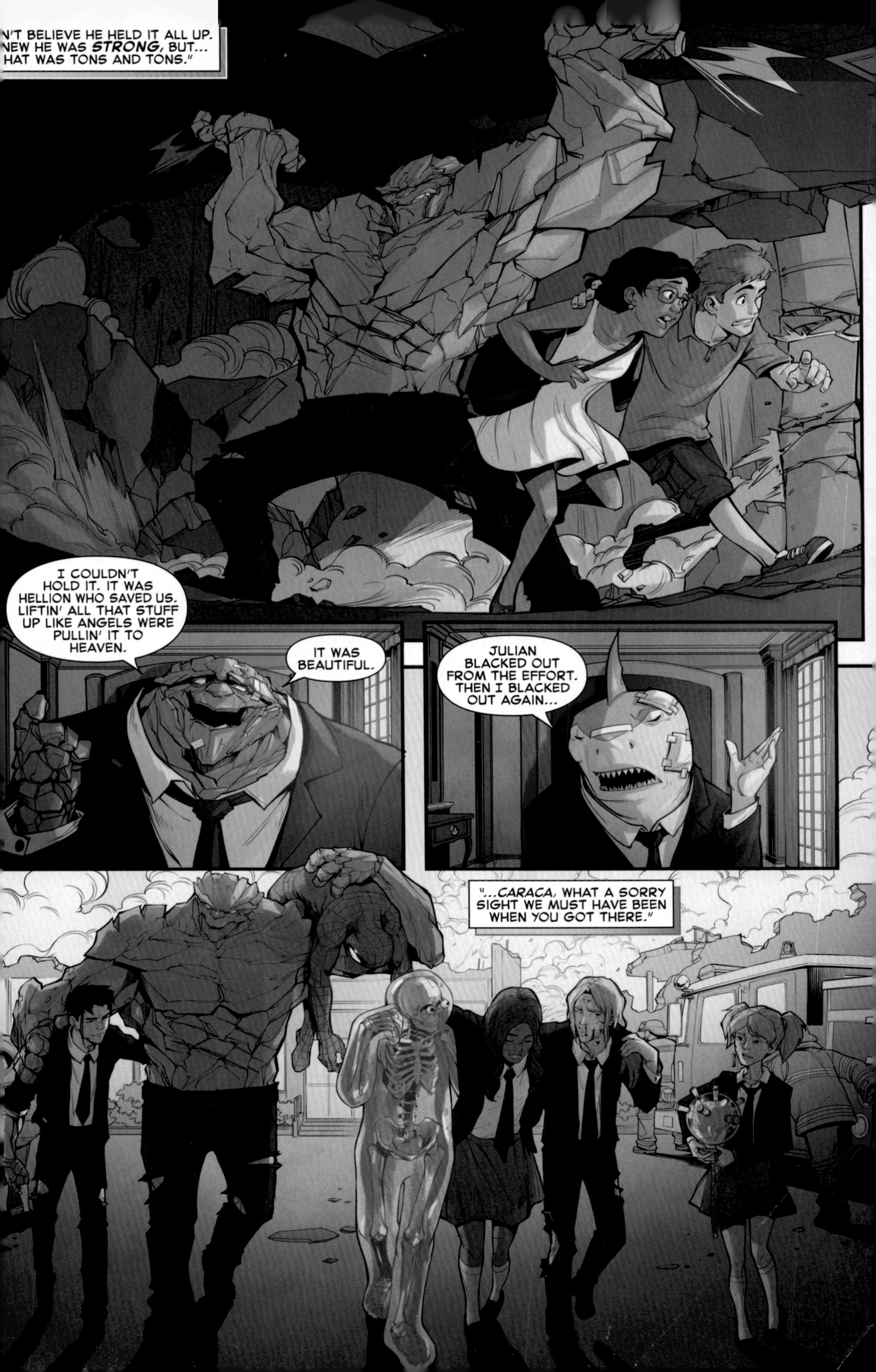

N'T BELIEVE HE HELD IT ALL UP. NEW HE WAS STRONG, BUT... HAT WAS TONS AND TONS."
I COULDN'T HOLD IT. IT WAS HELLION WHO SAVED US. LIFTIN' ALL THAT STUFF UP LIKE ANGELS WERE PULLIN' IT TO HEAVEN.
IT WAS BEAUTIFUL.
JULIAN BLACKED OUT FROM THE EFFORT. THEN I BLACKED OUT AGAIN...
"...CARACA, WHAT A SORRY SIGHT WE MUST HAVE BEEN WHEN YOU GOT THERE."

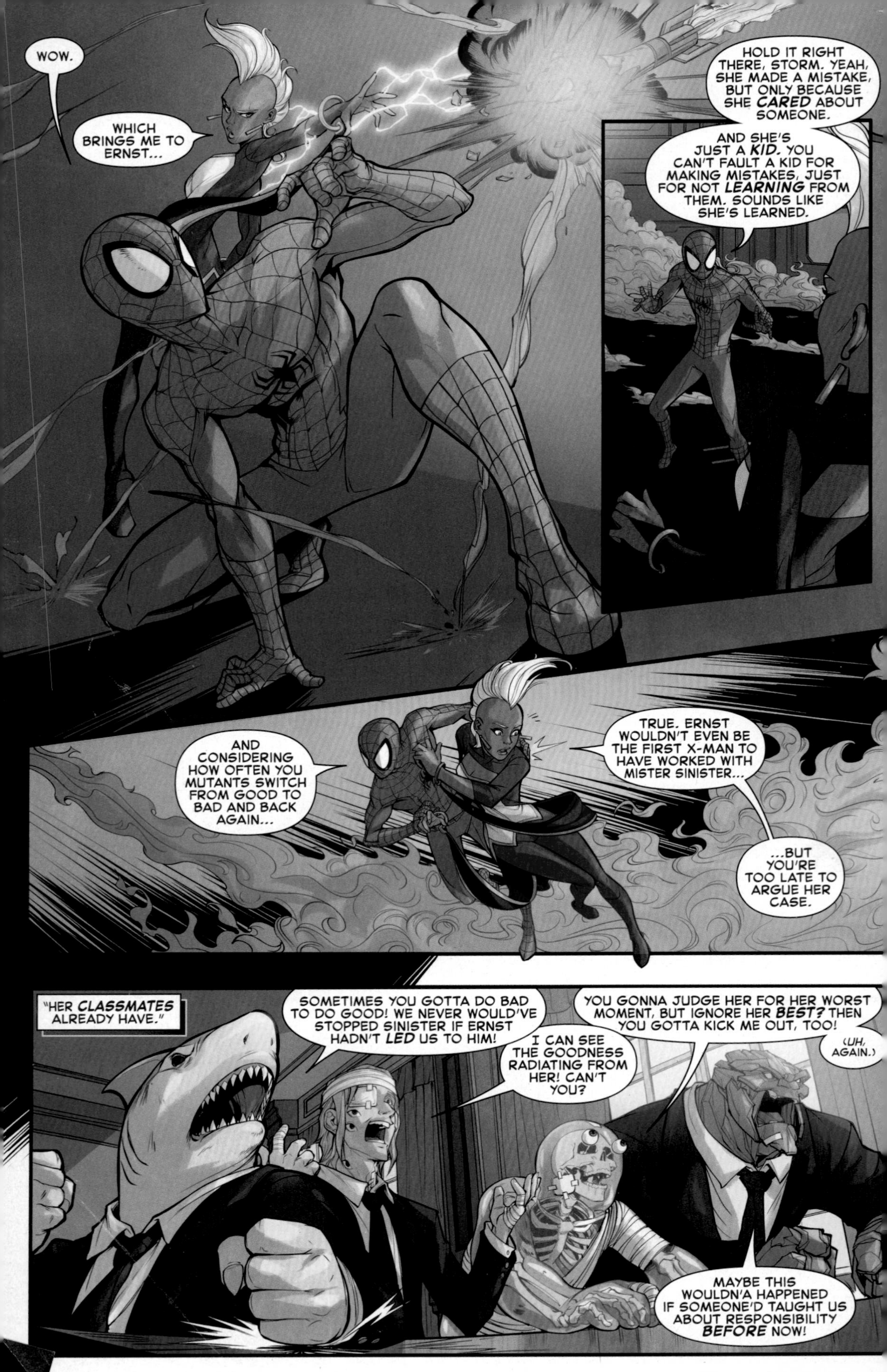
WOW.
WHICH BRINGS ME TO ERNST...
HOLD IT RIGHT THERE, STORM. YEAH, SHE MADE A MISTAKE, BUT ONLY BECAUSE SHE CARED ABOUT SOMEONE.
AND SHE'S JUST A KID. YOU CAN'T FAULT A KID FOR MAKING MISTAKES, JUST FOR NOT LEARNING FROM THEM. SOUNDS LIKE SHE'S LEARNED.
AND CONSIDERING HOW OFTEN YOU MUTANTS SWITCH FROM GOOD TO BAD AND BACK AGAIN...
TRUE. ERNST WOULDN'T EVEN BE THE FIRST X-MAN TO HAVE WORKED WITH MISTER SINISTER...
...BUT YOU'RE TOO LATE TO ARGUE HER CASE.
"HER CLASSMATES ALREADY HAVE."
SOMETIMES YOU GOTTA DO BAD TO DO GOOD! WE NEVER WOULD'VE STOPPED SINISTER IF ERNST HADN'T LED US TO HIM!
I CAN SEE THE GOODNESS RADIATING FROM HER! CAN'T YOU?
YOU GONNA JUDGE HER FOR HER WORST MOMENT, BUT IGNORE HER BEST? THEN YOU GOTTA KICK ME OUT, TOO!
(UH, AGAIN.)
MAYBE THIS WOULDN'A HAPPENED IF SOMEONE'D TAUGHT US ABOUT RESPONSIBILITY BEFORE NOW!

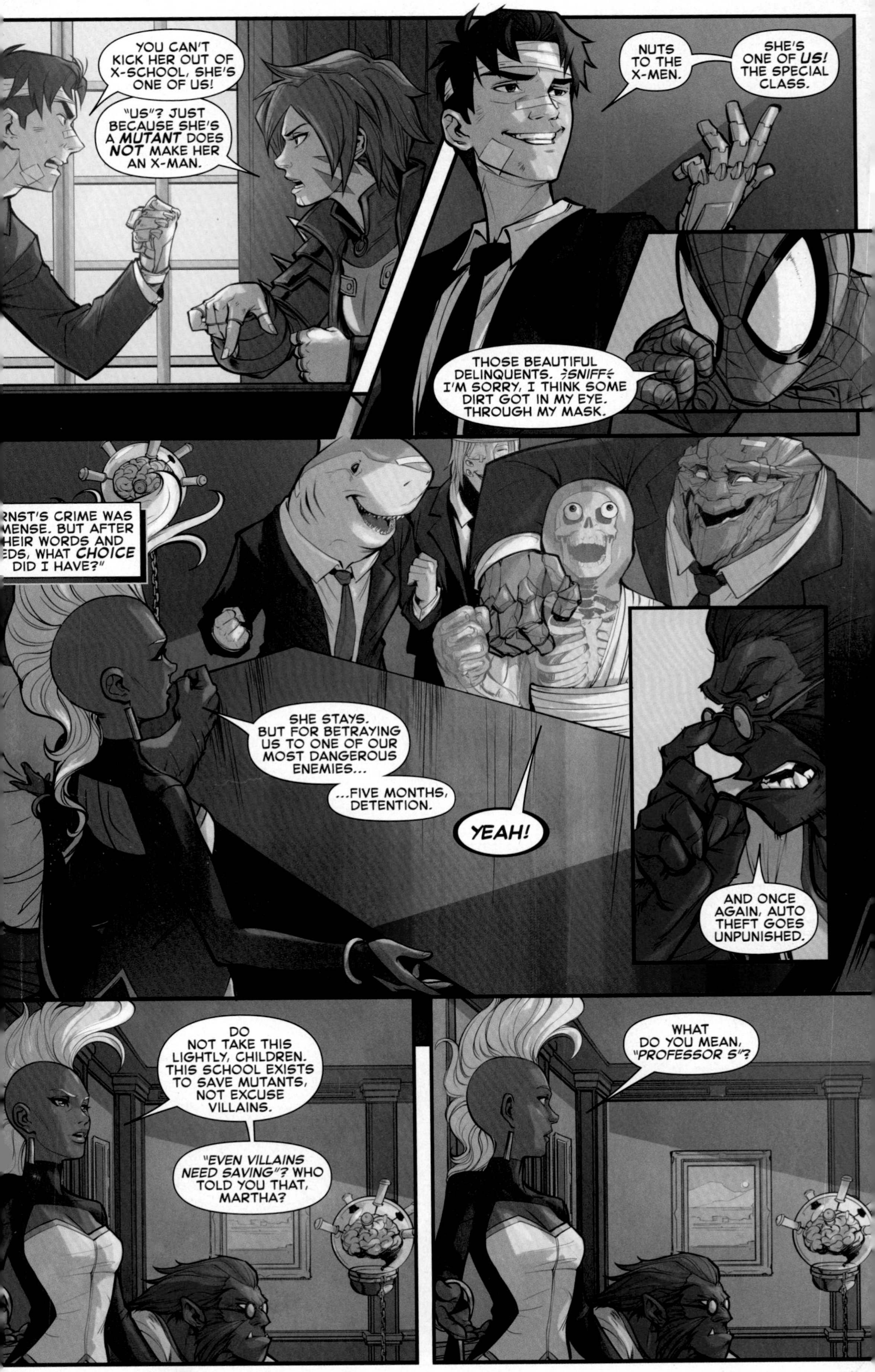

YOU CAN'T KICK HER OUT OF X-SCHOOL, SHE'S ONE OF US!
"US"? JUST BECAUSE SHE'S A MUTANT DOES NOT MAKE HER AN X-MAN.
NUTS TO THE X-MEN.
SHE'S ONE OF US! THE SPECIAL CLASS.
THOSE BEAUTIFUL DELINQUENTS. SNIFF I'M SORRY, I THINK SOME DIRT GOT IN MY EYE. THROUGH MY MASK.
RNST'S CRIME WAS MENSE. BUT AFTER HEIR WORDS AND EDS, WHAT CHOICE DID I HAVE?"
SHE STAYS. BUT FOR BETRAYING US TO ONE OF OUR MOST DANGEROUS ENEMIES...
...FIVE MONTHS, DETENTION.
YEAH!
AND ONCE AGAIN, AUTO THEFT GOES UNPUNISHED.
DO NOT TAKE THIS LIGHTLY, CHILDREN. THIS SCHOOL EXISTS TO SAVE MUTANTS, NOT EXCUSE VILLAINS.
"EVEN VILLAINS NEED SAVING"? WHO TOLD YOU THAT, MARTHA?
WHAT DO YOU MEAN, "PROFESSOR S"?

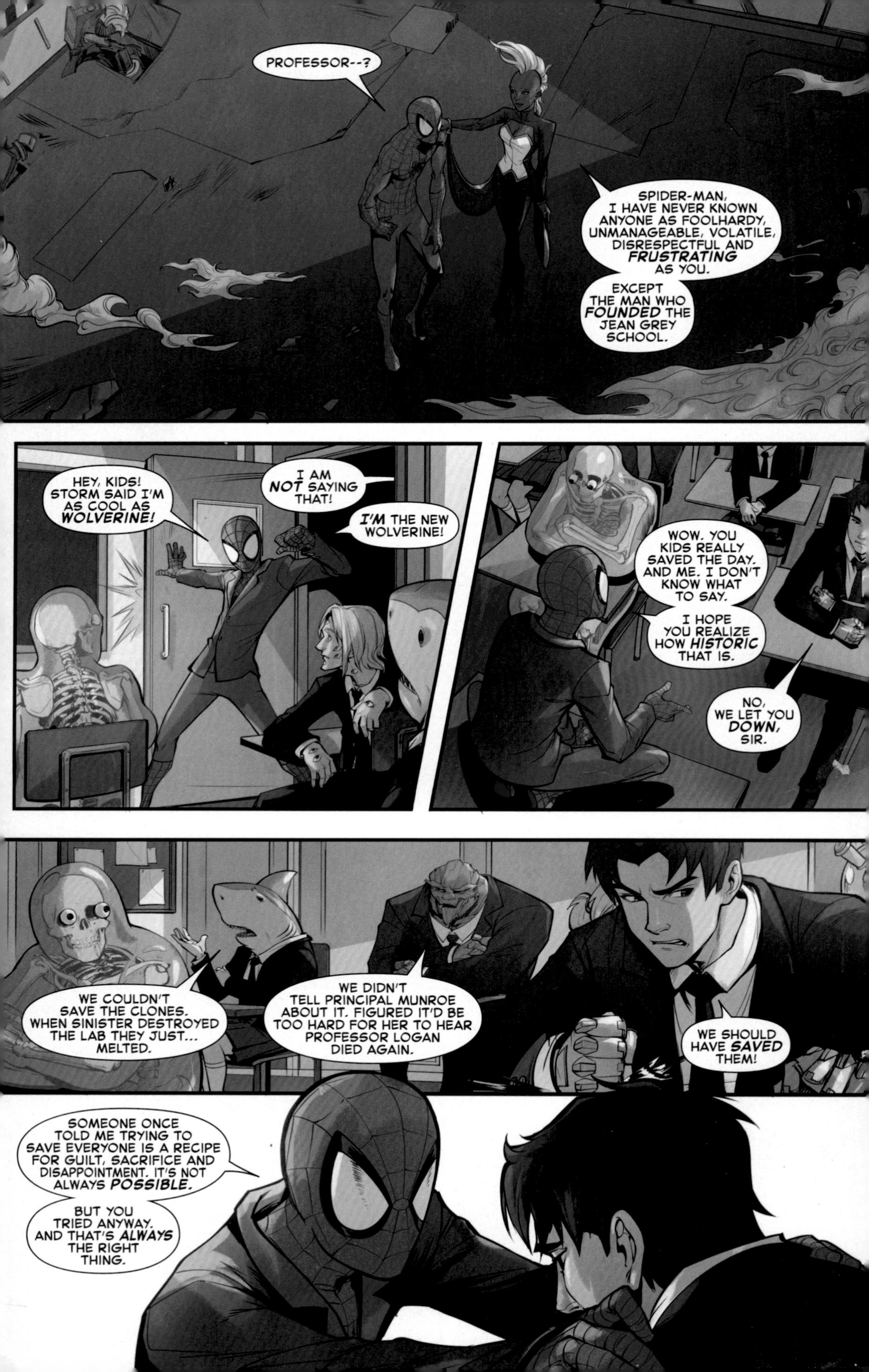
PROFESSOR--?
SPIDER-MAN, I HAVE NEVER KNOWN ANYONE AS FOOLHARDY, UNMANAGEABLE, VOLATILE, DISRESPECTFUL AND FRUSTRATING AS YOU.
EXCEPT THE MAN WHO FOUNDED THE JEAN GREY SCHOOL.
HEY, KIDS! STORM SAID I'M AS COOL AS WOLVERINE!
I AM NOT SAYING THAT!
I'M THE NEW WOLVERINE!
WOW. YOU KIDS REALLY SAVED THE DAY. AND ME. I DON'T KNOW WHAT TO SAY.
I HOPE YOU REALIZE HOW HISTORIC THAT IS.
NO, WE LET YOU DOWN, SIR.
WE COULDN'T SAVE THE CLONES. WHEN SINISTER DESTROYED THE LAB THEY JUST... MELTED.
WE DIDN'T TELL PRINCIPAL MUNROE ABOUT IT. FIGURED IT'D BE TOO HARD FOR HER TO HEAR PROFESSOR LOGAN DIED AGAIN.
WE SHOULD HAVE SAVED THEM!
SOMEONE ONCE TOLD ME TRYING TO SAVE EVERYONE IS A RECIPE FOR GUILT, SACRIFICE AND DISAPPOINTMENT. IT'S NOT ALWAYS POSSIBLE.
BUT YOU TRIED ANYWAY. AND THAT'S ALWAYS THE RIGHT THING.

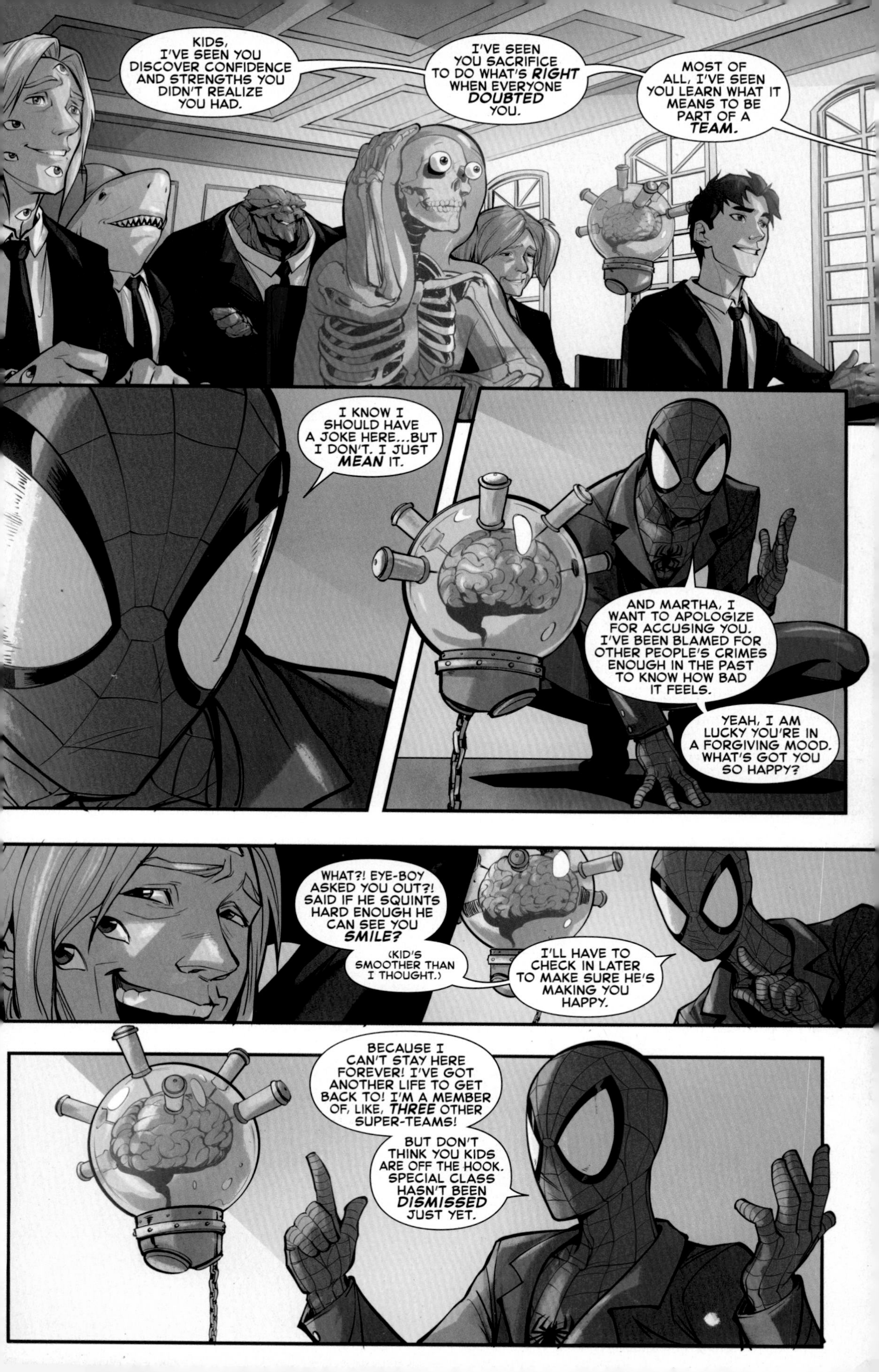
KIDS, I'VE SEEN YOU DISCOVER CONFIDENCE AND STRENGTHS YOU DIDN'T REALIZE YOU HAD.
I'VE SEEN YOU SACRIFICE TO DO WHAT'S RIGHT WHEN EVERYONE DOUBTED YOU.
MOST OF ALL, I'VE SEEN YOU LEARN WHAT IT MEANS TO BE PART OF A TEAM.
I KNOW I SHOULD HAVE A JOKE HERE...BUT I DON'T. I JUST MEAN IT.
AND MARTHA, I WANT TO APOLOGIZE FOR ACCUSING YOU. I'VE BEEN BLAMED FOR OTHER PEOPLE'S CRIMES ENOUGH IN THE PAST TO KNOW HOW BAD IT FEELS.
YEAH, I AM LUCKY YOU'RE IN A FORGIVING MOOD. WHAT'S GOT YOU SO HAPPY?
WHAT?! EYE-BOY ASKED YOU OUT?! SAID IF HE SQUINTS HARD ENOUGH HE CAN SEE YOU SMILE?
(KID'S SMOOTHER THAN I THOUGHT.)
I'LL HAVE TO CHECK IN LATER TO MAKE SURE HE'S MAKING YOU HAPPY.
BECAUSE I CAN'T STAY HERE FOREVER! I'VE GOT ANOTHER LIFE TO GET BACK TO! I'M A MEMBER OF, LIKE, THREE OTHER SUPER-TEAMS!
BUT DON'T THINK YOU KIDS ARE OFF THE HOOK. SPECIAL CLASS HASN'T BEEN DISMISSED JUST YET.

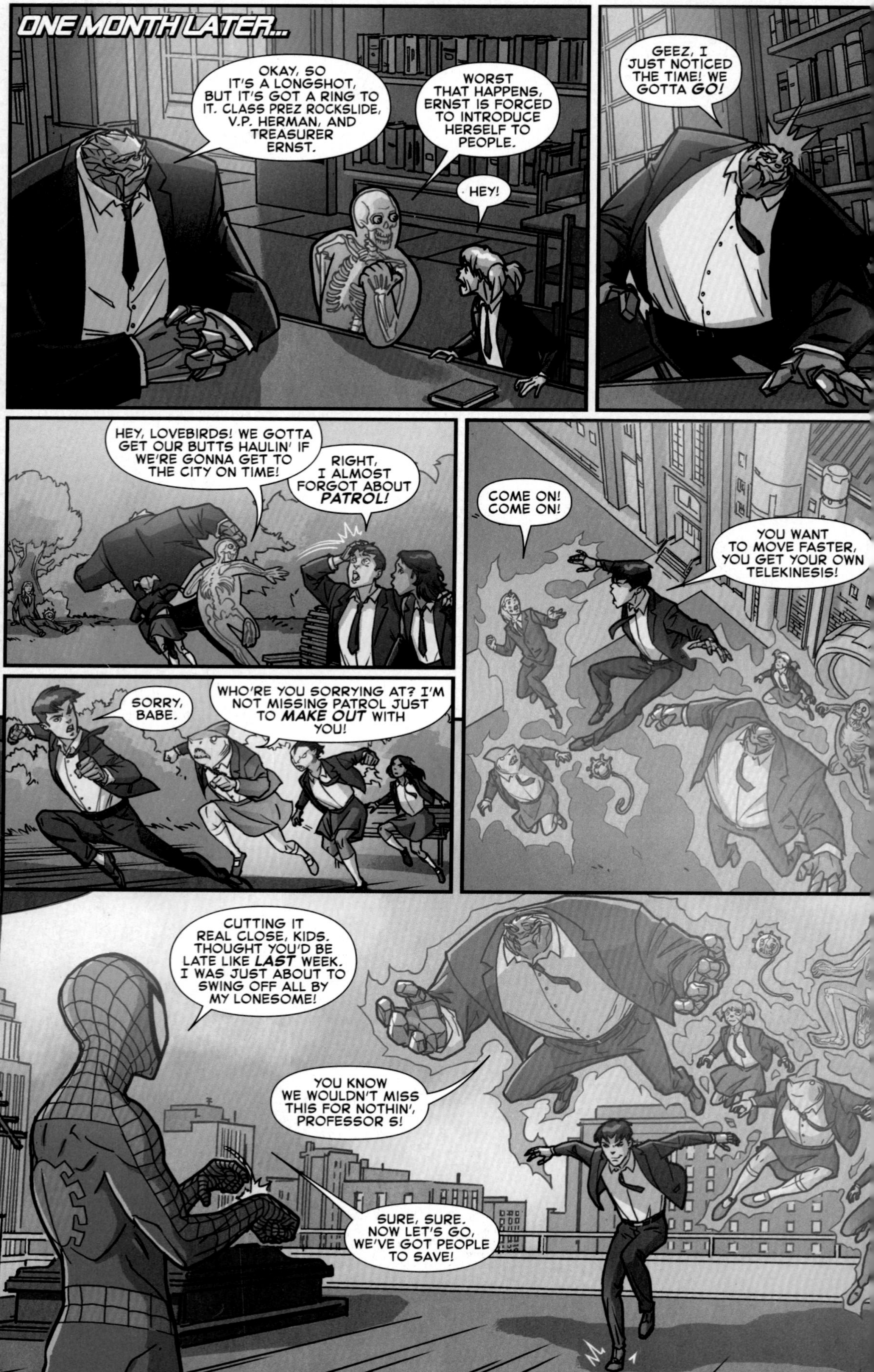

ONE MONTH LATER...
OKAY, SO IT'S A LONGSHOT, BUT IT'S GOT A RING TO IT. CLASS PREZ ROCKSLIDE, V.P. HERMAN, AND TREASURER ERNST.
WORST THAT HAPPENS, ERNST IS FORCED TO INTRODUCE HERSELF TO PEOPLE.
HEY!
GEEZ, I JUST NOTICED THE TIME! WE GOTTA GO!
HEY, LOVEBIRDS! WE GOTTA GET OUR BUTTS HAULIN' IF WE'RE GONNA GET TO THE CITY ON TIME!
RIGHT, I ALMOST FORGOT ABOUT PATROL!
SORRY, BABE.
WHO'RE YOU SORRYING AT? I'M NOT MISSING PATROL JUST TO MAKE OUT WITH YOU!
COME ON! COME ON!
YOU WANT TO MOVE FASTER, YOU GET YOUR OWN TELEKINESIS!
CUTTING IT REAL CLOSE, KIDS. THOUGHT YOU'D BE LATE LIKE LAST WEEK. I WAS JUST ABOUT TO SWING OFF ALL BY MY LONESOME!
YOU KNOW WE WOULDN'T MISS THIS FOR NOTHIN', PROFESSOR S!
SURE, SURE. NOW LET'S GO, WE'VE GOT PEOPLE TO SAVE!

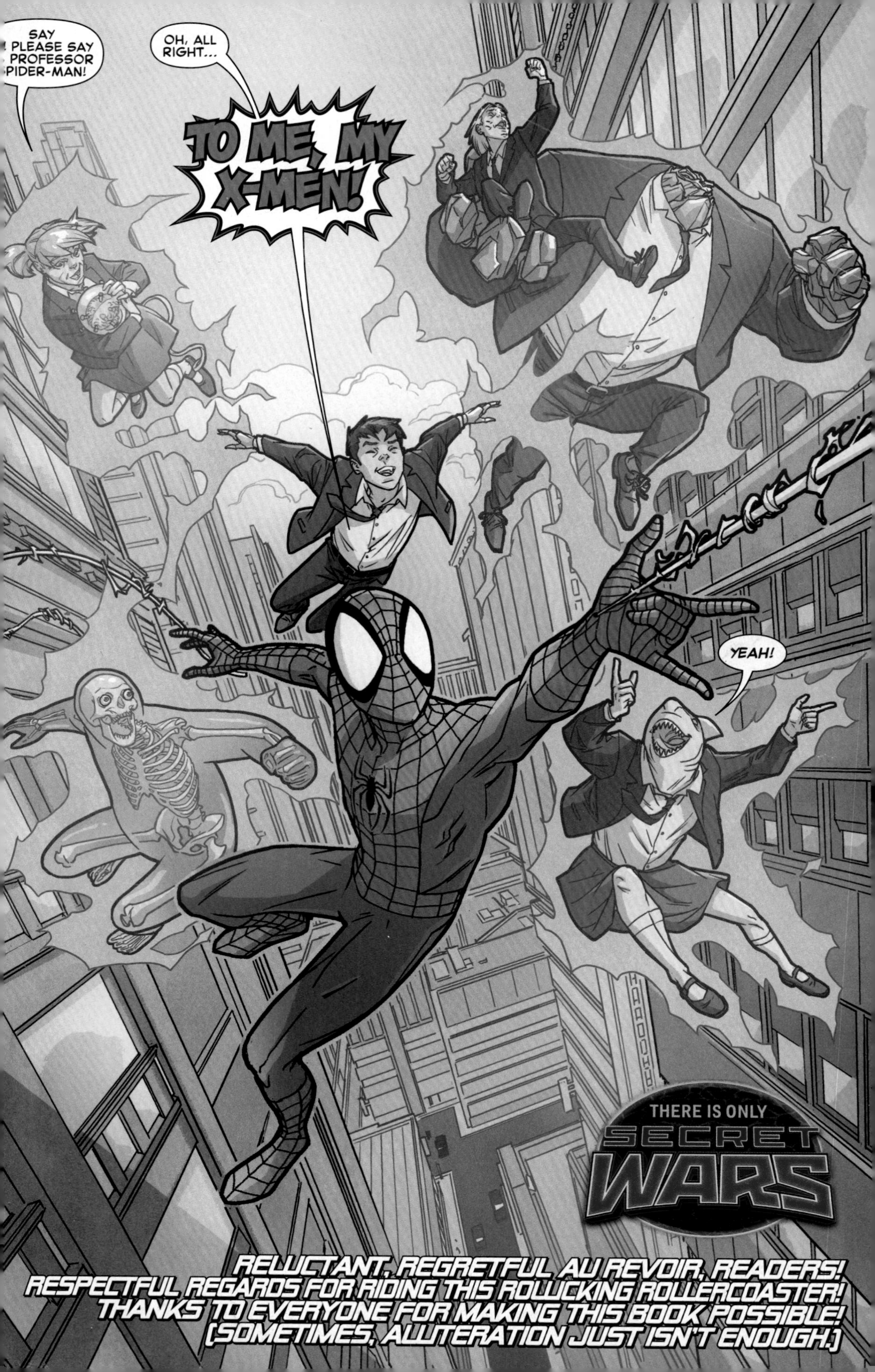
SAY PLEASE SAY PROFESSOR SPIDER-MAN!
OH, ALL RIGHT...
TO ME, MY X-MEN!
YEAH!
THERE IS ONLY SECRET WARS
RELUCTANT, REGRETFUL AU REVOIR, READERS!
RESPECTFUL REGARDS FOR RIDING THIS ROLLICKING ROLLERCOASTER!
THANKS TO EVERYONE FOR MAKING THIS BOOK POSSIBLE!
(SOMETIMES, ALLITERATION JUST ISN'T ENOUGH.)

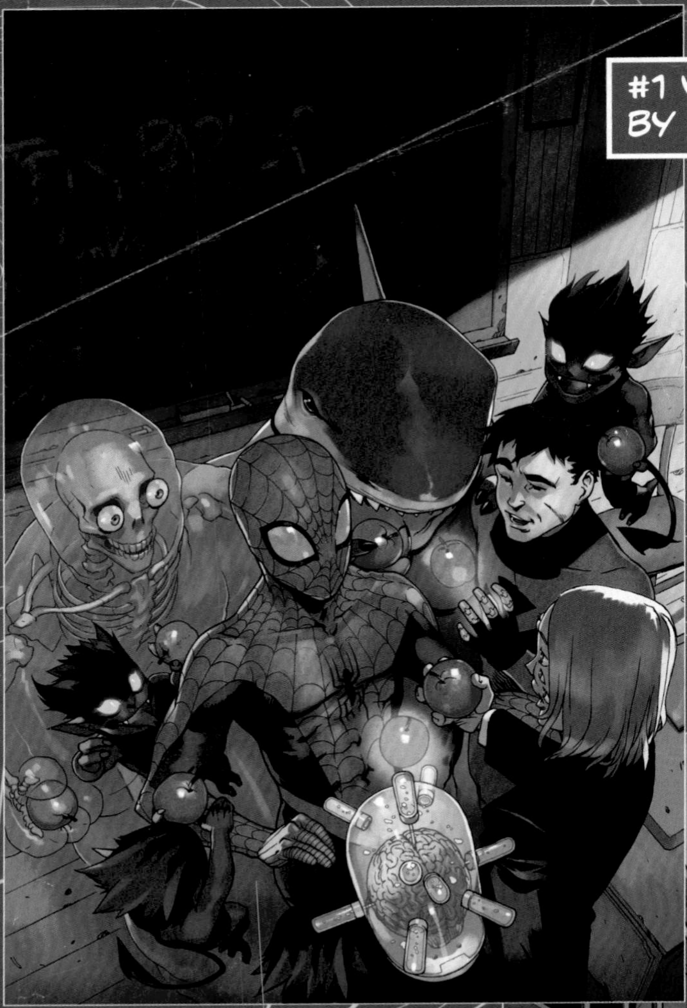

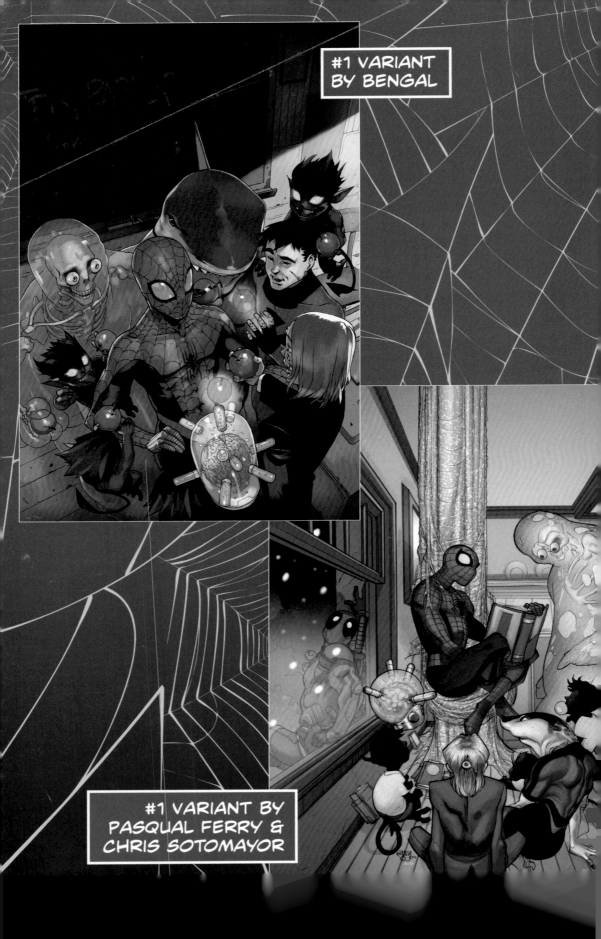

#1 VARIANT BY BENGAL

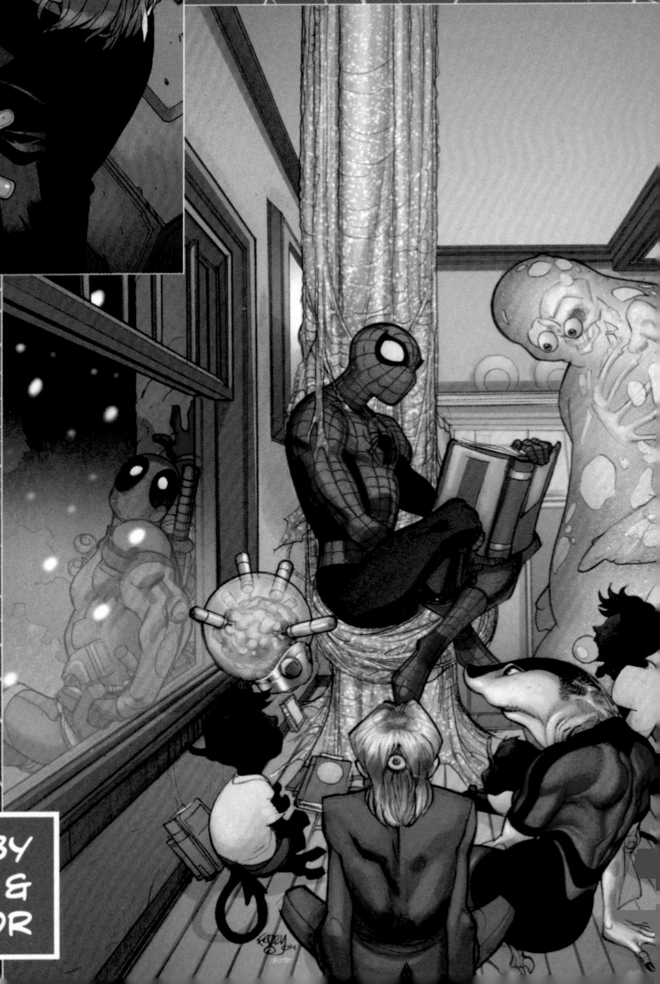

#1 VARIANT BY PASQUAL FERRY & CHRIS SOTOMAYOR

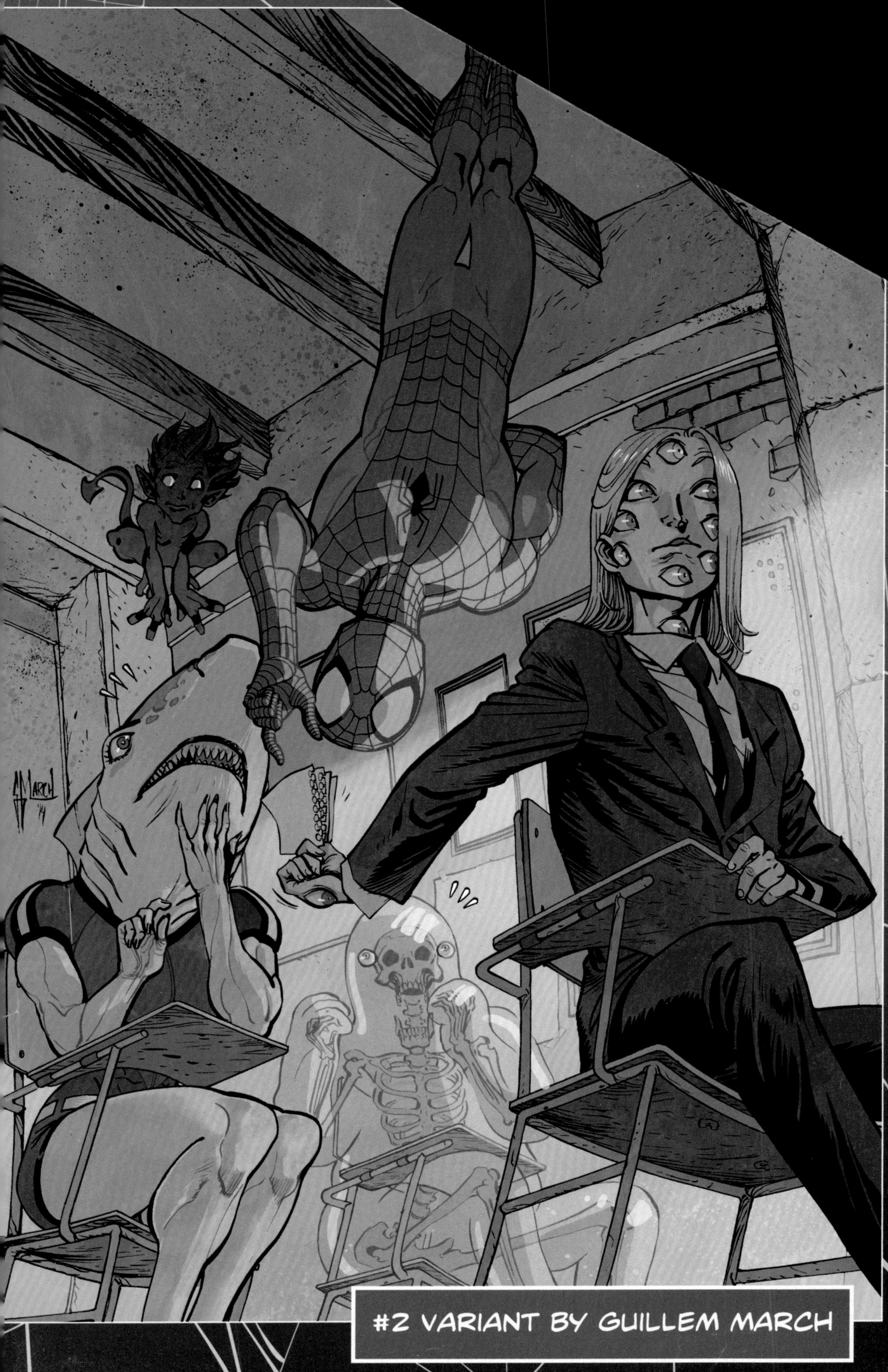

#2 VARIANT BY GUILLEM MARCH

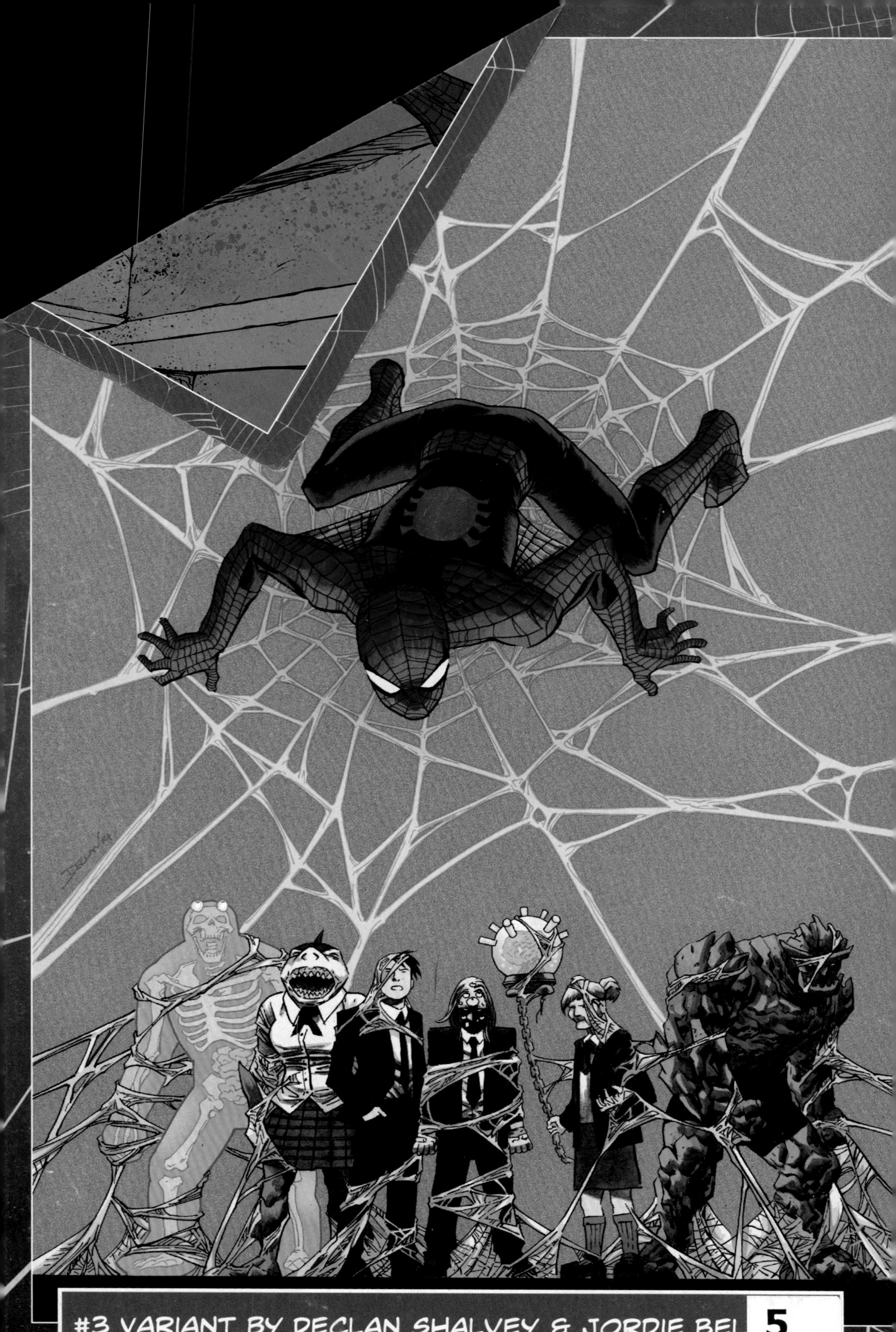

#3 VARIANT BY DECLAN SHALVEY & JORDIE BEL